THE COMPLETE BED BUILDING BOOK

No. 1124
$12.95

THE COMPLETE BED BUILDING BOOK
BY HYDEE SMALL

TAB BOOKS

BLUE RIDGE SUMMIT, PA. 17214

FIRST EDITION

FIRST PRINTING—MARCH 1979

Copyright © 1979 by TAB BOOKS

Printed in the United States of America

Library of Congress Cataloging in Publication Data

Small, HyDee.
    The complete bed building book.

    Includes index.
    1. Bedroom furniture. I. Title.
TT197.5.B4S57   684.1'5   78-20992
ISBN 0-8306-9822-1
ISBN 0-8306-1124-X pbk.

Contents

Introduction 9

1 No-Frills Bed Projects 11
   Quickly Converted Bedroll 14
   Fold-Up Chair Bed 14
   Rocking Chair Bed 16
   Lean-To Chair Bed 19
   Hammocks 20
   Sling Beds 22
   Materials 42
   Cots 51
   Children's No-Frill Beds 56
   Quickie Lounge Bed 59
   Bundle-Board Bed Couch 62
   Convertible Bed Couch 64
   Simple Out Sized Bed Platforms 66
   Bed Dimensions 70
   Safety 71
   Resiliency 72
   Putting It All Together 73

2 Advanced Bed Projects 75
   It's Your Choice 75
   Handy Information 77
   A Family Fun Project 81
   Shaker Style Doll Cradle 89
   Baby Box Cradle 94
   Swinging Cradle 100
   Folding Bassinet 105
   Broomstick Roll Up Cradle 112
   Knockdown Bassinet 114
   Rock-A-Bye Cradle 117
   Bedside Cradle 119
   Off-The-Floor Play Pen 122
   Multilevel Play Pen 124
   Gated Cribs 126

Sliding Side Crib 130
Spool Crib 131
Scooter Bed 131
Children's Yoke Bunks 138
Stacked Beds 144
Bed In A Box...150

3 **Designer Bed Projects** **155**
Siamese Twin Guest Accommodations................................155
Shoji Partitions...177
Shutter Doors...182
Hang-Up Clothes Closet 185
Built-Ins 186
Portable Library...190
Folding Luggage Rack..192
Lighting the Siamese Twin Guest Quarters 197
Waterbeds..199
Waterbed Pillow Chair 234
Beanbag Bed..234

4 **Conversation Piece Beds** **238**
Pivoting Twins..238
Guest Cube Squared..256
Sleeping Wedges..258
Attic Sleeper..258
Fold-Up Sling Pipe Bed..259
Siesta Tree House 261
For Floor People Only 262
Zoom-Zoom Bed...264
Bolted All In One Set-In..276
Alternative Set-In 279
Another Fold-Up Pipe Sling Bed 279
Bed of Roses 280
A Bed of Nails..281
Wheel Bed..282
If You Like To Whittle 282
Coat Hanger Tester 284
Period Beds 286

5 **Custom Beds and Surroundings** **314**
Headboards..314
Room Dividers 323
Let There Be Light! 324
Building Lamps 340
For The Ears 365
Total Involvement...371
BioAquatic Bed...386

Glossary of Terms...**389**
Appendix A—Details of Common Nails **396**
Appendix B—Wood Screw Holes..**397**
Appendix C—Fastenings **398**
Appendix D—Finishing..**407**
Appendix E—Wood For Your Bedroom Furniture................**417**
Index **429**

Introduction

Almost one-third of your life is spent in bed. Are you comfortable enough? If not, within the pages of this book, you will find possible solutions to some of your sleeping problems.

If you find your store-bought bed is too short, too narrow, too low or too high to the floor, or your mattress is simply no longer worthy of your body—delve into the following pages and find the bed that best suits your individual life style. Not only will you have fun with your own creativity, but you'll be rewarded with tremendous financial savings by building your own bed.

Each project is complete and easily modified to meet the needs of virtually any size bedroom. Step-by-step instructions and detailed illustrations make almost every project an easy one, whether you are a beginner or a pro at bed building.

No-frill projects ranging from hammocks and quickly converted bedrolls to the more advanced ones including a guest cube squared and an elaborate BioAquatic waterbed are detailed.

Family fun projects include building and decorating baby cribs. Family bed builders will enjoy making a Shaker style doll cradle, baby box cradle, broomstick roll up cradle, knockdown bassinet, children's yoke or stacked bunks, a bed in a box or even a scooter bed.

The third chapter offers designer bed projects which will provide unparalleled comfort as well as amazing utility to almost any room. Unique Siamese twin guest accommodations leads to an array of accessory projects including Shoji partitions, shutter doors, hang-up clothes closets, built-ins, a portable library and a folding luggage rack.

Several designs and many of the sleeping benefits of waterbeds are also given in the text.

For those with limited space, a bolted all in one set-in provides all the bedroom necessities in close quarters.

Before selecting the best bed for you—study the conversation piece beds. You could even try your hand at reproducing "periods beds." Or, consider pivoting twins—they quickly convert to one king-size bed.

This volume does not end with the mere plans for custom made beds. Unique bedroom surroundings are also covered. Headboards, mattresses, room dividers, lamps and even the proper placement of stereo equipment in the bedroom add to the conclusion of this book.

A glossary of wood and building terms has also been included to help you with your project—whether it is your first endeavor as a bed builder or one of many successes.

HyDee Small

Chapter 1
No-Frills Bed Projects

The Saxons used the phrase "hitting the hay" as a sort of code for going to bed. They felt lucky that they could sleep in the hay with the horses that the invading Normans, led by William the Conqueror, had brought with them across the English channel. The enslaved Saxons had been turned out of their homes by the Normans and the lucky ones welcomed the refuge during cold English nights in the hay of the Norman barns, warmed by the bodies of the fine Norman horses. The Norman lords would probably have objected had they understood what "hitting the hay" meant.

During the intervening nine centuries beds were often filled with hay. A hay-stuffed mattress offered resiliency as well as warmth, but the stuff tended to break up when it dried out. A succession of various mattress stuffings followed, from feathers, down and cotton to the polyurethane foam pads of different thicknesses and designs used today.

In discussing the building of beds, keep in mind the many different purposes to which beds are put besides a sound night's sleep. Beds can be daytime places for resting and relaxing, comfortable havens for those who are ailing, spots for love-making at any time of day or night, even as foundations for conversational groups of friends.

A couple of lucky friends of mine stopped off in Las Vegas on their vacation drive from Missouri to Southern California, coming away from the casinos with their winnings in paper sacks. When they got to my place, they trouped in with the paper bags filled with coins and dumped them on a bed. That bed was used as a counting house for their loot.

On a motor trip through Mexico we arrived in an old town one chilly night after driving through a storm. The pencione where we had reservations had one beautiful antique Spanish bed topped with a deep featherbed. We drew lots for this and I won—or perhaps lost. Although I snuggled down into its welcome folds that night, the next morning it was...oh my aching back!

After this experience, I realized why chiropractors advise that too-soft beds are responsible for more bad backs than anything, unless it is the automobile bucket seat. To fulfill the desire to accommodate the contours of the human body, we now have modern furniture that is contoured, sectionally raised or lowered and water-beds.

Probably one of the reasons our forefathers used featherbeds was because our fore*mothers* could stitch up the ticking and stuff them with feathers they pulled from the geese they raised. Since their bedrooms were generally unheated, these featherbeds offered warm sleeping as well as fitting to the contours of various sized people.

The human body bends naturally at only three points: upward or downward at the hips, usually upward at the knees and either upward or downward at the neck (Fig. 1-1). The contours generally follow these bends, which also affect or are affected by the individual's preferences and activity or inactivity at the time. Hospital beds crank up or down in sections designed to promote the comfort and the treatment of the patient.

Most available human body measurement statistics have been compiled by the military and so do not take into consideration the frailer bodies, the obese, children, or babies. Why not take your own measurements and build your furniture to fit your family and friends who will be the potential users?

Another consideration is the space available in which to put the bed. Sometimes this is a problem since beds take up more room than most other pieces of furniture. In rural Mexico I have stepped carefully over and around children and sometimes adults soundly sleeping on pallets unrolled at bedtime on the floor as I entered the casa of an amigo late in the evening.

In Japan the floor may be covered by *tatame'* that serves both as an indoor stocking-feet walking surface and a bed. Upon entering such an area one is expected to remove the shoes, as patrons of Japanese restaurants probably know. For more luxury the Japanese may add a *futon*, which is a sort of soft sleeping bag. The *futon* is rolled up and put away in the daytime.

Sleeping bags are popular extra beds today in the United States, especially with the younger set. When double occupancy is desired, two bags are zipped together. It pays to buy good quality sleeping bags that can be dry-cleaned and will keep the user comfortable in rainy or cold weather.

No longer do people sit primly erect; the designs of our modern beds and chairs reflect our tendency to sprawl. There are a few of the more formal occasions, such as sitting at a dining table, when we do tend to sit more or less erect; and then we must consider the people who find it difficult to get up and down from lower furniture.

The type of beds that we use seem, however, to be more a matter of fashion, ethnic background, or class, somewhat modified by individual preferences. For this reason you have a wide choice, not only in the matter of style and height from the floor, but in the manner of supporting and covering your bed.

While the human body can probably get a good night's rest on beds ranging in style from Early American or French Provincial to waterbeds, few people will admit it. Your choice in the type of bed you want to build will probably be influenced a great deal by your ideas on the subject. After all, maybe you would enjoy building a bed that can become a conversation piece, the one-of-a-kind sort. For this reason this book touches on a wide variety of beds. Use these ideas as "launching pads" for your imagination and build yourself a bed.

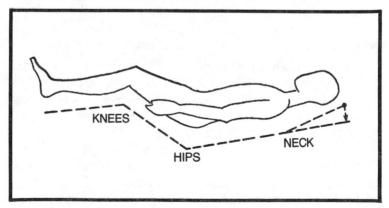

Fig. 1-1. Natural contours of the average human body.

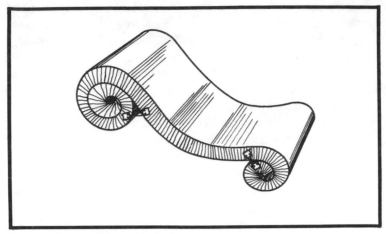

Fig. 1-2. Quickly converted bedroll.

QUICKLY CONVERTED BEDROLL

This bedroll can be quickly converted from a portable bedroll to a lounge or a bed. As shown in Fig. 1-2, it consists of a solid foam pad confined in a flat canvas bag on which are sewn tabs with ties to hold it in the desired position. When a large roll is left at the top, it serves as a lounge; when laid out flat except for a smaller roll as a pillow, it makes into a bed. The ties hold it in either position.

When rolled up it can be easily carried or stowed away. It will delight most children and be appreciated by jean-clad adults, especially for relaxed TV watching. Experiment with the placement of the ties. Upper and lower pairs should be exactly opposite each other and a third set can be provided to hold the roll when it is carried or stored.

FOLD-UP CHAIR BED

Another easily converted chair bed that can be constructed without carpentry is the fold-up design. It can be made from a recycled mattress or a thick foam pad. A certain amount of stiffness is needed for this bed to also serve as a satisfactory chair. Figure 1-3A shows how it is made into a chair.

The fabric covering must be strong enough to withstand the pull of the ties on the tabs (Fig. 1-3B). Make two of these tabs from heavy canvas or duck and securely sew on two rings along the center line of each. Firmly sew a tab to each corner of the mattress bottom. Catch the stitches into the mattress itself as well as the cover, unless you plan to remove the covering for laundering. To make the cover removable, sew in a zipper across the top edge.

After you have attached the tabs, make a heavy canvas strap (Fig. 1-3C) that is long enough to reach completely around the back, front and sides of the mattress allowing enough slack so it can be drawn up and tightly laced. Place two grommets in each end of the strap after hemming all the sides. To use grommets it will be necessary to use split rings. Heavy duty keyrings will do very well since they are split and can be slipped through the grommets. For the best appearance, the rings should match.

Cut four lengths of quarter-inch rope long enough to be doubled through both back and front rings and tied. You will be tying and untying the ropes, so use a "shoestring bow" knot. Firmly bend the mattress into four nearly equal sections. Use the strap to tie the bundle into the "chair" position, and make any needed tension adjustments.

This low chair will quickly convert to a bed by merely untying the bows. The pad should lie flat on the floor. If after a period of use the mattress tends to sag or become floppy from being tied as a chair, slip a piece of plywood between the sections forming the back of the chair to add stiffness. The width of the mattress determines whether the chair bed will accommodate one or two persons.

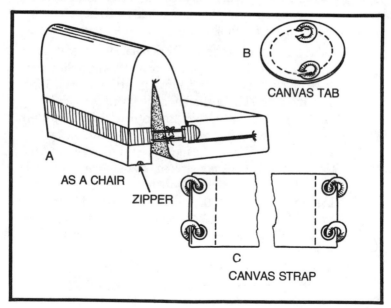

B

CANVAS TAB

A

AS A CHAIR

ZIPPER

C

CANVAS STRAP

Fig. 1-3. Fold-up chair bed.

ROCKING CHAIR BED

Another low-to-the-floor piece of furniture that can be easily built is the rocking chair bed. Although the project requires only minimal carpentry in building the rocking base, it does require some planning.

Before you even get out the saw, lay out the pattern for the base on heavy manila paper that will lie flat. You can recycle a heavy grocery sack for this purpose; but you must get the creases out, or they will throw off your measurements. The pattern need only be a little over half the rocker size because it can be turned end over end and completed by duplication. The paper for the pattern should be at least 50 by 15 inches.

Use light lines at first, then heavy ones when you are sure they are right. Use a soft pencil with a sharp point (so the lines aren't too wide) to lay out a rocker pattern as shown in Fig. 1-4A. Carry the curve at the middle of the rocker bottom beyond the center line to insure smoothness.

Each rocker can be sawed from either an 8 foot length of 2-by-12 or ¾-inch plywood. A 4 by 8 foot plywood sheet will be enough to cut both rockers, with usable scrap left over. Do not attempt to piece a rocker as this will cause a bump and interfere with its comfort. The rockers must be able to withstand the strain of the shifting pressure of supporting a relaxed human body.

Lay out the pattern as follows:

1. Along a straight line draw a horizontal line at least 1 inch from the bottom of the pattern paper. Using a 90 degree angle, draw a right angle line rising vertically about 1 inch from the right side of the horizontal line.

2. Measure exactly 48 inches to the middle of the pattern paper and draw another vertical line parallel to the one you drew in step 1. This will be the center line of your pattern.

3. Using a cord that will not stretch, lay out a curve with a 48 inch radius from the right edge of the paper at least as far as 12 inches to the left of the center line. To do this, hold the cord with a tack or nail 48 inches above the bottom line where it meets the center line, then swing your pencil in a smooth arc.

4. With the cord still swinging from the same tack, draw a shorter arc 6 inches above, extending over both sides of the center line a few inches.

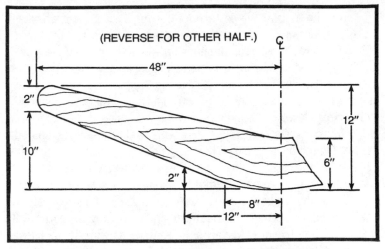

Fig. 1-4A. Half of the rocker sawing pattern for a rocking chair bed.

5. Using a straight edge, connect the lower curve to a mark 10 inches up from the bottom line at the left vertical line and smooth out the curve.
6. Again using the straight edge, connect the curve you have drawn 6 inches up from the bottom line to a point 12 inches up from the bottom line and 48 inches to the left of the center line.
7. Round off between the left ends of the two lines drawn in steps 5 and 6.

Additional dimensions are given on Fig. 1-4A to assist you in drawing a smooth curve for the rocker. You now have a pattern for half the rocker. Tape the pattern (or tack it) securely to the plywood panel and transfer the outline for sawing.

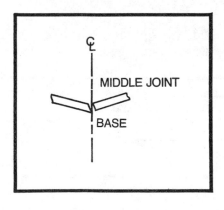

Fig. 1-4B. Middle joint base of a rocking chair bed.

17

You can transfer the pattern for sawing by using carbon paper or by brushing on carbon powder between the paper and the wood. When you have transferred the lines on which to saw to the left side of the plywood panel, turn the pattern upside down and trace the right side. Be sure that the center line on the pattern and the center line on the wood correspond exactly and you will have a smooth curve reproduced on the wood as a sawing guide.

Do your sawing carefully and with a sharp saw for smooth edges. Do not be in a hurry because at this point you can spoil the plywood or the rocker by too much haste. Unless you are sure that you can control it, do not attempt to use a saber saw for this job.

To insure that both rockers are exactly the same size and have the same curves, be careful about placing and tracing the pattern. If you trace the second rocker around the first, saw inside the lines.

Sand both rocker pieces, especially the edges. If you intend to use the rocker on a concrete floor, it is a good idea to face the bottom edge of both rockers with metal weatherstripping that is thin enough to bend smoothly to the curved bottom of the rockers.

The base must be cut from two pieces of ¾-inch plywood to accommodate the curve at the middle of the top of the rockers. One way to do this is to cut two pieces 30 inches wide by 48 inches long. Leave the inner edge (middle) of one of these pieces square, and shave the second piece so that when it butts against the first, it will fit snugly where they join (Fig. 1-4B). Nail and glue these pieces to the top of the base at each side.

To prevent the rockers from springing out at the bottom when weight is put upon them, dowel glue in four ¾-inch wooden rods about an inch from the bottom, 6 inches in from each end and halfway to the middle as shown in Fig. 1-4C. The rocker bed is now ready to be finished and covered. Sand, paint, or stain as desired, and allow to dry thoroughly.

The base can be covered with either solid or cored polyurethane foam pad. Cut the pad larger than the dimensions of the

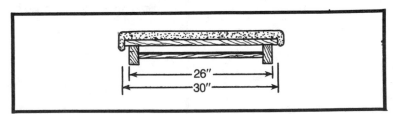

Fig. 1-4C. End view section of a rocking chair bed.

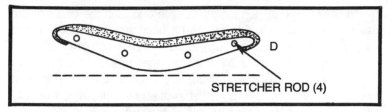

Fig. 1-4D. Side view of a completed rocking chair bed.

base so that you can crowd the foam toward the center rather than stretch it. Bring the foam pad over the edges of the base and glue underneath.

Cover the foam with canvas, bringing it smoothly over the edges on top of the foam, fold under and tack beyond the foam on all sides. When completed, your rocking chair bed will look like Fig. 1-4D from either side.

LEAN-TO CHAIR BED

Until about a century ago it was the habit of many people to sleep sitting upright. Today folks think they must lie flat for a night of restful sleep.

The motion picture industry introduced the slant-board; it isn't exactly for sleeping, but it does enable a star to relax between takes without getting wrinkles in the garments he or she is wearing. Resourceful nonconformists have been known to press (no pun intended) an ironing board into this service.

While the ironing board is usually too short for the comfort of tall people, it gave rise to the idea of a suitable board that can be built in an hour or two—and it can accommodate tall, short, fat or thin people. Like the slant-board, the lean-to chair bed leans against the wall when used for sitting. Used as a bed, the frame lies flat on the floor. The loose canvas conforms to the contours of the body. Measurements can be adapted to suit potential users.

Components of the lean-to consist of a frame and a length of heavy canvas fastened at each end to stretchers. The stretchers slip into notches on opposite sides of the frame about 14 inches in from the ends to provide a chair (Fig. 1-5A). As a bed, the stretchers are moved to the pair of notches located 8 inches from the ends (Fig. 1-5B) and the frame is laid flat on the floor. Gravity and the "fanny" of the occupant make the canvas conform to the body contours.

To build the frame cut two 8 foot lengths of 2-by-6 or 2-by-8 stock, with opposing angles at each end. The angle is determined by the fronts being 6 inches longer at each end than the backs of the frame. This enables the frame to tilt back from the floor (at the bottom) to the wall (at the top), resting solidly on both surfaces.

Cut the four notches to take the bare ends of the stretchers. The two stretchers should be cut from 2-by-2s of a strong grained wood, about 96 inches long so that each end will protrude from the frame far enough to be grasped. Cut the notches in the opposite sides of the frame on the long sides 8 inches from the ends and the second pair of notches 4 inches further along toward the middle (Fig. 1-5C).

Cut the top and the bottom of the frame from matching lumber, 30 inches long (Fig. 1-5D). These pieces fit inside the side pieces to complete the frame. From scrap cut four corner reinforcement triangles as shown in Fig.1-5E. Prebore two holes at an angle through each of these and ream at the top slightly to seat woodscrews. Use flathead screws long enough to pass through the corner blocks and bite into the frame.

Assemble the frame using nails, woodscrews and glue. Sand and finish by staining or painting. Allow to dry thoroughly.

To prevent the lean-to from slipping on the floor, you can glue carpeting to the bottom. If the floor is slippery, hooks, such as used on screen doors, can be installed at the top to secure the top to screweyes in the wall when the lean-to is being used as a chair, but this is seldom necessary and limits the mobility of the lean-to. The weight of the occupant should be enough, plus the carpeting at the bottom, to prevent it from slipping.

Hem heavy canvas on all sides, the top and bottom hems being wide enough to slip the stretchers through them. The canvas should be 30 inches wide by 76 inches long when finished so that it will fit inside the frame. Should you want to add the ability to adjust the length of the canvas, and at the same time do less sewing, tack-glue the canvas to the spreaders. This will enable you to use a slightly longer canvas and adjust its length to the occupant. The canvas should curve downward when the lean-to is used as a bed so that it misses the floor by about 2 inches. Add foam padding if you wish, but it is surprising how comfortable this lean-to can be either as a chair or a bed.

HAMMOCKS

Some people object to sleeping on the floor and prefer some sort of suspended bed. A hammock may be the answer for them.

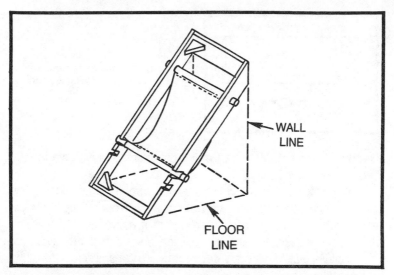

Fig. 1-5A. A lean-to chair bed leans against the wall when used for sitting.

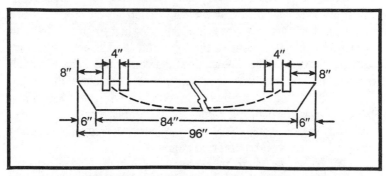

Fig. 1-5B. As a bed, the frame of the lean-to is laid flat on the floor.

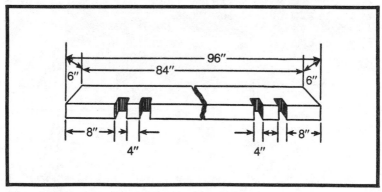

Fig. 1-5C. Notches are cut on the long sides of the frame.

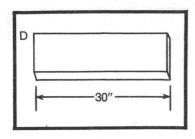

Fig. 1-5D. The top and bottom of the frame, cut from matching lumber.

Hammocks are not difficult to make using any of a wide variety of materials and designs.

When the subject of hammocks comes up, most people think of a woven or canvas sling with a stretcher at each end, slung between two structural uprights or two trees if out-of-doors (Fig. 1-6). When the sag is deep enough and the spreaders are sufficiently wide, an older child or agile adult can safely get in and out and lie comfortably in this style of bed.

Since the hammock can be easily detached at one or both ends, rolled up and stashed out of the way when not in use, they are popular on boats where there is limited space in the cabins. The sling sways with the movement of the boat and the sleeper, held in by gravity, is less apt to be thrown out than were he sleeping in a bunk attached to the deck that swayed with the movement of the boat.

A sling hammock can be contrived from strong fishnet, heavy twine, canvas or even macrame. Books detail how to make just about any of these slings. Add two spreader rods, strong rings and hang it from each end by marine rope.

The chief objection to a sling hammock is that some measure of agility and practice is needed to successfully get into it. It seems to be easy enough to fall out of according to some folks. Sling beds overcome some of these objections.

SLING BEDS

Sling beds differ from hammocks in that they are suspended from above rather than the two ends, thereby having more stability

Fig. 1-5E. Cut four corner blocks and bore holes for woodscrews.

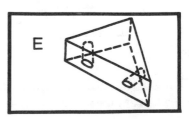

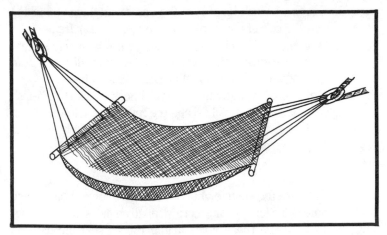

Fig. 1-6. A typical sling hammock.

and are not so apt to offer the evasive action to attempts at getting into them. Since they are suspended rather than sitting on legs, they take up no floor space. Sling beds have frames or bases. We will discuss two distinct types of sling beds: the head-foot frames and the flat-base slings. Since the head-foot frame types are more like the hammock, we will discuss these first.

Head-Foot Framed Slings

The head-foot framed sling bed, as the name suggests, consists of two frames, one at the head and one at the foot, connected by two pipe side rails. The head frame and the foot frame are suspended from the ceiling by marine rope hanging vertically to each upper corner. The occupant lies in the sling suspended on both sides by the side rails.

The frames can be constructed three ways: from wood 2-by-4s, either joined with the 4-inch way vertically or horizontally, or they can be constructed from ¾-inch common plumber's pipe. All three versions can be suspended with the ropes attached to individual hooks in the ceiling or with the two ropes at the foot and at the head hooked to yokes suspended from a ceiling hook. This method of suspension requires only two hooks in the ceiling.

The wooden frames with the 2 inch side of the 2-by-4s uppermost is built as shown in Fig. 1-7A. Proceed as follows:

1. Cut two 30 inch lengths of Douglas Fir or hardwood 2-by-4 with 45 degree mitered ends so that the 2 inch widths will be vertical.

2. Cut two 12 inch lengths of the same wood with matching mitered corners to complete the rectangular frame.
3. Drill four 5/16-inch holes through the 4 inch way so that they escape the miter joint and are an equal distance from the ends, one in each end of each 30 inch piece.
4. Drill a hole through the 2 inch thickness to take the ¾-inch pipe side rail that will escape the miter at the lower end of each 12 inch piece. These holes should be exactly the same distance from the end of the board.
5. Form two rectangular frames, 30 by 12 inches, from these components.
6. Cut from the scrap eight corner reinforcement blocks and bore holes for installing screws at an angle as shown in Fig. 1-7D. Ream these holes at the top to seat the flathead screws.
7. Install corner blocks using glue and flathead screws long enough to bite into the frame.
8. Obtain two ¾-inch common plumber's pipes 78 inches long. They should be threaded on each end to fit pipe caps. Paint to prevent corrosion.
9. Install in holes at lower ends of head and foot frames and secure by screwing on the caps. If the pipe side rails tend to slide too easily through the holes in the frames, shim them.
10. If you have made the frames from Douglas Fir, you will probably want to paint them; if you have made them from a hardwood, you will want to merely lacquer them, but the pipes must be painted. Before painting be sure that all edges and corners are rounded and the wood smooth. Allow to dry thoroughly before proceeding.
11. Measure off two lengths of ¼-inch marine rope. The length will depend on the height of the ceiling and the distance from the floor you want your sling bed to hang. It will also depend on the length of the chain you use at the ceiling hooks or whether or not you use the yoke arrangement in the suspension. This will be discussed under Suspension Methods for Head-Foot Framed Slings. Since the covering and sling for the three versions are the same, these will be discussed under the next heading.

To build the alternate head-foot frame sling bed proceed as follows:

1. Cut two 30 inch lengths of 2-by-4 but this time so that the miters will join them with the 4 inch widths horizontal as shown in Fig. 1-7B. Miter corners at 45 degrees.
2. Cut two 12 inch lengths of the same wood with matching miters to complete this frame.

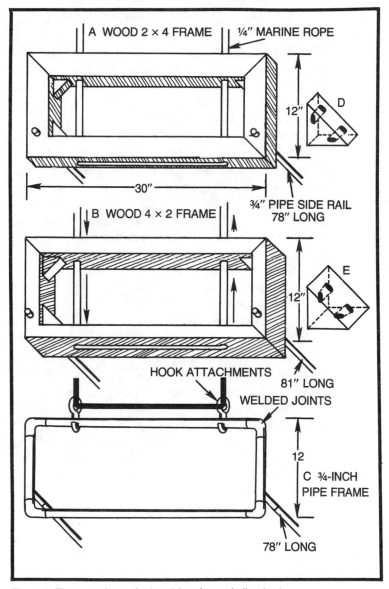

Fig. 1-7. Three versions of a head-foot framed sling bed.

3. Drill 5/16-inch holes through the 2 inch way so that they escape the miter joint and are an equal distance from the ends of the bottom of the top of the 12 inch pieces. The holes should be exactly in a line.
4. Toward the bottom of the 12 inch pieces drill a hole in each corner to snugly take the ¾-inch pipe side rails. The pipe should fit tight enough not to readily pull through or be shimmed.
5. Cut eight corner reinforcing blocks as shown in Fig. 1-7E. Bore two holes in each at angles to take the shanks of the woodscrews and ream at the top so that the flatheads do not protrude. The threads should bite into the frame to hold the corner blocks securely.
6. Obtain two ¾-inch common plumber's pipe 81 inches in length and threaded on each end to take caps. Force these through the holes drilled in step 4. If they do not fit snugly so that they will not slip through readily or turn, shim them. Screw on the caps tightly.
7. If you have made the frames from Douglas Fir, you will probably want to paint but if you have used hardwood, you will only want to lacquer. Sand smooth, rounding all corners before finishing and allow to dry thoroughly.
8. Since all variations of the head-foot frame sling are rigged and suspended similarly, refer to the paragraphs entitled Suspension Methods for Head-Foot Framed Slings. For covering refer to Covering for Head-Foot Framed Slings.

The third method of building the head-foot framed sling bed is using pipe frames. It is best to have the ¾-inch common plumber's pipe fabricated by a professional welder. This will not be expensive and much safer unless you are set up to do your own metal work and have all of the equipment and know-how.

Have the pipe formed into the two frames (Fig. 1-7C) with side rails, 78 inches long, welded to the frames at the lower end of each. Have the frame wire brushed and paint to prevent corrosion.

Holes bored through the pipe will tend to cut through rope, so install hooks to which to attach the suspension rope. Suspension methods are similar to those for the other two versions of this sling.

Covering for Head-Foot Slings

To provide the sleeper with a comfortable surface on which to relax it is slung between the two side rails. The sling should hang

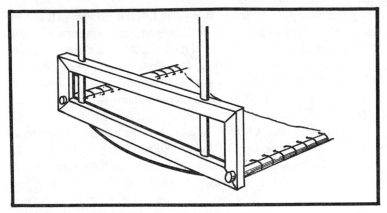

Fig. 1-8A. Canvas laced covering.

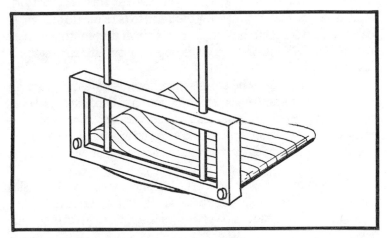

Fig. 1-8B. Webbing covering.

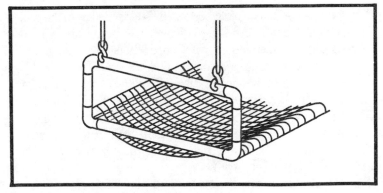

Fig. 1-8C. Interwoven rope covering.

free and must support the entire weight of the occupant. It can be made of heavy canvas, laced onto the side rails rather than sliding onto them through wide hems. This is best since the canvas may have to be replaced or, at best, laundered, which lacing permits. Hem the canvas on all sides. Install grommets lengthwise on each side at least every 2 inches. The ends should be left unattached to permit some sag.

Using upholsterer's rope or leather thongs, lace the sides to the pipe rails as shown in Fig. 1-8A. Allow about three times the length of a side for the lacing material so that it will not have to be pieced. Tie knots securely underneath.

If you choose to use webbing Fig. 1-8B, it must be wound continuously on a side. The problem here is in securing it on the pipe at the start and finish on a side. The best way is to take a double turn around the pipe and securely sew the doubled back turn to the end. A dab of glue will help to hold it. The webbing must be with no gaps between strips because it will not be interwoven. Use upholsterer's heavy thread.

Rope will probably be more satisfactory than webbing because it can be tied off at both ends, but the same objection holds true here, it cannot be fastened to the head and foot frames in interweaving (Fig. 1-8C). Plastic rope tends to stretch and will sag too much under the weight of a body. Lacing on heavy canvas will prove to be more satisfactory.

Rope or macrame can be woven but must be covered by muslin or a fabric to make a comfortable sleeping surface. A thin polyurethane foam pad can be placed on top of this and covered with fabric.

Suspension Methods for Head-Foot Framed Slings

A head-foot framed sling bed can be suspended from the ceiling using either two or four hooks, however the four point suspension method provides the sleeper with more stability.

In the four point suspension method, the ropes go vertically up from each corner of the sling to three or four links of a strong chain, which hook onto individual ceiling hooks (Fig. 1-9A). The ceiling hooks must be securely embedded into a structural member and have sufficiently deep threads to take the weight of the occupant of the sling. Knots in the ¼-inch marine rope must be tied off securely and the tap ends wound with cord.

The two point suspension method only requires two ceiling hooks, but these must share the total weight. The suspension ropes

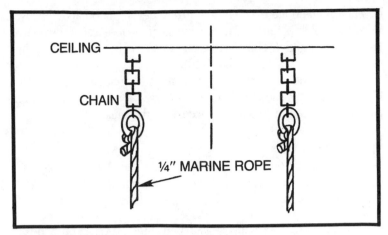

Fig. 1-9A. Four point suspension method.

again go up vertically, but to the yoke instead of to the ceiling. The yokes at the head and foot are suspended by an inverted V of strong chain, the top links of which hook onto the ceiling hooks (Fig. 1-9B). Be sure that all knots and attachments are secure so that they will carry the weight and not come loose when the sling swings.

Head-Foot Framed Sling Cradle

By varying the dimensions for adults, it is possible to build a head-foot framed sling cradle by using any of the three frame designs, but there is the problem of preventing baby from falling out of

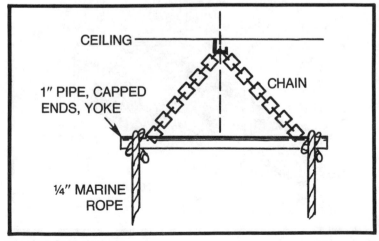

Fig. 1-9B. Yoke rigging.

it. This can be done by rigging a strong netting hood above baby. From the middle of the head to the middle of the foot frames stretch a strong cord tightly. The netting hood can be held off of baby by draping it over this cord (Fig. 1-10).

Fashion the hood from strong fishnet so that air can circulate freely over baby. Secure it to three sides by sewing, lacing or pinning. Pin the fourth side for access to the child.

Flat Base Sling Beds

There are three basic types of flat base sling beds that you can build. Two of these bases are made from wood, one as a frame and the other a plywood platform. A pipe base frame can also be built of pipe.

The wood framed flat base sling bed (Fig. 1-11) can be made of Douglas Fir or hardwood as follows:

1. Cut two lengths 72 inches long and two 30 inches long, mitering and doweling the corners from a 2-by-4. These dimensions can be increased, but not by more than 3 inches if you want your sling to be larger.
2. Cut four reinforcing blocks for the corners and predrill holes on the slant for the shanks of two woodscrews. Ream at the top to seat the flat heads flush. The screw threads should bite into the frame.

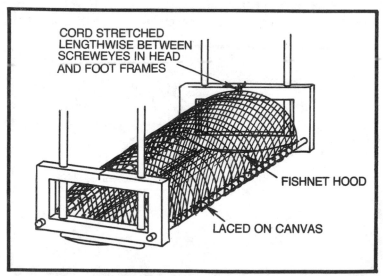

Fig. 1-10. Head-foot framed sling cradle.

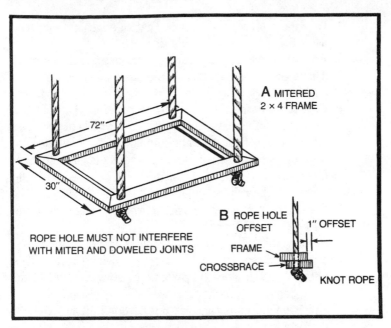

Fig. 1-11. Wood framed flat base sling bed.

3. Assemble these components into a frame as shown in Fig. 1-11A. Glue and allow to thoroughly dry.

4. Cut two more pieces of the 2-by-4 for crossbraces that jog inward 1 inch (Fig. 1-11B) and slightly round off the ends.

5. Nail crossbraces so that they jog inward 1 inch (Fig. 1-11B) to permit the rope holes to better escape interference with the mitered corners of the frame and the dowels.

6. Bore rope holes 5/16-inch in diameter through this double thickness formed in step 5.

7. Sand frame and paint or stain as desired. Allow to dry thoroughly.

8. Cover frame base as described under Covering the Flat Based Sling Bed.

9. Rig suspension using one of the methods discussed under Suspension Methods for the Flat Base Sling Bed.

The plywood base flat sling bed version (Fig. 1-12) is built as follows:

1. Cut two panels of ¾-inch plywood 72 by 30 inches. These dimensions can be increased but by no more than 3 inches each way.

2. Glue these panels together so that all edges are even and allow the glue to thoroughly dry.
3. From the scrap cut four triangles to reinforce the corners. These should be 6 inches on the sides adjoining the right angle.
4. Glue these corners to the bottom panel so that they are even with both edges. Unless you are certain of your glue job, a couple of short, flathead wood screws inserted toward the outer points of the reinforcements will help. Seat these screws so that the heads will be even with the surface of the reinforcements.
5. Bore 5/16-inch holes at each corner through the three thicknesses of plywood.
6. Sand so that all edges and surfaces are smooth. If you cannot attain smoothness with no splintering at the edges of the plywood, glue on halfround molding to cover them. (See step 8.)
7. Finish any portions that will not be covered and allow to thoroughly dry.
8. Spot glue polyurethane foam pad of the desired thickness to the top of the upper panel, crowding the foam toward the center rather than stretching it. Bring the pad around and over the edges, around the suspension ropes and glue underneath. If you prefer, instead of bringing the foam pad around the suspension ropes, proceed to step 9.
9. Locate the rope holes bored in step 5 from underneath the base at each of the four corners and extend them up

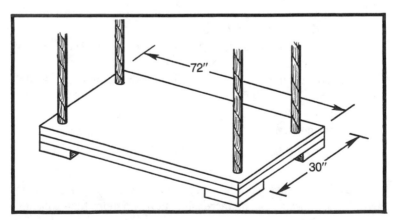

Fig. 1-12. A plywood base flat sling bed.

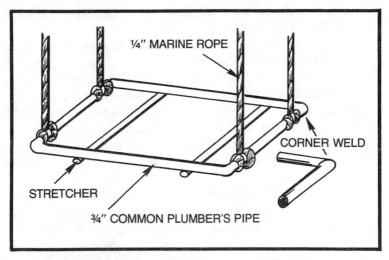

Fig. 1-13. Pipe framed sling bed.

through the pad carefully and without tearing the foam or loosening the pad from the panel.

10. Thread the suspension ropes through these holes and follow the instructions under Suspension Methods for the Flat Base Sling Bed.

11. Cover the sling as discussed in Covering the Flat Based Sling Bed.

The third version of the flat based sling bed is the pipe frame (Fig. 1-13). Construct it as follows:

1. Construct a rectangular frame from ¾-inch plumber's pipe 72 inches in length by 30 inches in width. It is a good idea to have this done by a professional welder unless you are set up to do your own metal work.

2. Weld in two stretchers of the same pipe, each 30 inches long, about 24 inches from each end of the frame.

3. Buff pipe and all welded joints clean and paint to prevent corrosion. Allow to thoroughly dry.

4. Rig suspension and cover.

Suspension Methods for Flat Base Sling Beds

The flat base sling can be suspended by any of several methods, all of which use ¼-inch marine rope, short lengths of strong chain and heavy hooks with sufficiently deep threads to bite deeply into the structural members. These hooks may be in the ceiling or in the wall.

Either four or two hooks are required depending on which method of suspension you prefer to use.

To swing freely the flat base sling is best suspended with the ¼-inch marine rope rising vertically from each of the four corners to three or four links of heavy chain (Fig. 1-14), hooked to heavy hooks embedded into structural members in the ceiling (Fig. 1-14A). These hooks should have deep enough threads to hold the weight. Paint the chain and hook to prevent corrosion and tie the rope securely. This method of suspension is the most foolproof since, should one rope fail, the other three will prevent the sling from falling.

If for some reason you prefer the two point ceiling method, run the ropes from each corner of the sling vertically up to two yokes suspended by three or four links of heavy chain hooked to two ceiling hooks (Fig. 1-14B). The yoke, suspending a rope at each capped end, should be 1 inch common plumber's pipe. Paint chains, hook and pipe to prevent corrosion. Twice as much weight must be carried by each hook and should one fail, the occupant of the sling will be let down with a crash that could injure him.

Should you desire to use the sling for seating as well as for sleeping, use the two point wall hung suspension method (Fig. 1-14C). In this method the front ropes must be longer than the back ropes, which go up vertically to the chain. In rigging this suspension follow this procedure:

1. Embed two strong hooks into structural members of the wall at points equal to the distance between the head and foot ropes.
2. Measure down to the desired distance you want the sling to be from the floor, about 18 to 24 inches.
3. Make up back head and foot ropes, tie off to the chains and secure to the sling so that the sling is horizontal. Test this by placing a carpenter's level lengthwise on the sling and adjust until the bubble in the level is exactly centered.
4. Rig the front ropes to their chains, testing to be sure it is level. Measuring up from the floor will not ensure the levelness.
5. Re-check all tieoffs and attachments.
6. Since the sling now contacts the wall at the back, to prevent marring it needs a bump-board. Cut a piece the length of the sling base and bolt it to the wall. By painting it the same color as the wall, it will not be noticeable but will

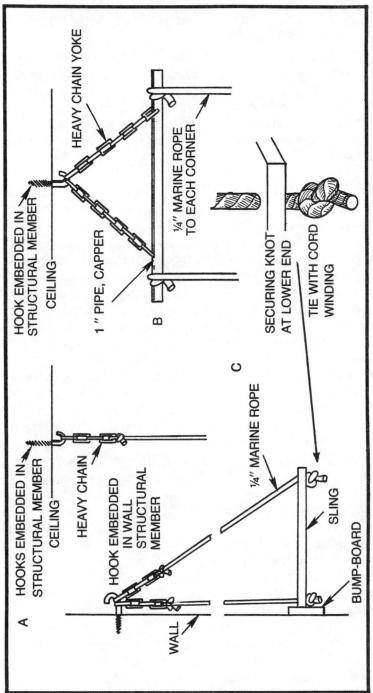

Fig. 1-14 A. Four point suspension for a flat base sling bed. B. Two point suspension method for a flat base sling bed. C. Two point wall hung suspension method for a flat base sling bed.

protect the wall from marring as the sling will be bumping against it frequently.

This method of suspension has the advantage of not swinging free. When a person backing up to the sling to sit down lowers himself into the sling base, it will not swing away from him. It also overcomes the objection some people have to slings and hammocks—the swinging sensation that makes some sleepers fear that they will fall out. Since all of the weight is held by the two hooks, they must be strong and well embedded.

Covering the Flat Base Sling Beds

All three versions of the flat base sling can be covered with webbing, rope or canvas. Since the wood and pipe bases are frames, they lend themselves best to interwoven webbing or rope while the solid base plywood sling gains little by either of these coverings.

The plywood based flat sling needs only polyurethane foam padding and a fabric cover. The thickness of the foam depends on how soft you want the bed to be. The cored type of foam pad will not only provide softness on which the occupant will lie but can be drawn nicely over the edges to pad and finish the plywood thickness. This will need to be covered in some manner as plywood tends to splinter at the edges. Figure 1-15A shows how the cores of a foam pad can be deformed to fit around the edges. Solid pads, of course, can also be drawn over the edges if you prefer to use this type (Fig. 1-15B).

Using either type of foam pad, spot glue it firmly to the top surface of the upper panel of the plywood base. Be sure to push it toward the center, not stretch the pad. When you come to the edges, bend the pad gently around to the underneath side, leaving all of the surplus possible, tack and glue solidly. This will not only make the top surface more comfortable to an occupant but take care of the sharp edges.

Over the foam pad spread a heavy fabric, such as a canvas covering. Carry it around the edges over the pad to beyond the end of the pad. Turn the edges of the fabric under and tack it about every inch. Spread the covering so that it will not bind on the pad yet fit smoothly. The tacks can be removed should you later want to remove the covering for laundering.

Webbing covering can benefit both the wooden and the pipe frames, but it is more difficult to anchor on the pipe frame. It will hold better if you take several turns around the pipe and hold it with glue at the start and finish of each length of webbing. One continuous strip

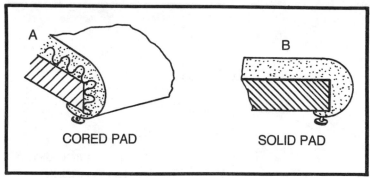

Fig. 1-15. Foam pad edge treatment.

of webbing should cross on top as well as underneath the frame, and this will double the amount of webbing you will need. Interweave it at right angles (Fig. 1-16A) as well.

Begin by winding the webbing, just behind the suspension rope at the corner, several times around the pipe and secure it with glue. It will be even better if you sew it with heavy upholsterer's thread. Come out over the pipe and across to the opposite side, keeping the webbing as taut as possible. Bring the webbing back across the frame underneath and repeat until you have filled the length of the pipe frame edge-to-edge with the webbing. Anchor by extra lapping and sew as before. Leave no gaps between strips of webbing above or below the frame except for the slight angle as you bring it back underneath so that the next strip will fall right next to the previous one.

Anchoring the webbing in the same manner as at the start, interweave it lengthwise until you have filled the width of the frame. At the end, anchor as before. Now you have a double thickness of webbing interwoven to fill the frame. If you only used a single thickness of webbing, every other crossing would come from beneath the pipe, leaving an uneven appearance and the pipe bare in these spots.

In covering the wooden frame with webbing it can be tacked underneath at each side (Fig. 1-16B) or wound continuously as described for the pipe frame design. Tacking should be reinforced by glue. Obviously, continuous winding is the strongest method and is certainly a lot less work.

Should you decide to tack glue each strip of webbing to the wooden frame, leave a square around the suspension rope and, turning the frame upside down, place five tacks about 1½ or 2 inches

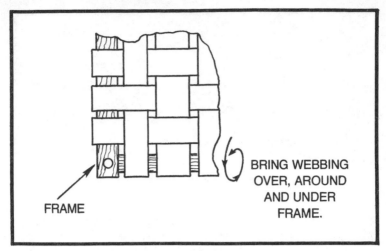

Fig. 1-16A. Interwoven webbing on a pipe frame.

back from the end of the webbing to secure the webbing exactly at a right angle to the length or width of the frame. Put in these tacks about the middle of the board and in a straight row across the webbing. Fold the webbing back over this and secure the tag end with four more tacks, also in a straight row but nearer the outer edge of the frame so that they will not interfere with the row of five. Reinforce tacking with glue. When you have completed the installation of the webbing by continuous winding or by tacking each strip, it will look like Fig. 1-16C.

Both open frames, the wood and the pipe, benefit from the use of interwoven ¼-inch rope. It should be woven in at least two directions and can even have a few diagonals for added strength and to help to keep the rope from bunching. Never leave more than 2 inches between strands, less is better. To prevent the covering from going down into the gaps, a piece of muslin should be stretched over the rope before putting on a foam pad and fabric covering.

The rope must be anchored to the pipe frame securely. Leaving a 20 inch tail to be used in the final tie off, loop the rope around the pipe twice, with the second loop over-lapping the first and the knot held in place by both of them (Fig. 1-17). Use ¼-inch rope that will not stretch, such as marine rope. To counteract the tendency of the rope to slip on the pipe, it is a good idea to anchor it with glue.

With the knot stabilized against the inner side of the pipe, bring it around and over the outer circumference and across to the opposite side of the frame. Stretch it tautly over that pipe and take it back

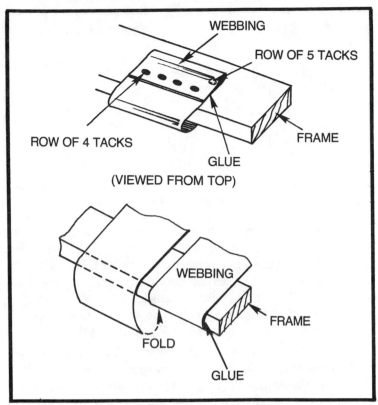

Fig. 1-16B. Tacking webbing to a wooden frame for flat base sling beds.

from underneath, stretching it to a position about 1½-inches along the opposite pipe rail. Continue down the length of the frame until you have filled it to within about 2 inches from the end. If you have plenty of rope left, start the crossweaving, if not, tie off securely.

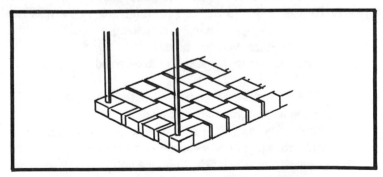

Fig. 1-16C. Completed interwoven webbing on a wooden frame.

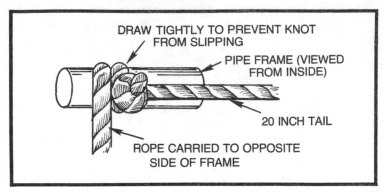

DRAW TIGHTLY TO PREVENT KNOT FROM SLIPPING

PIPE FRAME (VIEWED FROM INSIDE)

20 INCH TAIL

ROPE CARRIED TO OPPOSITE SIDE OF FRAME

Fig. 1-17. Anchoring the rope on a pipe frame.

Always before tying off the rope re-check the tautness of what you have woven. It is always better to carry on with the rope rather than cutting it. Whenever you must tie on another piece, make sure that the knot is secure and lies underneath the frame. The final tie off will be to the 20 inch tail left at the start.

The wooden frame base probably benefits the most from rope lacing. Install the lacing as shown in Fig. 1-18 as follows:

1. Drill ¼-inch diameter holes every 1½-inches in a straight line (closer will weaken the wood) about 1¼-inches in from the inner edge. The sling will be more comfortable if you slightly groove out channels for the rope from the top of each hole to the inner edge of the frame.

2. About 20 inches from the end of the rope tie a sizeable knot as shown in Fig. 1-14C that will not slip into the hole in the frame. Snug the knot up to the first hole beyond the suspension rope. If the knot tends to be drawn into the hole, tie a larger one before proceeding.

3. Pass the rope up through the first hole and across the frame to the opposite hole, stretching it taut. Thread the rope down through this hole.

4. Take the rope to the next hole and thread it up through it, drawing it tight.

5. Take the rope across to the opposite side of the frame and thread it down through that hole.

6. Here is where a helper will come in handy to hold the rope taut with a pair of pliers while you are threading it up and down through the holes. Continue until you have filled the length of the frame.

7. Re-check tautness of what you have done before proceeding to interweave lengthwise.
8. If you have a length of rope left, carry it around the corner and proceed to fill the holes widthwise, interweaving as you go. Tie any knots needed on the underside of the frame securely.
9. When you have laced the entire frame, tie off the rope to the 20 inch tail you left at the start.

Adding a few diagonals strengthens the lacing. Diagonal lacing will assist in keeping the interweaving in place if it is tied to ropes where they cross, but, unless you use a thick foam pad, they may provide uncomfortable bumps in the surface.

No matter which method of covering you use on the plywood base frame, if you leave the corners around the rope bare, the edges will need attention. Since plywood is made of laminated layers of wood, they should be covered. Slightly round them and glue on upholsterer's beading or thin weatherstripping that will curve smoothly with the arc of the corner.

Another way to cover the corners of the plywood sling is to extend the foam pad and fabric covering and pass the rope up through it. No matter which version of a flat base sling bed you have made, it should now be ready for you to take a well deserved nap.

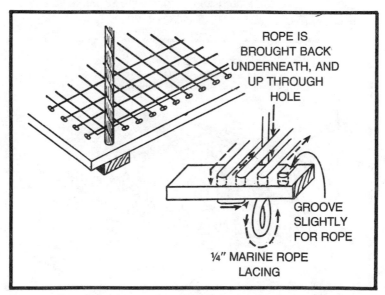

Fig. 1-18. Rope lacing in a wooden framed flat base sling bed.

Flat Base Sling Cradle

Any of these flat base sling designs can be adapted to use for a cradle with appropriate dimensions and the addition of a fishnet hood to prevent baby from falling out (Fig. 1-19). The fishnet hood should be rigged above baby and secured permanently on three sides. The fourth side is pinned to give access. Leave plenty of space for baby's movements and for taking him or her out of the cradle.

MATERIALS
Metal Springs

In general there are three types of metal springs. All of them offer resiliency and support providing that they are properly installed. Two of these are coil: the hourglass type and the gang mounted cone type. The flat type springs are called no-sag, and are probably the easiest for the amateur to install. All of these springs are also available in standard bed sizes.

When you build a bed that needs a surface 6 or 7 inches above the base or slats, and you do not want to use a prebuilt box spring, hourglass springs, named for their shape, will give you added height (Fig. 1-20A). Since each hourglass spring is separate, they must be sewn to the webbing to hold their place.

The cone spring also gets its name from its shape (Fig. 1-20B). These springs are mounted and do not have to be sewn into the webbing.

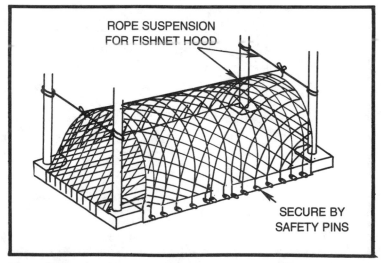

ROPE SUSPENSION
FOR FISHNET HOOD

SECURE BY
SAFETY PINS

Fig. 1-19. Flat base sling cradle with a fishnet hood.

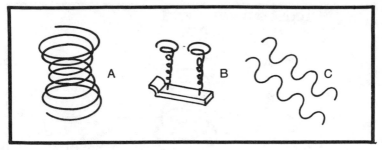

Fig. 1-20. Three types of metal springs.
A. Hourglass Spring
B. Cone Spring
C. Flat no-sag spring

The flat no-sag spring probably came from a trade name (Fig. 1-20C) and requires hardware or a sling to be held in place.

To install hourglass springs, fill the bed frame with interwoven webbing spaced so that each spring is located where webbing crosses. The webbing must be at least a ½-inch wider on each side than the spring. If the spring measures 3 inches across the bottom, the webbing must be 4 inches or more in width. This spring must be placed with the top side up. The top has a loose end while the bottom coil is a solid circle.

Using upholster's sewing twine and a curved needle (Fig. 1-21A) install the hourglass spring as follows:

1. Position the hourglass spring in the center of the square formed by the crossing of the interwoven webbing, making sure that the solid circle end of the spring is down and the one with the loose end is uppermost and turned toward the center of the bed. Start with the middle lengthwise row of the webbing.

2. Holding the spring flat against the crossed webbing, insert the curved needle through both pieces of webbing and take three or four stitches over the bottom circle of the spring at 9, 12, 3 and 6 o'clock.

3. Do not depend on a knot in the end of the thread to keep it from slipping through the webbing. Tie the thread securely to the spring wire. After installing one spring, carry the thread over to the next. At the last spring in that row, securely knot the tail end of that piece of thread to the next length of thread. Do this also if you run out of thread along a row.

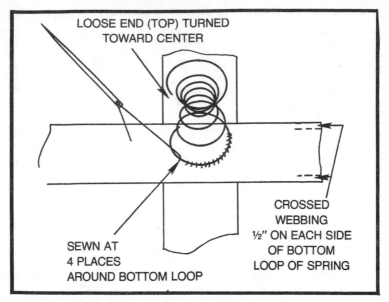

LOOSE END (TOP) TURNED
TOWARD CENTER

CROSSED
WEBBING
½" ON EACH SIDE
OF BOTTOM
LOOP OF SPRING

SEWN AT
4 PLACES
AROUND BOTTOM LOOP

Fig. 1-21A. An hourglass spring sewn to crossed webbing.

The gang mounted cone type springs carry their own attachment so require only woodscrew attachment to the bed frame (Fig. 1-21B).

The flat, no-sag springs are attached by a hardware cleat to the frame (Fig. 1-21C). They should be overlaid with webbing tacked to the bed frame on each side. These springs can be cut in lengths to fit the need, therefore are ideal for use on odd-sized beds or cradles.

Tying Coil Springs

All coil springs, including the hourglass and cone-type, must be tied to keep them upright and properly spaced at the top under a flat surface. Use 6-ply tying twine for this purpose and start with the middle lengthwise row. Anchor the twine at the end of this row leaving about a 20 inch tail and loop it between a pair of no. 12 or 14 webbing tacks driven halfway into the wooden frame about a ½-inch apart (Fig. 1-22A).

Before cutting off a length of twine about three times the distance of the row, loop the twine below and well under the heads of the two tacks. Draw it tight and drive the tacks in to firmly hold the twine (Fig. 1-22B).

After measuring a length of the tying twine three times the distance across the tops of all the springs in that row, plus a 20 inch

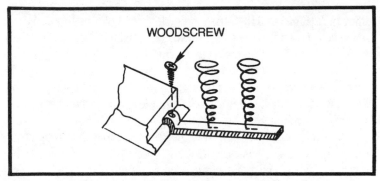

Fig. 1-21B. Gang mounted cone springs carry their own attachment.

tail, you will have a long piece to work with so keep it from getting tangled. Bring the longer end of the twine from the anchoring tacks to the nearest spring and loop it over the top coil, around and back to the left (Fig. 1-22C). Hold it firmly (Fig. 1-22D), between the thumb and forefinger.

Still holding firmly, loop the end of the twine over, than under (Fig. 1-22E) and pull firmly to the left. The tie will then look like the one in Fig. 1-22F. Be sure to pull the twine tight, leaving no slack in it between the springs, but not so tight as to pull the springs out of line. The spring should be properly distended vertically.

Draw the twine across the top of the coil and repeat the tie at the opposite side. Continue the process down that row to the end of the frame. Anchor the twine at the frame by looping it around and under the head of a pair of tacks driven halfway into that side of the frame (Fig. 1-22G). Complete the anchor by looping it under the

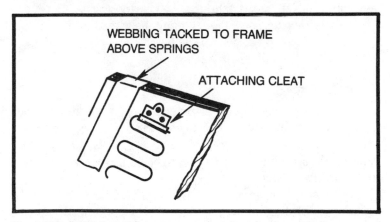

Fig. 1-21C. Installation of flat, no-sag springs by a hardware cleat.

other tack (Fig. 1-22H). Drive the tacks in to hold the loops. When you reach the end, tie off by knotting the twine (Fig. 1-22I), then drive the tacks in to hold the anchoring knot.

You should now be able to press down on any of the springs in the row and have them rebound satisfactorily within the limits of the ties. If the tops of all the springs are not level after they have been tied off, you will have a bumpy bed.

No return ties are needed in the row you have just completed. If there is twine left, you can carry it over along the frame to the next row. When you have completed tying all of the head-to-foot rows, proceed in the same manner to tie the coils in the side-to-side rows.

This method of tying the top of the coils applies to both hourglass and cone type springs. Depending on the height of the coils and the size of the bed, diagonal tying can be limited to squaring up the edges. Make diagonal ties from corner to corner in every other parallel row at each place that ties cross. Tie the twine around the cord being crossed. This prevents rubbing and consequent breaks.

After tying, cover coil springs with a burlap type material. Tack the burlap to the wooden bed frame to prevent it from wrinkling or bunching up. Start tacking from the middle and work toward the edges, placing the tacks about 1½-inches apart. Fit around any posts and do not depress the springs in stretching the fabric.

Some bed builders prefer to sew the burlap covering to the top of the coils to reduce the friction. For this purpose use a curved needle about 4 to 6 inches long and heavy sewing thread. Take several stitches at three or four places on the top ring of each coil and go on to the next spring without cutting the thread. A mattress or foam pad can then be placed on the burlap.

Tying Flat Sprrings

The flat, no-sag springs also need tying, but with extension coils. These are made of finer wire and coiled to provide expansion and contraction. Use at least two extension coils between each length of the flat springs. The last rows should also be attached to the bed frame with extension coils (Fig. 1-23).

A fabric cover, preferably cotton, should be spread on the webbing installed above these springs. Webbing should be stretched above the flat springs and tacked to the bed frame (Fig. 1-21C).

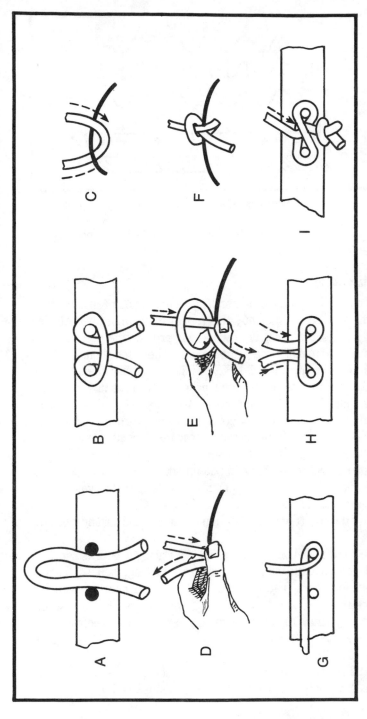

Fig. 1-22 A. Loop twine between tacks placed ½-inch apart. B. Catch twine under tacks, draw tightly and drive in tacks. C. Loop twine around top of coil of spring. D. Hold twine firmly. E. Make a knot. F. Draw knot tightly around wire of top coil. G. Anchor twine at opposite end of frame. H. Complete the anchor by looping twine under second tack. I. Tie off twine and anchor the knot by driving in the tacks.

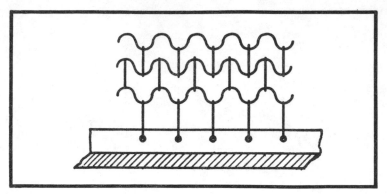

Fig. 1-23. Install extension coils between lengths of flat, no-sag springs.

Some people do not bother with this and use a thick foam pad directly on the flat springs.

Webbing Stretcher

To do a first rate job of installing webbing you need a webbing stretcher. You can either buy this tool or make your own. Making one is not a difficult job. Hardwood will provide the pressure and stress needed to make the webbing taut. The wood should be ½ to ⅝-inch thick because it will have to take some punishment.

Cut the stretcher out of the hardwood as shown in Fig. 1-24A. Into one end drive six evenly spaced 10d nails (Fig. 1-24B) and cut off the heads evenly ½-inch beyond the board. With a metal file taper the ends to a sharp point. Be sure that these points are even.

Cover the opposite end with heavy felt, rubber (a piece of innertube is fine) or leather and pad it underneath. This end should be soft enough so that when you put pressure against it, you will not bruise the palm of your hand.

Use this tool (Fig. 1-24C) when stretching and holding webbing taut.

Secure the webbing at both ends by placing five tacks 2 inches from the end, fold the tail end back over the tacking, then tack a small hem with four tacks. The four tack row should not interfere with the five tack row. Use No. 12 or 14 tacks with sharp points and space them evenly across the webbing in a straight line. The webbing must be secure enough to withstand the pull in stretching it as well as when in use.

When you have secured the webbing at one end and completed the necessary operations to bring it to the opposite side of the frame, repeat the tacking operation without allowing any slack to develop. This can be done by holding the webbing under the stretching tool with one hand and tacking with the other. If a helper is handy, have him or her hold the webbing taut with the stretching tool while you do the tacking.

In most cases webbing should be interwoven at right angles. If the webbing goes over one strip, it should go under the next. This can be done by flattening your hand and pushing the folded back webbing with your fingers extended or using a short piece of lath as a pusher. Your helper can often hold a piece of webbing with a pair of pliers when there is nothing to push the stretching tool against. It should seldom be necessary to add diagonal lacings of webbing.

Foam Padding

When we speak of foam padding today, we refer to polyurethane, either solid or cored. This plastic material overcomes the objections to rubber foam in that it is durable, allergy-free, mildew proof, bacteria proof, lightweight and comfortable to sleep or sit on. These plastic pads do not lump, mat or sag. They do not readily shift or slip and can be washed. Polyurethane foam is easy to use because it can be cut with scissors, tacked or glued and will resist tearing.

Rubber pads will harden and disintegrate in time and cannot be dry-cleaned. Never combine rubber and plastic foams. If you must use both pads, place a piece of muslin cloth between them. However, combining these two materials can cause a chemical reaction

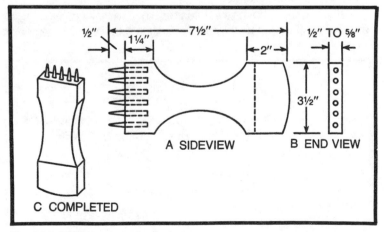

Fig. 1-24. Webbing stretching tool.

that will destroy the rubber, or at best make it turn brittle and discolored. For the same reason, rubber padding under nylon carpet is often unsuccessful.

Foam shees come in a variety of thicknesses and several layers can be cemented together. Where a deeper layer of foam is desired, the cored pads are best because they can be easily molded to the edges. The molded open cores on the underside that give cored pads their superior resiliency, can be easily distorted in bending.

A cored foam pad laid directly on a plywood base can make a quite comfortable bed. When foam is applied directly to plywood, it is a good idea to bore ¾-inch holes for vents every 4 inches to enable it to "breathe."

People insist on perching on the edge of beds. To prevent the edges from sagging when this is repeatedly done, cut a wedge from solid foam and glue it with the wider side along the edge under the covering pad (Fig. 1-25). This can be done whether solid or cored pads are being used as a covering for the bed. If you do not want to glue the wedge to the top pad, secure it with a few tacks to the frame or spot glue it to prevent slippage. This treatment will prevent any tendency to bed sag along the edges. If the wedge is wide enough and extends back far enough, slippage is unlikely even without tacking or gluing as the two pads will tend to stick together.

Methods of obtaining a neat edge treatment have been discussed under Covering the Flat Based Sling Beds. Some people like to overlay the foam pad with muslin cloth and tack it to the frame. If you do this, be sure not to depress or distort the foam pad or you will rob it of some of its resiliency.

If you want to push twin beds together to make a queen sized sleeping surface, the legs of the beds should be lashed together or

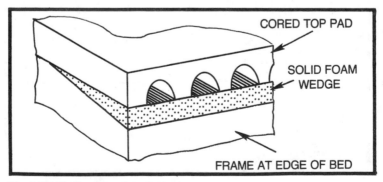

Fig. 1-25. Firming the edge of a bed.

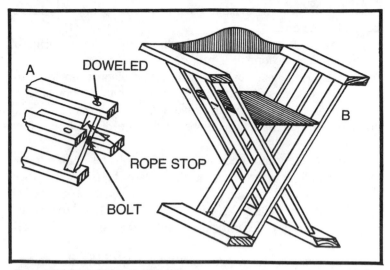

Fig. 1-26A. Straight line X-shaped base.
B. Savanarola—a royal folding seat.

connected by hooks and eyes, such as is used to latch screen doors. A queen sized box spring can be used to provide a smooth full width sleeping surface, or a full width mattress could bridge the gap between the two beds. Beds of exactly the same height will provide the best sleeping surface. If they are not the same height, laying a full width foam pad across the two beds will help. If you use a very thin pad, the valley between the two beds may still be discernible. A ¼-inch plywood panel under a thin solid foam pad will produce a hard but smooth surface.

COTS

The ancient Egyptians used folding beds. These had straight line X-shaped bases that were also used for stools (Fig. 1-26A). The Romans adopted the idea, softening the straight line X-shaped legs into curves. By the Renaissance the design had become a royal folding seat called "Savanarola" (Fig. 1-26B).

Because of its simplicity, the X-shaped, straight leg design is still used today for collapsable bases. A familiar example is the army cot.

Army cots are not particularly expensive, they are light in weight and easily stored. You can pick one up at a garage sale, swap meet or salvage store. Most likely it will need a new cover and a part or two may be missing or broken but these deficiencies are easily remedied. However, should you want to make one from scratch, here's how to do it.

Use a tough, long grained wood with a minimum cross section of 1¼ by 1¼-inches to form the straight X-shaped leg bases at each end of the cot. Use a heavy carriage bolt as the pivot where the legs cross. The top of each leg should be formed into a tenon at least ¾-inch in diameter. The side rails need matching holes at the head and the foot into which the tenons on the top of the legs will fit snugly.

To limit the width the X will spread and to take some of the stress off the canvas covering, install a cord or light chain between the legs above the pivot point. The cord or chain can be inserted in holes bored in the legs and secured on the outer sides so that the limiting cord can be pulled through for folding the legs when the cot is to be stored.

While you may have seen army type cots of slightly different design, this is a simpler way to assemble and disassemble the cot. If you prefer, there can be doweled cross pieces at each end that fit over the ends of the side rails and limit the spread of the pivoting legs, but these make setting up more difficult. They also make it uncomfortable for the feet and make a pillow necessary between the head and the end brace. Just be careful that the legs do not overlap or interfere with each other in folding.

The heavy canvas covering that forms the surface of the bed must be hemmed on all sides. There are two ways to assemble it to the cot: provide wide hems down each side through which to slide the side rails or lace it to the side rails. If stretchers are used at the head and foot, those hems must also be wide enough to take them. Lacing can be used here if desired, but a more comfortable sag will be produced without this stiffness. If you have wrestled with these pieces in assembling such a cot, you will probably want to do it the easier way. There will be more resiliency in this sleeping surface if it is attached only at the two sides.

To lace on the canvas topping, place grommets about 2 inches on center down both sides in the hems. Use ¼-inch marine rope or leather thongs as lacing; plastic will stretch too much.

Here is a tip that I discovered in sleeping on such a cot at camp. A layer of newspapers laid on the canvas beneath the bedding will not only insulate you from any chill that may creep up from below but make the cot softer. It's amazing how much warmth can be added by using newspapers, as Washington's soldiers learned at Valley Forge.

Peg-block Cot

The peg-block cot is similar to an army cot but instead of having X-shaped legs at each end, the legs are vertical (Fig. 1-27). The four pieces running lengthwise are of 2-by-4 with the ends morticed underneath to take the leg's ¾-inch dowels and on the inner faces to take the dowels of the crosspieces.

The canvas sleeping surface can either be hemmed or laced onto the side rails. The dimensions can be varied to suit but customarily the cot sleeping surface is 6 feet long by 28 inches wide. Heavy dowels can be used as legs or 2-by-2s, doweled at both ends; the same for the spacers. Take care that the dowels for these do not interfere with each other. Offsetting is one way.

Roll-up Bolster Bed

Some people might not call the roll-up bolster bed a cot, but it is portable and can be easily stored. The design is most simple and it requires almost no carpentry. The components are a roll of foam pad, encased in canvas, that can be rolled at each end to the desired contour on ¾-inch common plumber's pipes (Fig. 1-28).

The rolls are supported above the floor by side pieces of ¾-inch plywood with slots in which the ends of the pipes fit snugly. These side pieces are connected by cross braces. The pipe slots should be snug enough to prevent the pipes from turning freely. Yet they need to be able to be turned-slightly in order to adjust the height of the

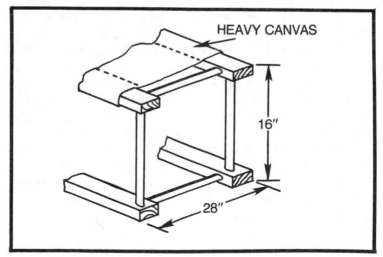

Fig. 1-27. Peg-block cot.

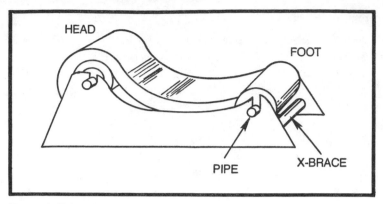

Fig. 1-28. Roll up bolster bed.

bolster at the top and the contour of the sleeping surface. To store, merely lift out the pad on the pipes, roll up and tie.

If you make the side pieces about 6 feet long, there should be about 10 feet of pad crammed into a 9½-foot flat canvas bag. The bag should have a zipper at one end so that the pad can be removed when you want to launder the covering. Roll the bagged pad on the pipes and set them in place in the slots and the bed is ready for occupancy. Any width from 28 inches may be used.

Rustic Cot

If you have access to sufficient lengths of tree limbs with the bark still on them and of uniform diameter, you can build this rustic cot. If you do not have such tree limbs, the bark can be faked by staining portions where the bark would have been left intact.

The legs are of X-style, pivoting on a bolt with a lock nut. Their spread is limited by a rope that stretches between them at the bottom. This rope is doubled so that a stick can be inserted. By turning this stick end over end the ropes are twisted until the desired tension is reached, then the stick is held by wedging it against the X formed by the legs at both the head and foot (Fig. 1-29A).

The rustic cot is easily disassembled and stored or carried. The heavy canvas topping has wide hems on both sides and at the bottom a smaller hem. The side hems should be wide enough to take the side rails. The cover is cut out at joint holes to permit insertion of the legs (Fig. 1-29B).

Buck Saw Cot

The buck saw cot (Fig. 1-30) is made from two beechwood poles 2 inches in diameter and 6 to 7 feet long, two leg assemblies and a heavy canvas topping. The canvas is hemmed on each side to take the side rail poles and is cut out where the legs fit into these poles. The hems at the ends can be narrower.

Cut the legs for this cot from 2-by-4s of solid beechwood preferably. You can make your carpentry as fancy as you want, shaping the legs, making knobbed feet and ends for the poles. There are several requirements however. One of these is the groove on the lower end of each leg to hold the limiting rope in place and the curving of the tops of the legs to fit the circumference of the poles.

Note that Fig. 1-30 shows the legs further in toward the center than the other cots. There may be drawbacks to this positioning however. The greater the overhang at the ends, the greater the chances of throwing anyone who sits on the end of the cot to the floor.

Locate the legs as near to the ends as you want, but be sure to dowel the legs into the side rail poles. If you will want to disassemble the cot for storage, do not glue these dowels in. The head and foot leg assemblies are identical with a round or square stretcher doweled between them about 6 inches up. Tension is provided by a rope, ¼-inch marine rope is suitable, that loops around a tension stick. This stick is left loose so that it can be turned over and over to tighten the tension on the rope. It is easily held at the desired tension by resting against the stretcher.

The heavy canvas covering is hemmed down each side deep enough to take the poles and with cutouts for the legs. The ends need only small finishing hems.

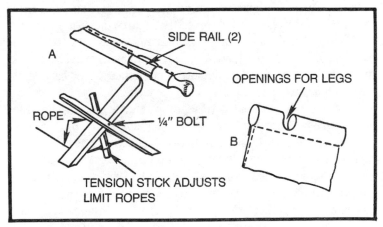

Fig. 1-29. Rustic cot.
    A. X-frame components.
    B. Canvas top.

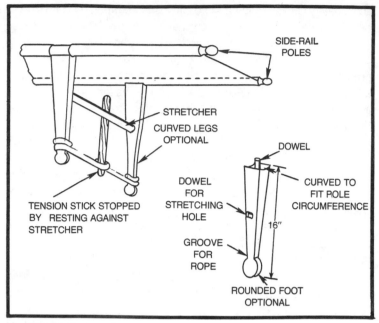

Fig. 1-30. Buck saw cot.

CHILDREN'S NO-FRILL BEDS

Sleeping Tubes

Nap time is made more enchanting when children can crawl into a sleeping tube. Like animals, they usually feel more secure in these confined sleeping places and the tubes capture their imaginations.

Fiber hardboard tubes of different sizes can usually be scrounged from shippers and recycled or obtained from the manufacturer. If they are recycled, be sure to ascertain if they have at any time contained chemical substances. Dry chemicals are sometimes shipped in such containers and if so, they must be thoroughly cleaned and assured to be safe for contact or breathing before they are used for this purpose. After some chemicals, all that will be needed is to add a lining to prevent any contamination, but make sure.

These fiber tubes come in all sizes so you can get them to fit the children who will be using them. Stack these tubes in convenient gangs with the smallest on top and glue them together to keep them in position (Fig. 1-31). A crosspiece of plywood at the front and back will lift them off the floor and help to keep them stationary. Line the tubes up in front.

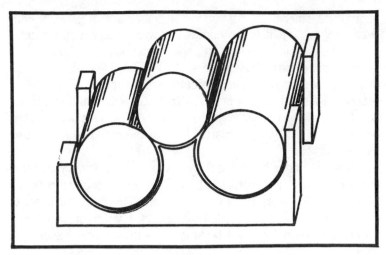

Fig. 1-31. Children's nap time tubes.

Prepare the tubes by lining them with a thin foam pad and smooth all of the edges. Cut the front and back from ¾-inch plywood or from 2-by-8s and connect them with 1 inch dowels or 2-by-2s.

Fiber Drum Crib

A fiber drum can also be made into a baby crib by cutting away a third of the circumference and gluing the bottom to 2-by-8s at the back and the front (Fig. 1-32). This can be made into a rocking cradle by sawing the bottom edges of the 2-by-8s in a curve. Cut the ends, if the originals are not intact, from hardboard and glue into place. Perforated board can be used for the ends if more ventilation is desired for baby.

Glue in foam padding and cover this with fabric. Bring the lining around the edges and glue well. A decorative fabric can be glued to the outside surfaces or it can be painted and decals applied. If the drum is recycled, be sure to find out what it has previously contained and thoroughly clean before lining.

Egg Cup Reversible Crib

Here is a crib that can "grow" with baby. The egg cup reversible crib (Fig. 1-33) is merely turned upside down when baby grows too big for the smaller side. This is convenient for those who have only one child and do not have a circle of friends with whom to trade sizes when their babies outgrow their cribs. Use your own idea of appropriate dimensions, but you will be limited as to maximum width because plywood panels only come 4 feet wide except at a premium.

The same width of the center board must be used in both cases. Dowel in this piece and reinforce with glue. Use ¼-inch dowels. Use ¼-inch dowels for the topmost sidebar and for the upper and lower sections. Below that, in a line parallel to the edge, drill five holes about 1 inch in on each side at the smaller end and six holes on the larger end for lacing. One-quarter inch marine rope is safest to use for this purpose.

Line both cribs by gluing them with foam padding. Cover with fabric as desired, waterproof is best. Paint the outside after being sure that all edges are rounded and smooth. Decals can be used to decorate each end board, but they should have no up and down pattern because the crib will be standing with only one side up at a time.

QUICKIE LOUNGE BED

This quickly converted couch-to-bed consists of a mitered frame across which is stretched webbing, rope or flat springs. The bed should be at least 30 inches wide. For comfortable sitting the sitter's back needs to be supported not more than 24 inches in from the front edge, therefore a wedge shaped back rest is supplied.

Build a frame 29 inches deep by 75 inches long from solid 2-by-6 inch stock, hard or softwood, with mitered and doweled corners (Fig. 1-34A). Before assembling this frame, rabbet the inside edges 1 inch in and ⅜-inch down for installation of the webbing. If you are going to use thick foam padding, the webbing can be attached flat to the frame but this will not result in as neat a job as if you rabbeted.

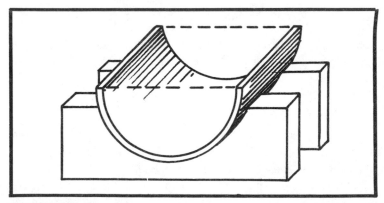

Fig. 1-32. Fiber drum crib.

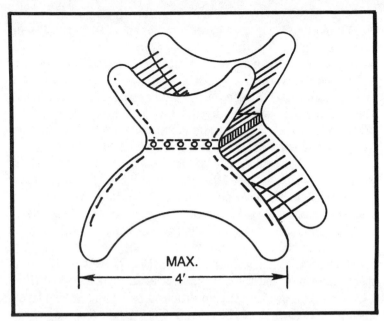

Fig. 1-33. Egg cup reversible crib.

Cut five arched supports (Fig. 1-34B). The curve of these pieces is to allow the webbing to clear when pressure is put on the sitting or lying surface above. Install these supports to the underside of the frame with countersunk No. 8, sufficiently long flathead wood-screws and glue. The two endmost curved supports should be placed just inside the legs and the other two evenly spaced between them.

Allow all glued joints to thoroughly dry before installing the webbing. Nail and glue webbing to the rabbet inset or on top at the front and run it tautly to the rabbet or the frame at the back (Fig. 1-34C). For this job you will need to use the webbing stretcher tool already described. Use at least 2 inch wide webbing and place it 2 inches apart if you interweave or 1 inch apart if you do not interweave.

Obtain six preformed metal legs at the building supplier, of not more than 10 inches in height. Assemble these to the frame with flathead woodscrews 9 inches in from each end and at midpoint, back and front. Although these preformed metal legs come in various heights; the 10 inch is recommended. Position them to run with the width of the couch as they will withstand the pressures better than if they run the lengthwise way.

Comfortable seating requires a maximum of 24 inches at seat level between the front of the seating area and the back rest. To provide for this without interfering with the comfort when used as a bed, a back rest is provided. It can be built to be removed when used for sleeping or raised 8 inches above the sleeping level (Fig. 1-34D). This back rest is supported by three ⅝-inch steel pipes or rods. (Figure 1-34E.) If you want to be fancy, use chrome finished steel rods, otherwise use ¾-inch pipes and paint them.

Each of these rods must be attached to the back rest in two places. Cut ¾-inch plywood 10 inches wide by 64 inches long to back up the back rest. This provides ample room to attach the rods in two places. The back rest cushion is glued to the face of the panel later.

At your hardware store or building supplier you should be able to find suitable hardware with which to attach the rods. The top bracket must have a closed cap (Fig. 1-34F) to prevent the rod from sliding through it and the bottom bracket a capped bottom (Fig. 1-34G) to prevent the rod from dropping below the needed level. The middle bracket should be open (Fig. 1-34H) so that the rod can pass through it. All of these brackets should have flanges on both sides with screw holes for attachment to the back rest panel. With a little ingenuity you can fashion these brackets yourself or adapt store-bought ones to your purpose.

Another way of attaching the rods at the bottom is to bend them at right angles and notch out grooves in the ends of the arched cross braces so that the bent portion of the rods will fit under the frame. This will preclude removal of the rods when the lounge is used for sleeping. Check that the bent portion of the rods will not interfere with the bolt or screw that attaches the arched cross brace under the frame. While this method does not permit removal of the rods, the back rest can be arranged to lift off of the rods by placing a stop at the bottom instead of using a capped top bracket.

To build up a pad, cement several thicknesses of polyurethane foam together, trimming as needed to arrive at the correct dimensions. Always leave more foam than the final dimensions so you can just cram the extra into the canvas covering. Cement the foam to the back board.

The fabric covering can be tack-glued over the edges to the back board or it can be made in a sort of hood with elastic on all sides to snugly fit over the cushion of the back rest. This will enable you to remove and launder it easily.

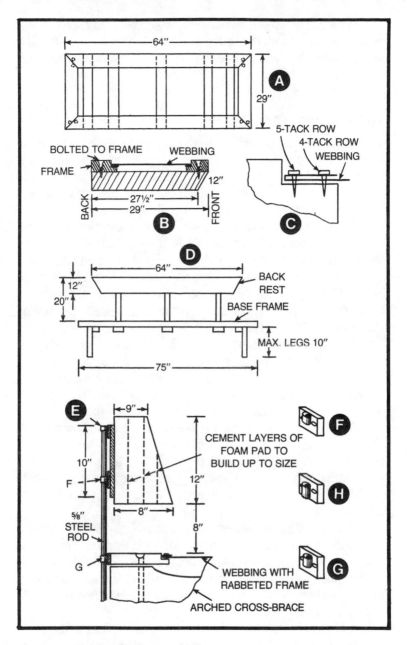

Fig. 1-34. Quickie lounge bed.

A. Frame

B. Arched supports.

C. Rabbet detail and webbing, tacking.

D. Raised back rest.

E. Back rest support details.

F. Closed cap bracket.

G. Capped bottom bracket.

H. Side-thru bracket.

As with any project, no matter how simple it may seem at first glance, before you start, sit down and think it out, make sketches and final decisions. You are building this bed to fit your own particular needs. If you would be satisfied with someone else's decisions, you could just go out and buy a bed.

BUNDLE-BOARD BED COUCH

The bundle-board bed couch is a two faced seat that converts to a double bed with a separating board, hence the name of bundle-board, derived from the old time piece of courting furniture. It needs to be in a large room, such as a studio where several conversational groups may gather, such as at a cocktail party.

The two sections are back-to-back, one facing one way and the other the other way. The back rest is in the middle and usable by those sitting on either side so it must be cushioned on both sides. When used as a double bed, the back rest can be arranged to be pulled out, but when used for two separate individuals, the back rest is left in place. However, a 6 foot or more long back rest will be clumsy to handle, especially if you make it so that it can be pulled out.

The bundle-board bed takes the place of bunk beds, which also have their problems and disadvantages. It should come in handy at any vacation cabin or studio where there is floor space for it. Individual sleeping accommodations are provided and your guests do not have to climb up any ladders to get to one of them.

Another advantage is the storage space offered below the bed. Here is an ideal place to store a card table or poker table top because of the width. A shelf can be built under the bed frame and the table slid in with plenty of room to get good handholds on it (Figs. 1-35A, 1-35B). There can also be drawers to store the bedding or other items.

The total width suggested is 55¼ inches. This allows an inch for the bundle-board rods and 27 inches for each sleeper. The dimensions are predicated on the 48 inch limit for the width of the shelf for the stowing of a card table. Plywood is only 48 inches wide unless specially ordered. However if the shelf is not included the total width will not be limited.

A bonus comes with building in the shelf—room at the other side for drawers as wide as 24 inches. Building instructions will presume that you want to build in the card table shelf.

Within this limitation the shelf can be no more than 48 inches wide, so attaching it to the 4-by-4 legs, cut 10 inches high, the total

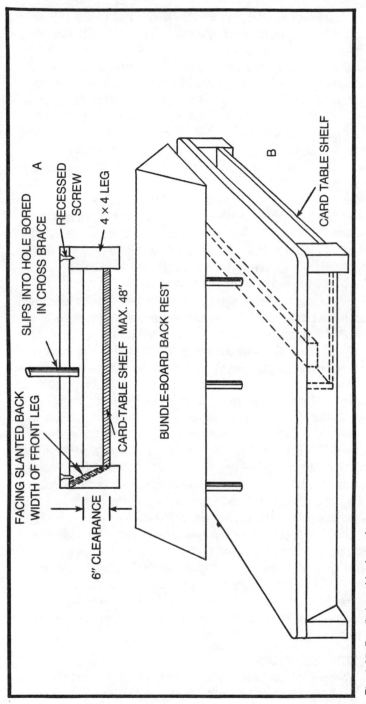

FACING SLANTED BACK
WIDTH OF FRONT LEG

SLIPS INTO HOLE BORED
IN CROSS BRACE

A

RECESSED
SCREW

4 × 4 LEG

CARD-TABLE SHELF MAX. 48"

6" CLEARANCE

BUNDLE-BOARD BACK REST

CARD TABLE SHELF

B

Fig. 1-35. Bundle-board bed couch.
A. Cross section from end.
B. Elevation.

width of the two beds will be 55¼ inches wide. This means that the frame must be 55¼ inches wide by about 75 inches long. Secure the 48 inch shelf between the two legs at one end. At the inner end of the shelf nail a 1-by-4 to act as a stop at the back. Support the shelf at the inner end, about 50 inches in, by a scantling below the cross braces.

Although there will be room at the other end of the couch for drawers, they are beyond the scope of no-frill projects and will not be discussed here. At least 6 inches vertically must be allowed to grasp the card table in getting it in and out of the shelf. Allowing for the 3⅝-inch depth of the cross brace, the frame will go on the top of the 10 inch high legs.

From 2-by-6s cut two 75 inch lengths and two 55¼-inch ends, miter and double peg the corners to form the frame, putting the 6 inch sides up. Center 2-by-4 cross braces under the frame. They should be 24 inches in from each end and across the middle bolt. Exactly at the middle point of each of these bore snug holes; insert the pipe or rods that will support the back rest.

The webbing can be installed flat to the frame, tacking with the five tack row an inch from the end and the four tack row about an inch inside that. Or it can be tacked to a rabbeted frame as described earlier. Avoid interfering with the line of back rest pipes. Interweave as directed. Don't forget to use the webbing stretcher tool to stretch the webbing taut.

Since the back rests are back-to-back, they can be bolted between the backing boards by using holes through the pipes instead of hardware. If rods are used to support the back rests, hardware will be needed, but in any case the two back rests should be made as a unit. Three supports will be needed. To ensure their stability 2 inch thick blocks can be placed on the cross braces with corresponding holes so that the pipes will penetrate deeper at the bottom ends.

Use thick polyurethane pad, extending full width and covering the edge of the frame. Cement tack underneath as already described. The fabric covering goes over this, around the edges and should be tacked beyond the pad underneath. Holes must be provided for the penetration of the back rest supporting pipes, and these can be finished with tape. It will be easier to find the holes for placement of the back rest supports if the fabric is glued down around these holes.

CONVERTIBLE BED COUCH

A simple platform single bed can be quickly converted to a couch by adding a bolster for back support (Fig. 1-36). This design

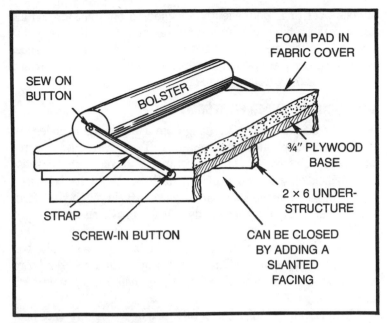

Fig. 1-36. Convertible couch bed.

overcomes the objection to using loose pillows or bolsters because it is attached, yet is easily moved off the sleeping area.

Build a simple frame of ¾-inch plywood, supported on legs or 2-by-6s on edge and slanted back to allow for heel room at the front. Top the plywood base with a thick pad of cored foam and cover with fabric, all of which has been detailed before.

The real feature of this bed couch is the attached bolster. Unless you have the know-how, have an upholsterer make it up for you. It should be the length of the couch and at least 12 inches in diameter. The enclosed ends should have a large button in the center.

In the drapery department of your favorite store you can find screw-in tie backs with decorative heads about 1½-inches across. You will need two with screw-ins and two matching buttons of the same size. If you cannot find matching buttons, cut off the screw-in portion on two of them and sew these to the center of each end of the bolster. Screw the other two into the front legs of the couch at the side (Fig. 1-36).

Place the bolster 20 to 24 inches back from the front edge of the couch and measure the distance between the buttons. This should be the same on each end. Make up a strong, decorative strap that buttons over or is permanently attached to both bolster and leg buttons. When the couch is used for seating, the bolster is held in place to shorten the depth of the seat to a comfortable distance. When the couch is used as a bed, the bolster is brought forward and laid on the floor in front of the legs.

SIMPLE OUT SIZED BED PLATFORMS

Bed platforms can be anything from a simple frame on legs to much more complicated arrangements. There is always one requirement, however—that the structure be strong enough to satisfactorily hold up whatever is placed on them. Using this book as a "launching pad" for your imagination, you can build your bed platform to suit your fancy and your needs, always providing the required stability.

A simple out sized bed platform can be built to fit a king size box spring merely by constructing slotted 2-by-8s in a checker board pattern with the open squares no more than 18 inches in each direction (Fig. 1-37A).

In the rafter type of substructure for a queen or king-sized bed, the open squares should never be more than 16 inches each way on center. If flat, no-sag springs are installed, each of these squares can be done separately, but to prevent the occupants of the bed from feeling these hard places, a thick core type foam pad is needed.

To keep the matress or box springs in place, install metal stops at the end of every other rafter (Fig. 1-37B).

In building the rafter type substructure, the slots must be cut so that the top of all are level and even (Fig. 1-37C). If they are not, the bed will be bumpy. Likewise, the legs or foundation on which the bed rests must be even or the bed will rock annoyingly. Even with legs the same length the floor may be uneven, requiring the shimming of one or more legs.

Platforms for round beds can be built in the same manner, using the rafter technique. Everything that has been said about the king-sized rectangular bed substructures will hold true for the round beds. The only difference is the shape.

It is a good idea to take the dimensions for the round bed by directly measuring the mattress and building to fit it. If you are making a round bed and covering it yourself instead of using a box spring or round mattress, your first decision is what diameter you are going to use (Fig. 1-38).

Even a plywood base must be made up in sections. Remember, standard plywood panels are 48 by 96 inches. A pattern is easier to

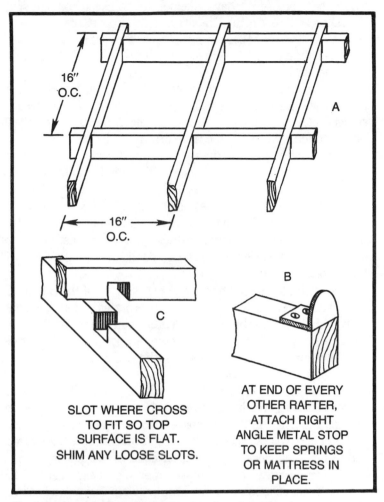

Fig. 1-37. Simple rafter type substructure for out sized beds.
    A. Checkerboard pattern.
    B. Box spring stop.
    C. Slotting.

follow, but if you are planning to build a rather large round bed, it may be difficult to get a piece of paper large enough even for a pie section. One way to solve this problem is to use chalk on the garage floor or the driveway to lay it out.

Clear a level space on the pavement large enough to contain the dimensions of the bed plus room for you to work around the circumference. Locate a center point and mark it with a firmly chalked X. Using a cord that does not stretch, either secure it with a nail exactly where the X crosses or have a helper hold it exactly on that spot. With chalk at the end of this line, at a distance from the center exactly equal to what you have chosen as the radius for your round bed, draw a circle on the pavement. Remember that the radius of a circle is half its diameter, in case your geometry is rusty.

Even the occupant of a round bed will tend to lie in more or less of a straight line. Make the rafters of the substructure also follow straight lines. The circular shape is obtained by cutting off these rafters to form the circle you have drawn on the pavement.

Do not attempt to build a round bed with rafters radiating out from a central point or you will meet with a number of frustrations. Some of these are: few professional carpenters can build a truly round structure; lumber is straight and advanced carpentry is needed to bend it or form it into a circle and, last but not least, a bed or any piece of furniture for that matter with a central post and others at the end of radii seldom will sit level and this teetering in a bed will haunt you.

Following the steps shown in Fig. 1-38, lay out the center line on 16 inch centers to fill the circle you have drawn on the pavement. Start with diameters through the center point of the circle in both directions (Fig. 1-38A). These are center lines and, since you should use 2-by lumber (preferably 2-by-6s), there will be about ⅞-inch of wood on either side of the center lines.

By measuring the length of these lines you can determine the approximate length of the pieces needed for the round bed of the size you want to build. In the example shown in Fig. 1-38 of an 8 foot diameter bed, you will need roughly: two 96 inch pieces, four 92 inch and four 76 inch pieces for the rafter checkerboard substructure.

Starting exactly at the midpoint of each of these, mark off and saw out slots, exactly on 16 inch centers, slots that extend halfway through the pieces. These slots should take the crossing rafter snugly and so that they sit flat on the top, otherwise your bed will be bumpy.

Lay out the rafters on the pattern, make any needed adjustments and nail them securely together as shown in Fig. 1-38B. The ends will roughly conform to the circle on the pavement. Trim the ends as needed so that the circle you have drawn is just barely visible beyond the ends of the rafters. Put in "stays" between the rafters as shown in Fig. 1-38C. Do not put the stays at the ends of the rafters but insert them even with the trimmed ends.

Supposing that the bed is 96 inches in diameter, two 48 by 96 inch panels of plywood can be pieced to form the base (Fig. 1-38D).

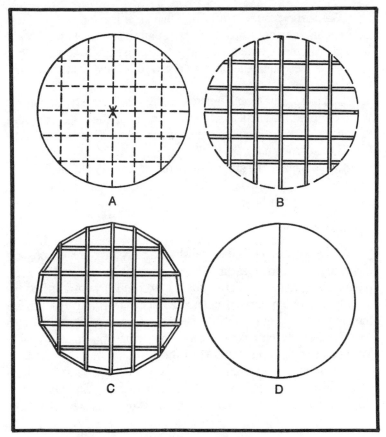

Fig. 1-38. Substructure and base for a round bed.
   A. Draw diameters beginning at center point.
   B. Lay rafters on the pattern.
   C. Put "stays" between outermost ends of rafters.
   D. Cover substructure with ¾-inch plywood base.

Join them together as closely as possible and round the edges to conform to the circle you drew on the pavement. You will need to mark the line firmly with a pencil. Saw slowly to maintain smoothness as you round off the circumference. Nail or screw the plywood base to the substructure, setting the finish nails and countersinking the flathead woodscrews so that the surface will be absolutely even.

A rounded skirting can be supplied to cover the substructure by using thin plywood (⅛-inch) that you have soaked at least over night in water so that the surface does not crack as you bend it to fit. Using finish nails and setting the heads, nail it to the edge of the plywood base and the substructure.

The skirting can be painted or stained, or if you really want it to be fancy, use a veneer. For that matter any pliable material that can be applied to the rounding structure can be used as a skirting. For a spectacular bed paint the skirting a dark color and cement on mirrored shapes.

Complete your round bed by shaping a thick core type foam pad to fit the base. It should not be cemented at the edges because unless you obtain contour round sheets, you will need to tuck in the bedding underneath.

In this manner any size or shape of bed can be built, but don't fail to take into consideration that bedding comes in standard sizes and having it made can be expensive.

BED DIMENSIONS

While nonstandard sized and shaped beds are coming more and more into use, the sizes of mattresses, box springs and bedding remain pretty much standard. The use of cored foam pads is lessening the need for box springs and mattresses that regularly determine the size of beds, but available bedding sizes must be taken into consideration. Another consideration is to equate the space available for the bed against the comfort of the sleeper.

It has long been assumed that a single adult can sleep comfortably in a bed 28 to 30 inches wide by 75 inches long. With this in mind the following dimensions have been developed as bed-size standards:

Cot for a single adult occupant, 30 by 75 inches
Single bed, 36 by 75 inches
Twin bed, 39 by 75 inches
Three-quarters bed, 48 by 75 inches
Double bed, 54 by 75 inches

These dimensions do not take larger individuals into consideration, and people seem to be getting larger all of the time. Neither do they consider the sprawlers or the spreaders. This has given rise to the following bed sizes:

Queen-size, 60 by 80 inches
King-size, 72 by 84 inches
"California" King-size, 84 by 84 inches
Round beds in many sizes, usually custom made

Children's bed sizes range from baby cribs and cradles to youth sizes. Remember, children grow quickly, and unless you have stair step sizes or a circle of friends with an exchange arrangement, you must carefully select the size of the bed you will want to build for your child.

In building beds for infants and smaller children, you must also consider how to keep them from falling out, especially out of double deck bunks. The old standby guards against these tumbles have been hinged and sliding sides that can be raised or lowered.

SAFETY

An important element in successful bed building is strength and stability. It is difficult to relax if the bed to which one entrusts one's body even wobbles a little. A person who has once been dumped to the floor in the middle of the night knows the importance of bed stability, even if it is low to the floor.

The strength and stability of a bed depends on the solidity of its framing. This includes such things as the evenness of the legs and the stability of the slats, everything that holds if up off the floor.

The apparent lack of stability of waterbeds takes some getting used to. In the case of double deck bunks, a collapse of the upper bunk can have serious consequences for both the occupant of the upper level and the one sleeping below.

Safety demands that you not only build your beds with a good grade of lumber and put them together with the proper hardware but that you use dowels and miters as well as reinforcements. This is good carpentry practice. An engineer considers a safety factor of six none too great for the safety of suspended members.

Nails can pull out with the shifting of weight. Woodscrews can split lumber. Butt joints are far from fail-safe unless doweled. If you do not have the tools or know-how to properly mortise a joint, it pays to have it done at the lumber yard. It only take a slight spread of the side rails of a bed, even on store-bought beds, to cause the slats to fall out. This forces the mattress, springs and the occupant to fall to the floor. This can be startling when one is sound asleep.

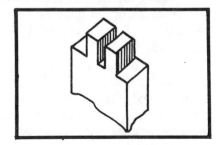

Fig. 1-39. Slotted tenon.

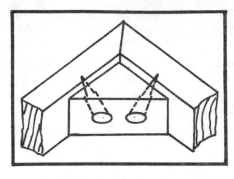

Fig. 1-40. Reinforcing corner block.

Just because youngsters weigh less does not mean that safety precautions in building their beds can be relaxed. Children are prone to jump up and down and subject furniture, especially beds, to tremendous stress.

Ladders in general, including those that give access to upper deck bunks, should never be painted. A solid paint covering hides cracks or splits, especially in the rungs, that indicate failure.

When wall or ceiling fastenings are needed, they should be made into structural members of the building. Woodscrews will hold little weight unless the threads are deep and bite into wood. Always use the proper fastener for the purpose and the material. Molly bolts are needed to fasten things into concrete or masonry walls. When a butterfly bolt is called for, its opening flanges are needed to hold in cavity walls. Few of these will be held sufficiently by merely lath and plaster.

Ignoring safety considerations is not worth a broken arm or worse. Be safe rather than sorry.

RESILIENCY

Any piece of furniture designed to receive the human body will benefit from built-in resiliency. It can be provided by springs, loose padding, webbing, plastic foam, lacing or a combination of these.

Webbing can also be used, especially when it is interwoven in both directions, or as a base for other resilient treatments. When the webbing is used to support coil springs, it should be at least 3½-inches wide.

Another method of distributing pressure to the mounting frame is rope lacing. Many bed builders turn up their noses at this time tested method of supplying resiliency, but for the money it is still hard to equal it. Resiliency lends the effect of softness in a bed without permitting distortion of the body.

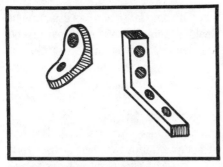

Fig. 1-41. Two types of metal corner braces.

PUTTING IT ALL TOGETHER

A slotted tenon (Fig. 1-39) will hold a joint firmly, especially when glued. The slot tends to swell and thus insures a tight fit.

Corner blocks (Fig. 1-40) can be cut from scrap pieces. They will reinforce a corner, whether mitered, doweled or both, and so prevent disruption of the joint. It keeps the joint at right angles. It is always a good idea to predrill two screw holes at opposing angles to take the shaft of the screw. This allows the flathead of the screw, providing the top of the hole is reamed out, to be flat with the surface. The threads then bite into the wood on either side of the corner and thus draw the block up snugly. Corner reinforcing blocks add considerable strength to a frame.

Metal corner braces (Fig. 1-41) can be used to reinforce a 90 degree angle and flat metal bars can reinforce butt joints, but there are much more efficient ways of doing this. This kind of hardware just doesn't result in enough strength to warrant their use. To begin with, usually there are only two screw holes in the bracket and these

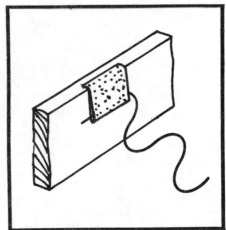

Fig. 1-42. Sling attachment for flat, no-sag springs.

73

are in a line on the bar type. When putting large screws in a straight line, the wood usually splits. Besides, this type of hardware must be applied to the surface. When it then protrudes beyond the surface, it gives an unfinished look to the job. From time to time these screws will need tightening because the metal on metal does not hold them tightly.

Before leaving this advice to the amateur bed builder, let me stress the convenience of using flat, no-sag springs. The cleat has been given as a method of attachment, but you can devise your own—a sort of sling (Fig. 1-42). This sling allows the springs to rise or lower as weight is applied to the surface above it, and it takes up almost no space. These springs can be cut and adapted to many uses in places where it would be inconvenient to use the more cumbersome coil springs. Flat no-sag springs are usually available at any upholstery supply house.

Chapter 2
Advanced Bed Projects

The bed builder has a number of alternatives. His "druthers" will be influenced and often times depend on his needs, his ambitions, the time he has available, the tools that he owns and his ability to use them. Of all of these his success as a bed builder will greatly depend on his woodworking ability, his experience with the tools and materials, but most importantly, his ability to follow directions.

IT'S YOUR CHOICE

If he is wise, he will choose a project that is within his capabilities. When he is too ambitious and begins a project that is too difficult or that requires too much time to complete, he may become discouraged. Such frustrating experiences often result in half-finished projects or worse, a slap-dash finish-up-quick item that is of no use, only a waste of good materials.

Every time you successfully complete a project you will be rewarded, not only by the exhilaration of a victory won and the joy of having whipped the inanimate material into usable shape, but you will experience such feelings every time you use or see someone in your family using the item you created.

After all, only a few of the early settlers who came to the shores of the New World or who traveled across the country to open up the West were expert carpenters or cabinetmakers, yet their homes were mainly furnished by their home-made furniture. They usually had only a few crude tools and they could not run down to a handy building supply store when they wanted or needed something. There were no lumber yards where they could get dimensioned wood, fabricated fasteners and hardware, or even have a bit of joinery done for them. These folks had to find a suitable stand of trees, hew down what they needed and shape the wood into usable components. They had to make just about everything they needed, their own nails and hardware, and they felt lucky if they had rope that they could spare from which to weave the springs for their beds.

Of course, everyone worked. The neighbors, if there were any within horseback or horse-and-wagon traveling distance, gathered to help with the larger projects such as a house or barn raising, but the smaller projects like furniture had to be done by the family. These cooperative tasks drew people closer together and tightened the family bonds. Why not take a leaf from the history book, let your enthusiasm for a project enthuse the whole family and let the kids help. It will do you and them a lot of good.

There are a lot of jobs where you could really use a few helpers. No one really gets much satisfaction unless he or she actually participates in the creation of a project. Plywood panels need to be held steady while being sawed to keep them from vibrating, sliding or breaking off. While doing this you can smell the newly-cut wood and see at close range how the saw cuts through, hopefully on the line, and learn how to keep the kerf open behind the saw so it won't stick and burn the blade. Not only can youngsters learn by doing but you will find that their presence and partnership in a project will encourage you to set a good example that they will long remember and later in life pass along to their children.

Family fun is only one of the many benefits of home projects. What could be more useful than for one of the projects to be the creation of a bed? After all, we spend about one-third of our lives in bed, and if we get sick or injured these hours are multiplied.

This book offers you a wide choice of bed projects and companion items from which to choose. Give that choice some serious consideration including your needs, availability of materials, their cost and the amount of time you can spend. Your woodworking ability will grow as you follow the directions and accrue experience, and acquire the tools and equipment. You must also furnish the enthusiasm that will sustain you to a successful completion of your project. Unless you are enthusiastic about what you are doing it becomes drudgery. Have fun...family fun!

HANDY INFORMATION

Before we start with the discussion of various advanced bed projects, we want to share some handy information. Although you may already know these things, reminders and the convenience of the tables will help you make your project successful.

Wood Screws

Predrilling for the installation of wood screws will differ according to whether you are working with hard or soft wood. The appearance and sturdiness of your bed will depend on how you follow the simple rules governing when and how to predrill, especially the shank hole diameter in the top member of two joined boards or the need or diameter of the guide hole in the board that is to receive the screw.

When you are working with hard wood, an anchor hole in the bottom board is needed to prevent any possible cracking or splitting in the wood when you install the screw, yet this guide hole must be small enough to allow the threads of the screw to get a good bite into the wood so that it will firmly hold. The top board hole must be large enough to accept the shank of the screw when inserted by hand, yet not so large a diameter that it will permit an undesirable wobble.

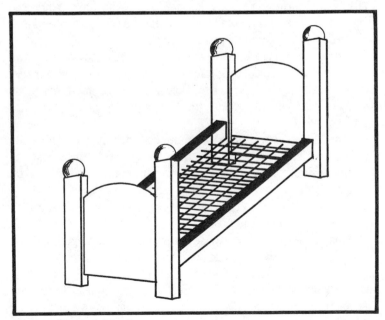

Fig. 2-1. Simple doll bed.

Even hard wood can shrink or swell that infinitesimal amount needed to loosen the bond of the joint.

It is desirable that the length of the shank of the screw and the thickness of the top board be the same and that the threaded portion of the screw from where the threads start to the tip of the point be the same as about two-thirds or three-fourths of the thickness of the lower member. If both of these conditions are not possible, do not worry, but make sure that the screw is not so long that the tip of the point will penetrate the opposite surface.

Flat-headed screws should be countersunk so that their heads are flush with the surface. Countersinking of round-headed screws is optional because you do not use them where surfaces need to be finished. If you countersink too deeply so that a depression remains above the head of the screw after it is installed, you will need to fill this level with the surrounding surface before applying the finish.

When you are working with a soft wood, the size of the guide hole in the board that is to accept the threaded end of the screw is of less importance, except that it should not be too large in diameter. If you are installing a wood screw near an edge or into the edge of a board, the guide hole will keep the screw going straight regardless of the grain of the wood and lessens the chances of it going through and marring the surface, thereby losing some of its hold. When the diameter of the screw is small and not near the edge, a center punch will mark the exact entry spot for the point.

Wood screws are used to achieve a better bond between two members, but to fulfill this purpose they should be the correct screws and be properly installed. Select the size that will carry the weight or withstand the stress yet will not put too great a pressure on the wooden members.

Use Table 2-1 to select the best screw for the job. This table does not include brass wood screws, only steel, since brass is seldom needed except where there is a danger that the steel will be subjected to rust or corrosion after the members are finished.

Should you need to remove a wood screw that is damaged or stubborn, here are a few tips:

Sometimes the slot of a wood screw has been damaged so that it is impossible to fit the screwdriver into the slot to extract it. If it is a round-headed screw, a few strokes of a hacksaw will usually remedy the slot. A hacksaw blade used carefully can usually remedy the head of a round-headed screw if it is protruding above the surface without marring the surfaces around it.

Table 2-1. Woodscrew Sizes and Drilling.

No.	SHANK DIA	SHANK HOLE HDWD	SHANK HOLE SFTWD	ANCHOR HOLE HDWD	ANCHOR HOLE SFTWD	1/4	3/8	1/2	5/8	3/4	7/8	1	1 1/4	1 1/2	1 3/4	2	2 1/4	2 1/2	2 3/4	3	3 1/2	4	4 1/2	5
0	1/16	1/16	**CP	1/32	**CP	X	X	X																
1	5/64	3/32	1/16	1/32	CP	X	X	X	X	X	X	X												
2	3/32	3/32	1/16	1/32	CP	X	X	X	X	X	X	X	X											
3	7/64	1/8	3/32	1/16	1/32	X	X	X	X	X	X	X	X	X										
4	1/8	1/8	3/32	1/16	1/32		X	X	X	X	X	X	X	X										
5	1/8	1/8	3/32	1/16	1/32		X	X	X	X	X	X	X	X										
6	9/64	5/32	1/8	3/32	1/16		X	X	X	X	X	X	X	X	X	X								
7	5/32	5/32	1/8	3/32	1/16			X	X	X	X	X	X	X	X	X								
8	11/64	3/16	5/32	3/32	1/16				X	X	X	X	X	X	X	X	X	X						
9	3/16	3/16	5/32	3/32	1/16				X	X	X	X	X	X	X	X	X	X						
10	13/64	7/32	3/16	1/8	3/32				X	X	X	X	X	X	X	X	X	X	X	X				
11	13/64	7/32	3/16	1/8	3/32				X	X	X	X	X	X	X	X	X	X	X	X				
12	7/32	7/32	3/16	1/8	3/32					X	X	X	X	X	X	X	X	X	X	X	X			
14	1/4	1/4	7/32	1/8	3/32					X	X	X	X	X	X	X	X	X	X	X	X	X		
16	9/32	5/16	1/4	5/32	1/8							X	X	X	X	X	X	X	X	X	X	X	X	X
18	5/16	5/16	1/4	3/16	5/32								X	X	X	X	X	X	X	X	X	X	X	X
20	21/64	3/8	5/16	3/16	5/32									X	X	X	X	X	X	X	X	X	X	X
24	3/8	3/8	5/16	7/32	3/16															X	X	X	X	X

LENGTH OF SCREW (inches) * ***

* Brass screws are measured differently.

** On soft woods, a centerpunch (CP) to mark point of entry is sufficient.

*** The length of flat-headed wood screws is measured from the top of the head to the tip of the point; for round-headed screws from the base of the head to the tip of the point.

When the slot of a flat-headed wood screw is counter-sunk below the surrounding surface so that you cannot get at it with a hacksaw, often it can be started out by placing the point of a small nail in the slot near the edge of the head of the screw. Using a nail set, tap the nail until the screw starts out far enough to be grasped by the jaws of diagonal-cutter pliers. The screw can then be worked out. If this does not do it, drill out the screw.

Nails

Common nails are the ones with larger, flat heads and larger diameters than finishing nails. They are seldom used in building furniture. Finishing nails can be and are usually nailset so that their heads are even with the surface. You cannot nailset the large-headed common nail. Like wood screws, the length should be selected so it does not penetrate the opposite surface of the member that receives them. To help you select the right nail for the job, consult Table 2-2.

Wire brads are smaller than finishing nails. For this reason they are used in working with light, thin wood that might otherwise split even with the entry of finishing nails. Wire brads are available in lengths from 3/16 to 3 inches. Their diameter is by wire gage and ranges from No. 24 to No. 10. The smaller number designates the larger wire.

Dowels

Wooden dowels, used in connecting and reinforcing many joints, range in diameter from ⅛ to 1½ inches and are 3 feet long. They are cut into short lengths for insertion at the joint. When longer stock is needed, they are called poles. Poles also come in larger diameters.

To secure the joint, the dowels are glued in place in both members, and there is a trick to this. When the dowel is pushed into the predrilled hole, the glue tends to either be forced out or com-press in the bottom of the hole. Unless there is no way for the glue to come up the hole, it will go down to the bottom ahead of the dowel and prevent it from properly seating. Also it will not be distributed along the sides of the dowel and therefore not hold the dowel secure.

To avoid this situation rough up the sides of the dowel or scrape tiny striations down the circumference for the glue to flow into. If you prefer, the hole can be made slightly larger than the dowel to make space for the glue, but be sure that it fills this overlarge space.

Table 2-2. Nail Sizes.

SIZE d**	LENGTH	
	COMMON	FINISHING
2	1	1
3	1¼	1¼
4	1½	1½
5	1¾	1¾
6	2	2
7	2¼	---
8	2½	2½
9	2¾	---
10	3	3
12	3¼	---
16	3½	3½
20	4	4
30	4½	---
40	5	---
50	5½	---
60	6	---

* Per "Catalog of U.S. American Nails," American Steel & Wire Co.

If you encounter difficulty in starting a dowel into a predrilled hole, shave off the edges of the end. This will help you guide the dowel into the hole.

A FAMILY FUN PROJECT

Even dolls need beds and such a bed will provide you and the children with an excellent family fun project and, at the same time, give you good practice in using the techniques you will need to build a full-sized bed project. If you already know these techniques, you can elaborate on this simple bed design (Fig. 2-1). In any case so little material is involved that, should you make a bobble, little will be lost.

Lone advantage in making your first advanced project a doll's bed is that you can use soft wood. This material is much easier to work with although it is seldom suitable for full-sized beds that are expected to take the weight of adults or even children.

To be authentic, any period furniture requires research. If you are going to do a period piece, use the true design so you can show it off proudly even to people who know all about such things.

If you have both the equipment and the know-how but are a little rusty on your craftsmanship, a basic design of a turned bed post can be used on an Early American style or a canopy doll bed. This will give you the opportunity to brush up on your use of a lathe or do a bit of hand carving by fashioning fancy round or contoured bed posts (Fig. 2-2). The trick here is to make all four of the posts match each other exactly.

There is a simpler way than doing this on a lathe or by hand carving, and it will save you a lot of work if you are interested in that. At the building supply store you will usually find an assortment of wooden balls, rings and spindles. They either can be screwed or glued together or mounted on an armature. Since this is a bed for a doll these components can well support the weight. However, in order to support a person, strength must be supplied by a stronger armature up through the center. In shopping for the spindles do not overlook their assortment of wooden furniture legs.

If you have never used this method, you may be amazed at what you can make up from such components. By mounting parts that have been preformed on at least ¾-inch steel pipe, the four legs should be strong enough to support considerable weight.

Make a paper pattern for the head and foot boards of the doll bed so that the curves will match (Fig. 2-3). A heavy manila paper is best for this. You can open up a grocery sack and press out the creases for this purpose. Draw light pencil lines until the pattern checks out, then draw heavier lines and transfer them to the plywood panels.

A full-width pattern is not necessary if you plainly mark the center line and only carry the curve far enough beyond it to ensure

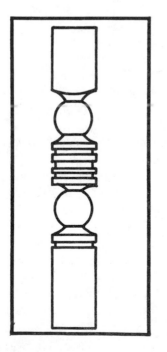

Fig. 2-2. A turned bed post.

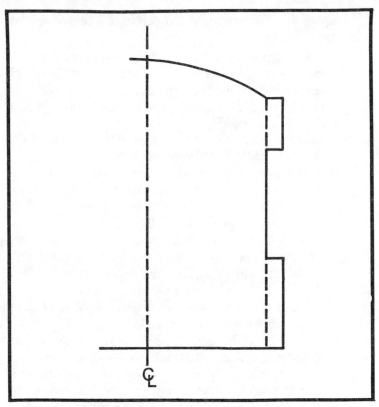

Fig. 2-3. Head and foot board pattern for a simple doll bed.

the roundness of the curve at the top. Transfer that half of the pattern and, being careful to place the center line of the pattern exactly on the center line marked on the panel, turn the pattern upside down and trace the other half of the pattern.

This simple doll bed will also require the following materials:

2 pieces ½-inch plywood 12-by-13 inches, head and foot boards
4 pieces 2-by-2 (1¾), 14 inches long, posts
2 pieces 1-by-4 (3¾), 20 inches long, side rails
2 pieces 1-by-2 (2¾), 20 inches long, lacing-frame sides
2 pieces 1-by-2, 11½ inches long, lacing-frame ends
4 pieces 1-by-4, 4 inches long, corner reinforcements
4 screw-in wooden balls, 1½ inches diameter
20 feet 3/16-inch nonstretching cord
2 decals
finish (stain or paint)

Prepare the components of the simple doll bed as follows referring to Fig. 2-4.

1. Cut the plywood head and foot boards out carefully following the saw lines. The tabs on either side should be square and the curve at the tops smoothly rounded. Be sure that the saw is sharp so that the edges of the plywood do not splinter (Fig. 2-4A).

2. Sand any rough spots and the edges of the plywood; check that they follow the pattern exactly.

3. With a sharp knife and steel straight-edge, reduce the thickness of the tenons at each side of the head and foot boards back to the straight line so that they are ¼-inch thick and will fit into the slots in the sides of the posts. This means only taking ⅛-inch off each surface, back and front, but not weakening the tongue that is left to act as a tenon.

4. Cut four posts from 2-by-2s, 14 inches long. (Figure 2-4B.) Be sure that all are exactly the same length.

5. Cut mortices in each post to exactly match the two tenons at each side of the head and the foot boards. Dig out the corners so that they are square to the ½-inch depth. Test by inserting tenons, which should fit snugly yet allow glue to collect on all sides. The best way to do this is to get a snug fit when hand-inserted, then scratch several slight striations up and down for the glue so it will not be pushed down to the bottom of the hole and prevent the tenon from seating squarely.

6. Bore two ¼-inch dowel holes in each post, again allowing for gluing.

7. If the knobs on top of the posts are to be doweled in, bore appropriate holes for their installation; if they are to be screwed in, centerpunch.

8. Sand any rough spots and slightly round off the corners of the top and bottom of the posts.

9. Cut two side rails from 1-by-4s, 20 inches long (Fig. 2-4C).

10. Cut eight 1-inch long, ¼-inch diameter wooden dowels. Two of these will be used at each end of each side rail.

11. Test dowels and glue into posts.

12. Drill both end edges of the two side rails to take the two dowels installed in Step 11. Measure carefully so that the bottom of the side rails will be 2 inches up from the bottom of the posts.

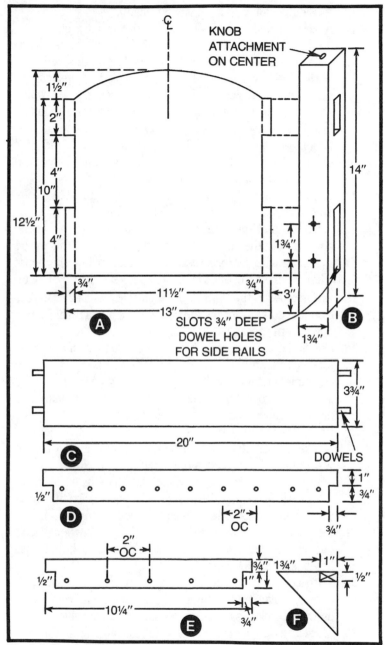

Fig. 2-4. Simple doll bed components.
A. Head and foot board detail.
B. Post detail.
C. Side rail detail.
D. Side view of lacing frame.
E. End of lacing frame.
F. Corner reinforcement

85

13. Assemble side rails to posts by gluing.
14. Assemble head and foot boards to posts by gluing the tenons. Now the outer portion of the bed is assembled. Allow the glue to thoroughly set while you proceed.
15. Without disturbing the already glued pieces, measure to verify the dimensions of the lacing frame (Fig. 2-4D, which should set inside the outer frame formed by the head and foot boards and the side rails. The lacing frame outside dimensions should be 10¼ by 20 inches, but should your measurements differ, make your lacing from conform to the actual dimensions so that it will fit snugly.
16. From 1-by-2 cut two pieces 20-inches long and two pieces 10½ inches long to form the lacing frame.
17. Note the L-shaped joints where each of these join at the corners. Cut the 10½-inch pieces from the side (this will be the inner side) across the board 1 inch below the ends. Then cut from the ends in ¾ inch. This notch ¾ by 1 inch.
18. Cut notches in the 20-inch pieces at each end (Fig. 2-4E), from the edge in across the board ¾ inch to a point ¾ inch down from the ends.
19. Check the fit of these notches to produce a square corner that will fit into the outer frame of the bed. Make any adjustment needed, nail and glue. Allow glue to thoroughly set while proceeding. Clamps will assist by holding the glued members while the glue is setting.
20. From scraps of 1-by-4, cut four corner reinforcement blocks (Fig. 2-4F). Since 1-by-4s are actually 3¾ inches wide, make these pieces the same length. Notch the 90-degree corner (the square one) so that the reinforcing blocks will fit against the posts. This will require the notch to be 1 inch in on one side and ½ inch in on the other.
21. Test the fit of reinforcing blocks to the posts when placed underneath the lacing frame with each edge of both frame and block exactly even.
22. Turn lacing frame over and apply a reinforcing block to each corner, nailing and gluing in place. Turn frame right-side-up with the blocks on the under side and allow glue to set.
23. Mark a straight line on all sides of the lacing frame ½ inch in from the inner edges. Find the center line of each side and mark with centerpunch. Continue both ways to center-

punch along the line for lacing holes every 2 inches on center toward the ends of each side.

24. Check your drill marks on the lacing frame and bore holes 3/16-inch in diameter. This should result in five holes at the ends and nine holes down each side. This uneven number of holes is necessary to end up the lacing at the corner where you started. This will be discussed in detail later.

25. You will probably want to install small metal glider buttons on the bottom of each of the posts. Carefully turn the bed upside down and tap these in to the center of each post. Make sure the bed will sit level on a level place on the floor. Adjustment of the glider buttons can prevent most teetering in the case of a doll bed.

26. The glue of the lacing frame should be now be set and the frame ready to be installed. Fit it into the outer frame so that the top edge of the flat frame is 2 inches below the top edge of the side rails on both sides. Secure with finishing nails entered from the outside surface of side rails, and head and foot boards. Also glue and nailset heads of nails.

27. When all glue has thoroughly set and the work you have done so far has been inspected, it is time to lace the springs. For this you will need about 20 feet of 3/16-inch rope. Plastic rope will stretch, resulting in springs that sag. Marine-quality rope is the best. To prevent having to piece the lacing rope midway in installation widthwise, measure off 10 feet. Tie a knot larger than the lacing hole about a foot from the end. Thread the rope up through the first hole at the lower right-hand corner and test to see if the knot is large enough. If it tends to be drawn up into the hole, retie it and test again.

28. Bring the rope out at the top of this first hole and drawing it snugly, take it across to the top of the first hole on the opposite side. Thread the rope down through this hole and draw it tightly.

29. Take the rope along the board to the next hole on that side and thread it through. Draw it tightly across the frame to the second hole on the opposite side, down through the hole and along the underside of the frame to the third hole.

30. Proceed in this manner to fill all holes on both sides of the frame and you will complete the lacing crosswise at the bottom of the last (ninth) hole at the head corner on the left-hand side.

31. Check the lacing you have done for tautness, meanwhile hold the rope so that the lacing retains its tightness. Here is where a helper will come in very handy. Your helper should be armed with a pair of pliers with a good grip and hold the rope right behind where you are working.

32. If you have a considerable length of rope left when you reach this point, take it underneath across the corner and start the first hole the other way, but if you have not had to piece the rope already, you will most likely only have a short piece left. Use this piece on the other half of the 20 feet of rope. Tie secure knots in joining the pieces, always so the knot will come underneath the frame.

33. You will be underneath the frame with the rope so thread it up through the first hole at the top left-hand side of the head of the lacing frame. Proceed to fill the length of the frame as before and you will end up at the lower (foot) right corner underneath, across the corner from the knot you tied when you started. Tie off to the 12-inch tail you left with the knot underneath across the corner.

34. Inspect the lacing job. In all cases the rope should come up through the hole and across the top side of the frame to the top of the opposite board where it should go down through that hole. Press down on the lacing at the center to test its tautness. One caution however, in pulling the lacing tight, remember that you are in this case working with lighter material than you would be with a people-bed so do not pull so tightly that you warp, bend or break the members of your creation. Good and snug is sufficient. Now your doll bed is ready to be finished.

35. Fill all countersinks and nail sets, sand any rough spots and finish as desired.

36. Install knobs on top of the posts. Two types of knob attachments should be available: screw-in and dowel. Choose whichever you want, but the balls should be about 1½ inches in diameter since the top of the posts will actually measure 1¾ by 1¾ inches. Knock off the corners and you will have a visual line leading up to the 1½-inch ball.

37. When the finish has thoroughly dried, install a 3 to 6 inch thick polyurethane foam pad as the mattress. Cut the foam 12 inches wide by 24 inches long so that it can be crammed in by pushing it toward the center, crowding it luxuriously

between the head and foot boards and the side rails. Apply decals if you want fancy head and foot boards.

The simple doll bed is now ready to be made up in preparation for dolly's nap, a job you will probably want to delegate to the new owner of the doll bed. This can be made a real family fun project while at the same time giving you the opportunity to brush up on your bed building abilities.

SHAKER STYLE DOLL CRADLE

This Shaker style doll cradle is an example of an authentic reproduction of ethnic and period furniture. When completed, it will look like the cradle in Fig. 2-5. The cradle sits on rockers and is 14½ inches wide. The rockers support the 8½ by 24 inch bed base that carries the sides. At the head the sides curve upward to support the partial roof at 13 inches above the floor.

Since four pieces of the cradle involve curves that need to be duplicated, patterns are needed for the two sides where they have a 6 inch radius curve upward toward the front of the roofed section, as well as their slants at both ends down to the base. Patterns are also needed for the head board, roof facia and foot board tops with their similar curves, and the two rockers. The rockers are the most complicated because they not only curve on the bottom edge but at the knobs of their outer extremities.

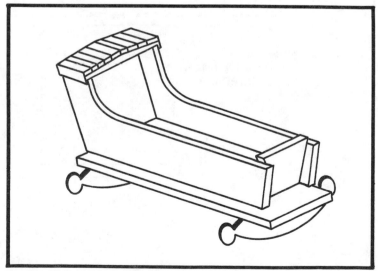

Fig. 2-5. Shaker style doll cradle.

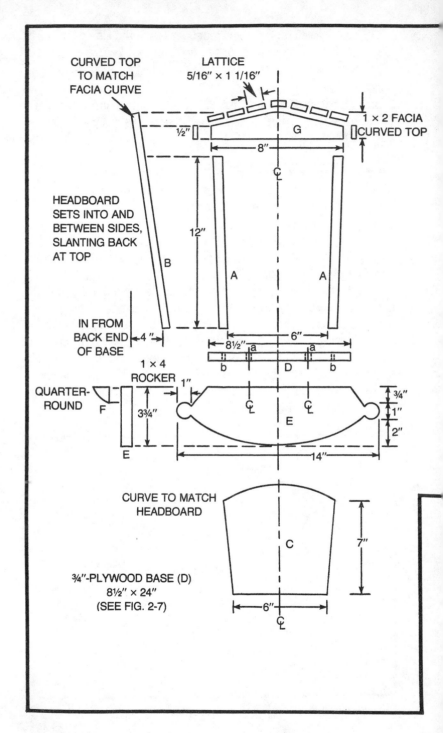

CURVED TOP TO MATCH FACIA CURVE

LATTICE 5/16" × 1 1/16"

1 × 2 FACIA CURVED TOP

½"

8"

G

HEADBOARD SETS INTO AND BETWEEN SIDES, SLANTING BACK AT TOP

12"

B

A

A

6"

IN FROM BACK END OF BASE

4"

8½"   a   a

b   D   b

1 × 4 ROCKER

QUARTER-ROUND

F

1"

3¾"

E

E

¾"
1"
2"

14"

CURVE TO MATCH HEADBOARD

C

7"

¾"-PLYWOOD BASE (D)
8½" × 24"
(SEE FIG. 2-7)

6"

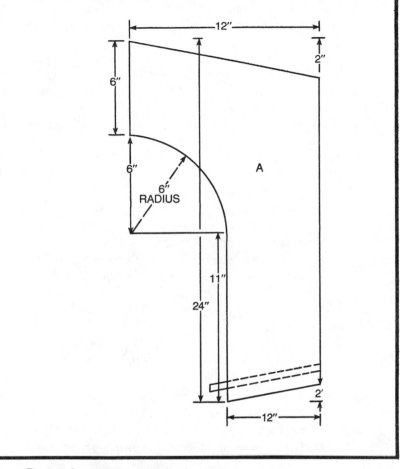

Fig. 2-6. Components of Shaker style cradle.

Again these patterns need only be for a little over half the component so that both sides will match exactly. See Fig. 2-6 for the dimensions and details for all of the components of the Shaker style doll cradle. Follow these directions and you will be able to create a satisfactory project. The specific details that have been previously given will not be repeated here.

The placement of your patterns will help you to utilize the materials most economically in addition to achieving exact matches of duplicate pieces. Saw slowly on the curves so that you can follow the saw lines transferred from the patterns. Before starting, check the saw's sharpness and teeth alignment.

The materials and sawing lengths are as follows:

1. Two pieces of ½-inch plywood for the sides, 12 by 24 inches (you will be able to utilize the scrap from this later) (Fig. 2-6A).
2. One piece of ½-inch plywood for the head board, 8 by 14 inches (Fig. 2-6B).
3. One piece of ½-inch plywood for the foot board, 7 by 7 inches (Fig. 2-6C).
4. One piece of ½-inch plywood for the base, 8½ by 24 inches (Fig. 2-6D).
5. Two pieces of 1 by 3, 14 inches long, for the rockers (Fig. 2-6E).
6. Nine pieces of lattice, 5/16 by 1-1/16, 6 inches long for the top of the roof and side pieces (Fig. 2-6F).
7. Four pieces of 1 inch quarter round, 8 inches long, for rocker to base reinforcement (Fig. 2-6G).
8. One piece of 1 by 2, 8 inches long, for the facia (Fig. 2-6H).
9. Approximately 14 feet of ½-inch-beading for plywood edging.
10. Eight flat-headed wood screws No. 6, 1¼ inches long. See Fig. 2-7 for placement.
11. Finish nails (4d by 1½-inch), adhesive and finish.
12. Wire brads for attaching roofing slats (even the small finish nails may split the lattice).

Holes should be prebored in the base (Fig. 2-7) with countersinks for the heads. If you are working with hardwood, drill shank holes 5/32-inch in diameter and starter holes in the top edge into the rockers 3/32-inch in diameter and not quite ¼ inch deep. If you are making the cradle of soft wood, drill ⅛-inch diameter shank holes and the starter holes 1/16-inch or merely centerpunched to get the screw edge of the rocker. If you want to verify this, refer to Table 2-1.

Assemble the Shaker style doll cradle in the following order or you will not be able to get at some of the screws since they will be covered:

1. On Fig. 2-7 note the location of the holes marked "a" and check that the countersinks for them are on the underneath side of the base. These are the six holes lined up 1¼-inch from the edges. These must be assembled first or they will be covered by the rockers, which use the other holes in the base.

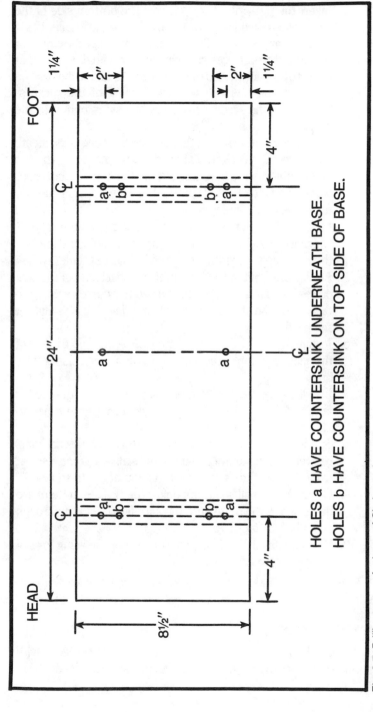

Fig. 2-7. Drilling pattern for base of Shaker style cradle.

HOLES a HAVE COUNTERSINK UNDERNEATH BASE.
HOLES b HAVE COUNTERSINK ON TOP SIDE OF BASE.

93

2. Insert the prescribed screws from the bottom side of the base upward and into the bottom edge of the cradle, being careful that you screw them in straight. Now they will not come out the surfaces and will get a firm hold. Check that the screw heads fit into the countersinks under the base so they will not interfere with the seating of the rockers. Tighten up the screws to secure the sides tightly to the base.

3. Measure in ¼-inch from the edge of the base underneath each side. The rockers extend to these marks. Using the screw holes with countersinks in the top of the base, assemble the rockers at front and back by installing the two prescribed screws in each.

4. Mark on the inner sides of the two side pieces the angle at which to install the foot board and the head board and set them in using prescribed finish nails. Nail set their heads.

5. Across the front of the top toward the back end of the side pieces, install the facia with curved top corresponding to the curved top of the head board. Use finishing nails and set the heads.

6. Joining the top of the back of the side pieces and the end of the facia assemble the lattice on both sides using wire brads.

7. Install the center lattice roof slat at the top of the arched facia and head board, front to back, using wire brads to attach this middle roof slat.

8. Spacing the other six pieces of lattice with equal gaps between the middle slat and the end slat, wire brad them at front and back to the facia and the top of the head board.

9. Check that all nail heads are below the surface. If there are dents above them, be sure they are filled. Sand any rough spots before finishing.

10. When the finish has dried, glue on the edge beading to all of the raw plywood edges.

This should complete your Shaker style doll cradle. Not only will it serve as a bed for dolly but as an authentic replica of the period.

BABY BOX CRADLE

If you have a small baby and want to take him or her along with you when you go on over night trips or visit the home of friends, build a box cradle in which you can carry him or her as well as provide a comfortable napping place. Ensconced in the box cradle, baby can be carried between two people without even awakening.

This bed has a substantial handle at each end (Fig. 2-8). When set down it can rock back and forth, head to feet, slightly. This cradle can also be slid in on the floor of the back seat of the family car where baby can ride safely right in his or her own bed.

The box cradle should be made from ¾-inch plywood because the joints will be more secure when wood screws join them. The flooring should be tongue-and-groove (T&G) maple and lined with 2 inch thick polyurethane foam padding that is carried up the sides and over the top edges. A thicker, preferably cored foam pad is fitted over this.

If you can find some worn out brooms with the broomsticks intact, they will make fine handles and reinforcing corner posts because, not only are they tough, they are just the right size, usually ⅞-inch in diameter. Since holes must be bored in them, you will need a good vise on your workbench to grip them in position while you are drilling them.

Prepare the components (Fig. 2-9) as follows:

Two pieces of ¾-inch plywood, 18 by 40 inches, for sides of cradle (Fig. 2-9A)
Two pieces of ¾-inch plywood, 16½ by 16 inches, for ends of cradle (Fig. 2-9B)

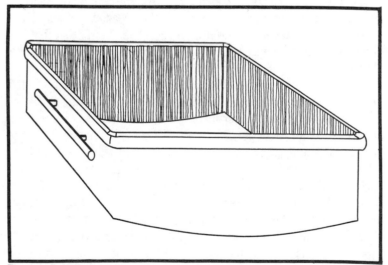
Fig. 2-8. Baby box cradle.

Seventeen pieces of tongue-and-groove (T&G) maple flooring, 18 inches long, for bottom of cradle, applied to curve (Fig. 2-9C)

Four pieces of ⅞-inch broomstick, 16 inches long, for corner reinforcement posts (Fig. 2-9D)

Two pieces of ⅞-inch broomstick, 12 inches long, for handles (Fig. 2-9E)

Four carriage bolts ¼-inch diameter by 2½ inches long, with two nuts and two washers each, to attach handles

Eight carriage bolts ¼-inch diameter by 2⅜-inches long, each with nut and washer, to attach corner reinforcement posts to sides and ends

Finishing Nails

Since the bottom edge of the sides is curved, a pattern is needed to ensure uniformity of both sides and smoothness of the rocking motion of the cradle. Use heavy manila paper that will lay flat. A piece 24 by 20 inches is sufficient because the bottom curve needs to be carried only a little beyond the center line.

Near the right edge of the pattern paper, draw a vertical line 18 inches long. At the top end of this line, at a true right angle, draw a horizontal line completely across the pattern. On this line, 20 inches to the left of the first vertical line, draw another vertical line. This is the center line. At a point 18 inches down on the center line, mark an X with the crossing points exactly at the measuring point. Place another X 2 inches up on the first vertical line. Verify that this X is exactly centered 16 inches down from the right end of the horizontal line.

To assist you in sketching in the curve at the bottom of your pattern, measure 17 inches down from the horizontal line at the top and halfway between the vertical line and the center line. Place a firm dot here. Now in light pencil lines sketch in the curve starting at the X 16 inches down the first vertical line, through the midway dot and the X that is 18 inches down on the center line. When you have achieved a true, smooth arc between these points, carry the curve to the left beyond the center line to the edge of the pattern. Check to insure the smoothness of the curve, especially at the bottom or your cradle or it will rock with a bump that is sure to awaken baby.

When you are satisfied with your pattern, lay it on the plywood panel designated (Fig. 2-9) and transfer the saw marks. Be sure that

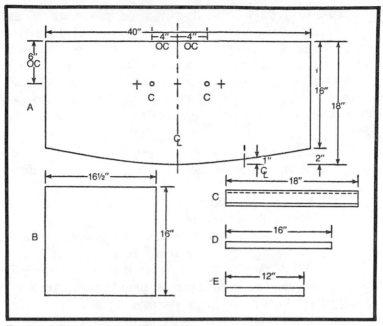

Fig. 2-9. Baby box cradle components.

the edge marks are exactly along the edges of the piece you have
sawed out in Step 1 when preparing the components. The mark for
the middle point of the curved bottom on the pattern should fall
exactly over the midpoint at the bottom edge of the piece you have
sawed. When you have transferred the curved saw marking on the
right-hand half of the piece, turn the pattern over in reversed
position, line it up with the top and left edges of the sawn piece and
transfer the other half of the curve. Again check the bottom of the
curve before starting to saw; you can't put back what you've sawed
off. Saw slowly enough to follow the saw line exactly on the curved
line you have drawn.

Now drill the broomstick components (Fig. 2-10). The four 16
inch pieces should be drilled to take ¼-inch carriage bolts. Centered
at 2 inches in from each end, the bolts (a) attach the corner post to
the end of the crib. Centered at 3 inches in from each end, bolts (b)
are at right angles to the other pair of bolts (a) so that they can attach
the posts to the side pieces of the cradle. Countersink the heads of
these bolts.

In the two 12 inch pieces of broomstick drill and countersink
two holes for the ¼-inch diameter bolts. The only difference bet-

ween these two bolts and those that attach the reinforcing pieces at the corners of the crib is the length. An inch needs to be left between the handles and the crib for a handhold. Drill these holes 3 inches in from the ends of the end pieces of the crib as seen in Fig. 2-10.

All that remains in the preparation of the components of the cradle is the drilling of the holes that match those drilled in the broomsticks. First, however, the cradle needs to be assembled as follows:

1. Square up the ends to the sides so that the top edges are even and assemble using finishing nails, setting their heads.

2. Install the T&G flooring across the curved bottom with finishing nails and set the heads.

3. Check that the bottom follows the curve smoothly. If there are any bumps, plane and round them off.

4. Drill matching holes for the corner posts into the sides and ends. Mark the position of these holes by putting a center-punch through the holes you have drilled in the corner reinforcing broomsticks and centerpunching.

5. Measure in on the endpieces and center the handle. Using the centerpunch, mark the holes in the cradle end pieces for boring. These holes should be 4 inches in from the edges of the ends and 6 inches down from the top edge, but in case you have not been too exact in your other measurements, make them agree with the holes you have drilled in the handles.

6. Install the corner reinforcements with a pair of bolts into the ends pieces and a pair into the side pieces. Tighten and check that nothing protrudes beyond the surfaces inside or out.

7. Install the handles to both ends so that one nut and washer leaves 1 inch between the handle and the outside surface of the end. The inside nut should rest fully within the countersink with nothing protruding beyond the inner surface of the end.

8. Sand all surfaces and fill all countersink and nail sets so that the inside and outside surfaces are smooth.

9. Cement a 2 inch thick polyurethane foam pad lining in place, carrying it up the sides, across the top edges of the sides and ends and down on the outside 1½ inches all the way around. Be sure that the adhesive you use for this has no

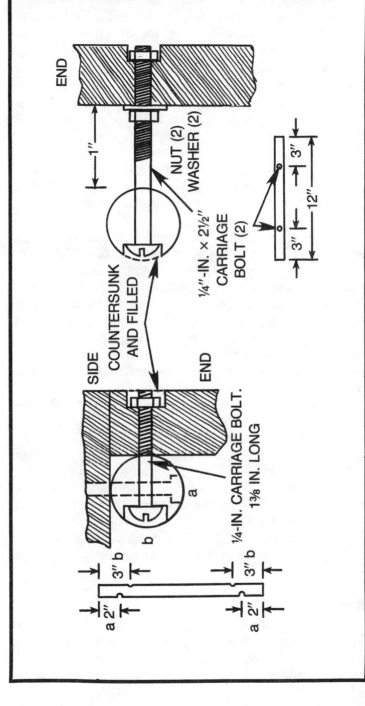

Fig. 2-10. Drilling broomstick components for baby box cradle.

allergic properties to which baby may have reactions. Allow it to thoroughly set. Do not stretch the foam padding, rather crowd it toward the center, but keep the surface smooth.

The best way to go about the lining job is to use a sheet of the 2 inch thick foam, cut at least 72 by 86 inches, and start to cement at the center of the bottom. Gradually work outward until you reach the corners. There will be surplus material here, and although you will have to cut some of it away, make only a diagonal cut as far as necessary as you work up the sides of the corners. Crowd the padding into the corners as much as possible, cutting away surplus material only as necessary. The faster the adhesive sets, the less you will have to wait, but you won't be able to loosen it to correct mistakes.

After the adhesive has set, the cradle must be lined. Use a water-repellant fabric for the lining. The fabric can be carried over to cover the outside as a finish. Or, if you prefer to paint the outside of the cradle, take the fabric over the top edges and down about ½-inch beyond the foam padding. Turn under the edges of the fabric, which should be cut with pinking shears, and glue to the outer surfaces down ½ inch beyond the foam. If you are using this fabric to cover the outside as well as the inside, carry it down and across the bottom. Lap the edges where they meet underneath. Be sure to cement all edges solidly.

Should you decide to paint the outside of the cradle below the carried over foam and fabric at the top, you can decorate the cradle with decals. Since this design has no definite head or foot, decorations should be the same at both ends as they should be on both sides.

When you are certain that everything is thoroughly dry and set, insert the mattress. This can be a conventional baby mattress or cut from core type polyurethane foam. If it is the latter, it should be at least 3 inches in thickness. Baby's head and flailing arms will be protected by the inner lining that has been carried over the top edges.

SWINGING CRADLE

The swinging baby cradle (Fig. 2-11) is supported by 40 inch standards at each end. Toward the bottom these standards are strengthened by a stretcher that keyholes in above the feet. Between the 18 inch deep solid ends of the swinging portion the doweled

Fig. 2-11. Swinging baby cradle.

in side rails contain baby by pickets that slant slightly outward from the lower rail leaving 20 inches at the bottom and 24 inches at the top rail for baby. Inverted V arms rise from both ends of the cradle to the bolt attachment to the standard. This arrangement allows the cradle to swing.

To build this baby bed you will need the following materials:

Two ends shaped from ¾-inch plywood 24 by 24 inches (Fig. 2-12A)
Two posts shaped from 2-by-4, 36 inches long (Fig. 2-12B)
Two feet shaped from 2-by-4, 26 inches long (Fig. 2-12C)
One stretcher, 2-by-4, 36 inches long (Fig. 2-12D)
Two top rails, 1-by-2, 36 inches long (Fig. 2-12E)
Two bottom rails, 1-by-4, 36 inches long (Fig. 2-12F)
Sixteen pickets, ¾-inch₁ diameter dowels, 20 inches long (Fig. 2-12G)
Two bolts, ¼-inch diameter and 3 inches long, with lock nuts and four washers each 1 inch across (Fig. 2-12H)
One base, ¾-inch plywood, 20 by 36 inches (Fig. 2-12I)

Adhesive
Finishing nails
6 feet of ¾-inch flexible edging to match plywood finish
Four metal gliders (optional)
Finishing materials

A stunning cradle can be built with this design by using solid maple or birch and plywood veneered on one side to match. Since the interior is lined, the plywood only needs to be veneered on one side. These woods can be stained or left natural. If you prefer, all or part of the cradle assembly can be painted one color or in contrasting colors with decal decoration. In any case the wood must be of a good quality.

Prepare the materials and assemble as follows:

If veneered plywood is used, be sure that you cut the end pieces of the cradle so that the grain pattern corresponds to that of the upright standards and the feet since these are viewed at the same time. If you plan to paint the whole thing, your concern will be solely for the strength of the wood and its straightness. Whenever possible, make measurement marks on the inside if you are going to apply a natural finish.

Working from the bottom edge of the end pieces, mark the center line and verify all of your measurements from this line. Be sure that this line rises from the bottom edge of the panel at exactly a right angle.

1. Measure along the bottom edge toward the center line 10 inches both left and right and mark on the profile (thickness) of the panel. Then check that it is exactly 20 inches between the marks.

2. Measure up 18 inches on the center line and mark.

3. From this mark measure 12 inches to the left and right and mark. Connect these marks with those you made at the bottom of the panel. This will be your saw lines for the lower portion of the cradle end piece. The cradle should be 20 inches across the bottom and 24 inches across where it is joined by the sides. This point should be 6 inches down from the top of the inverted V.

4. At the top edge of the panel mark 1 inch to the right and the same to the left of the center line. Connect these marks, which should be 2 inches apart, and check that this line is parallel to the bottom of the panel.

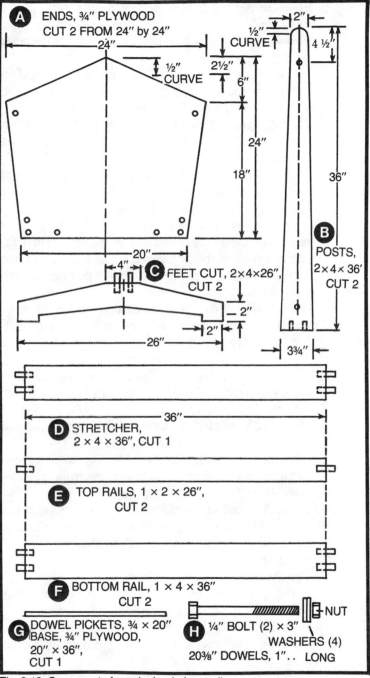

Fig. 2-12. Components for swinging baby cradle.

5. From the ends of the line made in Step 4, draw lines to connect with the ends of the 24 inch line drawn in Step 3. Now you have the rough outline or saw lines of the outermost cradle end.

6. On the center line, 4½-inches below the top edge of the panel, centerpunch for the hole to be drilled for the ¼-inch bolt on which the cradle swings.

7. The top of the inverted V will need rounding off after you have sawn out the end pieces, so sketch the limits of these curves.

8. The shaping of the standards from 2-by-4, 36 inches long is next. At the bottom these two pieces should form a rectangle 3¾ by 1¾-inches. Find the middle and draw a center line from bottom to top.

9. At the top edge of the center line, measure left and right 1 inch and mark on the profile of the board. Draw saw lines from these marks to the bottom corners that will shape the tapered post.

10. On the 2-by-4s that are 26 inches long, draw a center line across the narrow width. Measure 2 inches to the right and 2 inches to the left of the center line and mark on the profile.

11. Measure up from the opposite edge at each end 2 inches and mark on the profile. Draw a saw line across the profile to connect these dots.

12. Measure 2 inches in from each end along the bottom edge and draw a saw line parallel with the ends.

13. From the bottom edge on the center line, mark a point 1 inch up. Connect this point with the points marked 2 inches in and ½-inch up at both ends.

14. Check all of your saw marks carefully. Remember, you can saw it off but not on again. When you are sure that the markings correspond to the pieces as shown in Fig. 2-12, saw them out.

15. Drill the holes as centerpunched:
   at the apex of the cradle end pieces, a 5/16-inch hole, countersunk on the inside surface for the nut;
   at 4½ inches down from the top of the standards, a 5/16-inch hole, countersunk on the outer surface for the bolt head;
   twenty-four pairs of ⅜-inch dowel holes (Fig. 2-12) for the

insertion of strengthening dowels at joints; clamp the 1-by pieces in bench vice to drill.

16. Sand all edges and surfaces.
17. Assemble all components, cradle first.
18. Check that the bolts on which the cradle swings does not bind so that the cradle swings smoothly and freely. Enlarge hole if necessary. Check that nothing protrudes. The double washers should slide over each other between the cradle and the standard to assist in the smooth operation.
19. Finish the wood.
20. When everything is dry, install the lining. Use at least a 3 inch thick polyurethane foam pad and bring it up to the top of the lower side rail, which should keep it in place. Over this use a water-repellant fabric. Cut the foam padding oversize, just so you can cram it into the bottom of the cradle smoothly.

A helper will come in handy in hanging the cradle, to support one end of the cradle while you install the bolt at the other end. If you do not have a helper, prop the other end up on a box or something about 14 or 15 inches high that will be steady. All that remains to be done is to install the metal glider buttons on the bottom of the feet and the cradle is ready for baby.

FOLDING BASSINET

If you have a small baby and want to take him or her with you visiting the home of friends, build a fold-up bassinet. He or she will feel right at home wherever you are. This design is quite portable, is light to carry and will fit almost anywhere (Fig. 2-13).

Since there is a minimal amount of wood used, its choice is important. Probably your favorite lumber yard, like many today, carries a limited selection of woods from which you can choose, and most of that is probably of dubious quality for this purpose. The best thing to do is to find a knowledgeable salesman who knows lumber and after explaining just how you propose to use the pieces, take his advice. First you should understand a little about the different types of wood available.

Any wood you use for the folding bassinet must be straight, not bowed, free from knots and strong. Since this design requires little beyond sawing, drilling and rounding off the corners, workability is only a minor consideration. The same applies to the way the wood will take a finish since the bassinet will be folded and put away after serving its purpose on trips.

Here are a few general qualities of some types of wood that deserve your consideration:

Birch is popular for furniture because it looks smart whether it is stained to look like another wood such as walnut, left natural or painted. It has uniform density on the surface so it will take a high polish. Although it is hard and tough, it is easily worked for a hard wood.

Maple is another wood that is popular for furniture because it is heavy, fine-grained, does not tend to shrink or warp, yet it is easily worked. It also takes a nice finish.

Beech is still another popular wood because it is strong, yet bends well so it is adapted for use where pieces must be curved. It holds nails well and, when properly dried, it is hard and wears well. For this reason it is often used for floors and the sides of drawers. It takes any finish well.

Oak offers over 60 species of which only 14 are used for interiors and furniture. Since the descriptive names for these vary in different localities, they would only be confusing. Oak is one of the stronger of the hard woods but works well and takes a good finish providing you don't try for a light finish on a darker variety of the wood.

Western spruce is referred to as Sitka. It is usually straight-grained and free from warping and checking. It is light in weight, especially when compared to oak. These qualities make it worth your consideration in selecting the wood for any article that is portable.

Walnut takes the darker finishes well but is expensive. It is shock-resistant and offers little shrinkage. For these reasons it is popular for furniture in spite of its cost.

Elm is a very hard wood and varies in color.

Yellow poplar is often used for furniture since it does not easily split and takes a smooth, high finish.

Cyprus is resistant to decay and dampness so it is often used for exterior furniture although it is difficult to work. It is not recommended for furniture to be used indoors.

The strength of doweling is important in reinforcing joints as will be done with the folding bassinet. Since it is not seen when inserted between two members, only its strength need be considered. To reinforce the glued dowel, drive a finishing nail into it

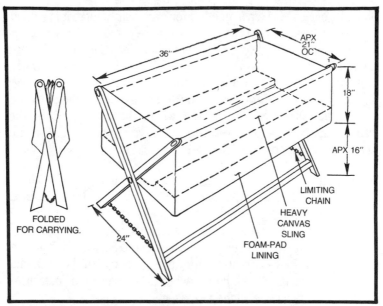

Fig. 2-13. Folding bassinet.

before the glue is dry. This is a good practice with any glued dowel to spread the holding quality and tighten up the joint.

The pivot pin that joins the two legs at both ends of the bassinet where they cross should be a ¼-inch bolt, 3½-inches long. Countersink both head and nut of this pivot. A locking nut will prevent it from loosening and dropping off. Double washers should be slid on the bolt between the two legs so they will turn easier.

The side rails are 1½-inch diameter poles to enable the canvas sling to slip over them easily. Wide hems in the top edges of the sling should permit this slippage. These rails should not turn but be solidly fastened to the top of the legs at both ends where they are joined by ¼-inch diameter, 4 inch long, wood screws that have deep enough threads to hold when screwed into the end grain of the poles that are the side rails. The head of this screw can be either flat or rounded, but in either case it should be countersunk.

The only other hardware needed are the limit chains. These are installed between each set of legs to control their spread. A light chain with link loops about ¼-inch across will be sufficiently strong and the link loops at the ends can be opened to fasten to the screw eyes that screw into the legs at least 1 inch. The finish of the chain and screw eyes should match; both come in chrome or brass. While about 22 inches of chain is needed for each pair of legs, it is a good idea to get 4 feet. Do not cut it until you have completed assembly of the bassinet and set the outer tips of the legs 24 inches apart or until the sling hangs properly. A good way of measuring the leg setting is to place the bottom of the legs on a yardstick with the outside of one leg touching 16 and the outside of the other leg touching the 30 mark.

Additional components needed will be the wooden pieces, the canvas sling and the polyurethane, core type foam lining. Prepare the wooden components (Fig. 2-14) as follows:

1. If a soft wood is being used, cut four legs from 2-by-2 (actually 1¾ by 1¾ inches), 41 inches long. If using a hard wood, a slightly smaller thickness and width will suffice.
2. Round off the top ends of these pieces.
3. If soft wood is being used, cut two pieces 36 inches long from 2-by-2 for stretchers that go between the back and front legs. Again, if hard wood is being used the measurements can be slightly smaller.
4. From 1½-inch diameter pole cut two lengths 36 inches long. Be sure that the ends are squared, not angled.
5. Drill 5/16-inch holes in all four legs up 21 inches from the square ends for the pivot bolts on which the legs swing to open and close the bassinet. Countersink on the outside surfaces for head and nut of the ¼ inch bolts.
6. So that the bassinet will sit flat on the legs, they must be sawed at an angle at the bottom. The safest way to determine this angle is to install the bolt (hole drilled in Step 5) and set the feet on a yardstick with one leg just touching the 16 mark and the other the 30 mark. Then determine how much must be cut off of the inside of the leg to slant it so that the bottom of the leg sits flat on the floor. If you know how to use a try square, the angle can be determined by that. I have even done it with a folding rule by placing the folded part flat on the floor and turning one of the sections upward until the correct angle is obtained. Holding it in this position, all you have to do is to transfer the angle to the bottom of the legs. Whatever method you prefer, be sure that your saw line is right, then saw the slant at the bottom of the legs.
7. Now for the drilling of the dowel holes. Checking dowels reinforce the joining of the stretcher to the legs at both ends, and these ⅜-inch dowels should have 7/16-inch

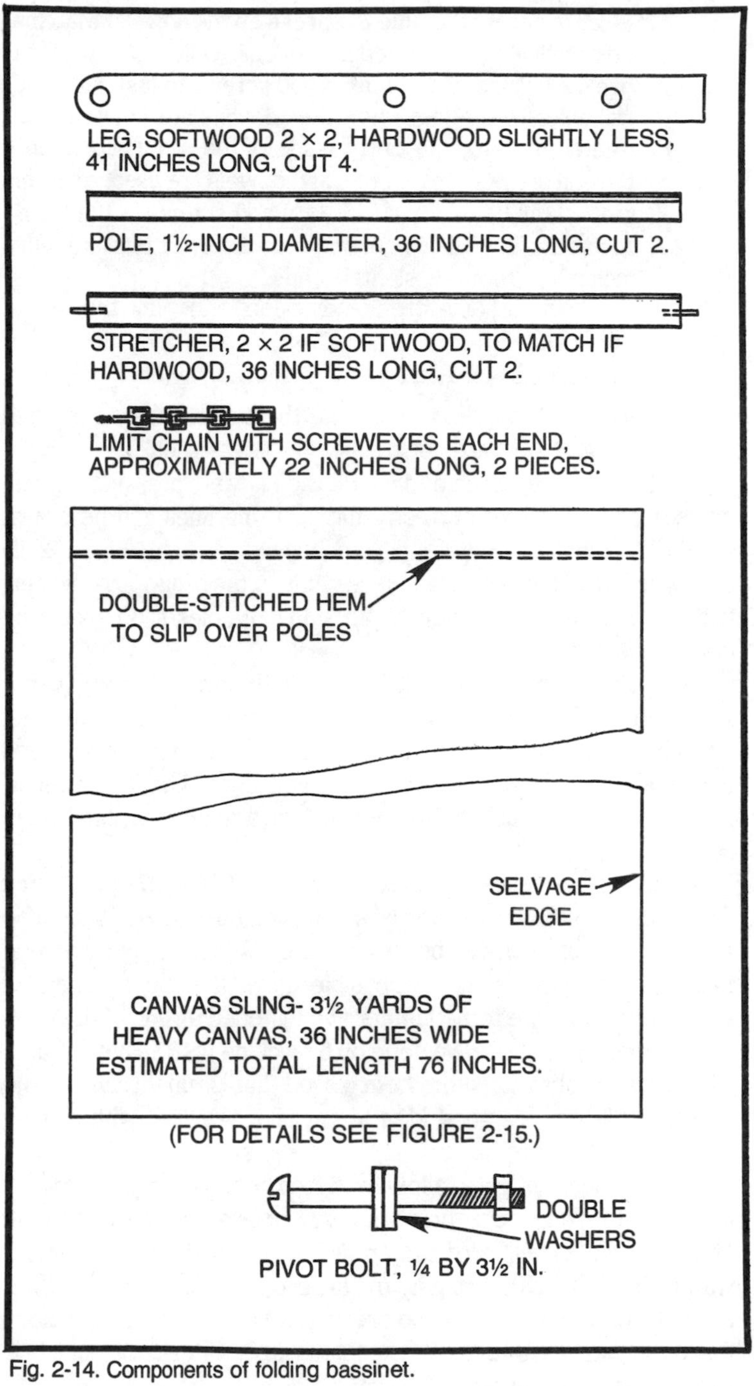

LEG, SOFTWOOD 2 × 2, HARDWOOD SLIGHTLY LESS, 41 INCHES LONG, CUT 4.

POLE, 1½-INCH DIAMETER, 36 INCHES LONG, CUT 2.

STRETCHER, 2 × 2 IF SOFTWOOD, TO MATCH IF HARDWOOD, 36 INCHES LONG, CUT 2.

LIMIT CHAIN WITH SCREWEYES EACH END, APPROXIMATELY 22 INCHES LONG, 2 PIECES.

DOUBLE-STITCHED HEM TO SLIP OVER POLES

SELVAGE EDGE

CANVAS SLING- 3½ YARDS OF HEAVY CANVAS, 36 INCHES WIDE ESTIMATED TOTAL LENGTH 76 INCHES.

(FOR DETAILS SEE FIGURE 2-15.)

DOUBLE WASHERS

PIVOT BOLT, ¼ BY 3½ IN.

Fig. 2-14. Components of folding bassinet.

holes to permit the glue to spread up the dowels. Matching holes will also be needed in the legs. Unless you prefer to use dowels instead of long wood screws to fasten the side rail poles to the legs, no other dowels are needed.

8. Centerpunch for the entry guide of the wood screws into the end of the side rail poles. (If dowels are used, omit this step.) Drill holes for shank of wood screws in the legs.

9. Install the limit chain screw eyes in each pair of legs about 4 inches up from the slanted ends.

10. Assemble all parts after sanding each and round the ends of the poles.

11. Finish as desired and allow to thoroughly dry.

All that is left to do is to fabricate the canvas sling. If planned before cutting, 3 1/3 yards of the heavy canvas should be enough. Clear off your work bench and unroll the canvas, pressing out any creases so that it lays perfectly flat. Cutting lines can be drawn directly on the fabric, but keep your pencil lines light. Figure 2-15 shows how to cut the required pieces. Since the sling will be holding baby, the hems through which the side rail poles slide should be double stitched.

The first 76 inches, the full 36 inch width, forms the width of the sling with the selvage edges at the back and front. Cut the remaining 44 inches in 22 inches from a selvage edge in two for the back and front ends. This leaves a piece 14 by 44 inches. Cut this into two pieces each 7 by 44 inches. These will form a reinforcing band when seamed together.

Stitch these pieces together as shown in Fig. 2-15 by hemming the edges and seaming the corners. The reinforcing band should be added to the sling midway between the ends, lapped over the side rails and continued as far as possible down the inside. The raw edges, of course, are turned under and fastened by one of the rows of stitching, which should be done on a machine with heavy thread.

Be sure not to stitch the hem closed that is run through by the side rail poles. It is a good idea to cut all raw edges with pinking shears to reduce raveling.

The dimensions given allow for 6 inch hems on either side and 2 inches for turn under of selvage edges. Check stability and strength before using. To help hold the cradle square at the bottom, line it with at least 3 inch thick polyurethane core type foam pad (Fig. 2-13). Cut the pad oversize and crowd it toward the center but keep the top surface smooth. Cover the foam with a water-resistant fabric before putting in the other bedding.

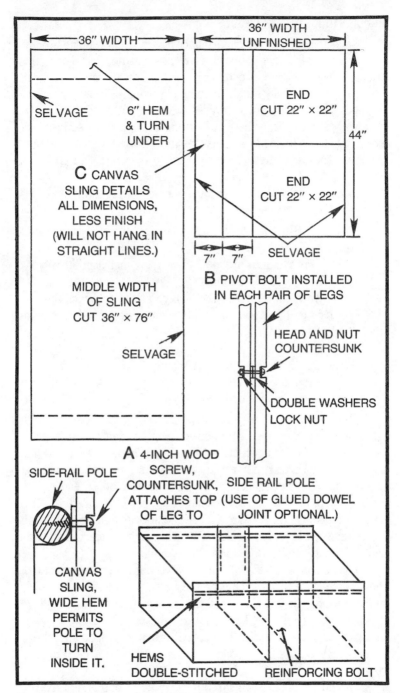

Fig. 2-15. Assembly details for folding bassinet.

BROOMSTICK ROLL UP CRADLE

Collect about a dozen old ordinary household sweeping brooms with the handles intact and you have most of the material for this cradle, hence its name, broomstick cradle. Dowels can be used but broomsticks are really tough, strong and usually already smoothly finished. Unless you want to refinish them, all you need to do is a bit of sawing, some drilling and a little sanding. No nails or screws, not even any glue is needed as the pieces are strung together on rope. When taken down, the broomstick cradle can be rolled up into a portable or easily stored parcel.

The materials needed to make a cradle with the dimensions shown in Fig. 2-16 are:

Twenty 16 inch lengths of broomstick (usually ⅞-inch diameter)
Four 36 inch lengths of broomstick or 1½-inch diameter poles
Six 1-by-2s, 16 inches long
1 2/3 yards of 36 inch wide heavy canvas or sail cloth
40 to 50 feet (depending on the suspension) of ¼-inch marine rope
Ceiling hooks
¾-inch common iron plumber's pipe
short lengths of heavy chain (depending on the method you want to use to suspend the cradle)

The preparation consists mainly of drilling the holes through which to thread the rope. To do this drilling you really need a bench vise. Use a 5/16-inch drill bit so the ¼-inch rope will slip through easily. Before drilling, centerpunch each hole and insure that the hole in one end is parallel to the hole in the other end of the broomstick or dowel. On the broomsticks, center the holes 1 inch in from each end. On the poles at the top and bottom that run the length of the cradle, the holes should be 2 inches in from each end. This allows for the carving of a knob at the ends.

The 36 inch wide canvas will put a selvage edge at each end of the crib. Each of these should be finished with a 1 inch hem. This brings the canvas just short of the rope. Both sides should be finished with a deep enough hem to allow the 1½-inch diameter poles to slip through them easily. The canvas must be slipped onto these poles at least before the second end of the crib is threaded onto the rope.

Thread the rope down through the hole at one end of the top side pole, then in this order: top 1-by-2, five broomsticks, the middle

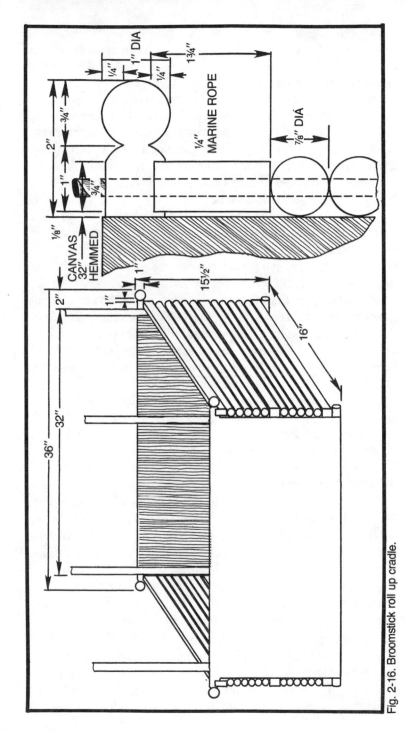

Fig. 2-16. Broomstick roll up cradle.

113

1-by-2, the bottom five broomsticks and the side pole. The rope then goes across the bottom of the canvas and up the opposite side in reverse order. While knots at the top of the side poles are not necessary, tie them if you like.

From where the rope emerges at the top of the side poles it is then taken up to whichever suspension system you have chosen (Fig. 2-17). The four ropes can rise vertically, each to the chain from its own ceiling hook or they may be ganged. This may be done by using two pipes each yoked to a single hook in the ceiling by the chain or a single pipe yoked to one or two ceiling hooks. The fewer the hooks, the stronger each must be.

Don't try to hang the whole thing on one hook. Not only is it unsafe, the cradle will tend to spin around. If it is impossible or inconvenient to place the hooks so that all four ropes, rising vertically, will connect with them, then use a yoke. Use either the one that gangs the pair rising from the foot and the pair rising from the head individually or the lengthwise yoke. The lengthwise yoke can gang the ropes from one side to one pipe and the ropes rising from the other side to another pipe, leaving all four ropes suspended from two hooks by chains. In any case, be sure that the hooks are of the correct type and are installed into structural members of the house to avoid any chance of the cradle dropping.

Line the broomstick cradle, not only for baby's comfort but to give the canvas bottom some rigidity. Use at least 3 inch thick polyurethane foam padding. The core type, 6 inch thick foam is preferred. Over this, lay a water-resistant fabric.

KNOCKDOWN BASSINET

For portability you can't beat this knockdown bassinet (Fig. 2-18A). Some claim that it can even be carried between two people, but the real advantage is that it comes apart and can be made into a light-weight, easily carried or stored parcel that can also be assembled easily.

The sling can be sail cloth, heavy canvas or fishnet. It is hemmed all the way around and lined with polyurethane foam padding. The sling can be made of reinforced macrame.

Tough rods, such as ⅞-inch diameter broomsticks, are slipped into the hems. The two 36 inch poles and the 18 inch cross poles can be 1½-inch diameter.

To set up the crib, the end poles are slipped into the holes and the lengthwise poles slipped into their holes so that they interlock in

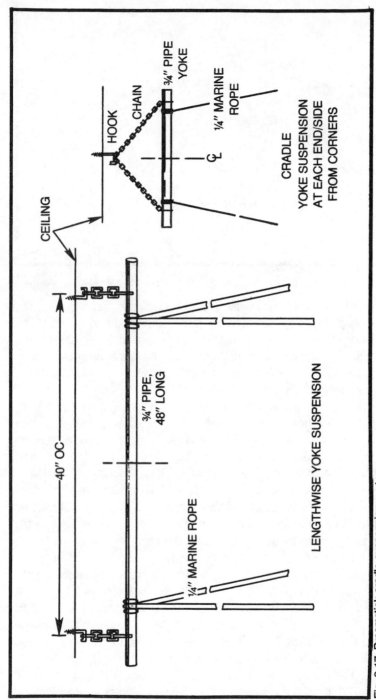

CEILING

HOOK

CHAIN

¾" PIPE
YOKE

¼" MARINE
ROPE

CL

CRADLE
YOKE SUSPENSION
AT EACH END/SIDE
FROM CORNERS

40" OC

¾" PIPE,
48" LONG

¼" MARINE ROPE

LENGTHWISE YOKE SUSPENSION

Fig. 2-17. Broomstick cradle suspension systems.

115

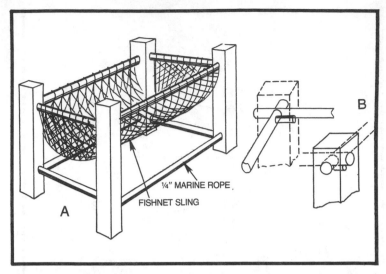

Fig. 2-18 A. Knockdown bassinet. B. Interlocking poles with latching dowel.

the notches of the widthwise poles. To lock this arrangement, the dowel, just below the widthwise poles, is slipped into its hole. The dowel presses the lengthwise pole upward so that it remains in the notch of the upper pole. This requires some pretty accurate drilling (Fig. 2-18B) and sufficiently large corner posts; a 2-by-4 is needed to accept all of these holes without weakening.

The notch in the 18 inch poles should be made about 1 inch from the end. The hole for this pole should be bored deep enough to stop the pole so that the notch is exactly on the hole drilled to take the lengthwise pole. The dowel hole must be such that it directs the dowel directly under the lengthwise pole, touching it so that it presses it upward and locks it in place within the 2-by-4. The dowel should be press-fit and of sufficient length so that it can be inserted or extracted by the finger tips. Although this seems complicated, with careful measurement you can make it work.

To prevent the legs from spreading, rope should be laced through holes about 4 inches up from the bottom of the legs. A knot on either side of the holes will prevent the rope from running through these holes. Even for these holes, careful measurement is required to make the holes from the two sides of the post meet at right angles in the center of the post. This right angle turn of the rope is supposed to keep it from readily slipping through.

There are parents who have made and used this design for their infants that claim that this crib is the handiest thing since safety pins.

They even insist that they can set it up on the floor of the back seat of their car so that their baby can ride safely in it.

ROCK-A-BYE CRADLE

The rock-a-bye cradle (Fig. 2-19A) will depend on your ability to find a pair of hangers. The type used to install stair rails are ideal because they are necessarily strong. Strength is a requirement when using the hangers for the cradle (Fig. 2-19B). These brackets are usually finished in brass and will go handsomely with a walnut stained wooden cradle.

It is a good idea to make patterns so that the four different curves will match each other. In fact it will be simpler if you make your pattern for half of the entire standard and another for half of the cradle end piece.

The standard has three curves: the one at the top with a 7½-inch radius, the side that slants down to a curve with an 8 inch

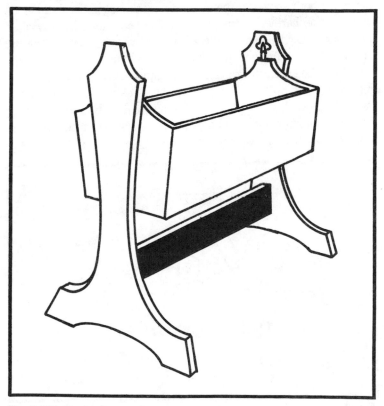

Fig. 2-19A. Rock-a-bye cradle.

radius, the foot contours and the curve at the bottom. While the end of the cradle only has one curve, it will be easier to draw the saw line from a pattern that includes the 7½-inch-radius curve toward the top and the slanted side. Since making saw patterns has been explained with other projects, it will not be detailed here.

The recommended dimensions and cutting requirements are given in Fig. 2-20. The entire cradle can be made of ¾-inch thick plywood, veneered if you like. This means that the raw edges must be finished with ¾-inch wide flexible tape to match. The stretcher reinforcing blocks can also be cut from the plywood scraps, although they will be stronger if cut from solid stock. Since they are not large, no doubt you will have some suitable scraps on hand.

While only the stretcher is shown for glued dowel assembly, the base will benefit from this treatment for added strength. Otherwise glue and finishing nails should suffice.

Regardless of how strong the brackets from which the cradle swings at both ends are, the strength of the fastenings to the ends and the other hardware attachments are of equal importance. Bolted fastening is always superior to wood screws, especially when the screw threads must get their bite from the end grain of plywood.

Line the cradle at least 12 inches up all the way around with 2 inch thick polyurethane foam padding. Cover this with water-resistant fabric before putting in the mattress or thicker foam pad. Sand everything smooth and finish the exterior and uncovered portions of the interior as desired.

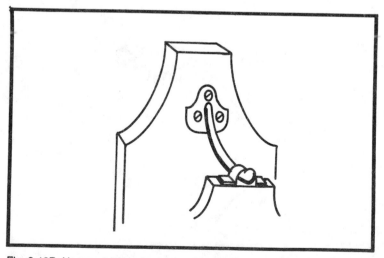

Fig. 2-19B. Hanger detail using stair rail brackets.

BEDSIDE CRADLE

When mother is bed-ridden, it is convenient to have a bedside cradle. It must be sufficiently low so that she can just reach across to get at the little one without getting out of bed. Using 1½-inch spherical casters also increases the mobility of the cradle.

The following materials are needed to build a bedside cradle (Fig. 2-21):

Two 2-by-4 posts, 24 inches long, with the top corners rounded

Two feet formed from 2-by-4, 19¾ inches long, shaped to repeat the curves at the end of the cradle end pieces

One spreader from 2-by-4, 30½ inches long, notched and doweled at both ends

Two cradle ends from ¾-inch thick plywood, 16 by 18 inches, shaped at the top

Two cradle sides of ¾-inch thick plywood, 11¼ by 29 inches

Two bolts, ¼-inch diameter by 3¼ inches long, with two large washers and one nut each

Six ⅜-inch dowels, 2 inches long

10 feet of ¾-inch wide flexible tape to finish raw edges of the plywood

Finishing nails

Adhesive

Prepare the components as follows:

1. Make a pattern for the curve at either side of the top of the cradle end piece and a pattern for the feet with the identical curves.
2. Mark saw lines after measuring carefully.
3. Centerpunch for all holes to be drilled.
4. Cut all components to shape.
5. Sand edges to knock off the sharp corners, especially the top of the posts.
6. Drill 5/16-inch holes in cradle ends and the posts and countersink for bolt head and nut.
7. Drill six matching holes for ⅜-inch dowels.
8. Prepare both ends of the feet to take the 1½-inch spherical casters.
9. Sand all components.

To assemble the cradle proceed as follows:

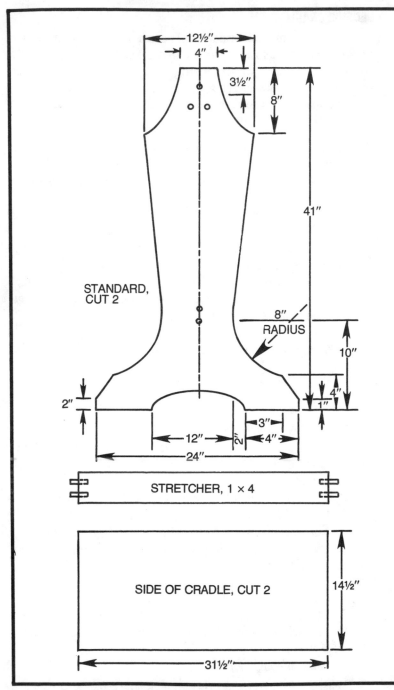

Fig. 2-20. Components of rock-a-bye cradle.

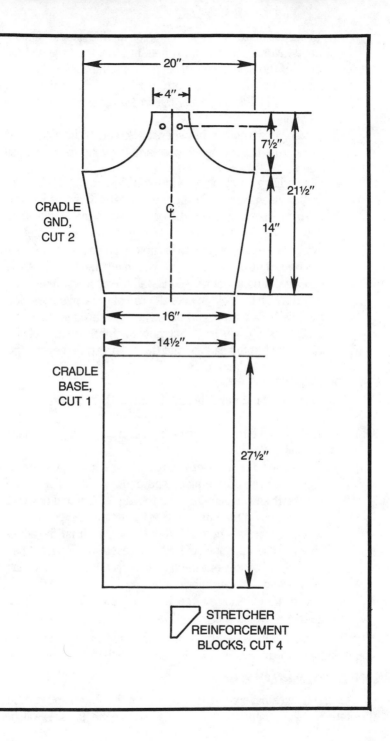

20"

4"

7½"

21½"

CRADLE
GND,
CUT 2

C
L

14"

16"

14½"

CRADLE
BASE,
CUT 1

27½"

STRETCHER
REINFORCEMENT
BLOCKS, CUT 4

1. Using finishing nails and glue, assemble cradle components. Note that the end panels fit over the base and the ends of the side panels. Nail set all nail heads.
2. Attach the feet to the bottom of the posts using glue, dowels and finishing nails, making sure that they are at a right angle.
3. Assemble stretcher between back and front assembled standards, using glue, dowels and finishing nails. Set nail heads.
4. Glue edging on all plywood raw edges.
5. Install assembled cradle between posts. For this job you need a helper to hold up the other end of the cradle while you fix the bolt in one end. If you do not have a helper available, set the other end of the cradle on something that will bring it up and level before you insert the bolt. This will be easier if done before you install the casters. Insert the bolt through the hole toward the top of the end piece, slide two washers onto it and pass the bolt through the post. Install the nut securely but not so tightly that it binds. Check that both head and nut do not protrude beyond the surfaces on either side.
6. Repeat at the other end.
7. Test that the cradle swings freely and that there are no rough spots.
8. Allow all glue to set thoroughly before applying the finish and lining the cradle.
9. Cut at least 3 inch thick polyurethane foam pad oversize so that it can run up the sides and ends of the inside of the cradle. It should also go over the top edges and down at least 1 inch on the outside. Start gluing at the center and work outward all the way around. Be sure that the adhesive you use will not cause allergic reactions. Push the pad toward the center but keep the surface smooth. Overlay with water-resistant fabric.
10. Finish the exterior as you wish. If you paint, decals can decorate the panels.

If you have a bedside cradle waiting when baby and mother come home from the hospital, it will be appreciated.

OFF-THE-FLOOR PLAY PEN

Some houses have persistent drafts on the floors and parents hesitate to allow baby to play or nap where he or she will be

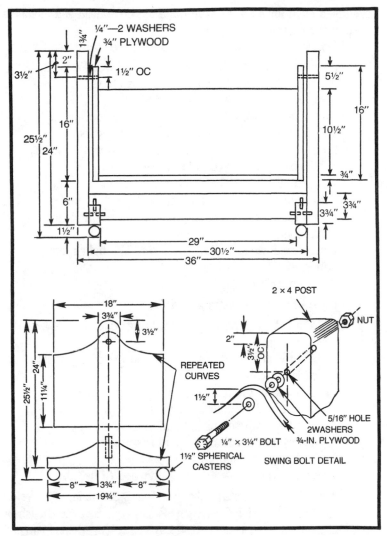

Fig. 2-21. Assembling a bedside cradle.

subjected to these drafts. For these situations the off-the-floor play pen is the answer.

The dimensions (Fig. 2-22) are such that the pen can be moved through doorways from room to room without having to disassemble the pen in spite of the legs that lift it up off of the floor.

To further fend off the possibility of drafts, one or two sides of the pen can be solid hardboard instead of pickets. One-quarter inch thick masonite is good for this purpose, but because it must be predrilled even for nails, the top rail must be routed and moldings used at the bottom to retain it.

Materials needed to build the playpen are: (using soft wood)

Four legs, 2-by-2, 32 inches long (if hard wood is used, 1½ by 1½ is sufficient for both legs and stretchers)
Four stretchers, 2-by-2, 28 inches long
One base, ¾-inch thick plywood or T&G flooring, 28 by 45½ inches (if plywood is used, raw edges must be taped)
Four top rails: two 26 inches long and two 44½ inches, 1¼-inch diameter dowel or pole
Ten pickets, 1 inch diameter dowel, 24 inches long
Two sheets of ¼-inch hardboard, 28 by 45½ inches
Two quarter round molding: one 28 inches long and one 45 inches long
Thirty-six dowels, ⅜-inch diameter, 1½ inches long
Adhesive
Finishing nails

Prepare the components as follows:

1. Rout (or have the lumber yard rout) one edge to take the ¼-inch hardboard.
2. Drill for installation of dowels and matching holes at the following joints:
   each end of the four stringers and in the four posts;
   each end of the four top rails and in the four posts;
   lower end of each picket and into base;
   upper end of each picket and into top rail.
3. Sand all parts smooth.
4. Apply tape to raw edges of plywood (if used).

Assemble components as shown in Fig. 2-22, gluing all doweled or routed joints and using finishing nails to install the base. Finish as desired and allow to thoroughly dry. Lay in a polyurethane foam pad and cover with water-resistant fabric.

If hard board is used as panels, decals can be applied after painting them. The off-the-floor play pen can be stored on end and only requires a space of about 2 feet, 8 inches by 2 feet, 4 inches. Glider buttons can be installed on the feet to protect the floor.

MULTILEVEL PLAY PEN

A similar play pen can be built that will grow with the child. This is accomplished by securing the base (floor) at a choice of levels by means of carriage bolts.

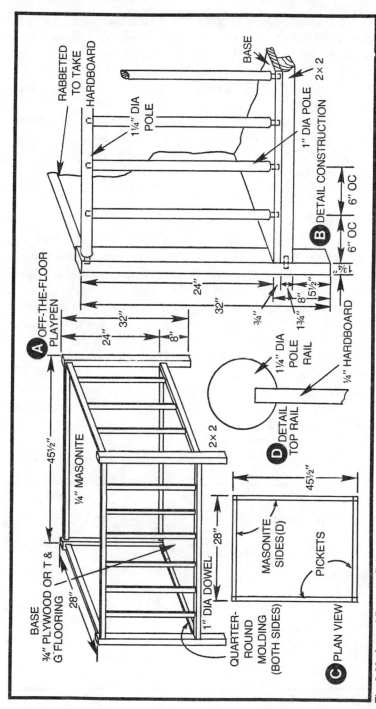

Fig. 2-22. Assembling an off-the-floor playpen.

125

To accommodate the infant, the floor is moved to the shallowest level and a hinged, fold-down gate allows easy access to this compartment. As the child grows, the floor is moved to the lower level. The dimensions can be made to accommodate a large crib mattress that is 28 by 52¾ inches, or any size of polyurethane foam padding (Fig. 2-23).

Because the pen is first used as a crib for a small baby, the upper pickets can be ⅝-inch dowels, but they must be spaced closer together than the 6 inches on center shown in Fig. 2-22 for the off-the-floor playpen. Otherwise the construction can be much the same. Be sure to use nontoxic finishes and adhesive.

GATED CRIBS

The bed builder for little ones has a wide choice of ways to gate cribs. Among the choices are the hinged side that folds downward, the sliding side, the vertical door-like gate and the hinged half gated cribs. This is in addition to an infinite variety of sizes.

Leg or post styles can vary, but in general, there are four of them. Between the legs are the stretchers, a base and four sides. The sides may be solid or made with pickets. The pickets are usually dowels of less than 1 inch diameter. The dimensions of the other components depend on the type of wood used and that choice will somewhat depend on the availability, the builder's ability to work with wood and the choice of finishes. Softer woods demand the use of larger dimensional pieces.

The size of the crib depends on baby's sleeping habits. Recommended lengths run from 36 to 48 inches and widths from 24 to 30

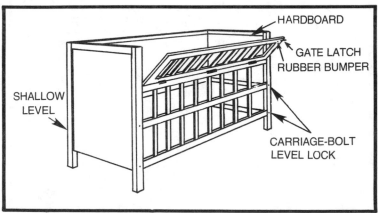

Fig. 2-23. Multilevel play pen.

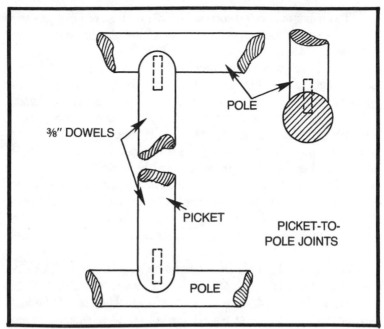

Fig. 2-24A. Cylindrical picket.

inches. One thing is certain, no matter what dimensions you chose to make your crib, baby will soon outgrow it.

We will discuss several examples of gated cribs, but first some building pointers that will apply to all types.

As with most conventional home-made beds, ¾-inch plywood makes a very satisfactory base. Top this with polyurethane foam padding of the thickness desired. A store-bought mattress should be your last choice for your home-made bed. For safety avoid using loose slats as a base. Even with store-bought bed frames it is not uncommon for the slats to drop out. The plywood base not only adds stability that is desirable but makes it easier to tie your bed components together. It also insulates the bed from underneath and keeps the dust out.

In building any bed it is always a good practice to dowel all joints. The dowel holes should be 1/16-inch larger than the dowel to permit the glue to spread down the sides of the hole. When the hole is the same size, air and glue will be compressed at the bottom of the hole and this will prevent the dowel from seating properly. Tiny grooves should be scratched in the sides around the circumference of the dowel. If the dowel is small, this can weaken it somewhat.

To further insure the solid hold of a dowel, it is a good practice to drive a small finishing nail into it before the glue has had time to set, but this can be done to only one in a joint.

In building cribs do not underestimate baby's strength. Very small infants cannot wreck much havoc on ⅝-inch dowels used as pickets, but there soon comes a time when you wish you had used larger ones, even 1 inch diameter. Always dowel in the pickets securely at the bottom and top. When a cylindrical picket is doweled into the top pole of a crib, it should be shaped to fit the circumference of the rail (Fig. 2-24A). Drill in first for the dowel.

A hinge can be installed between two 1½-inch diameter poles by leveling off the joining sides of both circumferences the thickness of one leaf of the hinge (Fig. 2-24B). Be sure that the leaves of the hinge are no wider than this level place or dangerous corners will protrude.

A crib should usually be mounted on casters so that it can be moved around easily and not scratch the floor. The best type of casters are 1½-inch diameter spherical ones. They should be just slightly smaller than the cross-section of the legs to which they are attached. For example, a 2-by-2 leg can take a 1½-inch caster with nothing sticking out to trip someone. Remember that a 2-by-2 actually measures 1¾ by 1¾ inches.

Unless a dense hard wood is used, posts of cribs should be at least 2-by-2, but they can take a little shaping. Keep in mind that the

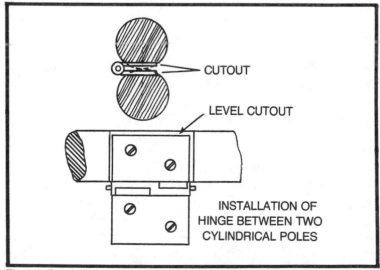

CUTOUT

LEVEL CUTOUT

INSTALLATION OF HINGE BETWEEN TWO CYLINDRICAL POLES

Fig. 2-24B. Installation of hinge between two cylindrical poles.

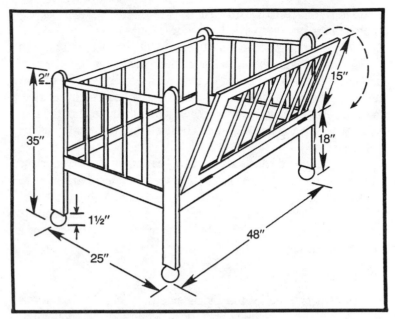

Fig. 2-25. Side hinged crib.

four legs must not only support the combined weight of baby and the bedding but withstand the stress of yanking around.

Side Hinged Crib

The side hinged crib (Fig. 2-25) should be sufficiently high to allow the fold-down gate to fall down completely vertically without being in the way of the person who is putting baby in or getting him out of the crib. This means that if the gate is 15 inches vertically, the hinged edge must be at least 17 inches from the floor when it is open. At least 2 inches of clearance are needed, to prevent stubbing the toes.

The foam pad should be contained on all four sides, including the gate side. The bottom of the hinged gate should be even or slightly above the top of the mattress pad. This will help to keep the bedding from falling out.

Half Gated Hinged Crib

In the half gated hinged crib (Fig. 2-26), one side is divided into two sections, the lower being stationary and the upper swinging down on hinges. The typical half gated hinged crib has pickets on two sides, the front or gate side and one end. The other two sides are solid with ¼-inch hardboard (usually Masonite) to keep out unwanted drafts or noise while baby is sleeping.

When hardboard panels are used, the upper rail, in this case a 1½-inch pole, is rabbeted so that the panel can be glued in. Hardboard must be predrilled to take nails or screws. This treatment is optional. The bottom of such panels is secured by quarter-round molding although it too can be rabbeted. Instead of the 1½-inch pole for the top rail, 2-by-2 can be used, but the edges must be well rounded.

The hardboard panels are usually painted on the exterior and lined on the interior. Decals can be used for decoration on the painted surfaces.

Line the interior, as usual, with polyurethane foam padding. Over this lay water-resistant fabric even if additional padding or a mattress is used above that.

SLIDING SIDE CRIB

Some people prefer the sliding side crib (Fig. 2-27), but this version presents problems both in construction and operation. First, it is almost impossible to lower the sliding side with baby in your arms because both catches must be operated and the side must be

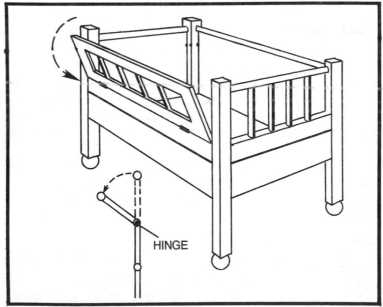

Fig. 2-26. Half gated hinged crib.

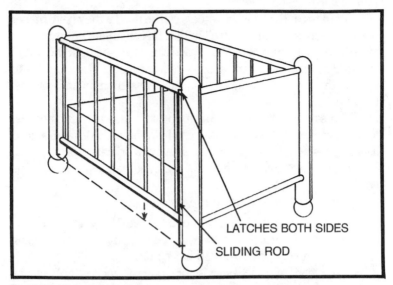

LATCHES BOTH SIDES

SLIDING ROD

Fig. 2-27. Sliding side crib.

raised evenly or it sticks no matter how well built it is. Some mothers say that baby can soon learn to trip the latches. Another disadvantage is that the crib must be higher to allow the side to drop its full width without hitting the feet of anyone standing by the side of the crib.

The typical sliding side crib shown has two solid ends and pickets on the two longer sides. This again is optional. Since bed building details have already been discussed, they will not be repeated here. Just one thing, since metal slides better on metal than wood on wood or even wood on metal, the sliding gate should be mounted on metal rods at each side. Use your ingenuity and you may be able to devise a sliding arrangement that will not stick at the wrong moments.

SPOOL CRIB

If you have access to a lot of sewing thread spools, you can string them on dowel and use them as legs or, better yet as pickets for a crib. This will at least be a conversation piece.

SCOOTER BED

There comes a time when the tot protests that he or she is too old to take that afternoon nap. A scooter bed (Fig. 2-28) could help overcome such protests. The sunshade is optional equipment.

Any 4 to 6 inch diameter wheels can be used if they have rubber tires. Wheels from an old stroller that the child has outgrown are ideal. The length and width of the base can be varied to fit the size of the tot that will be using the scooter at nap time. It is a good idea to restrict the use to nap times to enhance the attraction and maintain the novelty.

The safety belt can be similar to those used in automobiles. Your insistence that it be buckled can help the child develop a good habit. It also permits the use of a narrower base for the bed. Remember that the scooter must be "garaged" some place when it is not in use.

Materials needed to build the scooter bed are:

From ¾-inch thick plywood cut: a base 18 by 44 inches
Two head and foot boards 18 inches wide by 12 inches angling to a rounded point from 10 inches up
Four fenders, 8 inches wide, tapering to 5 inches by 16 inches long, curved out 6 inches lower for the wheels
Two sunshade supports (optional), 16 by 16 inches, in a fan shape
From 2-by-4 cut two 48 inch pieces for the beams and three 18 inch pieces for the crossbraces; from the scrap cut four reinforcing blocks 6 inches tapered to 2 inches; and six axle suspension blocks 4 inches long
½-inch common plumber's pipe for axles, with screw-on caps to retain the wheels; the length will depend on the wheels and the width of the base
Four wheels, preferably 4 to 6 inch diameter, with rubber tires
Seat belt and brackets
Corrugated fiber glass, 16 inches or more in width by 48 inches long
Two bolts with washers and nuts (can be thumb-screw type) ¼-inch diameter, 1 inch long if head and nut countersunk
Edge finishing tape for plywood, ¾ inches wide
Finishing materials, bright-colored paint

Note that the fenders are mounted on the outside edge of the base against the outside of the head and foot boards. This means that they must be cut out for the wheels, which they otherwise would touch. They are needed to retain the pad and any bedding used on the base, but need to be cut out at the middle to permit access without climbing over them. This means that only the exposed edges of the plywood base need be covered with flexible tape for finishing.

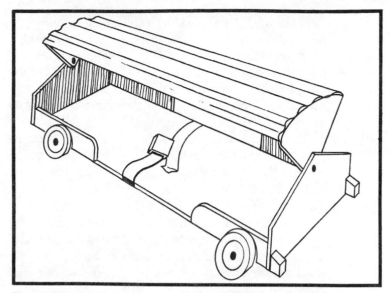

Fig. 2-28. Scooter bed with a sunshade and seat belt.

The sunshade is flexible so it can be moved as desired, but must not be so easily moved that it might fall down along the side. This is the reason why a thumb-screw nut is suggested for one or both of the bolts that attach the sunshade support to the head and foot boards. It is not too difficult to bend fiber glass sheet to fit the fan shaped support at each end if the sheet is warm. A short time in the sun will warm it sufficiently, just don't try to bend it against the corrugations.

Prepare the components as follows:

1. Cut the base from ¾-inch thick plywood (Fig. 2-29A).
2. Cut two pieces for the head and the foot boards from ¾-inch thick plywood the same width as the base at the bottom and up 10 inches, then tapering to a rounded apex the last 2 inches. On the center line down 2 inches from the top, drill a hole for the ¼-inch bolt that holds the sunshade support. If you use a bolt with a standard nut, both head and nut should be countersunk; however, if you use a thumb-screw nut that can be loosened or tightened when the sunshade is in place, countersink the head on the inner surface and leave the adjustable end of the bolt on the surface (Fig. 2-29B).
3. Cut two lengthwise beams from 2 by 4 so that they are 4 inches longer than the base. This allows them to stick out 2

inches beyond at each end for the mounting of the ¾-inch thick head and foot boards and the reinforcing blocks, which should come out even at the ends (Fig. 2-29C).

4. Cut three crossbraces from 2-by-4 the same width as the base. One of these supports the case just behind the axle supports at the front, another at the rear and one across the middle beneath the base, (Fig. 2-29D).

5. From the remaining pieces of 2-by-4 cut four reinforcing blocks to strengthen the vertical position of the head and foot boards. These blocks should be 6 inches high at the back, 2 inches at the front and taper from one of these planes to the other. It may be that the thickness will have to be narrowed slightly from the 1¾-inch dimension of the 2-by-4 in order to come out even with the face of the end of the beam on which it rests. If the blocks are installed with wood screws and glue, they will not require doweling (Fig. 2-29E).

6. From the remaining scrap of the 2-by-4, cut six axle supports, three for each set of wheels. These should be large enough to allow the axle to turn freely, yet not so large that they will extend below the level of the wheels. Usually 4 inches square will take the ½-inch pipe axle and not be too large for the wheels. If you prefer, the axles can be attached to the base by pipe strap (Fig. 2-29F).

7. Unless the wheels are already mounted on a satisfactory axle, use ½-inch common plumbers pipe. Have it threaded at each end to take pipe caps to retain the wheels. The length of this pipe will be determined by the width of the base and the thickness of the wheels. The less the axles protrude beyond the wheels, the less are the chances of barking an ankle on it (Fig. 2-29G).

8. While the sunshade is optional, it does contribute to the design of the scooter bed. Cut two sunshade supports from ¾-inch plywood. If you prefer, ¼-inch plywood will do just as nicely. Having encouraged the needed bend in the corrugated fiber glass under the heat of the sun, it should bend to the contour of the edge of each sunshade support. Secure it with brads and glue. If you want a wider sunshade, use a wider sheet of corrugated fiber glass and lengthen the arc of the sunshade support accordingly. In no case, however, should the sunshade be wider than 2 inches

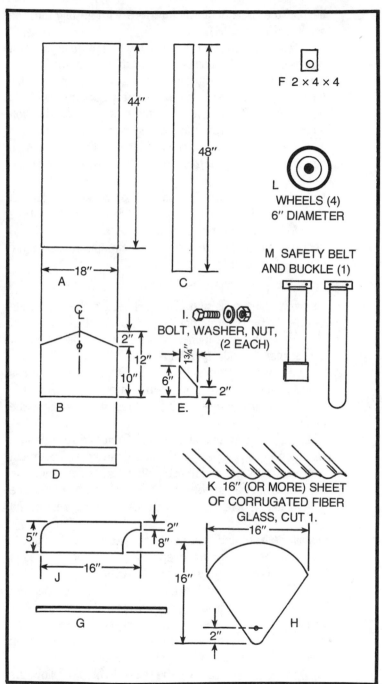

Fig. 2-29. Scooter bed components.

135

beyond the base or it will interfere with getting into the scooter (Fig. 2-29H).

9. The bolts that attach the sunshade to the head and foot boards should be countersunk at the bolt head (the interior surface). If common nuts are used at the other end, also countersink for these. If thumb-screw nuts are used, do not countersink for them. Install a washer on the bolt where it emerges from the board at the nut end. If countersunk at both ends, the bolt can be 1 inch in length. Under no circumstances allow it to protrude beyond the surface (Fig. 2-29I).

10. Cut four fenders from ¾-inch thick plywood, rounding off the corners. Leave a gap in the middle of each side of the base to facilitate getting into the scooter. The ends should be rounded inward to follow the circumference of the wheels (Fig. 2-29J).

Assemble the scooter bed as follows:

1. Using finishing nails and glue, nail setting the heads, assemble the two beams, one on each side of the base so that the beams extend 2 inches beyond the base at each end. Check that the side edges are even.

2. Turn the base bottom side up and position the three cross braces, one 4 inches from each end and one across the middle. Secure these with finishing nails, setting the heads.

3. Nail and glue the axle supports at front and rear. Insure that they line up properly by inserting the axles. They must also be exactly parallel to each other and at right angles to the wheels or the scooter will tend to run in circles. The axles must also be parallel with the front and rear of the base.

4. Install the front and rear head and foot boards so that the edges at the bottom are even with the bottom surface of the base. Use finishing nails and set the heads.

5. Install the reinforcing blocks at each of the four corners with the longest straight edges against the front, or rear board. The front lower vertical area should be even with the front of the beam below the base. Fasten securely with glue and finishing nails and set the heads.

6. Apply the fenders so that the curved cutouts follow the circumferences of the wheel but do not touch them. The

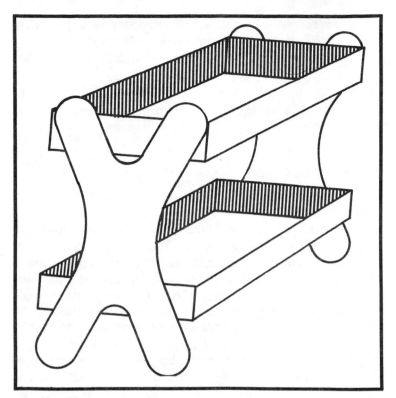

Fig. 2-30. Children's yoke bunk.

bottom edges should be even with the bottom of the base. Fasten securely with finishing nails and set the heads.

7. Mount the safety belt brackets at the middle of each side of the base using wood screws of sufficient length to give a good hold. Be sure that the brackets are exactly opposite each other.

8. The glue of the sunshade assembly should be thoroughly set by now and ready to be installed. Using the prescribed bolt, fasten the fan shaped support to the head and foot boards and test that it does not move too freely.

9. Install the four wheels on the axles. Check that the wheels do not spin too freely so that use of this bed as a scooter will not be encouraged.

10. Check everything and sand any rough spots, especially the edges.

11. Depending on how you want to finish the scooter bed, the rough edges of the plywood components should be finished

with a pliable beading. Acrylic paint may do the job. Bright colors on the exterior portions, perked up by decals, are quite suitable, but the interior should be a "quiet" color conducive to sleep.

This scooter bed should bring an end to protests "Do I have to take a nap?" It is an ideal family fun project, but you may have to build several of them.

CHILDREN'S YOKE BUNKS

For any family with twin babies or two children who are both small, the yoke bunk (Fig. 2-30) is an ideal bed project. By increasing the dimensions, the boxes can take twin 34 by 74 inch springs and mattresses and be used by older children.

Use of casters is not recommended with beds of this design. If dimensions are increased for use by older children, the head room between bunks must also be increased. The center of balance needs to be kept as low as possible to prevent any tendency to tip. The dimensions given in Fig. 2-31 will keep the upper bunk conveniently low for mother's access without the use of a stepladder.

For the use of older children who are of course heavier and require an increase in the dimensions, 2-by-4 side rails should be added for the bunks as well as other structural members, however the description and instructions for building these bunks will be confined to those appropriate to the small fry.

The main feature of this design is the free form X that conceals the structure. See Fig. 2-32 for explicit instructions for making the free form X pattern. As with the other patterns, this one need only be for a part of the piece to be shaped by sawing.

Start anywhere and locate the point where two coordinates given in the table meet and place a dot on the pattern paper there. The paper needs to be about 18 inches wide and 30 inches long. This is only a quarter of the whole panel to be cut out. Line up the vertical and horizontal center lines, and when you have transferred the quarter pattern, turn it over and line up the center lines and transfer that quarter. Repeat this for the lower two quarters and you have all four quarters exactly duplicated.

The first dot should be located where the vertical line marked 14 crosses the horizontal line marked 14. The next dot is placed where the horizontal line numbered 12 crosses the vertical line identified as 11. When you have placed a dot at all eighteen coordi-

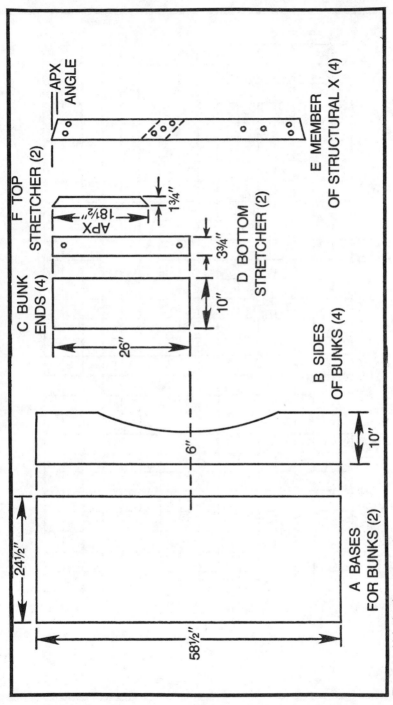

Fig. 2-31. Yoke bunk components.

139

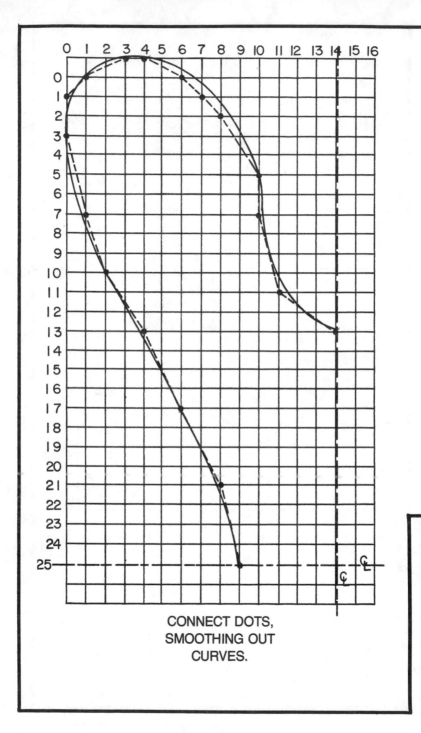

CONNECT DOTS,
SMOOTHING OUT
CURVES.

DOT POSITIONS	
ACROSS	DOWN
14	14
11	12
10	8
10	6
8	3
7	2
6	1
4	0
3	0
1	1
0	2
0	4
1	8
2	11
4	14
6	18
8	22
9	25

Fig. 2-32. Free form yoke pattern.

nates, sketch between them. This will be a jerky line so it must be smoothed out to form curves. Carry the outline slightly beyond the center lines for a smooth connection with the adjacent quarters.

Since this is a final step in building the yoke bunks, you can hold the pattern up to the X structure with the two bunk boxes installed to test that it covers the structural members completely. If there are any alterations you want to make in the sawing pattern before transferring it to the plywood, make them now.

Unless you are doing the cutting with a jig saw, you should use a saw with a narrow blade so you can get into the narrow curves smoothly. A helper will certainly come in handy for this job because you will be handling a large sheet of plywood. To prevent any chance of a part breaking off, the helper should support the sawn ends. By keeping the panel level the saw will be less likely to bind in the kerf. Unless the yoke bed is permanently set in a corner or next to a wall, two free form Xs will be required, one for each end.

The structural components should be prepared as follows:

1. Cut the two bases, 24½ by 58½ inches, from ¾-inch plywood and sand any rough spots, especially the edges (Fig. 2-31A).

2. Cut four bunk bed sides, 10 by 52½ inches, from ¾-inch plywood. Starting in 12 inches from each end, curve down to 4 inches from the bottom at midpoint for 34½ inches. A pattern will help you to make all of these curves alike (Fig. 2-31B).

3. Cut four bunk ends, 10 by 26 inches, from ¾-inch plywood (Fig. 2-31C).

4. Sand these pieces smooth and assemble into the two box-like bunks.

5. Cut two bottom stretchers, 26 inches long, from 2-by-4 (Fig. 2-31D).

6. From straight 2-by-4, cut four structural X pieces (Fig. 2-31E). Bore the center bolt as shown in Fig. 2-33.

7. Sand all surfaces and edges smooth.

8. To verify the position of the bolt holes in the X frame, install the center bolt loosely and set the frame on the stretcher with the outer edges even with the ends of the stretcher, even when it is placed flat on the floor with the 2¾-inch side down. Mark the inside angle so that the structural X pieces must sit flat on the stretcher to be cut. When they will sit flat together, nail securely in place. Now you can verify the position of all three center bolt holes in both X pieces.

9. Repeat with the other structural X member and bore all three center holes in each. Insert these bolts, checking that they are properly countersunk so that nothing will protrude on either side.

10. Now you can determine not only the exact measurement that the top stretcher should be, but also the angle that the ends must be cut. This piece will be approximately 18½

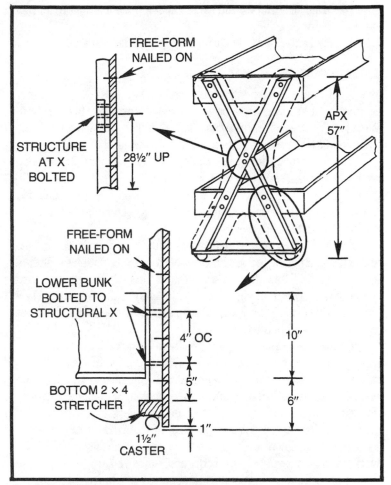

Fig. 2-33. Assembly details for yoke bunks.

       inches long and cut from 2-by-2 with both ends angled (Fig. 2-31F).

11. Drill the holes for attachment of both top and lower bunks. Countersink for these bolts on both surfaces.
12. Have a helper hold one end of the top bunk while you attach the other end. This will also be necessary in installing the lower bunk.
13. Check that nothing protrudes on either side of any surface.
14. Install the four casters, about 2 inches from each end of the bottom stretcher and on center widthwise.
15. Check that all bolts are tight.

16. Sand all surfaces and edges and apply edge tape to all raw plywood edges.
17. Finish by painting in bright colors and decorate with decals.

STACKED BEDS

A lot of people honestly feel that stacked beds are the bunk. Suppose you had two little boys but only floor room for one bed. Wouldn't you welcome the use of stacked beds that would provide the needed two bunks yet take up the space of only one?

Children usually like these beds too. I have heard them arguing over who could sleep in the top bunk. Perhaps it is the lure of the ladder. Climbing a ladder is an adventure usually denied small fry, but when you are sleeping in an upper bunk, climbing the ladder is not only permitted but necessary.

Stacked beds come in handy for adults too. In vacation cabins and hunting or fishing lodges stacked beds offer a solution for limited sleeping space. These bunks are often of the built-in type and need not be put away out of sight or camouflaged in the daytime. They certainly also come in handy in homes with only one guest room but two guests to be bedded down.

Usually the person responsible for the bed making dislikes the stacked beds the most. Did you ever have the job of making up an upper bunk? There is a simple solution to this objection. Make the one who sleeps in it responsible also for making it up. The secret to doing that is to smooth it out and pull up the covers as you are getting out of bed. The final smoothing can be done from the top of the ladder as he is getting down. I perfected this performance at camp. It also works with floor level beds and cots and, since you are already in the center of it, there is a minimum amount of reaching.

Any bed is easier to make up when you can do it from the head instead of the foot. You do not have to be on both sides at once as when you do it from the foot.

Not only is it easier to make up beds with the head board facing into the room instead of against a wall, but you also enjoy other advantages. The air flow is freer in the middle of the room and there are less drafts for the sleeper's head.

When you have stacked bunks, you need a ladder of some kind to reach the upper bed. After you've built a safe ladder, you are confronted with the problem of where to store it when it is not in use.

Why not arrange a hanger or a crossrail under the lower bunk and just slip the ladder in there when it is not needed? Other

144

solutions are suggested in various designs. The style of the ladder always follows the style of the bunks.

Safety of ladders is a serious consideration. Figure 2-34 shows one way that a ladder can be hooked to an upper bunk to minimize any chance of it slipping.

One quite reputable how-to magazine suggested making a ladder with 1¼ by ¾-inch rails and ⅜-inch dowels for rungs. It is hoped that those who follow this instruction won't sue the magazine for the resulting injuries when the ladder fails. Rails for any ladder should be from 2-by-4s and the rungs of 1 inch diameter dowels if a soft wood is used.

Even short ladders can present dangers. It is a safety axiom never to paint ladders, but when it is a part of the furnishings this accident prevention measure can hardly be observed. The reason is that paint will obscure faults in the wood. The paint covers up any developing cracks or splits in the wood that weaken members, especially the rungs. When an unsuspecting climber puts his weight on the weakened rung that developed because of the paint, it can suddenly snap with serious results.

When the upper bunk is not too high, you can build a ladder that converts to a chair (Fig. 2-35). This solves two problems at one

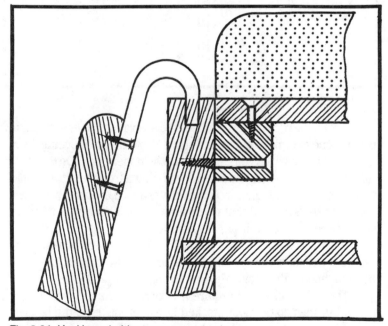

Fig. 2-34. Hooking a ladder to an upper bunk.

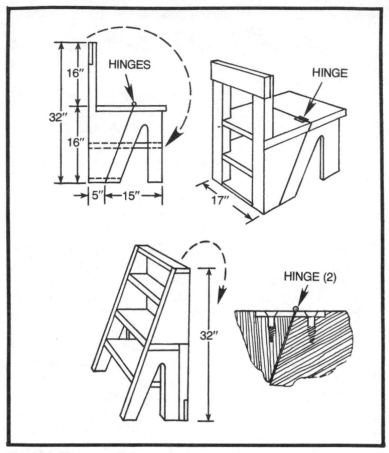

Fig. 2-35. Stepladder chair.

time. When the room is very limited, the stepladder chair serves as a seat for one to remove shoes and socks. Fold the back over and you have a ladder on which you can climb to the upper bunk. Do the same thing in reverse the next morning, climb down from the upper bunk, fold the back upright, and sit on the converted chair to don shoes and socks. There is no need to stash this ladder chair away when a ladder is not needed because it has become a chair.

Narrow rooms are ideal for built-in double deck bunks. They can be built into the walls and they can fold out of what looks like cabinets and fold in again when not in use (Fig. 2-36).

These fold-up bunks require a 7 foot, 6 inch ceiling height or more, but then so do most stacked beds. In this case the bedding must be strapped onto the beds before folding them up so they won't succomb to gravity. Firmly tucking in oversize blankets may do the job but it is better to use the two straps per bed.

The ladder chair just described is one way to reach the upper bunk, however with these bunks, it is better to use a self standing ladder.

If you have need for only one bed, the upper space may be used as a storage cabinet instead of installing a bunk. The doors then should be hinged to open and swing outward and be divided into two.

The handles of the lower bunk become the legs when it is let down. They can be arranged to swing out and, when the bunk is

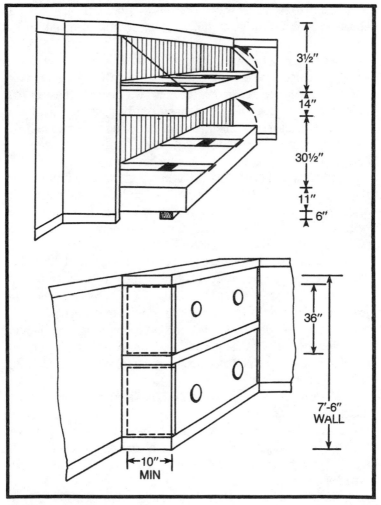

Fig. 2-36. Fold-up bunks.

147

folded, to swing into the surface of what appears to be the cabinet door. Note the heavy cables or chains that support the upper bunk when it is folded down. These must be able to take the weight. They must be securely fastened to the wall behind, to the side or bottom and to the top rails of the bunk. Since they fold away with the bunk, they should be selected more for their strength than their appearance.

The inside depth of the cabinet that contains the beds only needs to be 10 inches to take bunk and bedding. The cabinet itself, if built as a separate piece, must be well anchored to the wall so that it is not likely to topple outward. Besides anchoring them to the wall studs, they can also be anchored to structural members in the ceiling.

Depending on the space you have to work with and your needs and desires, a complete bedroom unit can be fitted into little space. Figure 2-37 shows an example of how two beds, a chest of four drawers and a place to hang clothing can be built into the space ordinarily occupied by one bed. Two of these beds are trundles (Fig. 2-37A and B), and can be moved elsewhere if you decide to do so at a later time. These are really rooms within rooms.

Most stacked bed designs can be unstacked and used separately. Dowels on top of the posts of the lower bed permit the stacking with safety. If a ladder has been built-in as in the stacked bed shown in Fig. 2-38, it must then be unmounted and stashed away. Removing a built-in ladder will require a remodeling job or at the least a bit of patching where you removed it. Some of these beds simply are not designed to be taken apart and used as twins.

When any stacked bunks are used separately, the doweled joints at the top of the four posts of the lower bed must be capped. Sometimes these dowels are wooden but more often they are steel pins because they are safer and won't break off as easily as the wooden dowels. Such typical joints and the pins are shown in Fig. 2-39.

The simplest way of finishing off these posts is by installing a matching ball or matching whatever is used on the upper posts. If one of the bunks used as twin beds is to be located in another room the ornaments on top of the posts of both beds do not need to be the same, but a finish is needed as the pins are not in themselves ornamental.

There is another problem that we might as well deal with here: how to attach head or foot boards that are too thin to be nailed or to

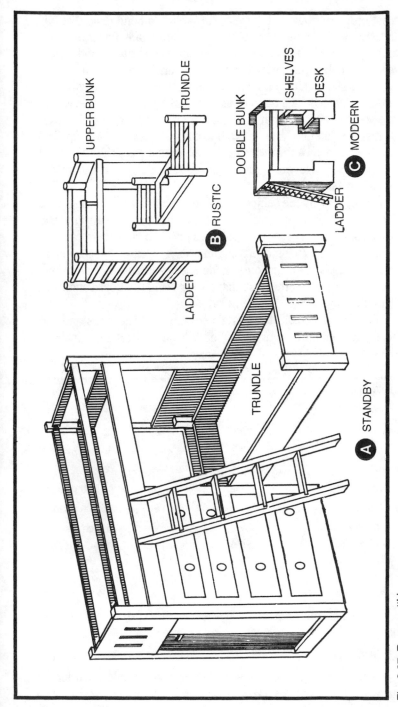

Fig. 2-37. Rooms within rooms.

accept ordinary dowels. Figure 2-39B shows a blind dado that will solve this problem and is customarily used by many furniture makers. The blind dado is a form of mortice and tenon that is both a neat and substantial method of joining a too thin panel to a larger member.

For a blind dado to take a ¼-inch thick panel it should have a mortice at least ⅜-inch deep to allow the glue to hold. Observe the same precautions here that you would for the ordinary glued dowel. The mortice must be large enough to allow the glue to flow upward along the surface of the inserted tenon, in this case the thin panel being joined. However, it must not be so large that it allows the tenon to wobble and loosen the glue.

Before leaving the subject of stacked bunks, the following table offers a typical bill of materials for building a bed project similar to the one in Fig. 2-40. These beds are designed so that they can use standard 39 by 72 inch store-bought springs (spring clips should be installed in this case), or home-made springs in any of the various varieties discussed in the first chapter, or using the board and foam pad method.

The following bill of materials covers only the beds and the ladder, using either hard or soft wood. All dimensions are in inches.

ITEM	NO. REQ	LENGTH	HARDWOOD	SOFT WOOD
(For two bunks)				
Posts	4	34¾	2⅜ × 2⅜	2 × 4
	4	25¼		
Siderails	4	72	⅞ × 4¾	2 × 6
Cleats	4	72	⅞ × ⅞	2 × 2
End rails	4	39¼	⅞ × 4¾	2 × 6
Head board	2	41¼	⅞ × 12	½-inch plywood
Foot board	2	41¼	⅞ × 62	½-inch plywood
Steel dowels	4	3¾	1 inch diam.	1 inch diam.
Safety rail (For ladder)	1	78	⅞ × 2⅝	1½ diam. pole
Side rails	2	54	⅞ × 2⅝	2 × 4
Steps, rungs	4	15	⅞ × 3½	1½ diam. pole

This should give you some idea of how the type of wood you use will make a difference in building requirements.

BED IN A BOX

If you have a folding bed no doubt you have trouble in working it into a closet. These beds are not exactly the kind of thing you want to

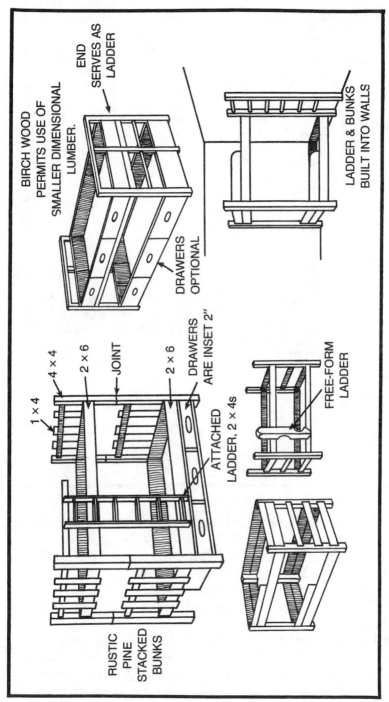

BIRCH WOOD PERMITS USE OF SMALLER DIMENSIONAL LUMBER.

END SERVES AS LADDER

DRAWERS OPTIONAL

LADDER & BUNKS BUILT INTO WALLS

1 × 4
4 × 4
2 × 6
JOINT
2 × 6
DRAWERS ARE INSET 2″

ATTACHED LADDER, 2 × 4s

FREE-FORM LADDER

RUSTIC PINE STACKED BUNKS

Fig. 2-38. Bunks with built-in ladders.

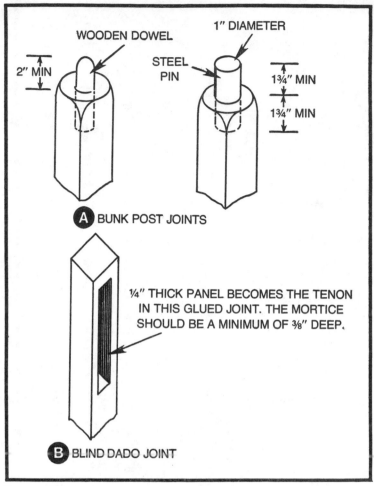

WOODEN DOWEL

1" DIAMETER

STEEL PIN

2" MIN

1¾" MIN

1¾" MIN

Ⓐ BUNK POST JOINTS

¼" THICK PANEL BECOMES THE TENON IN THIS GLUED JOINT. THE MORTICE SHOULD BE A MINIMUM OF ⅜" DEEP.

Ⓑ BLIND DADO JOINT

Fig. 2-39. Typical joints for stacked bunks.

leave out in the room when not in use, but where do you put it? Why not build a "box" for it?

This "box" is really a cabinet and can be fitted into a wall of shelves. It's a lot better than having to bark your shins on the folded-up bed every time you go into the closet.

The dimensions of store-bought folding beds make them a clumsy size. The inside dimensions needed to accommodate the bed when folded up usually are a minimum of 18 inches wide by 40 inches, by 42 inches high. The builder does have the option of putting the double doors of the cabinet at the end (the 18 by 42 inch way) or on the side (40 by 42 inch way). The latter has one advantage, the bed

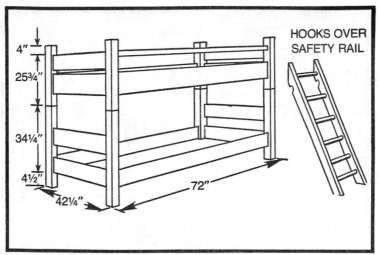

Fig. 2-40. Typical stacked bunks.

can be opened out right next to the cabinet. Figure 2-41 gives you an idea of how these cabinets work.

It is easier to build the cabinet into a wall shelf arrangement when the double doors face outward from the flat side, but since wall shelves are seldom 18 inches deep, some planning is needed to make it fit properly. If the bed did not require the cabinet to be so high, a television set could be set on top of it. Of course that would require a bit of strengthening to the top of the cabinet because television sets are quite heavy. It would be an ideal place for a lamp and bric-a-brac, especially pieces too large for the average shelves.

The structure inside the box should be of 2-by-4s. The outside covering should be ¾-inch thick plywood. It can be veneered with a finish to match the other furniture in the room. Veneering only needs to be on one side. The raw plywood edges should be covered with ¾-inch tape to match the finish. The top panel should cover the edges of the side panels.

Whichever door opening you choose, on the end or on the face, the bottom of the opening needs a sill. A sill is needed to prevent the sides from spreading. While the ordinary beveled edge wood door sill could be used, a metal strip will produce less obstruction to the casters on which folding beds roll. Consider a strip of a brass or a chrome weather-strip door sill when you are shopping for components. A thin metal strip no more than ⅛-inch in thickness would work, providing that it has holes in the right places to attach it to the bottom of the 2-by-4s that comprise the structure of the "box."

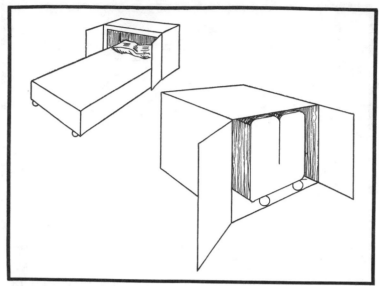

Fig. 2-41. Cabinets to hold folding beds.

Attach this strip by routing out for it on the bottom of the 2-by-4 on either side of the doors so that it will not add to the height of the structural piece and throw the "box" out of square. Also rout out for the hinges, which should be concealed when the doors are closed.

Before you start, carefully measure your folding bed to ascertain the minimum measurements of the inside of the box structure. You should do this with the bedding on and the bed folded. You will be glad you did later when you want to put the bed away without removing the bedding. This will mean that you do not have to make it up every day and find a place to stow the bedding. Be warned that the measurements given here may not be the same as for the bed you are boxing so use your own measurements.

Remember that your bed, when folded, must fit inside the frame. The thicknesses of the structural members must be added to the bed measurements and the thickness of the plywood covering. If your bed measures 18 inches across at the widest place with the usual amount of bedding folded into it for example, you must add at least the narrowest dimension of the 2-by-4 on each side and the ¾-inch for the plywood on each side. This means that on the outside the cabinet would measure at least 5 inches wider. It is always a good idea to allow a little extra for good measure, so if you have an 18 inch wide folding bed, the outside of your cabinet should come to 24 inches.

Chapter 3
Designer Bed Projects

When problems related to beds arise, the solution often calls for the exercise of ingenuity. These are the times that should bring out the designer in the bed builder. One such problem that demands solution is the lack of bedrooms. By the exercise of ingenuity and the ability to design, several guests can be provided with private sleeping quarters in almost any house.

Let us suppose that all of the bedrooms in your home are occupied already by your immediate family members when you find that you must prepare to individually bed down two guests who need separate bedrooms. What can you do?

You could sleep on the sofa and let the woman guest sleep with your wife, but the sofa isn't long enough for you to straighten out on and there still is the problem of where to put the other guest. If you have two boys of your own, the man guest could sleep with one of them while the other boy slept in a sleeping bag on the floor of the living room. You could give guests who are a married couple your and your wife's bed, let your wife sleep on the sofa and, well, hang yourself from a chandelier.

Obviously none of these makeshift arrangements turn out to be satisfactory as most of us have learned from experience. There is, however, an ingenious way of solving the dilemma: build Siamese twin guest accommodations.

SIAMESE TWIN GUEST ACCOMMODATIONS

Practically every house will have a small area that with ingenuity can be turned into usable space. Sometimes it is called the sewing room, a maid's room even though you may not have a live-in maid, a storage or junk room, even a breezeway. Although it is being used for another purpose, when the guests depart, it can revert to that purpose if you still find it needful.

A single bed requires only a space of 30 to 39 inches in width plus room to get into and out of bed, and a length of 72 to 78 inches, so the square footage must be at least that. Any more space will multiply your options on the arrangement.

Go about your house with this in mind and measure all such nooks and corners; then sharpen your pencil and get busy designing. This will require some planning but that will be better than being removed from your comfortable bed or members of your family giving up their own beds. Your guests will appreciate the privacy of the individual sleeping accommodations that do not require, like double deck bunks, having to climb a ladder to go to bed.

After you have accurately measured any likely spaces that could possibly be available, draw up scaled plans of them. Indicate accurately the position of all doors, windows and offsets and their dimensions, even up from the floor. Don't forget that needed access doors must have room to swing open. Every inch may count so make your measurements down to the fraction of an inch; you may need it.

Depending on the size of the paper on which you draw your plans, you could use a scale of anywhere from 1/32-inch equals an inch, 1/16-inch equals an inch or larger. The larger the scale you use the easier it will be to draw it accurately. A scale as small as 1/32-inch equals an inch may give you some trouble or cause an error that will vitally affect your planning. To aid you in avoiding arithmetic errors in converting to scale, refer to Table 3-1.

Using Table 3-1, for example, in drawing a bed that is 39 by 75 inches, refer to the equivalent of 36 inches under the ⅛-inch to 1 inch conversion column, which is 4½-inches. Since 39 inches is 3 inches more than 36 inches, add to this ⅛-inch (for 1 inch) and ¼-inch (for 2 inches) and you find that a line 4⅞-inches long will be, by the ⅛-inch scale, equal to 39 inches.

By the 1/32-inch to 1-inch scale, 39 inches would 1 7/32-inches. Many rulers do not show thirty-secondth inches. That is another reason why it will be better to draw your plan to a larger scale. Also unless you use a very sharp pointed pencil, it will throw you off an inch every time you draw a line.

Unless you are accustomed to drawing to scale, here is a better way to do your planning. Draw the outline of the space being

Table 3-1. Scale Conversions

Measurement		CONVERTED BY SCALE TO INCHES		
FEET	INCHES	⅛-IN.	1/16-IN.	1/32-IN.
	½	$1/16$	$1/32$	$1/64$
	2	¼	⅛	$1/16$
	6	¾	⅜	$3/16$
1	12	1½	¾	⅜
2	24	3	1½	¾
3	36	4½	2¼	1⅛
4	48	6	3	1½
5	60	8½	3¾	1⅞
6	72	9	4½	2¼
7	84	10½	5¼	2⅝
8	96	12	6	3
9	108	13½	7½	3⅜
10	120	15	8¼	3¾
11	132	16½	9	4⅛
12	144	18	9¾	4½
13	156	19½	10½	4⅞
14	168	21	11¼	5½
15	180	22½		5⅝

considered to scale as before, then from old business cards or file cards, draw the dimensions of two beds to the scale of your room outline and cut them out. Later, if you will have room for more furnishings, you can do the same for them, but since your planning will depend on placement of the two beds, cut them out first. By moving the two scaled bed shapes around on your plan of the available areas you will be able to figure out all possible arrangements and select the best one.

If the standard size items just won't fit in, remember, you are a bed builder so you need not be limited by store-bought sizes when it comes to the beds as well as the other furnishings. In working with limited sized areas one sometimes wonders why the manufacturers of furniture presuppose that everyone has unlimited sized rooms in their homes and apartments.

Speaking of apartments, do not despair if you live in rented quarters where the landlord will object to any permanent alterations or built-ins on his premises. It is possible to even install partitions so that they can be removed without leaving a trace.

One more thing before we leave the subject of building furnishings to fit the spaces you have. Bed sizes have been standardized by manufacturers after a lot of study on the requirements of the average human body. This does not mean that no one could get a restful, comfortable night's sleep on a bed of slightly differing dimensions. Sheets and other bedding, however, do come in standard sizes and, unless you intend to buy a lot of new linen and blankets or have them made up in a special size, it would be better to keep the dimensions of any beds that you build somewhat standard so that you can utilize the supply of bedding that you have on hand already in your linen closet.

To help you in planning your Siamese twin guest quarters, we will offer some examples of how different sized areas can be adapted to this purpose. At first we will assume that you are free to make any structural alterations and permanent installations that you wish. Later examples will take into consideration the necessity of keeping on the good side of the landlord. These suggested solutions to the lack of individual private sleeping quarters will not include the need for adequate bathroom facilities since that does not come under the scope of our discussions; these solutions are confined solely to bed and bedroom facilities.

For the first example, let us see how a breezeway could be converted to two Siamese twin guest quarters (Fig. 3-1). Let us say that the inside, wall-to-wall measurements are 7 feet in width by 13 feet in length. This will allow for a partition 1 inch thick.

The 77½-inch length of each area allows a bed 75 inches long, plus bedding, to be slid into the space at one side of one cell, yet leave clear the access door that enters from the rest of the house. In the other cell, there is also space left clear for the door that exits to the garage or the outside. Now you can see why every half-inch can be important. If both of these doors swing inward, this space is necessary.

The partition needs a doorway if one is to get from one cell to the other. If entry to one cell is planned to be from the rest of the house and the entry to the other cell from outside, this door is not necessary. This opening need only be 24 inches wide because no bulky furniture has to be moved through it. The bed can be disassembled to move and the other furnishings built-in.

With a 24 inch opening, a 21 inch space is left along the partition for built-ins. This is allowing for a bed that is 39 inches wide. If the bed is 30 inches wide, this space would be 30 inches, which is more adequate. Of course, the arrangement of the beds will also be affected by the location of the existing doors, also the width and swing of these doors. Usually such doors are 28 inches wide and, with their surrounds, will require no more than 30 inches. It is not always necessary for the doors to swing fully open.

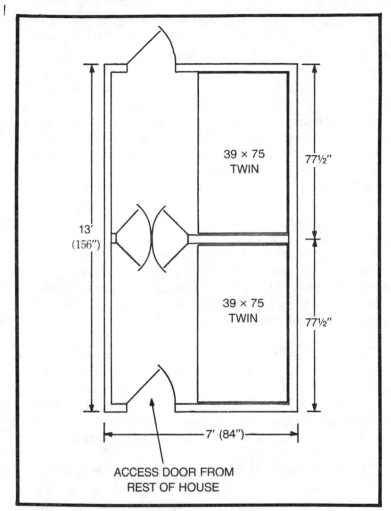

Fig. 3-1. Breezeway turns into quarters for two guests.

Most houses can easily do without the breezeway. The family may have to slightly alter their traffic patterns, but such passage ways seem to function mainly as dust catchers or the repository of an assortment of stuff that really belongs somewhere else. Converting it to needed Siamese twin guest quarters won't inconvenience the family very much.

Now that we've located the beds, possible built-ins that can be added will be discussed later. Since you will be building them, you can make them any size that you want. Let us now progress to the conversion of spaces of other sizes.

This time let us see what can be done with a space that measures 9 feet by 12 feet (Fig. 3-2). Depending on the location of the doors and windows, there is a lot more room for built-ins, such as a hang-up clothes closet, dressing table, stool, and a fold-up luggage rack. The dressing table should have drawers and a mirror. Incidental shelves can also be built-in.

If you are fortunate enough to discover that you have available a room with a 9 by 14-foot area (Fig. 3-3), you can really do a lot with it, especially if the access door from the rest of the house is centered in one 9-foot wall and the window centered in the opposite wall. Here you will have plenty of space for the beds and a good assortment of built-ins.

These examples should give you a fair idea of how to identify usable spaces that you didn't realize you had and that were probably going to waste while you were trying to sleep on a too short davenport and your guests were having to double up with members of the family and feeling that they were being an imposition. Now let us consider how to make these conversions and to make them so that the guest quarters are not only private, but also comfortable as sleeping quarters.

The first thing is the partition, presuming that it can be installed permanently. Soon we will discuss temporary installations. We will also talk about reading lights and area illumination and controls.

The partition is for the purpose of privacy, but it need be only an inch in thickness to ensure that. By using 1-by-2s for studs and facing each side with ⅛-inch particle board or hardboard, it will come out to be exactly 1 inch in thickness.

The studs should be placed a distance apart that corresponds to the material that is to be fastened to them. Wallboards are usually 4 feet wide so that if the studs are 24 inches on center, the wallboards will meet on every other stud. This permits the covering to be nailed along the edges and stayed in the middle.

The partition is installed between top and bottom rails whether it is permanent or temporary. These rails can be 2-by-2, with grooves routed according to the way you build the partition.

Figure 3-4 shows the various treatments of hardboard partitions. Note how the panels meet at the middle of alternate studs where they are nailed with wire brads. The seam can be covered with small half round molding. On the other studs merely passed over by the panel, it is tacked down the middle and the brads are also covered with half round molding. Where only one panel is used,

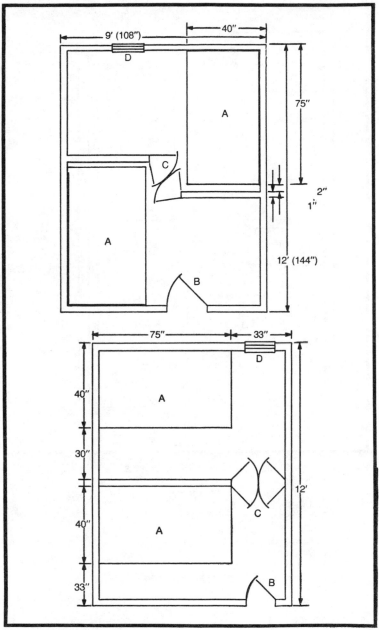

Fig. 3-2. Converting two small rooms into two guest bedrooms.
A. Single or twin bed.
B. Access door.
C. Swinging shutter door.
D. Window.

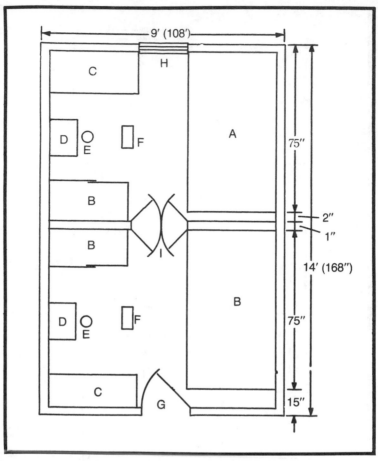

Fig. 3-3. A 9 by 14 room converts to two bedrooms.
    A. Single bed.
    B. Clothes closet (20 by 36).
    C. Chest of drawers.
    D. Dressing table.
    E. Stool
    F. Fold-up luggage rack.
    G. Access door.
    H. Window.
    I. Partition with swinging shutter doors.

there is no need for the molding (Fig. 3-4B). Where both sides have panels, the double facing permits the insertion of a fiberglass blanket for soundproofing (Fig. 3-4C).

When hardboard panels are used, the top and bottom rails can be rabbeted to take the panel or panels and the studs toenailed to the

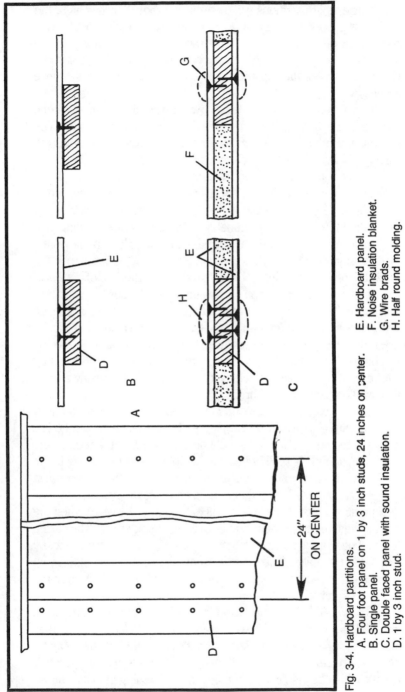

Fig. 3-4. Hardboard partitions.
A. Four foot panel on 1 by 3 inch studs, 24 inches on center.
B. Single panel.
C. Double faced panel with sound insulation.
D. 1 by 3 inch stud.
E. Hardboard panel.
F. Noise insulation blanket.
G. Wire brads.
H. Half round molding.

163

rails. Since most partitions will be around 7-foot, 6 inches high, the studs are needed for stiffening to prevent the panels from bowing and slipping out of the rabbets in the rails. This is the prime purpose of the studs since the partition does not hold up anything but itself. Figure 3-5 shows the top and bottom rails designed to take these panels.

Figure 3-5C and 3-5D show how intermediate splines can be used either alternately with studs or incorporating studs. The splines, which are 2-by-2s, act as vertical stays, especially when the partition is over 7 feet, 6 inches high.

In Fig. 3-5, "E" indicates the 2-by-2s; "F" indicates the panels of the partition; "G" indicates the 1-by-3 studs that are toenailed to the rails by "H," small finish nails or wire brads; "I" indicates the rabbets; "J" indicates the optional quarter round finish molding; and "K" indicates where alternate studs are toenailed to the intermediate splines. The width of the rabbets must be adjusted to fit the thickness of the panel plus 1/16-inch to allow for the flow of the glue.

If the partition cannot be permanently installed by toenailing the rails into the floor, ceiling and surrounds, the partition can be wedged between the floor and ceiling in the same manner as can be used for other temporary built-ins. T-bolts are installed in the top and bottom rails (Fig. 3-6) to wedge the partition or built-in tightly where you want it, yet be able to remove it without leaving a trace that would upset the landlord.

The T-bolt can be installed anywhere in the rail just so that it does not interfere with the rabbet. At least ¼-inch should be left between the hole drilled for the T-bolt and the rabbet that takes the partition panel. It is really better to be able to put the T-bolt in the center of the surface but that is not a must. The installation shown in Fig. 3-6 is for a 5/16-inch T-bolt. The depth of the hole needed will depend upon how far the screw will extend into the wood when the head is adjusted to produce the desired wedging effect. The casing for the bolt is held in place so that it will not turn with the screw, by tapping in the spike. The desired wedging pressure is obtained by using a flat crescent wrench to turn the head of the bolt after the partition is in place.

By using T-bolts in the top and bottom rails, the partition can be installed as securely as if it were permanently nailed in. To further insure that no scars will be left when it is removed, a shim may be placed between the bolt head and the surface against which it presses. T-bolts also come in handy in the leveling of installations.

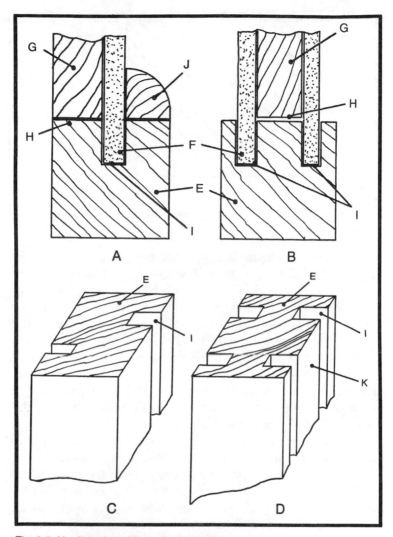

Fig. 3-5. Hardboard partition rails and splines.
　　　A. Top or bottom rail for single faced partition.
　　　B. Top or bottom rail for double faced partition.
　　　C. Intermediate spline for single faced partition.
　　　D. Intermediate spline for double faced partition.

This brings up the subject of gaps left between existing walls and the partition or between the partition and the floor or ceiling. Figure 3-7 will give you some ideas of how to fill these gaps.

When the gap between the end of a panel width and the existing wall is left, perhaps another stile will finish it off. If it is only a small gap not only between that wall and the partition but between the rail

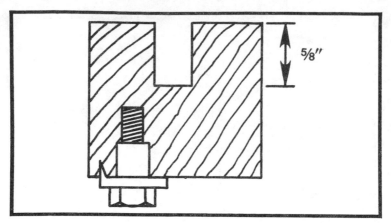

Fig. 3-6. Temporary T-bolt installation of partition rails.

and the ceiling or the rail and the floor, molding usually will fill the gap. You don't need to use expensive molding, and some of it is very expensive. Figure 3-7 B, C and D shows three inexpensive moldings that can be used to good effect. The quarter round molding comes in various widths, so does the half round. The cloverleaf molding, often called screen molding, is probably the cheapest and the most useful. Most lumber yards carry cloverleaf in several widths.

These moldings can also be used as decorative effects glued or nailed on panels. This is not only good for partition panels but as trim on cabinets and drawers. Figure 3-8 shows some of the effects that can be achieved with these moldings with little expense. Let your designer abilities guide you in these. You can paint them the same as the background on which they are applied or in contrast.

These edge moldings are especially good on plywood where they can be applied with small finish nails. Be sure to nailset the heads neatly. Look over the various shapes offered at the building supply store, including wooden knobs. You can also use vinyl or Formica type plastic strips and cutouts. Their edges should be beveled to blend into the background. These applied designs can be left natural, stained to match, painted or gilded to enhance panels, the fronts of drawers, cabinets or headboards.

Before buying the materials for your partition, you should check the levelness of the floor and the ceiling at the places that you intend to install the rails. Few houses are built absolutely square and they settle so don't be surprised if the ceiling and the floor are not parallel. To fit into an uneven space, especially if the partition is to be wedged into place for removal at a later time, you will have to build it to fit the

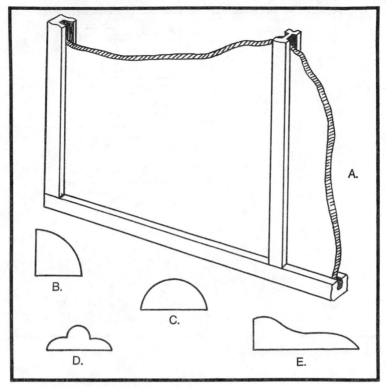

Fig. 3-7. Room partition installation and gap fillers.
    A. Splines with single panels against walls.
    B. Quarter round molding.
    C. Half round molding.
    D. Cloverleaf molding.
    E. Other types.

uneven space or shim it at the low places in the floor or the high places in the ceiling. The shims should not show when the panel rails are in place if you want a neat appearance, besides if the floor is not carpeted, a dust mop would catch on any rough edges that protrude. Another thing, when the shims stick out beyond the rail, you won't be able to get the molding to fit up snugly to cover the gap.

Sometimes a narrow strip of plywood, built up where needed, can be laid between the top rail and the ceiling or the bottom rail and the floor. This can neatly fill the uneven gaps and, at the same time, protect those surfaces. This strip need not be fastened separately but wedged in along with the partition. Should the ceiling be higher than the 8-foot length of the standard wallboard panel plus the rails, a 2-by-4 added at top or bottom, or both, should take care of the height deficiency.

Fig. 3-8. Decorative moldings.

If the inner of the two guest cells seems too dark in daytime because the window of the area is located in the other cell, you may elect to use translucent plastic panels in your partition. While these will maintain the privacy, they will admit light to the inner cell. Such panels can be used intermittently or exclusively in the partition. They can be decorated with decals, but remember that these decals will be silhouetted on the opposite side when light shines through the translucent plastic sheet. For this reason any applied decorations should be placed exactly opposite each other on both sides of the panel.

Translucent panels can also be easily installed almost any place, even into existing woodwork as shown in Fig. 3-9. The three steps are as follows:

1. Carefully cut out a strip ½-inch wide by ¼-inch deep in the surrounding woodwork (Fig. 3-9A). If possible, keep the strip intact because it is to be returned after mounting the plastic sheet.
2. Apply adhesive to the cutout place and lay in the translucent sheet that will form your panel (Fig. 3-9B). To secure

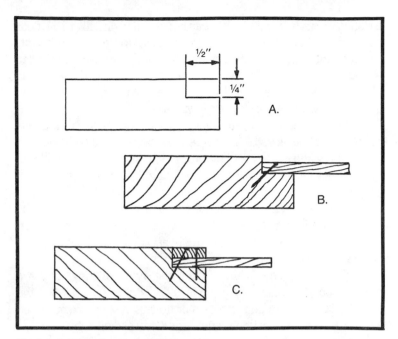

Fig. 3-9. Installation of translucent panel.

it in place while you are completing the job, you can tack it with wire brads in a few places. Plastic sheets are tough and the wire brads will tend to bend if you try to pound them through without making a small guide hole with an awl. Just be sure that the hole is no larger than the brad.

3. When the glue has set, replace the strip that you removed in Step 1. A little adhesive and wire brads will hold it in place. Be sure that you use only small wire brads so that they will not split the thin strip of wood. Nailset the heads.

The plastic sheet is about the same thickness as the kerf of the saw with which you removed the strip so that the difference in its width should about compensate for the added material. Before nailing in the strip, however, check that the surface will be flat. If it is not, lightly sand off enough material from the back of the strip to make it fit over the plastic sheet and still be even with the surrounding woodwork surface. Making and installing shoji panels will be discussed later.

While any of these partitions can be finished with fabric covering, or wallpaper for that matter, the fabric can be mounted on frame-like panels like those used in stage settings and called flats. This type of partition works better if the flats can be toenailed directly to the floor and ceiling, if you choose to carry the partition to ceiling height, which is not necessary for privacy. A crossbeam can be installed across the ceiling and the floor and the flats secured to those instead of rails as has been described. Each individual flat can be wedged in place with the use of T-bolts, but it will take at least two to each flat.

The width of a flat is determined by the width of the fabric that is to cover it. Both sides of the frame must be covered so it will take double the width of the partition times its height in material. Where the flats join each other the seam is covered by molding or a strip of lattice.

Figure 3-10 shows how a flat is constructed. Since the frame can be made from 1-by-3s and the two thicknesses of fabric that cover both sides constitute practically no additional thickness, the flats can be considered to form a partition ¾-inch thick.

Within the frame and between the two covering fabrics a noise-proofing blanket can be inserted. The cross brace at the middle of the flat can be moved up or down where there are to be attachments to the partition, such as a bed reading light.

In building the flats each piece must be sawed square and exactly to dimension or the flat will be out-of-square and not fit up to its neighbor properly. The corners should be mitered and reinforced by triangular blocks, which can be sawed from the scrap left over from the 1-by-3s used for the frame. Toenail in these blocks flat with the frame. Insert the middle cross brace also flat; remember you are building a flat so keep it flat.

Staple on the fabric, starting at one selvage, making certain that you keep it square with the frame. If you anchor the fabric with a staple at the middle of one side and at the top and bottom, it will help to keep it straight. Turn the raw edges at top and bottom under far enough for them to be caught and held by the staples. Bring the fabric right to the edge of the frame so that when it is butted to the next frame, the molding or lattice will fully cover the seam on both flats.

The fabric must be stretched taut so it will not sag in spots. In choosing the fabric you will be wise to buy the kind that does not stretch unevenly because that will make your job more difficult. Stage flats are covered with muslin and coated with liquid glue that contracts the material until it is so taut that you could drum on it. I have covered flats for use on the stage with burlap and then brushed on a solution of alum to tighten up the material so it would not sag.

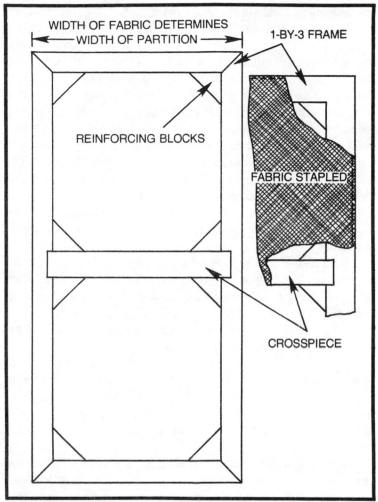

Fig. 3-10. Construction of a flat for a partition.

This is how stage flats are made to give the appearance of solid walls. Always test anything you propose to use on the fabric to tighten it, on a scrap to see if it stains. One other precaution, this treatment can shorten the life of the fabric, making it brittle.

Any of these types of partitions can really be made elegant by tufting fabric. This may be done on one or both sides of the partition. The luxuriousness of the tufts will depend on how much stuffing you use behind each puff.

Plywood panels will make the tufting job the easiest because you can use tacks and staples. Half-inch thick plywood will take upholstering tacks, the kind with the fancy heads. Since the puffs will give, no space will be lost. You can even tuft down only as far as the surface of the bed when the bed is against the partition wall and save yourself that much tufting. Of course you will want to run the fabric down to the bottom of the partition, but it can be flat.

It will be easier to work on the panel when it is laying flat across a couple of saw horses than to work on it after it is in place when you will have to stoop for some tufts and climb up on a ladder for others. However, when the panels are installed in place in the partition, it will be easier to line up the puffs straight across the entire partition and stop them at the top and bottom in the right places. Careful measurement and a little care will take care of this. Just follow the instructions that we offer and you will be able to successfully achieve a beautiful and rich tufted partition for your Siamese twin guest quarters.

First you lay out the pattern for your tufts. To help you to keep them uniform, make yourself a measuring tool, but first you must decide on the size you want to make the tufts. Only when you have done this can you make the measuring tool (Fig. 3-11).

Find a large enough piece of heavy cardboard. It should be tough enough to stand up until you have finished the job.

Make notches at the top edge the exact distance corresponding to the width and height of the tufts that you have chosen. Then make a curve at the bottom of the card to help you in gaging the uniform depth of the puffs. Notches at top and bottom of the center line will further assist you in keeping the tufts in straight lines both up and down.

If you find it difficult to visualize which size of tufts will look the best, you can cut out squares of paper in the various sizes you want to consider. Stick these squares up on a wall with Scotch tape. Usually the tufts will be somewhere between 6 and 8 inches. The larger they are, the fewer tufts you will have to make, but if they are larger than 8 inches each way, it will be difficult to make the puffs stand out and all your tufting will be wasted.

The fabric can be any type of material you wish, patterned or a solid color. The panels, such as plywood, come regularly 48 inches wide, so if the material is 50 inches wide, selvage to selvage, there will be 2 inches for puffing. The width of the panels will influence your selection of the size of the tufts. An even number across should be the simplest. The length can be taken care of as will be explained later.

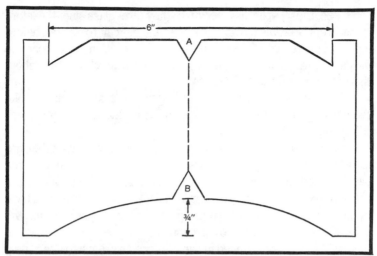

Fig. 3-11. Tuft measuring tool.
    A. Width and height of tuft.
    B. Depth of puff.

Another influence on the size of the tufts is that if the fabric is patterned, some patterns just don't fit into some size of tufts. Supposing that the fabric is 50 inches in width and the backing is 48 inches (Fig. 3-12), the piece can be divided into eight tufts across, if the backing is solid, or into two sections of four tufts, divided by a molding that will act as a stiffener should the backing be a flat frame. This leaves a 2 inch surplus for puffing the tufts.

The tufts should always start at the top rail and progress evenly down and across to the bottom rail with uniform puffiness. If there is any variation in size necessary, let it come at the bottom row. It will be less noticeable there. If a bed is against the partition, you have the option of stopping the puffs below its top surface where it will be covered. The fabric can be carried on down but without the tufts being puffed. The tufted partition makes an attractive headboard effect.

To make the tufts rich looking use 3½-inch fiber glass blanket without the vapor barrier facing. This will add a noise-proofing quality to the partition. While other padding can be used to puff out the tufts, by all means use the fiber glass. It will not pack or wad up and adds fire resistance to your partition. This is desirable if there are to be electrical installations or if your guest has the habit of smoking in bed.

There is one precaution about handling fiber glass, wear gloves. If the tiny threads of glass get under the skin, they can be nasty. You can't see these splinters because they are glass and therefore transparent. For this reason they are quite difficult to pick out before an infection results. There are some preparations that coat the hands that are supposed to be as good as wearing gloves. Ask about this where you buy the fiber glass.

If there are to be any electrical installations in the panel, make them before you cover the panel in any case. Electrical installations will be discussed later.

Take your choice of whether to cover the panels after they are installed in the partition or work on them one at a time with the panels placed across two saw horses. If you use the saw horses, you will have to complete the job after installing them and when you have tufted one side, carefully turn the panel over and rest it so that the puffs will not be flattened by pressure. Of course, if you work on them when they are installed in the rails, you will have to alternately stoop and use a ladder.

Using solid, preferably ½-inch thick plywood backing so that it will take upholstering tacks as well as staples, proceed as follows:

1. Temporarily tack the insulation blanket at one corner just below where the rail will come, about ¾-inch from the end of the backing. Straighten the blanket so that it is parallel with both that side and the top and insert another tack or staple.

2. Allowing for about an inch of turn under at the raw edge and bringing the selvage edge of the fabric even with the outer side edge of the backing, staple it in place. When you have insured that the selvage will be even with the edge of the backing all the way down the side, add another staple (Fig. 3-13). This should result in the fiber glass blanket being entirely covered with the fabric at the edges.

3. Crowd the insulation blanket smoothly down the stud or edge of the backing and staple every unit at the top of the tufts with the staple parallel to the edge. Do not staple at the bottom at this time.

4. Adjust the fabric over the padding, smoothing but allowing it to puff to the maximum, and staple it all except the bottom row. These staples should also be parallel to the edge and in the selvage of the fabric so that they will be covered by the molding.

5. Check what you have done and make any adjustments that seem to be needed before going on.

174

6. When you are satisfied, tap all staples in solidly.
7. Now progress to complete the first row of tufts by measuring toward the middle of the panel with the measuring tool. By this time you have the feel of just how much puffing will be required. Be sure to keep the tufts in line both vertically and horizontally as well as uniform. Check that the middle of the fabric width will reach the middle of the panel. To prevent yourself from using too much fabric in the puffs, you can temporarily tack the middle points, but do not draw the padding too tightly.
8. Continue to form the puffs across the panel, measuring both size and depth with the measuring tool and keeping the tufts in lines and rows. Then go to the next row down. The upholstery tacks at the abutting corners of the tufts should be lined up so that they form straight lines.
9. Fasten at the far stud or stile and at the bottom (Fig. 3-13), the same as at the top. By this time you will have cut off all surplus material.
10. When completed with the panel installation in the rails, finish with the quarter round molding as shown.

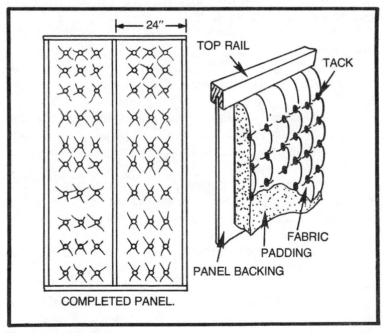

Fig. 3-12. Tufting the panel.

Fancy headed upholstering tacks often have sharp edges where they contact the fabric. If you strike them with too much force or too heavy a hammer, these edges can cut the threads of the fabric. Use a light-weight hammer and tap the tacks in place rather than pounding them in. This will also avoid the tendency of the wire shanks of the tacks to bend causing the head to set at an angle rather than squarely against the fabric.

If you have made your partition by assembling stage type flats, obviously the upholstery tacks cannot be used because there is nothing to nail into in the center of the frames. You will need a helper for this job to stand on the other side of the flat. In this case the tufts are formed and held by ornamental buttons that must be sewn through, creating tufts on the opposite sides of the partition in one operation. Your helper will need a duplicate measuring tool to use on his or her side.

Each side should have its own insulation blanket and fabric covering, otherwise the tufting will not only look skimpy when the job is done, but the padding will have to be split to go over the middle cross piece and the edges of the frame.

A long, straight needle is needed that will take heavy upholstering thread that won't easily break. Select ornamental buttons, the kind that have a ring shank on the back for attachment.

With your helper on the opposite side of the partition, tie the first button onto the thread leaving a tail of at least 6 inches beyond to use in tying off (Fig. 3-14A). Pass the needle through, keeping it straight. A short needle is much more apt to go at an angle or get lost in the padding.

Your helper then threads and ties his button onto the thread and passes the needle back through to you (Fig. 3-14B). You should then tie off the two buttons after drawing them up to form puffs on either side of the partition that will fill the curve of the measuring tool.

If the needle does not come out at the exact place on the opposite side, your helper should press it back through to you so you can try again. The same thing goes when your helper passes the needle back through to you to tie off (Fig. 3-14C). After you and your helper have satisfactorily formed several tufts, the process will usually go quite smoothly, but do not get careless or you will spoil the appearance of the elegant tufted partition.

When you have completed all but the top and bottom at the rails, finish off in the same manner as described for the solid panel. You have solid wood now to work on.

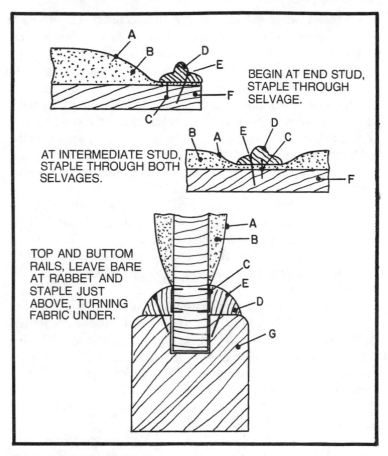

Fig. 3-13. Details of tuft edges.
- A. Fabric.
- B. Padding.
- C. Molding.
- D. Staple.
- E. Wire brad.
- F. Stud.
- G. Rail.

After you have made all of the tufts, do not lay the panel down so that there will be pressure against the tufts. This will tend to flatten them. That is one reason why it may be better to erect the partition and work on it in the upright position.

SHOJI PARTITIONS

Shoji screen walls are popular in Japan even today because they provide privacy without shutting out the light as do solid walls. Since the Siamese twin guest quarters are often converted from a room that has but one window, a solid partition would leave the side that had no window in comparative darkness in the daytime.

By using shutter doors that only reach from about 7 feet to 2 to 3 feet from the floor, privacy is provided between the cells and ventilation without shutting out all of the light from the window in the other side, but it does not admit as much light to the inner cell as a translucent partition would. Were you to build the partition on the shoji style instead of solid, the two sides would share the daylight from the sole window. Be warned however that building a shoji requires meticulous attention to details.

Like the partitions already discussed, the shoji can be permanently built in or installed between the ceiling and the floor by wedging so that it can be removed without leaving a trace. These translucent screen walls can be stationary or sliding, and in the latter case the two rooms can be thrown into one merely by sliding the shoji section open.

True shojis always run in hardwood tracks at top and bottom, but you can build them to suit your taste and purposes since you will be designing and constructing them yourself. You also will have a wide choice in the materials you use. You can build them to be authentic shojis, like the Japanese, covering them with rice paper, or with plastic sheets or with fabric. You can paint on designs, on both sides, or decorate them with decals. You have the option also of using a printed fabric as the covering.

Since the shoji is at least translucent, any designs painted on or applied should be directly opposite each other on both sides of the panel because they will otherwise be silhouetted through the translucent material, be visible on the other side and interfere with the designs on that side whenever light shines through. Such designs should be made to coincide exactly. When a printed fabric is used as the covering, the design must be considered in planning the panels, and if it is a large design, it should be centered if possible. Like wall paper, any design material must match with the adjacent panel design.

Another choice in the design is whether you use horizontal or vertical wooden strips in the shoji grid. Smaller panels mean that, should one panel become damaged, you will have less covering to replace. This is more apt to occur when the shoji is covered with rice paper. It is however a simple matter to cut out the damaged paper and replace it, providing you have kept enough for this purpose when

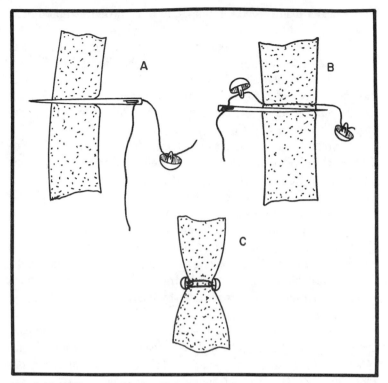

Fig. 3-14. Tufting a double faced panel.
    A. Thread, tied on to first button, is passed through fabric and padding.
    B. Thread picks up second button on opposite face of panel.
    C. Thread tied off to complete tuft.

you made the shoji. You just cut out the bad panel with a razor blade and glue the fresh piece into that grid.

Shojis can also be used for other purposes. If you have a window with an undesirable view or nosey neighbors who have an equally undesired view in, a shoji would be just the thing to solve either or both problems. While a shoji assures the benefit of privacy, it does not shut out the light. If you use a coarse-woven fabric as a covering, it will not interfere with the ventilation and the air will go right through it. Shojis are also ideal for cabinet doors, either swinging or sliding.

The authentic shoji consists of a hardwood frame that slides in hardwood tracks above and below. Inset into this frame is the grid (Fig. 3-15), which should be removable. The frame lifts out of the tracks and the grid slides out of the frame at the top. The grid and the panel divisions are also of hard wood so they can be thin, like ¼-inch, and no wider than 1½-inches. Maple, fir or redwood are appropriate woods.

For a screen, like a door or a window, to slide open, it must have tracks at least twice its width. Even if the sliding panel were to be hung from an upper track, it would need a track at the bottom to prevent it from swinging in and out of the opening. To be authentic the shoji panel should actually slide on the bottom track while the upper track merely keeps it in place.

If you use plastic in the panels, it is not mandatory that the shoji frames lift out of the tracks, but if you use rice paper or even a fabric in the grids, you should build them so that they can be removed in the case that a repair of the covering becomes necessary, otherwise you will have to dismantle the entire track to remove one pnael.

Figure 3-16 shows how a frame is removed from the track by lifting it off of the bottom track into the space allowed at the top within the upper track, and pulling the frame out at the bottom until it is freed from both upper and lower tracks. Note that when it rests within the bottom track, it is retained by the slight bulge of the outer lip of the track.

The tracks must make it possible for one screen to slide past the other when you open it. One panel can be stationary while the other slides past it, or both panels can slide to make an opening in either direction. By building sliding shojis you will not have to allow for the swinging open of a door for access to the area beyond the partition. The shoji framework is obviously not strong enough to permit the use of swinging doors, even lightweight ones.

If you have your heart set on the use of shutter doors between the Siamese twin guest quarters, yet you want to make your partition a shoji, build stationary shoji panels and set them into 2-by-2 stiles as you would with the partitions already discussed. This can be done in the same way as building in any stationary shoji, but in this case it is better to use plastic panels.

Figure 3-17 shows shoji construction details as keyed to Fig. 3-15. To build an authentic shoji proceed as follows:

1. Mount the screening material in a grid, using ¾ by ⅝ hard wood. The grid pattern may be either horizontal, or vertical. If you use sheets of plastic as the screening material, it may form the entire grid or be divided by strips vertically. Even in this case it is a good idea to use the integral grid that slides into the frame.

2. Only when you have completed the grids will you be ready to build the frames. It is the frame that slides between the upper and lower tracks and stiffens the grid. The screen grid fits into the 5/16-inch deep rabbet in the frame (Fig. 3-17E). For this reason the frame is a total of almost 4 inches wider than the grid, 2 inches on each side, less the two 5/16-inch rabbets, a net of 1⅜-inch. The bottom and two sides are made from 1⅛ by 2 inch hard wood. The thinness of the components makes it necessary to use a hard, tough wood. As has been previously pointed out, when working in hard wood, holes should be predrilled to take the shank of woodscrews and a smaller hole predrilled to insure the proper entry of the screw into the lower piece. This hole must not be so large as to prevent the screw from biting into the wood for a secure hold.

3. Carefully measure the opening to be filled by the sliding shoji. Be warned that houses are seldom built on the square and, even if they were, there is usually some

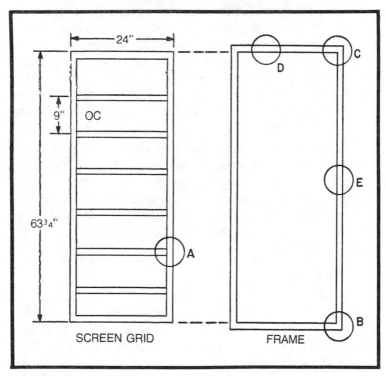

Fig. 3-15. Shoji frame and grid.

settling, so the opening will quite likely need some squaring up for the shojis to run smoothly. This will be the case in any sliding door or window. Shim out the opening before installing the tracks as has been discussed in the case of the other partition rails. In measuring don't forget the clearance needed at the top track to permit the frame to be lifted out from the tracks.

4. When you are certain that the opening is square and all height adjustments have been made, install the tracks and verify your measurements for the frame so that it will fit perfectly.

5. Now all that remains is to build the frame. The grid slips into the frame from the top and the frame, in turn, pulls out of the track. Use 1⅛ by 2 inch hardwood, rabbeted 11/16-inch deep on the narrow edge to take the grid.

6. As shown, the tracks have been made from 3¼ by 1⅜-inch hard wood for the full width of the opening. If one screen is to slide over the other, the track must be twice the width of a screen and the screens of equal width. The upper track has two rabbets to accept the sliding frames, separated far enough to allow one screen to slide past the other without scraping at any point. The sliding rabbet of the bottom track is formed into a sort of lip to allow the screen, when lifted into the upper track, to be pulled free; yet when the frame is resting in the rabbet, to hold it securely in place (Fig. 3-16).

Once your shoji is finished and installed, you will truly have a conversation piece that is also a useful asset to any home. You will have gained privacy for your Siamese twin guest quarters without shutting out the daylight from the one window and added true esthetic beauty in so doing. Every time you slide the shoji panels open or closed you will again experience the thrill of achievement from your own handiwork.

SHUTTER DOORS

Should you want to use shutter doors at the 24 inch wide opening between the Siamese twin guest rooms, do not feel that they must be full length for privacy. They are but visual barriers and therefore need extend from only a little above eye level to 2 or 3 feet from the floor. It will be better to use two doors because that will distribute the weight and stress of the doors and so require less

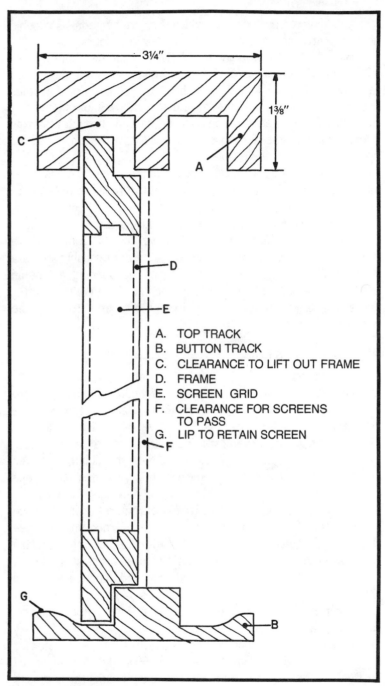

A. TOP TRACK
B. BUTTON TRACK
C. CLEARANCE TO LIFT OUT FRAME
D. FRAME
E. SCREEN GRID
F. CLEARANCE FOR SCREENS TO PASS
G. LIP TO RETAIN SCREEN

Fig. 3-16. Sliding shoji double track.

strengthening of the studs from which they are hinged. Also double doors require half the swing room of full width doors.

Since both cells will seldom each have a window, shutter doors will permit flow-through ventilation as well as admitting daylight to the inner cell. This door will not have to be the width of other household doors to permit the moving of furniture in or out because the bed will be taken apart and can be passed through a narrow opening and the other furniture will be built-in or the kind that folds up.

Note that in Fig. 3-3 space was left at the foot of the bed in the inner cell to permit the access door from the rest of the house to swing sufficiently open to allow passage.

Select shutter doors that are made of the lightest wood. Since this type of door will not require a heavy upright from which to swing, and if the partition is securely anchored, probably an extra 2-by-2 will suffice. Hopefully one side of the opening will be an existing house wall. This will simplify the installation of the shutter doors. No sill or lintel is needed except of course to carry the partition to the wall.

HANG-UP CLOTHES CLOSET

Your guests will want to hang up the clothing that they brought along with them, or at least the clothing they take off before going to bed, so you will need some provision for this. According to the space you have and the arrangement you have decided upon for the Siamese twin guest quarters, you can build in a closet of some sort.

To conserve space the doors should be of the sliding variety so you will not have to allow more space for doors to open. This space can be put to better advantage by making your closet deeper.

To hang clothing on hangers in a closet requires an inside space of 18 inches (Fig. 3-18A). When this depth is not possible, the clothing on hangers must be hung parallel to the backing. In such a case the hooks must be spaced about 10 inches apart to allow each item on a hanger the 18 inches in width needed. This means that a shallow clothes closet measuring 60 inches wide on the inside by about 16 inches deep would be capable of hanging no more than nine garments, three to a hook, one over another.

If the depth could be increased by 2 inches and to 18 inches for the inside dimension, a closet of the same 60 inches in width would be capable of hanging twice as many garments without the necessity of hanging one over another. The garments would be less likely to

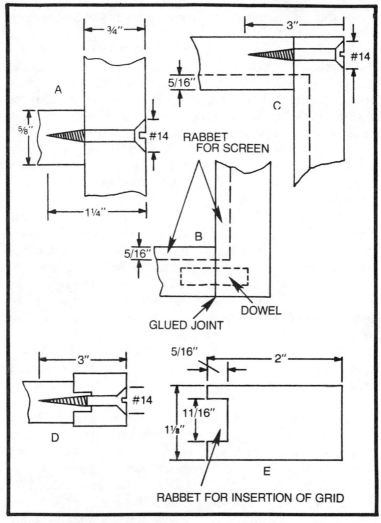

Fig. 3-17. Shoji construction details.
   A. Grid joint.
   B. Bottom corner of frame.
   C. Upper corner of frame.
   D. Top of frame.
   E. Side rail of frame.

become wrinkled from having another garment hanging on top and pressing it into the backing. The individual hanging of the garments on hangers on a pole the length of the 18 inch deep closet also permits any one garment to be taken down without disturbing the others. It therefore behooves the thoughtful host to provide his guests with clothes closets in which to hang up their clothing comfortably.

Another consideration in building clothes closets or wardrobes is at what height the pole or the hooks for the wire hangers should be placed. Today's dresses seldom require more than 48 inches of vertical space plus a few inches for the hook of the hanger. Men's or women's slacks are usually folded over hangers when hung in a closet or wardrobe so they will fit within this length.

Women guests these days seldom travel with floor length evening gowns, but if they should have brought one along for a special occasion, no doubt there will be some place in the house where it can be hung full length.

The ideal height for a closet clothes pole is from 60 to 64 inches above the floor. This leaves about 16 inches below the hung-up garments that can be utilized for drawers or a shoe rack. A shoe rack is always good and drawers will probably be built elsewhere.

There should be a shelf about 6 inches above the clothes pole. There will be room for more than one shelf if the closet goes to the ceiling. Clothes closets should always be ceiling high, otherwise things get piled on top or it collects dust.

The average ceiling in a house is 7 feet, 6 inches, or 90 inches. That leaves about 26 inches above the shelf, enough to store luggage or hat boxes. This shelf will come in quite handy, but it should be well supported.

Note the 20 inch deep 36 inch wide clothes closet shown in Fig. 3-18. It will be larger than some closets found in the bedrooms of some homes. Just don't be surprised when you discover some day how, when no guests are occupying the Siamese twin guest quarters, these convenient closets get filled up with the overflow from the closets of members of your family. If this is allowed, there will have to be a hurried clearing out of all this overflow when guests are expected.

BUILT-INS

Other possible built-ins include shelves, drawers and vanity with stool. The vanity can be store-bought, finished or unfinished, but is really quite easy to build. It can be a shelf incorporated with others, either open or with drawers. The main thing is that it offers a mirror. This will ease the popularity of the bathroom mirror, if you happen to be short on bathrooms.

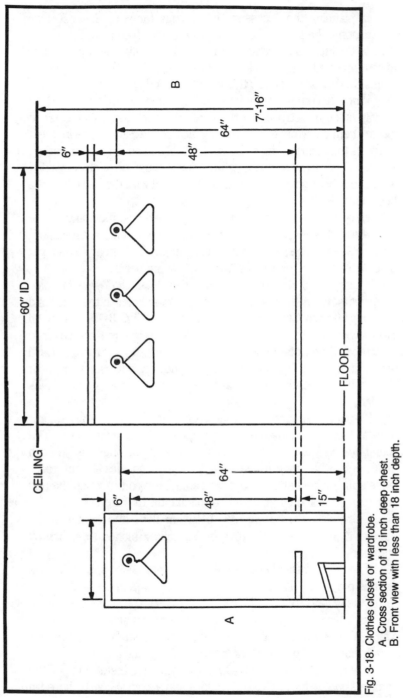

Fig. 3-18. Clothes closet or wardrobe.
A. Cross section of 18 inch deep chest.
B. Front view with less than 18 inch depth.

187

In planning the accessory furnishings for your Siamese twin guest rooms, be sure to keep the passageway free from the access door to the interconnecting door to the outer cell. With the possible exception of a luggage rack, everything should be kept around the edges. In such small areas, this will still fill the center of the rooms.

When it comes to shelves, never build shelves that will be heavily laden directly above the head of a bed. It is much safer to locate them elsewhere, especially since in the Siamese twin guest quarters the heads of the beds will probably be against the partition, which will not be strong enough to mount attached shelves solidly. There may be room to build a small shelf level with the bed to act as a bedside table.

One good way to build shelves, perhaps including some cabinets with doors, can be done without permanent installation. Such shelves can be strong enough to support fairly heavy loads, yet be capable of being removed without leaving scars.

This method of building shelves uses 1¾-inch dowels or poles as uprights. Each shelf is supported by boring holes in the poles and inserting ⅜-inch dowels to support them (Fig. 3-19). Plywood ¾-inch thick makes good shelves but the raw edges must be covered with tape. If you need ends on a shelf, you can use particle board where little strength is required. Square pegs can be used to support the shelves, but the problem here is making the square holes needed.

To make a square hole ⅜-inch each way, it is necessary to first bore a ⅜-inch hole, then dig it out square with a small chisel. The round dowels will be better because they are stronger as you can figure out for yourself if you know stress mechanics. In any case, leave a finger hold sticking out far enough for you to grasp the peg and remove it should you want to dismantle the shelves.

The poles can be wedged between floor and ceiling in the manner shown in Fig. 3-20 or permanently attached to structural members.

The building supply store will have compression spring devices for this purpose. These devices can be installed in the bottom and top of the wooden pole, or if you prefer to use pipe as the stanchions for your shelves, they can be installed in that by using a cotter pin as a stop. To prevent damage to the floor or ceiling surfaces, get rubber crutch tips and slide them over the wedging ends.

If you prefer, use 2-by-2s as stanchions. Installation of the compression spring device will require that a ½-inch hole be bored in

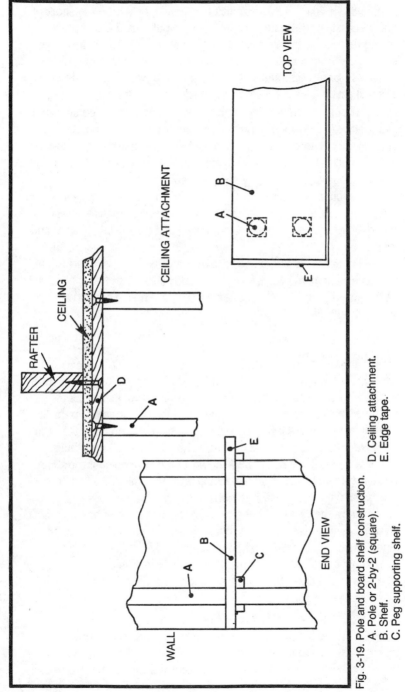

Fig. 3-19. Pole and board shelf construction.
A. Pole or 2-by-2 (square).   D. Ceiling attachment.
B. Shelf.   E. Edge tape.
C. Peg supporting shelf.

189

both ends. If your measurements turn out to be a little too short of that necessary to obtain a tight wedge, pull out the compression spring device and insert a little packing into the hole, then reinsert the device. Another way is to use a screw, a woodscrew in the hole or 2-by-2, or a machine screw in the pipe. If you hit the right spot, this will act as a stop at the place needed to secure a tight wedge.

If you prefer to use pipe for the stanchions, it can be common plumber's pipe, ¾-inch aluminum tubing or electrical conduit, depending on the load you expect to put on the shelves. It is always best to build shelves strong enough for any purpose because their purpose may change after you have them built.

The building supply store will also have a variety of shelf support systems. Some of them will turn out to be expensive and by using either of these methods, you can build them a lot cheaper and just as good.

The subject of building in drawers will be discussed later. The movable shelf units just discussed are no place for drawers because of the stresses drawers will exert as they are pulled out and shoved in when fully filled.

PORTABLE LIBRARY

Presuming that your books are housed elsewhere in the house and your guests will be given the opportunity of selecting his or her bedtime reading matter from them, why not furnish a portable carrier and rack? As with the other accessories you build for your Siamese twin guest quarters, you will need two of everything.

For those who read in bed the portable library is just the thing. You can tote your selection of reading matter to the bedside where it is at your finger tips without getting out of bed.

You can get two of these portable libraries out of one panel of plywood easily. Use the ¾-inch thickness, two dowels, some edge tape, finishing nails, glue and finishing materials. It is possible to use ½-inch plywood, but books are heavy so ¾-inch is better and you won't have to adjust the dimensions given in Fig. 3-21.

Proceed as follows:

1. Cut out a backboard 12 by 24 inches.
2. At the bottom edge of the backboard cut a slot ¾-inch wide on the center line, upward for 6 inches. Be sure to square the corners and test that the slot will take the width of the plywood.

3. Toward the top of the backboard, 2 inches down from the edge and centered, cut a handhold. It should extend 3 inches on each side of the center line and be 2 inches wide. Round the hole at each end and smooth the edges.
4. Drill two dowel holes in the backboard 10⅜-inch up from the bottom edge, ⅜-inch in diameter.
5. Cut out the foot extensions.
6. Cut the shelf 12 inches long, slanting back and front edges to fit the angle at the dowel end of the shelf.

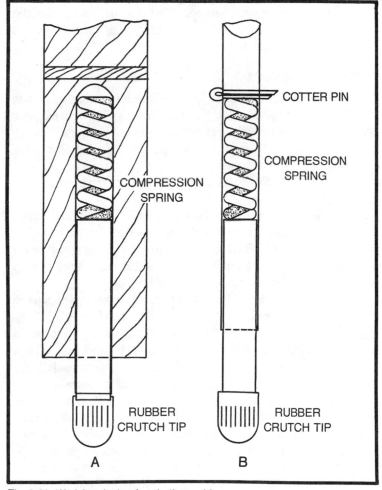

COMPRESSION SPRING

COTTER PIN

COMPRESSION SPRING

COMPRESSION SPRING

RUBBER CRUTCH TIP

RUBBER CRUTCH TIP

A

B

Fig. 3-20. Wedging device for shelf stanchion.
    A. Wooden stanchion.
    B. Pipe stanchion.

7. Drill the slanted edge of the shelf to take the two dowels that hold it to the backboard.
8. Cut out two end pieces and angle the edge to fit the slant of the shelf from the backboard.
9. Sand all pieces smooth.
10. Assemble the components, using finish nails and glue, by slipping the backboard slot over the foot extension so that the two pieces are at right angles. Install the shelf so that it dowels into the backboard and rests on the upper slant of the foot extension. Nail glue the end pieces to the edges of the backboard and the shelf. When you have completed the assembly, it should be ready to carry your guests' selection of bed reading matter.

FOLDING LUGGAGE RACK

Every guest room needs a luggage rack if for no other reason than to get the guest's bag off the bed. You should not make your guest stand on his or her head to get things out of his luggage on the floor. Since suitcases are usually packed until they are heavy, the rack must be capable of bearing up under a load. It should also be of the fold-up type so that it can be stored away when it is not needed for luggage.

The folding luggage rack shown in Figs. 3-22 and 3-23 will fill the bill on all of these particulars. When it is opened up, it will hold a good load because it will be made of hard wood. Using soft wood would make it too cumbersome. When it is folded up, it will take up practically no space in a closet or under the bed.

To build two of these convenient folding luggage racks, you will only need less than two 16-foot lengths of hard wood, milled to 1¼ by 1¼ inches. You will probably have to buy that much to get the 13 feet, 3 inches that you will really have to have in usable lengths. Then you will need almost 2½-yards of 2 inch wide webbing for each. You'll find this in upholstering supply stores. Doweling comes in 3-foot lengths although you won't use all of that. While ⅜-inch diameter dowel is indicated on the drawings, you can use ½-inch diameter by boring the holes that size. Lastly you need large washers, at least 1 inch diameter because they must go over the dowels between the legs and are the pivots on which the legs open and close when you fold up the rack. The usual finishing materials, upholstering tacks, finishing nails and glue complete the list of materials that you will need.

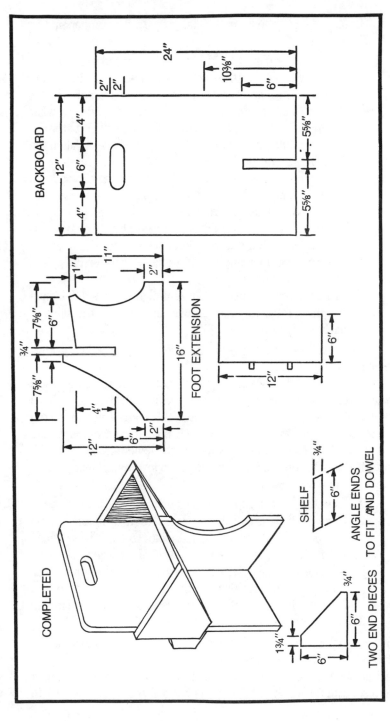

Fig. 3-21. Portable library bookshelf.

193

Having gathered these materials, prepare the components as follows:

1. Cut four legs from the 1½ by 1½ hard wood, 21 inches in length. Centered, 10½-inches from each end, drill a hole 9/16-inch in diameter (1/16-inch larger than the dowel used) to take the dowels on which the legs pivot. At what will be the top end, drill for the attaching dowel. Later the other end must be angled so that the rack will sit flat on the floor but do not do this until the rack is completed.
2. Cut two stretchers from the 1¼ by 1¼ hard wood, 22 inches in length. Drill for the dowels 2 inches in from one end and 3¼-inches in from the other end on center.
3. Cut two bottom stretchers from the 1¼ by 1¼ hard wood, 15½-inches in length, and drill each end for the dowels.
4. Cut from the doweling two 2¾-inch lengths for the pivots and lay aside.
5. From the rest of the doweling cut eight lengths 1¼-inch in length. Scratch tiny glue flow channels down the sides of each.

Assemble the components of the folding luggage rack as follows referring to Fig. 3-22:

In assembling the two pairs of legs, notice that the outer leg is joined to the top stretcher by a dowel at the hole that is 2 inches from the end of the stretcher. The other leg of the pair is joined to the top stretcher by the dowel at the 3¼-inch hole from the end of the stretcher. This arrangement means that the lower stretcher in both cases is the same length, 15½ inches. Each lower stretcher joins an inner and an outer leg.

1. Glue the legs to top stretcher using the dowels.
2. Connect the legs by the lower stretchers using the dowels and gluing in. Allow the glued joints to thoroughly set.
3. Insert the pivot dowels with a washer between the legs.
4. Either drill small holes in the legs and thread limiting cords through, knotting these at one end at the far side of the legs; or, insert small screweyes and attach the limiting cord to these.

When the glue has set thoroughly, open the rack so that the top stretchers are 15 or 16 inches apart and tie the limiting cords off to that position. A sizable knot in this ¼-inch cord should prevent it from slipping through the holes you drilled in the legs. It is best to

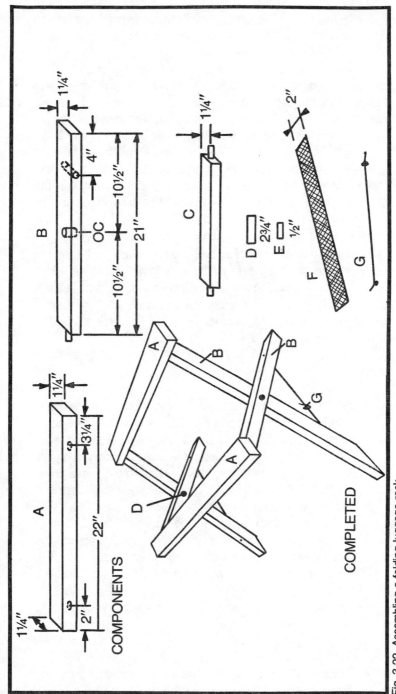

Fig. 3-22. Assembling a folding luggage rack.

195

use ¼-inch marine rope as limiting cords because it will not stretch and ties well. Strain will be put on this limiting cord when luggage is on the rack so do not use light cord.

Now the bottom of the legs must be sawed at an angle to allow them to sit flat on the floor. The simplest way to gauge this angle is to set the rack on two straight 2-by-4s and, using a straight edge held parallel to the 2-by-4, mark the minimum amount that must be cut off, usually only a corner. If the bottom of the leg was square in the first place, the cut off piece should be the same for all four of the legs.

You will probably want to either paint or stain the luggage rack. Take care that this finish does not interfere with the pivoting of the legs in opening and closing. Sand all surfaces smooth, and round the edges of the top stretchers for the webbing. When the finish has thoroughly dried, you can start installing the webbing.

There are two methods of installing the webbing on the luggage rack: gluing and tacking each individual strip at both sides, which requires a little less yardage of webbing but more tacks and gluing, thereby taking more time; or, returning a continuous winding of webbing from one top stretcher to the other and back again. The continuous winding method is the stronger.

To install the webbing by the continuous winding method, proceed as follows:

1. Glue and tack with upholstering tacks on the inside of the underside of the stretcher at the end escaping the leg by about ⅜ inch (Fig. 3-23), so that it will not interfere with the leg. Bring the webbing under the stretcher and over the outside to the top. A spot of glue should be placed on each of these surfaces to anchor the webbing before it is stretched across to the opposite side.

2. Take the webbing across to the opposite stretcher, over and around it, securing it with spots of glue and on the outside with an upholstering tack.

3. From underneath the top stretcher carry the webbing back across to the underside of the opposite top stretcher, angling it slightly to leave about ½-inch between that strip and the first one when you bring it up and around the stretcher, anchoring it with a spot of glue and an upholstering tack on the outer surface of the stretcher.

4. Continue this process until you have crossed from the top side six times.

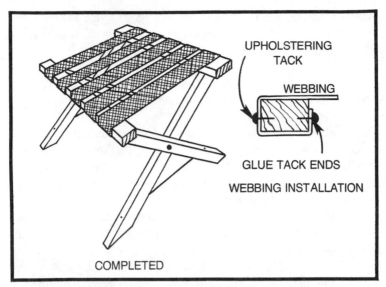

UPHOLSTERING
TACK

WEBBING

GLUE TACK ENDS

WEBBING INSTALLATION

COMPLETED

Fig. 3-23. Webbing installation and a completed folding luggage rack.

5. Do not bring the last crossing back but glue and tack as you did at the start, behind and under the stretcher.

When you have finished, there should be six strips on top and five crossings underneath, each tacked on the outer side of the top stretcher. This row of upholstering tacks should be straight and the webbing should be drawn tightly but to maintain the limits of the opening as governed by the limiting cord.

The alternate method will end up with much the same appearance, except that there will be no crossings underneath. Each strip is firmly anchored at one side and again at the other side where it is cut off and the next strip anchored and crossed in the same manner.

Before you use the luggage rack, be sure that all gluings have thoroughly set. Meanwhile let it stand opened to the limits.

LIGHTING THE SIAMESE TWIN GUEST QUARTERS

Since bed lighting will be discussed later, along with television and stereo installations at the bed, only that specifically related to the Siamese twin guest quarters will be touched upon here. First, some kind of general illumination is needed. This should be controlled for each room within easy reach of the door so that the guest will not have to stumble about in the dark hunting for the light.

Many people must get up in the night for a trip to the bathroom. There should therefore be a light that he or she can turn on before getting out of bed. At the same time this light should, in so far as possible, not disturb the occupant in the neighboring cell. A bed light will answer this purpose and will also provide illumination for reading in bed.

If you build a bedside table where you can set a lamp, that will serve the purpose nicely. This arrangement requires convenient plug-ins that are available to both rooms.

Installation of electrical wiring will require the services of a licensed electrician unless you are willing to jeopardize the validity of your fire insurance. Any junction of electrical wiring should be made properly in a UL-approved junction box. The householder, however, can always legally plug in extension cords.

A junction box can be installed in the partition between the two guest cells, even if the wires to it are connected to the house power by a plugged-in extension cord. You can use a junction box that allows the lighting fixtures to be fastened to it on either side of the partition and the wires run directly from the box into the fixture. If you use this arrangement, cut a hole in the partition for mounting the box and then fasten the fixtures on both sides of the partition to it.

If the partition is of the stage flat variety, be sure to change the location of the cross piece to the correct height. The best way to do this is to install a piece above and a piece below, then to run pieces on either side like a frame and mount the junction box within this. The light fixtures can then be mounted either to the cross pieces or to the junction box.

If you plan to buy the bed light fixtures, consider the type used to illuminate paintings (Fig. 3-24A). These are ideal because the shades can be adjusted and they are provided with clamps or means to attach them. They use small wattage bulbs that do not heat up as much as bulbs of higher wattage.

Fluorescent strips, such as are often installed over kitchen sinks, also are comparatively cool lights. These fixtures are mounted flat on the partition and incorporate a control switch.

Although they will be more expensive, you can use the kind of spot-light lamps that have hinged necks that extend the reflector and the bulb away from the partition on which they are mounted (Fig. 3-24B). These lamps will use more electricity and the reflectors will get quite hot because they are usually metal, but they do give more light by which to read and can be adjusted to almost any angle. You may be able to find these spots with fiberglass shades that will not burn your guest should he or she happen to touch the shade. These lamps also incorporate switches.

Take precaution when locating any electric light so that there is no danger of the hot shade or bulb touching or even coming close to any flammable surface. If the heat does not actually start a fire, it can leave a scorched spot very quickly.

Do any electric wiring with care even when the current is only plugged-in. A short circuit can easily cause a disastrous fire. It is always better to be safe than sorry. For more details on bed lighting see Chapter 5.

WATERBEDS

Before you seriously consider a waterbed, whether it be to build it all from scratch, buy components and assemble them, store-buy the entire unit or combine these, you should know at least a little about them. No matter what put the idea into your head, you've heard a lot of rumors about flotation sleeping. Some of these will be true, some will have only a small element of truth and some will be totally erroneous.

The measure of relaxed rest that a person's body can get from lying on a bed, especially for a protracted period of time, depends

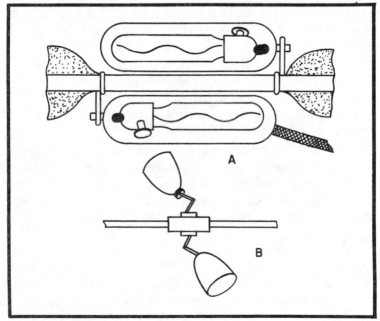

Fig. 3-24. Bed lighting.
    A. Picture frame light on tufted partition.
    B. Hinged neck spot lamps.

upon how much pressure the surface on which one lies returns in relation to the weight, or nonweight, upon it. The human body is not a flat plane, like a board; it sticks out in places and goes inward in other places. For this reason the mattress on which he or she is lying must be able to fill the hollow places of the body while also accommodating the protrusions. The more constant this upward pressure, the more restful is the mattress.

Throughout the ages man has been seeking a better surface on which to rest his body. In very ancient times when the Persians travelled their trade routes in caravans, they solved this problem by filling animal skins with water and slept very well on these. The Egyptians were quick to take up this idea, but somewhere along the passage of time the idea of flotation sleeping was lost. Perhaps leaky or bursting water bags tended to discourage the indoor use of this mode of sleeping.

It was not until recent times that the development of a tough sheet from polyvinyl chloride made waterbeds practical and popular. Meanwhile men tried straw, feathers, cotton, down and a variety of springs to make their mattresses more sleepable. They got up in the morning, after tossing and turning all night as their bodies tried to find a comfortable position on these surfaces, tired or perhaps even more tired than when they went to bed. Then someone thought up a posture bed that was jointed at strategic places in the attempt to accommodate the ins and outs of the contours of the average human body. The average body was determined from statistics compiled by the Armed Forces so they pertained mainly to the well-developed masculine proportions. Statistics were lacking on women's and children's bodies.

There are other troubles with these expensive, so-called posture beds. Few people sleep in just one position all night and to change the contour of the bed for different positions that the body assumes while sleeping, the occupant had to wake up sufficiently to press the right button or turn the crank every time he or she changed sleeping posture.

From experience I know that although you succeed in getting these mechanical adjustments to your liking so you can go to sleep comfortably, sooner or later you will change your position in your sleep. Then you are awakened later by a cramp or a strain caused by your body spanning a hollow that fitted nicely in your original position. Half asleep and often in pain, you grope for the switches or the crank that controls the gyrations of the bed and try to adjust it to fit your new position only to have the same thing happen all over again after you have succeeded in getting back to sleep again.

Waterbeds require no such adjustment; they automatically fit the body contours. Scientists have studied the pressures that a relaxed body exerts on its sleeping surface and the pressures returned by the mattress to the various contours of the body. These pressures are measured in milimeters of mercury (mmHg).

Figures 3-25 and 26 show the principle points of the body that are concerned whether the sleeper is on his or her back or on the side, with or without a pillow under the head. The conventional mattress leaves the hollow at the small of the back unsupported while pressing up mightily at the hips, tailbone and heels. In addition to this variable pressure, the bedding is at the same time pressing down heavily on the toes, causing the feet to cramp. The added pressure from the bedding was not taken into account in the recording of the pressures by those studying the problem.

Scientists, such as those at the Rehabilitation Institute of Tufts New England Medical Center, studied the various postures that the sleeping body assumes and the pressures exerted against this body by conventional sleeping surfaces and waterbeds. In one such study the scientists reported that a sleeping body on a conventional mattress, sleeping on the side and with a pillow under the head, experienced 56 mmHg of pressure upward on the tailbone-sacrum and 63

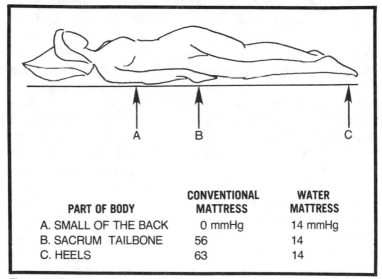

PART OF BODY	CONVENTIONAL MATTRESS	WATER MATTRESS
A. SMALL OF THE BACK	0 mmHg	14 mmHg
B. SACRUM TAILBONE	56	14
C. HEELS	63	14

Fig. 3-25. Sleeping surface pressures on a sleeping body when on the side with a pillow under the head.

mmHg on the heels while no pressure at all supported the small of the back. In contrast, the same body in the same position sleeping on a waterbed mattress was supported at all three of these points by a constant pressure of 14 mmHg.

When you consider that any upward reciprocal pressure from a sleeping surface of over 30 mmHg shuts off the surface blood vessels, it is no wonder that we so often awaken with a foot asleep, a cramp in the leg or a lame back. But you say, "I sleep on my back and without a pillow; what then?"

When you sleep flat on your back, there are five body points to consider (Fig. 3-26): the shoulders, the small of the back, the tail bone, the hips and the heels. The conventional mattress was found to exert a reciprocal pressure of 47 mmHg at the shoulders, again none at all to support the small of the back, 58 mmHg at the tail bone, 78 mmHg at the hips and 63 mmHg on the heels. In contrast the waterbed mattress supported the shoulders with 25 mmHg of pressure, the small of the back with 17 mmHg, the tail bone with 12 mmHg, the hips with 24 mmHg and the heels with 14 mmHg. Note that none of these reciprocal pressures approach the 30 mmHg shut off point for surface blood vessels.

Soon the medical profession realized that here was a beneficial sleeping surface, especially for badly burned patients where the least amount of pressure magnified their pain. Here also was a way to prevent that bane of the bedridden, bed sores, and to promote healing. The semi-weightless support provided by water-filled mattresses was found to relieve back aches, just one of its therapeutic values, and those who slept on one found that they reached a state of relaxation conducive to restful sleep much quicker. Then it was found that water mattresses were ideal for post-operative brain and eye patients and for premature babies. Soon the waterbed became "what the doctor ordered." Even the Income Tax people allow such beds as a medical deduction when they are prescribed by the doctor.

The evolution of sleeping surfaces form the bare ground to the featherbed always left man wanting something more satisfactory, yet he was always skeptical of any innovation. Would you believe it, when the innerspring mattress was introduced, some people hesitated to risk sleeping on one for fear that the springs might break loose inside the mattress, come through and stab them while they slept.

Water weighs a lot and tends to throw that weight around. It is not a simple matter to contain it, support it and it is an even more

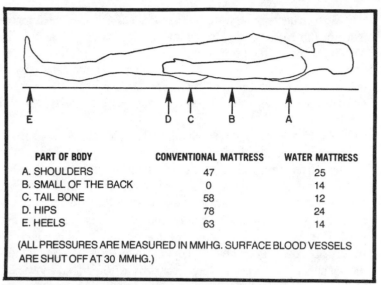

PART OF BODY	CONVENTIONAL MATTRESS	WATER MATTRESS
A. SHOULDERS	47	25
B. SMALL OF THE BACK	0	14
C. TAIL BONE	58	12
D. HIPS	78	24
E. HEELS	63	14

(ALL PRESSURES ARE MEASURED IN MMHG. SURFACE BLOOD VESSELS ARE SHUT OFF AT 30 MMHG.)

Fig. 3-26. Sleeping surface pressures on a sleeping body when body is sleeping on back with no pillow under head.

difficult job to heat it. It does not pay to fool around with nearly a ton of water that; if turned loose, can cause thousands of dollars in damages. Satisfactory containment became possible with the perfection of polyvinyl chloride (PVC), a strong, tough, yet flexible material that can be produced in sheets.

Scientists have found that the average person's internal body temperature actually drops one degree below normal during an eight hour sleep. This fact explained why people who slept on unheated waterbeds, as they were at first, complained of a "morning drag" until their bodies could work back to a normal temperature.

In spite of the generally accepted idea that it is dangerous to mix water and electricity, manufacturers of waterbeds tackled the problem of heating the water in the mattress. The fact that the PVC covering offered only a small barrier helped in the solution of the heating problem.

The Chemelex Division of the Raychem Corporation was the first to market a waterbed heater that was approved by the Underwriters Laboratories and soon others that were UL listed followed. These heaters are thermostatically and accurately controlled, and although they are rated at 300 to 400 watts, they only use current when they are on, and then no more than three or four 100-watt light bulbs.

With no heater, the water in the mattress assumes the temperature of the room, probably somewhere between 65° and 75°F. That is 20° below the normal body temperature. Furthermore, the water can absorb a great deal of body heat. This means that an unheated waterbed will feel cold. The temperature needs to be brought up and maintained at body temperature for relaxation and comfort.

The temperature should also be adjustable to the pleasure of the occupant and the thermostat enables him or her to choose the setting. From there on that temperature is automatically maintained, warm in winter and cool in summer, within 0.2°F, without the sleeper noticing any variation nor hot spots. This of course is assuming that a high quality heater and controlling thermostat are used. Overheating can shorten the life of the PVC liner and the watermattress. A good heater, controlled by an equally good thermostat should have a broad range from 75° to 100°F, but above all it should be UL approved.

For use in Europe, Japan and Australia 100 and 240-volt waterbed heaters are available. Special heaters are also available for baby incubators, baby dish warmers, safety showers, copy machines, hot trays and nuclear-power facilities from the same manufacturers.

At first, the waterbeds required a lot of room due to the bulky frames and reinforced construction, but today there are a great variety of styles that look like any bedroom furniture (Fig. 3-27). No longer need one expect the waterbed to not match the other furniture in the bedroom. These beds can look just like any other bed. Even the firmness of the sleeping surface can be controlled. Scented mattresses are even available.

Some people, and that includes landlords, have been fearful of waterbeds, especially upstairs. To meet these objections the manufacturers called upon structural engineers. Tests were conducted and building codes were studied. Here is an excerpt from the resulting report:

> "...providing that the building was constructed in conformance with the Uniform Building Code, the Southern Building Code, Basic Building Code, or other codes requiring a 40 pounds-per-square-foot minimum live load...(and) occupants do not exceed 250 pounds for twin size and 500 pounds for all others...(the maximum live load for a waterbed should not exceed) 38.0 pounds per square foot."

The live load rating for most dwellings today is higher than the minimum required by law.

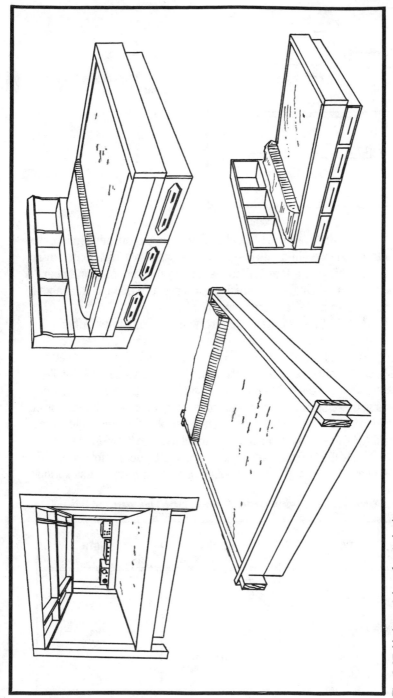

Fig. 3-27. Various styles of waterbeds.

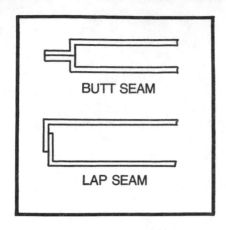

BUTT SEAM

LAP SEAM

Fig. 3-28. Waterbed mattress seams.

When the waterbed stands on four legs, on pedestals or a platform, the weight of the bed plus its occupants is distributed over a number of square feet and spans numerous structural members, such as rafters. Unless you are living in a rat-trap, have no fear about it bearing up under a normal waterbed.

In 1972 the California Department of Consumer Affairs developed standards for manufacturers and retailers of waterbeds and accessories. Industry-sponsored organizations like the American Association of Waterbed Manufacturers and the Waterbed Retailers Association have established sets of standards based on research. Among these standards are those governing the inside dimensions of standard, rigid type waterbed frames (Table 3-2) and rigid frame decking (Table 3-3). Miscellaneous standards are listed in Table 3-4.

The waterbed mattress is the crux of the successful waterbed. The chances of today's store-bought air and water mattress spring-

Table 3-2. Inside Dimensions of Standard, Rigid Type Waterbed Frames

TYPE	WIDTH	LENGTH
King	72	84
Queen	60	84
Double	54	84
Super single	48	84
Single	39	84
Jumbo	84	108
Round	94½ diameter	
Polygon	94½ flat to flat	
Baby crib	27	52

Table 3-3. Waterbed Pedestal Decking Dimensions

TYPE	WIDTH	LENGTH
King	71¾	85⅜
Queen	59¾	85⅜
Double	53¾	85⅜
Super single	47¾	85⅜
Single	38¾	85⅜
Jumbo	83¾	109⅜
Round	95⅞ diameter	
Polygon	95⅞ flat to flat	
Baby crib	26¾	53⅜

(Ridig frame; only head and foot dado is allowed; all dimensions are given in inches.)
Acceptable tolerance +⅛"; −0"
Corners may be cut to accommodate four poster frames.

ing a leak is less than that of a good automobile tire going flat. Waterbed dealers can often provide insurance on their products against any accidental damage, but if you try to build your own, you'll probably have to take your own chances.

The waterbed mattress must be really tough; moreover, it must be flexible. Polyvinyl chloride (PVC) seems to be the only appropriate material for the purpose. Specifications for waterbed mattresses set forth by the Waterbed Manufacturers Association are given in Table 3-5. The California Department of Consumer Affairs has set the minimum standards for these mattresses as given in Table 3-6.

The seams may be of two types: butt and lap (Fig. 3-28). Two pieces of PVC, which are to form the top and bottom of the mattress, are cut exactly the same size. They are placed together, the valve inserted and the seam welded by the process known as thermo welding. The butt seam is less expensive to manufacture. The California Department of Consumer Affairs requires that the seam strength be no less than 25 pounds.

An awful lot of engineering has gone into these mattresses to make them foolproof and able to withstand not only the water pressure but the human stresses that are usually put upon a mattress. When you stop to consider that a king-sized water mattress holds around 235 gallons of water, you can see why they must be well-built. While this is less water than would be needed for five tub baths, it means a total weight of around a ton, about the weight of twelve people.

The frame of the waterbed is built solidly and totally lined so that, should the water-filled mattress experience total failure, the entire volume of water can be retained within the confines of the bed. While such a failure has never been reported on today's waterbed mattresses, which are guaranteed, it is a safety measure for reliability.

The store bought watermattress is not only water-tight but it is air-tight so that no splashing can occur. There can be splashing only

Table 3-4. Miscellaneous Standards for Waterbeds

ITEM	LOCATION	MINIMUM
Dadoes	Underside of frame rail that sits on decking	¾ by ½-inch (inside to outside)
Screws	Holding corners of frame together	Threaded screw bite into wood on end of each board or part a total of 3 inches
Hinges	Holding corners of frame together	3½-inch height
Heater cord	Exit through pedestal decking	On each set
Safety liner	Means of affixing to frame or mattress	Each frame PVC 8-mil. thickness
Mattress	Labeled	Full instructions and warnings
Mattress	Material	Polyvinyl chloride (PVC) 20 mil. (0.20 inch) in thickness
Mattress	Seams	Thermo welded
Heater		115 VAC, 300, 400-watts, 2 to 3 lb. weight, setting range of 65° to 105°F
Complete set of instructions	With each unit	for each component

Table 3-5. Specifications for Waterbed Mattresses

TYPE	DIMENSIONS (In inches)	ALL-WATER		AIR-WATER	
		Gal	Pounds	Gal	POUNDS
King	72 X 84	235	2028	168	1450
Queen	60 X 84	196	1690	134	1161
Double	54 X 84	176	1520	118	1013
Super single	48 X 84	152	1301	97	832
Twin	39 X 84	128	1101	76	652
Round	96 diameter	282	2428	216	1861

at the surface of contact of air and water. When a mattress is properly filled with water, all air bubbles should be pushed out at the filler vale if the instructions are followed.

The air frame mattress (Fig. 3-27) is designed to eliminate the "drop-in" effect to a person sitting along the side of the bed. It is claimed that it also makes it easier to sit up in a waterbed to read or watch television. It does not increase or reduce the cost of heating, although one might think that it would take less heat to warm the smaller volume of water.

Certain manufacturers have overcome the "drop-in" effect without the use of the air frame mattress by incorporating a double wedged foam frame foundation that goes on top of the edges of the watermattress. The top wedge is made of a polyurethane that possesses a built-in memory for shape, density and firmness. The lower wedge has a beveled top surface on which the upper wedge rests. The two wedges are attached to the base in a manner that

Table 3-6. Waterbed Matress Minimum Standards

ITEM	NO LESS THAN
Weight	17.5 oz per sq. yard
Thickness	0.020 inch (20 mil.)
Hydrostatic resistance	55 lb. per sq. inch
Puncture test	20 lb. with ¼-inch dia. rod
Single-sheet tear force	5 lb.
Elongation	Initial, 275%
	Subsequent, 10%
Tensile strength	2000 lb. per sq. inch
Seam strength	25 lb.

produces a hinged effect. This arrangement allows the use of conventional flat or fitted sheets.

This double wedge arrangement also allows the occupant of the waterbed to sit up easily and comfortably on the edge of the waterbed as he takes off or puts on his or her bedroom slippers, or to sit up in bed to read or to watch television. The only trouble encountered has been that, when subjected to the ozone from light or air, the useful life of the polyurethane foam was shortened and the manufacturers wanted to be able to guarantee their waterbed for at least five years and to tell their customers to expect a life of at least fifteen years. The problem was solved be sealing the foam in air-tight PVC. This eliminated the need for the heavily upholstered sides of a waterbed frame.

Some consider the air filled edges that form the air frame more stable than the edges of a water only mattress. This dual filling requires two fill valves, a water fill (Fig. 3-29) and an air fill (Fig. 3-30). Because air tends to leak more readily than water, a special lap seam is incorporated in the PVC mattress.

There are two types of air frame mattresses. In the self-supporting type the air chamber functions as the frame. This type requires the use of a contoured safety liner to safeguard against seam leaks. The other type is air-inherent in design and must have a wooden frame to which the safety liner is attached.

When the mattress has been completely filled with water, the plastic valve is gently pushed down below the PVC surface so that it will not be felt by anyone lying on the surface of the bed. This is part of the filling procedure that will be given later.

The basic components of the most common type of waterbed consist of a pedestal base, pedestal decking or platform, a frame containing the safety liner and the water mattress (Fig. 3-31). To these components are added the heater and its controlling thermostat. The pedestal base may contain inserts or drawers for storage.

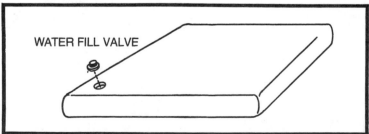

WATER FILL VALVE

Fig. 3-29. Water only mattress.

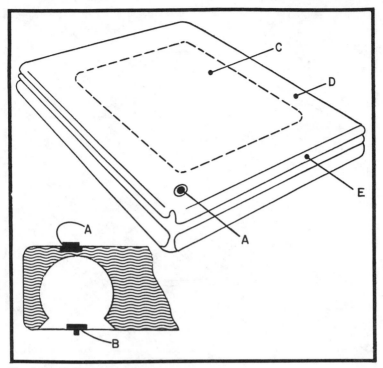

Fig. 3-30. Air fill frame mattress.
   A. Water fill valve.
   B. Plug.
   C. Water chamber.
   D. Air chamber.
   E. Lap seam.

The basic function of the pedestal is to raise the bed to a comfortable height and with the decking to distribute the weight across the floor. Two different types of pedestal beds are shown in Fig. 3-32.

The function of the frame is to contain the mattress and the safety liner. The liner completely covers the inside of the frame and forms a reservoir that will contain anything from the entire volume of water in the mattress should it fail, to a trickle from a pinhole leak. The latter is more in the realm of possibilities with a store-bought water mattress.

Among the accessories is an algae inhibitor. With this algae inhibitor in the water, it never need to be changed. Once filled and the temperature adjusted, no maintenance is required. When you need to move the waterbed, first pull the plug to the heater, drain the water from the mattress by syphoning, allow the mattress to dry,

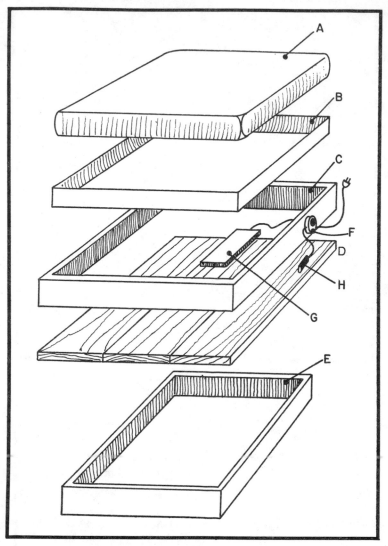

Fig. 3-31. Basic waterbed components.
A. Waterbed mattress.
B. Safety liner.
C. Frame.
D. Pedestal decking or platform.
E. Pedestal base.
F. Thermostat.
G. Heater.
H. Sensor capillary tube.

disassemble the other components and roll up the mattress. Never leave the heater plugged in unless the mattress is filled with water.

Today, a waterbed can be any style. Figures 3-33 and 3-34 show two examples, an Early American four poster and a novelty child's bed called the "Night Racer" designed by Chase National. Manufacturers vie with each other on innovations and a wide variety

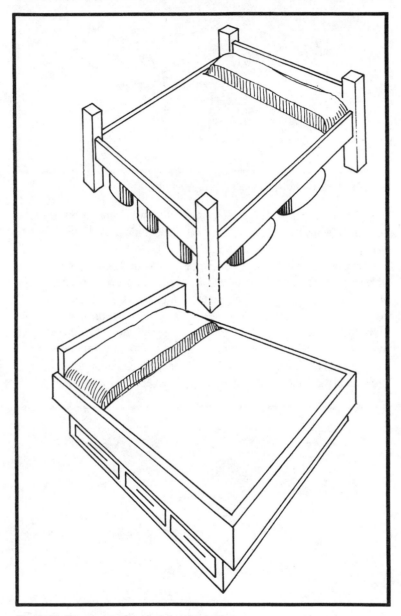

Fig. 3-32. Two types of pedestal water beds.

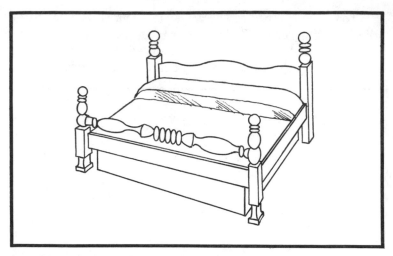

Fig. 3-33. An Early American four poster waterbed.

of styles for their waterbeds. Some offer a full line while others specialize and still others do custom jobs that include just about everything but the kitchen sink.

One waterbed dealer is building a large round bed in anticipation of his coming marriage. This bed will incorporate everything imaginable. Such a wide variety of waterbeds is available at prices quite comparable with conventional beds that little is to be gained from starting from scratch and building your own. There are, however, available sources for the components and companies that specialize in components and aids to the do-it-yourselfers. These are listed in the lists of manufacturers and suppliers in Table 3-7 and Table 3-8.

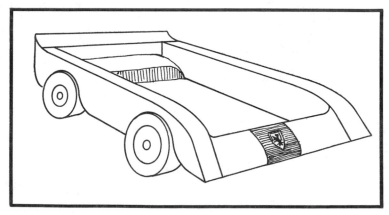

Fig. 3-34. "Night Racer," a child's waterbed.

The most common mistake, I am told, that do-it-yourselfers make is in the measurements of the frames. If the inside dimensions are not exactly right to take the safety liner and the watermattress, special ones have to be made up to fit the frame and this is expensive (Fig. 3-35).

Waterbed manufacturers say they work to a tolerance of +1/64 inch, −0 inches. Various frame corner treatments used and approved are shown in Fig. 3-36 and approved hardware is shown in Fig. 3-37.

Be warned, if your frame is not an exact fit, you are in for trouble. Components are not expensive and they are available all across the country and in many foreign countries. These people can also supply algaecide, water conditioner, fill-and-drain kits, UL-aproved heaters, thermostatic controls and patch kits, all of which you will need. These items will be guaranteed and their professional advice is free.

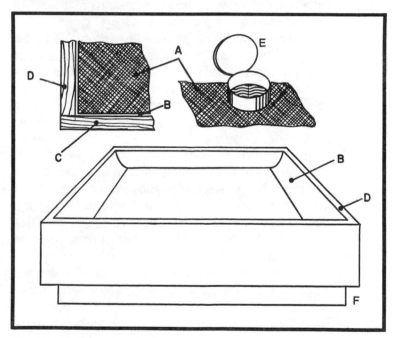

Fig. 3-35. Waterbed mattress and safety liner components.
    A. Waterfilled mattress.
    B. Safety liner secured by T-molding.
    C. Decking.
    D. Frame.
    E. Water fill and drain valve.
    F. Safety liner installation.

If you want to build a part of your waterbed, the pedestal will be your wisest choice. You can build it with drawers or cubical inserts for storage as shown in Fig. 3-38. That will give you plenty of work as you must have begun to realize from our discussion so far. There is a lot more to a waterbed than to a conventional bed, although probably no more trouble than those that will be discussed in Chapter 4.

To assemble the store-bought components of a waterbed you will only need a hammer and a screwdriver. The manufacturers are required to furnish complete instructions for assembly and use of their components. You can get the parts unfinished and finish them to match the decor of your bedroom.

The assembly procedure is, in general, as follows:

1. Decide on the exact location for the waterbed. It should be within 5 feet of an electrical outlet if possible. If this is not possible and you have to use an extension cord, use only a heavy-duty appliance cord that is no longer than is necessary to reach from the outlet to the heater cord. This is the cord that must be unplugged whenever the mattress is not filled with water. Always do this the last thing upon installing the bed and the first thing before starting to empty the mattress so that you run no chances of damaging the safety liner and the PVC of the mattress and perhaps also charring the frame or decking.

2. Position the pedestal exactly where you will want the bed to sit and insert any parts that fit into it. If the style of waterbed you have selected has no pedestal base, protect the floor or carpet beneath the bed with an old rug or a sheet of insulation. Do not mistake any condensation that may form with water from a leak in the mattress. When the bed is cooler than the room, drops of water may appear. This is only condensation and the drops of water will disappear as soon as the bed heats up to room temperature or higher.

3. When the pedestal base is all set, lay the decking on top of it.

4. Assemble the frame and attach it to the base decking with at least three screws on each side or, better yet, with eight 1 by 1 inch right-angle brackets. Screw two brackets to the inside of the frame on each side, near the middle and 18 inches apart. This will add support and prevent the sides of

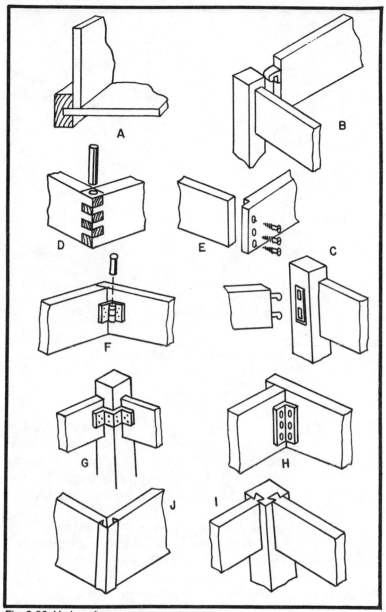

Fig. 3-36. Various frame corner treatments.

A. With 2 by 4 nail.
B. Snap together.
C. Bed hook.
D. Knuckle or finger joint with dowel.
E. Leg screws.

F. Loose pin|hinge.
G. Metal double-U bracket.
H. Keylock corner retainer.
I. Dovetail corner block.
J. Metal spline.

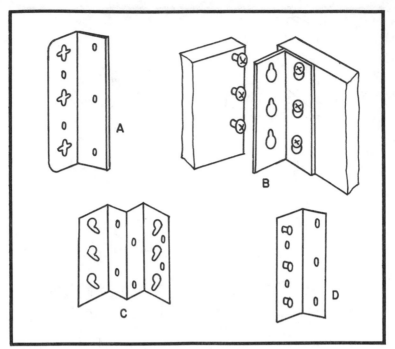

Fig. 3-37. Approved waterbed frame hardware.
  A. Keylock retainer.
  B. 6 inch high retainer.
  C. W-retainer, 6 inches high.
  D. 6 inch high retainer.

the frame from bowing outward. Insure that the decking fits into the grooves that are cut for it in the bottom of the frame. Should you be unable to fix any gaps between the decking and the frame, let them occur in the middle rather· than near the edges, and permit no gaps larger than ½-inch.

5. A hole or slot should be provided for admittance of the heater cord and the thermostat sensing tube. If these holes are not provided, drill or cut them into the frame. Whatever you do never crease, fold, pound or drill holes in the heater. Do not pull it by the cord or use nails, staples or other metal fasteners near it. Never immerse the heater in water. Never install a full-sized heater in beds smaller than 36 by 72 inches. When no hole has been provided for the entrance of the heater cord, make a 2 by 2 inch notch at the corner of the base platform at least 12 inches from any side

(text continues on page 224)

Table 3-7. Waterbed Manufacturers and Suppliers and What They Offer

Aegean Designs Inc.
  Los Angeles, CA

Classical and brass frames

Air Bed Inc.
  1992 Junction Ave.
  San Jose, CA 95131

Inflatable airbeds

American-National Waterbed Mattress Corp.
  1940 N. Glassell St.
  Orange, CA 92667

Aqua-Mate, Confor-Pedio, Supreme, Infinity, Four-T, Float-A-Pedic, American Centennial, seamless fitted linens, contour linens

Northeast Div: Stone Street Industrial Park
  276 Stone St., P.O. Box
  138, Walpole, Mass 02081
  Southeast Div: 2007 Southwest 11th St.,
  Ft. Lauderdale, FL 33312

American Poly-Seal Co.
  878 Susex Blvd., Broomall, PA 19008

Electrofilm heaters, Aqua-float air water mattresses

Aqua Queen-Electrofilm, Inc.
  7116 Laurel Canyon Blvd.
  North Hollywood, CA 91608

American Thermoseal
  Los Angeles, CA

Associated Furniture
  1213-B West Struck Ave.
  Orange, CA 92667

Avant
  372 Martin Ave.
  Santa Clara, CA 95050

Vibratune, heaters, sheets, bedding, accessories, algaecide

Blue Magic Products
  P.O. Box 4175
  Stockton, CA 95204

Water conditioners, accessories

Calco-Hawaiian, Inc.
  148 Beacon St.
  South San Francisco, CA 94080

Airfactor flotation mattresses

Casual Bedding
  37433 Centralmont Rd.
  Fremont, CA 94536

Chemelex Div., Rayehem Corp.
  837 Second Ave.
  Redwood City, CA 94063

Chase National   Children's special beds
  P.O. Box 1070
  Fontana, CA 92335

(N. CALIF)
  1990 N. California Blvd.
  Walnut Creek, CA 94596

Closco Manufacturing   Sheet attaching system
  27132 Belvedere Ct, No. 3   (can be installed with
  Hayward, CA 94544   mattress water-filled)

Classic Products Corp.   Flotation Sleeper
  1233 2 Conway Rd.
  Boltsville, Md 20705

Continental Case, Inc.
  1565 Sunflower Ave.
  Costa Mesa, CA 92626

E & S Vinyl Manufacturing
  2920 S. Kelson
  Santa Ana, CA 92707

Gahm Industries Inc.
  25 Bidwell Rd.
  South Windsor, Conn 06074

Gillespie Furniture Co.
  Waterbed Division
  Los Angeles, CA

Hallmark General Corp.   Water sleeper, custom
  17120 Alburtis   designs
  Artesia, CA 90701

(WEST COAST) 6910-B Arayon Circle
              Buena Park, CA 90620
(EAST COAST) 251 Welsh Pool Rd.
              Lionville, PA 19353

Hammond Furniture Co.   Bed frames
  792 Montague Ave.
  San Leandro, CA 94577

Heritage House
  146 E. Emerson
  Orange, CA 92665

Hodel and Company
  1580 Davidson
  San Francisco, CA 94124

Super Valve, Custom Aire,
"Everything but the water"

Hydro-Dynamics
  32 N. Pima Square
  South Lake Havasau City, AZ 86403

Waterbedding

Intimate Sleep Products
  Santa Clara, CA

Water mattresses to
fit baby cribs

R. L. Kuss & Co., Inc.
  1331 Broad Ave.
  Findlay, Ohio 45840

Water mattresses

Laguna Manufacturing
  17622 Von Karman Ave.
  Irvine, CA 92714

L & M Metal Products, Inc.
  5108 Calmview Ave.
  Baldwin Park, CA 91706

Hardware, Aquarius
waterbeds

Land and Sky
  P.O. Box 2754,
  Lincoln Industrial Park
  Lincoln, Neb 68502

Safeway heaters

Lee Con Manufacturing
  2027—35th St. South
  Clearwater, FL 33520

Bedspreads

Liberty Vinyl Corp.
  Santa Clara, CA
  also: Kent, WA
      Fountain Valley, CA
      Mundelein, IL
      Denver, Colo
      Irving, TX

Solid-state and thermal heaters,
mattresses, liners, fill and
drain kits, Comfort-Aire, Natural-
Air

Mo-Zar Industries, Inc.
  15002 S. Avalon
  Gardena, CA

Contemp frames

Neptune Waterbeds, Inc.
  244 Mt. Vernon St.
  Dorchester, Mass 02125

New World Manufacturing Inc.
P.O. Box 484,
123 N. Cloverdale Blvd.
Cloverdale, CA 95425

Air Cushion mattresses,
crib to king sized and
rounds

Northwest Waterbed Distributors
7960 SW Cirrus Dr.
Beaverton, OR 97005

Calco-Hawaiian distributor

Odyssey Distributors
16218 E. 14th St.
San Leandro, CA 94578

Ody-Loc, pedestals,
solid, plywood or
unfinished frames,
Velcro sheet straps

Pillow Pleasure, Inc.
1440 NW 45th St.
Seattle, WA 98107

Water pillows and cushions

Raintree Distributing
11705 Meridian South
Puyallup, WA 98371

Hydro-Dynamics, Wavecrest,
Wacco products, Jiffy linen
grippers, Safeway frames, 6-drawer
pedestals, pillow furniture
frames, comforters, bedspreads

Riverwood Frames & Furniture
410—18th St.
Washougal, WA 98671

Frames, pedestals, 5⁄8-
aluminum extrusions, padded rail caps

Safeway Products Inc.
440 Middlefield
Middlefield, Conn 06457

Heaters and controls

Shallow Waterbeds Inc.
1406—19th St.
Lubbock, TX 79401

Sheer Comfort
286 Charoot Ave.
San Jose, CA 95131

Sequoia Woods
1331 E. Pomona
Santa Ana, CA 92705

Frames

**Sleep Machine Div,
Ortho Medical Labs**
5711 NE 14th St.
Ft. Lauderdale, FL 33334

Water stabilizer,
thermal covers

222

M & J Sokolou Manufacturing Co.
738 S. San Pedro St.
Los Angeles, CA 90014

Comforters

Thermal Technology Inc.
103 Independence Dr.
Menlo Park, CA 94025

Sundown UL-listed heaters

Triad Manufacturing

Padded rails (Naugahyde, foam, plywood)

Tucker
436 Ardmore Ave.
Hermosa Beach, CA 90254

Tuck-a-Liner, safety locks, Quick-Tucker bedding, Tite-Nites, headboards, pedestals

Ultrarest
851 Shasta St.
Redwood City, CA 94063

Massage systems

UltraTherm
2630 Seaman Ave.
El Monte, CA 91733

Solid state and deluxe comfort systems

Undercurrents
515 N. La Salle
Chicago, IL 60610

Frames

U.S. Frame and Furniture Co.
15604 S. Broadway
Gardena, CA 90248

Pedestals (with storage pockets)

Vinyl Products

3-D Infinite-Lap mattresses

Water and Wood
1555 S. Figueroa St.
Gardena, CA 90248

Water Dealers Institute
430—32nd St.
Newport Beach, CA 92663

Information

Wasco Products, Inc.
1831 S. State College Blvd.
Anaheim, CA 92806

Jiffy liner gripper, do-it-yourself frames and pedestals kits, gripper aluminum extrusions, keyhole brackets

Table 3-7. Waterbed Manufacturers and Suppliers and What They Offer (continued)

World Wood   Frames
  10540 Fern St.
Stanton, CA 90680

Watercloud Bed Co., Inc.
  15581 Computer Lane
Huntington Beach, CA 92649

Waterworth   UL-approved vibrators,
  Los Angeles, CA   accessory systems, conditioners

Wavecrest   Mattresses
  5877 Rodeo Rd.
Los Angeles, CA 90016

Wave Master   Bio-massage

Western Wood Turning, Inc.   Bed posts, spindles,
  433 E. Banning   rails, finials
Compton, CA 90222

Woodstock Furniture Manufacturing Inc.
  1395 Colorado Ave.
Long Beach, CA 90804

(Telephone numbers are listed by area in Table 3-8.)

board. Try to keep the cord and sensing tube straight and
free from kinks. Leave a minimum amount of the sensing
tube exposed outside the frame of the bed. If the thermostat has a sensing bulb, keep it at least 6 inches from the
heater. Secure it to the base platform with the clamp and
screw that is provided. If you are using a combination
air-water mattress, insure that both the heater and the
sensing bulb are beneath the water-filled section of the
mattress.

6. Attach the headboard if one is to be used.

7. Adjust the frame and decking so that the overhang is equal
   on both sides of the pedestal base and check that the bed is
   level.

8. Place the heater pad on the decking on a relatively
   nonflammable flat surface, such as plywood, that is slightly
   larger than the heater. Put it near the center of the bed if
   the decking is solid. If the decking is not solid, do not place

the heater where it will straddle any gaps. Run the cord and the copper sensing tube through the openings provided or which you have made. Do not plug in the heater yet, wait until the mattress has been filled with water. Check that there will be no pressure on either the cord or the sensing tube and that the heater is right side up.

9. Lay the safety liner over the heater and the copper sensing tube and bring the liner up the sides of the frame right to the top. There should be an attaching arrangement, but if not, you must obtain this. Do not use staples, tacks or any sharp objects that will puncture the liner or that may come loose. Using an approved method of attachment, fasten the safety liner to the top edge of the frame on all four sides. Approved methods of attachment are: plastic molding, wood molding attached by duct tape or small nails, or a patented attachment strip such as Velcro. If Velcro attachments are used, they will allow for adjustment of the sleeping surface to suit the individual, from taut firmness to loose softness.

10. Smooth out any wrinkles in the liner, especially above the heater. Insure that the safety liner is securely fastened all of the way around the frame so that it will perform as an emergency reservoir in the event of mattress failure.

11. Place the mattress squarely inside of the frame so that it will fit snugly when it is filled with water. Check that there are no folds, especially above the heater.

12. At one corner on the top of the mattress locate the fill valve. A fill kit is needed and a length of garden hose that will reach from a source of water. The hose is merely pushed into the fill valve. It does not screw onto the valve so you may want to secure it with tape. If you use cold water to fill the mattress, it will take the heater 40 to 48 hours to bring the temperature up to 90°F. Figure that this temperature change will be at about 1°F per hour. To avoid the use of this amount of electricity and the delay in using the bed, which you are anxious to try out, you can use a mix of hot and cold water from the bathroom or kitchen faucets, but in order to do that you must have a mixer attachment to fit your hose. Do not use water solely from the hot water faucet because it will become over 90°F and that can damage the mattress fill valve, which is plastic. If you are

(text continues on page 229)

Table 3-8. Manufacturers and Suppliers by Areas

SOUTHERN CALIFORNIA TELEPHONE NUMBERS

Aegan	(213)632-5816
Aeolus	(714)526-5033
American Frame and Furniture	(714)639-5912
American National	(714)998-7300
American Theroseal	(213)629-3647
Animan Designers	(213)232-2661; Except California (800)421-5968
Aquatic Slumber	(213)233-5865
A.R.B. Wood Products	(213)795-8331
Associated Furniture	(714)997-0851
Bal Harbour Manufacturing	(714)973-0988
Bedspread Story	(714)645-1079
Bedding Concepts	(213)749-0234
Beehive Manufacturing	(213)774-1970
BRED	(213)588-1941
Brinkley's Manufacturing Company	(213)633-3701
Catalina Furniture Company	(213)583-6057
Chase National	(714)874-4095
Continental Case	(714)751-9922
Coronado Wood Products	(714)835-5306
C & P Waterbed Manufacturing	(213)751-0134
Custom Designer	(714)522-8920
Daydream Designs	(714)497-2636
Day-Kor Manufacturing	(714)956-9340
Dooley & Co. Lumber	(213)336-1261
E & S Vinyl	(714)751-3123
F & J Wood Products	(714)646-3919
Fortano, Inc.	(213)581-8268
Gemini Products	(213)434-9445
Gillespie Furniture	(213)233-3151
Hallmark General	(714)521-2152
Heritage House	(714)974-1003
I Am Waterbeds	(213)372-9540
India Ink.	(213)589-5471
Kare-Free	(213)626-1966
Laguna Manufacturing	(714)540-6384; (800)854-3584
Lambeck & Co.	(213)566-5502
Latin Industries	(714)623-4456
LCM Company	(213)660-3672
L & M Metals	(213)960-1821
Madera Manufacturing	(213)537-9660
Marina Marine	(213)532-2780
Martinez Enterprise	(213)634-0220
Masterpiece Concepts	(714)997-5670
Mollura Industries	(213)968-0555; 686-1808
Mo-Zar Industries, Inc.	(213)538-5510
Natural Design	(714)630-4641
Natural Rest Furnishings	(714)645-0061
Natural Grain	(213)538-4760; (800)421-1840
Pacific Frames	(213)776-7363; (800)421-1413
Perfect Fit Industries	(213)728-8445
Permafit Water Bedding	(714)556-4142
Phoenicia	(714)751-1563; (800)854-3907
Pillow Patch Manufacturing Co.	(714)232-5009

226

Table 3-8. Waterbed Manufacturers and Suppliers by Area (continued)

Rarewood Designs	(714)497-2810
Regency Furniture	(213)532-0101
Roberts Company	(714)633-4422
Ross Industries	(714)270-3123
Sea Breeze	(213)341-4703
Sequoia Woods	(714)547-7157
Shelley's Custom Quilting	(231)232-6110
Skinner Wood Turning	(213)566-3161
Smith Distributing Co.	(213)531-6577
M & J Sokolow Manufacturing	(213)622-8936
Space Saver	(714)639-1780
Thronton Company	(714)984-8317
Timberline Manufacturing	(213)928-1919
Timewood Products	(213)679-3791
Tite Nites	(213)376-7668
Tomorrow Furniture	(714)638-4860
Trendwest	(213)949-7802
Ultratherm	(213)443-9379
U.S. Furniture and Frame	(213)538-5805
Wasco Products	(714)634-1134
Water & Wood Manufacturing	(213)532-8230
Waterbeds, Systems and Accessories	(213)532-7213
Watercloud Bed Co.	(714)898-6792
Waterworth	(213)532-7213
Wavecrest	(213)559-8250; (800)421-4181
Wavemaster	(714)646-2913
Western Wood Turning	(213)631-1532
Westwood	(714)673-4363
W.G. Manufacturing	(714)995-2107
Woodstock Manufacturing	(213)498-2453
Wood Tec	(714)793-2671
World Wood Products	(714)827-9032

NORTHERN CALIFORNIA AND NEVADA TELEPHONE NUMBERS

Agatha, The Living Age	(408)998-1848
Air Bed Company	(408)279-1444
Americana Designs	(408)946-2222
American Waterbed	(209)948-1947
Aqua-Mite	(916)446-4075
Avant	(408)246-2710; (800)428-6450
A-Z Automatic Woodturning	(209)948-9685
Blue Magic	(209)948-8075
Calco-Hawaiian	(415)837-1505
Carson Manufacturing	(415)453-7313
Casual Bedding	(415)796-4555
Chemelex, Inc.	(415)329-4713
Closco	(415)783-1311
Cosmos Designers	(209)948-8534
Evans Manufacturing	(408)264-3038
Frame-Up	(408)998-2827
Future-Rest	(916)381-3450
H2O Bed Cleaner	(415)457-2578
Hamex	(415)525-6088
Hammond Furniture	(415)483-8530
Hodel & Company	(415)826-7200
Intimate Sleep	(408)988-2091

Table 3-8. Waterbed Manufacturers and Suppliers by Area (continued)

S.M. Kadas Ltd.	(408)354-0533
Liberty Vinyl	(408)249-1234
Logvy Manufacturing	(415)883-6814
New World Manufacturing, Inc.	(707)894-5259
Odessey Distributor	(415)278-8808
Panelcraft Wood Products	(408)295-5959
Penn International Industries	(415)453-6666
Sheer Comfort	(408)363-7222
Slaton's Ruofic Shop	(209)532-2819
Slumberland of Nevada	(702)825-5252
Soft Machine	(415)647-5160
Soma Manufacturing Co.	(415)824-8339; (800)227-4760
Thermal Technology	(415)321-7640
Triad Manufacturing	(408)688-3691
Ultrarest	(415)365-5614
Vinyl Products	(415)647-2520
Winn Manufacturing	(408)263-5500
Wood & Bolt Furniture	(707)544-1789
Woodcraft Industries	(408)248-5400

PACIFIC NORTHWEST TELEPHONE NUMBERS

Pillow Pleasure	(206)782-9373
Raintree	(206)834-3409
Riverwood Frame	(206)835-8000
Spectrum Industries, Inc.	(206)767-6336
Water and Wheel Manufacturing	(503)884-5741

MOUNTAIN AND SOUTHWEST TELEPHONE NUMBERS

Atlantis Manufacturing Co.	(208)343-7547
CLC Corp.	(303)289-2961
Flotation Concepts	(602)881-6771
Hinds-Carlisle	(303)353-3740
Hydro-Dynamics	(602)855-6161
Pillow Shoppe	(303)573-7325
Shallow Waterbed	(806)744-4012
Tops	(303)399-2610

MIDWESTERN TELEPHONE NUMBERS

Easyrest	(812)282-4388
Inflate-A-Bed	(913)384-0714
R.L. Kuss & Co.	(419)423-9040
Mauve Caterpillar	(319)338-9321
Natural Sleep Products	(816)842-3858
New Dawn Trading Co.	(517)351-3100
One Sweet Dream Ent. Ltd.	(414)654-6578
Sunrise Woodcraft	(715)386-3561
Undercurrents	(312)329-9283
Uni Con	(216)834-5050
Waterbed Frame Co.	(321)421-7509
Wertz Crafters	(614)885-9209
Woodcrest Manufacturing	(612)469-4964
Word Products Warehouse Co.	(913)394-0714

Table 3-8. Waterbed Manufacturers and Suppliers by Area (continued)

ATLANTIC TELEPHONE NUMBERS

American Poly Seal	(215)543-1827
Classic Products Corp.	(301)539-9500
Environs	(703)653-4937
GAHM Industries Inc.	(203)289-9521
Gel-Bed	(914)969-1629
Neptune Waterbeds	(617)825-4198
Safeway Products, Inc.	(203)346-6601
Waterbeds By Aquarius	(516)281-9616
Waterbed World	(716)342-2700
Waterbrothers	(716)833-2222

SOUTHEAST TELEPHONE NUMBERS

Lee Con	(813)536-9307
Pace Industries	(404)696-1331
Sleep Machine	(305)372-1017

TOLL-FREE NUMBERS

Aquarius Manufacturing	(800)231-2303
Avant	(800)438-6450
Commodore	(800)227-4760
Laguna Manufacturing	(800)854-3584
Natural Grain	(800)421-1840
Pacific Frames	(800)421-1413
Phoenicia	(800)854-3907
Agatha, The Living Age	(800)227-4760
Wavecrest	(800)421-4181

using the hot-cold water mix, check on it every so often to see that it is not too hot or too cold. When you exhaust the hot-water heater's supply of hot water, turn off the water and wait about a half an hour to let the hot-water heater recycle is supply. Do not plug in the heater until the mattress is completely filled.

13. The best way to determine when the mattress is filled is to lie on it. When you do that, your body should lie in a straight plane from head to toes. If the mattress is not full enough, you will feel like you are sinking in the middle. This could cause you to get a backache. On an overfilled mattress your body will arch and your stomach will feel higher than your head. Fill the mattress until it is comfortable for you.

14. When you have turned off the water and removed the hose from the fill valve, you will need to "burp" the air bubbles out. Bubbles left in the mattress will encourage the growth of algae and also make disturbing noises. The valve probably telescoped into the water when you were testing the

firmness by lying on the bed, so fish it out and open it. Don't worry about the water spurting out, it won't. With a broom push any bubbles toward the open valve. You can do this with your hands or the hands of your helper or even by lying on the bed, but it will be easier to do with the flat side of a broom. If you have an air frame type of mattress, the air bubbles will form mostly where the air and water meet so pay particular attention to those places. The "burping" job will be much simpler when two people do it, one to hold up the fill valve on one side of the bed and urge the bubbles out while the other pushes the bubbles from his or her side.

15. When the mattress has been satisfactorily filled with water, plug in the heater and set the thermostatic controls. If you have a dog that enjoys flotation sleeping, don't worry about his claws puncturing the mattress; however, his chewing the vinyl will damage it. Cat's claws can puncture a mattress so use a pad or keep them off while you are changing the sheets.

16. Today most store-bought waterbeds use regular linen. To use foam pads or blankets underneath a sleeper will tend to inhibit the true feeling of flotation. For those who insist on a cold bed, a mattress pad will absorb the body ash and moisture from condensation, the result being a too cold bed. While this reduces the clammy feeling of the sheets, it will tend to accelerate the deterioration of the vinyl.

If you suspect that you have a leak in the mattress, check that it is not condensation. If the beads of moisture disappear when the bed heats up to warmer than the room temperature, check if it is condensation. If the beads of moisture do not begin to disappear, you have a leak. If new dampness appears, you are sure to have a leak. Some leak patch kits claim to stop small leaks without the necessity of draining the mattress of water. Finding the leak so that you can patch it is a time consuming job at best, although patching the leak is simple.

To drain the mattress, first unplug the heater. Insert one end of the garden hose in the fill valve and tape it so it won't slip out. To start the syphoning action the hose must be filled with water so attach it to a faucet and turn on the water until it comes out at the bed end, then turn off the tap and the water will start to flow through the hose, draining the mattress.

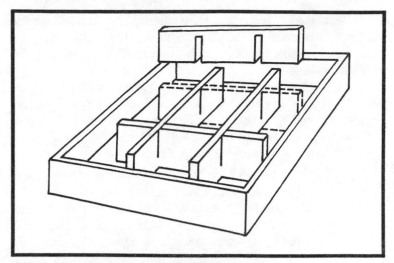

Fig. 3-38. Pedestal base waterbed with storage inserts.

To hasten this draining, the other end of the hose should be lower than the mattress, the lower the better. If the bed is below ground level, you will have to pump the water out. You can probably borrow a syphon pump that operates against gravity, from your waterbed dealer. The syphoning process operates with, not against gravity. It is a good idea before you start the draining to consider the best place to dispose of the several hundred gallons of water. A greater drop will empty the mattress faster, so if it is available, you can attach several lengths of hose together.

Once the mattress has been emptied of water, the best way to test for the location of the leak is to use the leak test of an automobile inner tube. If you have or can get hold of a canister vacuum cleaner, use that to inflate the mattress with air. With the mattress filled with air, spray it with soapy water, especially the seams. Any leaks should become evident by bubbles formed with the air escaping through the soapy film, even pinhole leaks.

A very small leak may be mended by applying glue from the patch kit applied in several layers. Let each layer dry several hours before applying the next unless you hasten the drying with a hair dryer set on cool. When you have patched one leak, do not stop testing until you are certain that there are no others. This is too lengthy a process to have to repeat because you overlooked another leak or a bad place in a seam. The same thing that caused the leak you discovered and mended may have caused another.

If you should need to store the waterbed mattress, do not fold it. Empty it of water and let it thoroughly dry, then roll it loosely. Do not store it or the safety liner in a hot or cold place—room temperature is the best.

Earlier I suggested that you use components, both store-bought ones and unfinished. If you do the finishing yourself, you can use some wood finishing tips. As in the case of finishing any wood, careful preparation of the surface is the secret of success.

For a successful staining job proceed as follows:

1. Fill all of the small cracks in the grain and any knots with wood putty to match the color of the wood.
2. Sand off any rough spots with a final sanding with fine grit paper. Too much or too little sanding in one spot will result in a blotchy appearance when you apply the stain.
3. When you buy stain or paint, always have the store shake it well in their vibrating machine, then when you open the can before you apply it, stir the pigments thoroughly.
4. If you are staining the wood, wipe it on, covering all surfaces evenly.
5. Give the stain a few minutes to penetrate before wiping off all excess with a dry, absorbent rag.
6. Allow this to dry at least a few hours, preferably over night.
7. Apply the sealing coat or coats.

When you are painting the wood, fill and sand it, as in steps 1 and 2 for staining, before applying the paint. Always allow each coat of paint to dry thoroughly before applying the next. Unless you want a higher gloss than will be produced by the paint alone, you will not need to use a seal coat.

Among the seals are varnish, lacquer, urethane and oil. The varnish, lacquer and urethane produce a hard, glossy appearance. For this reason they need to be applied carefully in two or more coats. Between each of these coats, fine sand after allowing substantial drying time, which is usually around 12 hours. Follow the instructions on the can and the advice of the salesman where you bought it. Be sure to remove all sanding dust before applying the next coat.

The oils, linseed or Danish, produce a softer sheen. Apply them with a dry, clean rag in several coats, one right after the other. After more fine sanding, you can apply wood wax over the oil.

Always work with finishing materials in a well-ventilated area and away from fire, heat or pilot lights. Turpentine and oil-soaked rags must be disposed of safely and at once. They can ignite spontaneously without a spark or flame. A friend of mine had her "dream house" gutted from leaving an oily rag, which she had been using on the furniture, for only the few minutes that it took to run over to the neighbor's for a little more oil to finish the job. Spontaneous combustion did it.

Waterbed manufacturers have not been content to rest on their laurels, or should we say mattresses? Figure 3-39 shows two examples of what their designers have to offer in king and queen sizes.

The Wavecrest people have turned out a watermattress that is hydrodynamically engineered to calm the wave motion of the water within the mattress and to prevent what is called "bottoming out." This watermattress carries the trade name of "Tranquil Rest."

Within this lap-seamed mattress are diamond-shaped chambers that interrupt any wave action and make "bottoming out" impossible. One dealer offers to combine the advantages of this design and that of the one shown in Fig. 3-39.

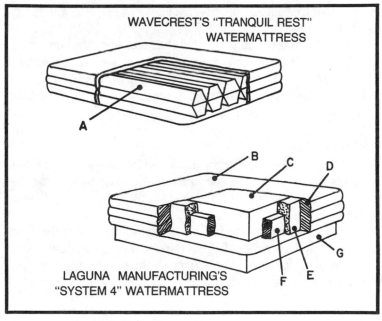

Fig. 3-39. Two waterbed innovations.
    A. Diamond-shaped chambers.
    B. Removable damask cover.
    C. Wedge shaped sides.
    D. Safety liner.
    E. Wedge shaped from soft sides.
    F. Solid wood frame from embedded foam sides.
    G. Platform.

Laguna Manufacturing has developed this second mattress. It is a heated, soft sided waterbed in a variety of styles that will fit into the decor of any bedroom. They have given this one the trade name of "System 4." It is identical in size and appearance to conventional innerspring mattresses so that standard king or queen sheets and other bedding can be used on it.

The high density foam creates soft sides to the bed to overcome the objection that some waterbeds are difficult to get into or out of and almost impossible to sit on the side of while removing or putting on one's slippers. Imbedded in this soft side frame is a solid wood beam for added support and stability. The foam framing is wedge shaped. The conforming wedge shape of the watermattress cuts down on the volume of water needed to fill the mattress by about 25 percent, which decreases the weight and the time required to fill or empty the mattress of its water.

The entire unit is encased by a damask cover that can be removed for cleaning. A lot of technology is going into waterbeds these days.

If you have made up your mind that you want the comfort of sleeping on the flotation surface provided by a waterbed, don't waste your money on a cheap bed. Now that you fully understand what is involved, build or buy, but our advice is to investigate personally before you come to a decision.

WATERBED PILLOW CHAIR

Waterbed pillows are also available, in fact several firms listed in Tables 3-7 and 3-8 specialize in them. Why not build a chair to contain such a pillow and enjoy flotation sitting and snoozing? Figure 3-40 shows one such chair.

Unless you want a waterbed pillow custom made to fit the chair you build, you will be wise to find out the size that these pillows come in that are in regular stock. The chair can be built for two persons and makes a cozy snuggle spot.

BEANBAG BED

The beanbag bed is something that you can easily make from scratch because it is filled with styrene foam pellets that won't leak. These pellets are light in weight, statically charged and make a comfortable sleeping surface. You can make this bed any size you want by using dimensions other than those shown on the pattern in Fig. 3-41.

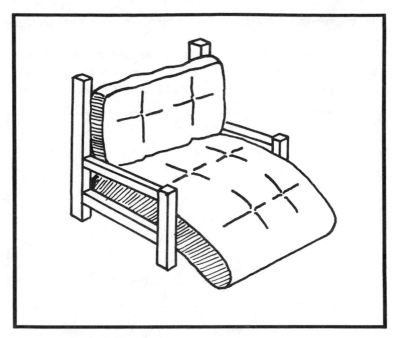

Fig. 3-40. Waterbed pillow chair.

To make this giant cushion in a double bed size and extra long, 54 by 78 inches, with a thickness of about 8 inches, you will need about 8 yards of 60 inch wide closely woven fabric for the outer covering. The inside bag takes 8 yards of muslin, and 30 pounds of styrene foam pellets. Two 72 inch long zippers are needed and these are the most expensive items. The zippers will enable you to remove the cover for laundering and to get at the styrene pellet stuffing in the inner bag.

The beanbag can be placed on a bed or chair frame if it is made to fit, or it can be put on the floor like a sleeping bag. The cover can be of sailcloth, a heavy canvas, corduroy or even Naugahyde.

One of the advantages of the beanbag is that it can be emptied and folded up to store on moving day. It offers a sleeping surface that yields easily to body pressures. It comes closer to offering the flotation sensation of the waterbed than any other sleeping surface, yet it is simple to make.

To make a beanbag bed, cut out the ten pieces as shown in Fig. 3-41 and sew them into a tube. The seams in the muslin inner bag should be 5/8-inch and those in the cover ½-inch. This ⅛-inch difference results in a slightly smaller inner bag that will slip into the outer covering, however it will be a snug fit that does not encourage creases.

Sew the zippers into the seams at the bottom center of both inner and outer bags so that they will be opposite each other and when you open the outer bag the zipper in the inner bag will be right

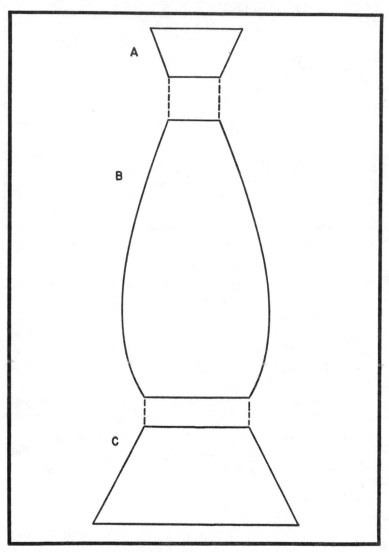

Fig. 3-41. Beanbag bed patterns.
    A. Top (2).
    B. Sides (6).
    C. Bottom (2).

there. Place the muslin inner bag inside the cover and straighten it out before filling.

From heavy brown (manila) paper, such as a large grocery sack, make a funnel. Using this funnel, fill the muslin liner about two-thirds full of styrene foam pellets and zip it up. Check that the filled liner extends to all parts of the cover, then zip it up. Your beanbag bed is now ready for use.

The beanbag can be used on a chair in the same manner as the waterbed pillow shown in Fig. 3-40. It can be used in the place of a mattress on flat bed springs or a woven, laced base. If you build the bed or chair first, adjust the dimensions of the beanbag to crowd into the frame snugly. It can stand plenty of fullness as long as the frame is built to retain it. Any capable bed builder can make this beanbag bed successfully.

While your scope of designer beds is wide, you can no doubt think up many variations. You will find that your success in building one of your own designs will encourage you and spur you on to exercise your design abilities further. Chapter 4 will deal with more complicated designs, exotic bed arrangements and accessory comforts surrounding the sleeping quarters.

Chapter 4

Conversation Piece Beds

Successful completion of any pet project is always sweeter if it solves a problem as well as fulfilling a desire. Since we spend around one-third of our lives in bed, it follows that a similar proportion of our problems will involve beds. It is the purpose of this book to aid you in solving this third of your problems.

Frequently these problems involve twin beds. When one of a couple prefers to sleep in a cold bed and the other feels the need of a warm bed to sleep comfortably; when one of a couple tosses and turns in his or her sleep, the other bed partner cannot get the rest required; when one of a couple likes to read himself or herself to sleep but doesn't want to disturb the other; when...but then you are already aware of the problems to which twin beds appear to be the answer.

But, twin beds can cause other problems. The physically separated pair will at times desire and need the intimacy afforded by a double bed. Also, when made up, a king-sized bed looks grander to visitors. Here is a way to "have your cake and eat it too."

PIVOTING TWINS

Your options in creating pivoting twin beds will depend on what you have to start with and what you want to end up with. First you need the adequate square footage, at least 9 by 12 feet, in your bedroom. If you are converting twin beds that you already have, the construction of their frames will determine how to proceed in converting them to pivoting twins. If you are building the headboard storage piece and the beds from scratch, you will proceed in another way. For this reason we must approach the projects separately as well as the options offered by each situation. In any case, you will end up with what appears to be a king-sized bed that looks something like the one in Fig. 4-1.

Whether you are converting existing twins or building from scratch, the frames should be constructed from or reinforced by 2 inch thick lumber. Another requisite is that each bed be mounted on orbital casters that permit them to move easily. The choice of casters is an important factor in the success of your project. Shepherd casters are the only kind that I am aware of that will fill the bill.

Orbital Casters

If the floor of your bedroom is carpeted, get eight Shepherd Planet-style casters (Fig. 4-2A). This is an all-metal caster, 2½-inches in diameter, with a metal tread and a 1½-inch mounting plate, that has a maximum mobility load rating of 100 pounds per caster.

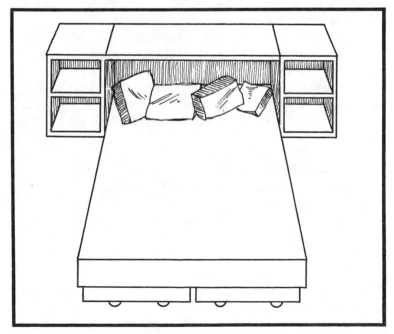

Fig. 4-1. Pivoting twin beds look king-size.

Allow 3 inches from the mounting to the floor. Although this caster is designed for use on carpeting, the manufacturer recommends that the load be moved every once in a while to prevent indentations in the pile of the carpet from the bed standing too long in one place.

If your bedroom has a hardwood or tile floor, get the Shepherd Saturn-style casters (Fig. 4-2B). This caster has a rubber tread that raises the overall mounting ¼-inch higher over the Planet style. This style has the same maximum mobility load rating of 100 pounds per caster. This means that the four casters together will take a 400 pound load under its 25 year guarantee. The diameter of this caster is 3 inches.

Should the bedroom floor be surfaced with a thin vinyl or linoleum, any caster will cause indentations to the depth of the surfacing. In this case, install carpeting at least over the area of the beds. Cement floors will tend to abrade any casters.

If you are using beds that you already have and they are fitted with grip or threaded stem casters, replace them with the orbital type. Plug the holes and cover them with a small square of wood that will provide a bit for the woodscrews that secure the mounting plates of the orbital casters. In figuring the height of the beds, do not forget to allow for the casters and the wood plate. The important thing is that you end up with both beds exactly the same height.

Do not try to move a bed while it is occupied. Not only will this put an undue strain in the pivoting structure and the bed, but it will do no good to the floor or the casters.

The casters will not be visible underneath the beds so their color and type of finish usually is immaterial. Details on mounting the casters and how you can control the heights of the beds will be given later.

Converting Existing Twin Beds

The conversion of existing twin beds to pivoting twins can be a simple job, providing the beds have existing sturdy frames. The frames must be reinforced and corner blocks installed to withstand the pull of the pivoting. The corner blocks can be utilized for the mounting of the casters as will be explained later with the discussion of building the beds from scratch.

Once you have sufficiently sturdy frames, reinforced by corner blocks, you can install on the head posts four heavy door hinges, but the beds will still look like twins (Fig. 4-3). The pins of the hinges must be put so that the beds can pivot properly.

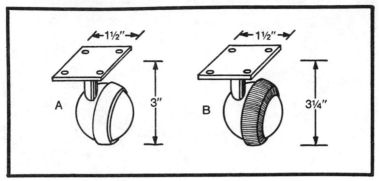

Fig. 4-2. Orbital casters.
    A Planet, for use on carpets.
    B Saturn, for use on hardwood or tile floors.

There will be a slight gap between the beds when they are closed up together. The width of this gap will depend on the thickness of the hinges at the head post. A slight overhang of the mattress and bedding should take care of this providing that the beds are latched together closely at the foot. A strong screw hook can be installed on the under edge of the foot rail of one bed so that it latches into a screw eye on the foot rail of the other bed. This arrangement will keep the two beds securely together when that position is desired, yet it will permit them to be quickly converted to twins or back to king size. The latch will eliminate the danger of the two beds sliding apart and letting an occupant fall into the crack.

The procedure of quickly converting existing twin beds to pivoting beds will depend on the structure of the beds at their heads. Strip the beds down to their frames and inspect how sturdy they are when pulled in a pivoting direction. Determine how well they will be able to withstand the stress of pivoting even on orbital casters with occupants. This will depend a great deal on the strength of the inside corners.

If the existing beds that you propose to use have headboards or if you propose to build a headboard as shown in Fig. 4-1, the headboards should be removed. They won't be needed and will only be in the way. Besides, two separate headboards and footboards will destroy the appearance of the two beds being a king-sized one, as shown in Fig. 4-3.

Beds that have headboards usually have head posts. These can be left if you do not plan to build the uniting headboard. They can be connected as shown in Fig. 4-4, using several heavy hinges. The

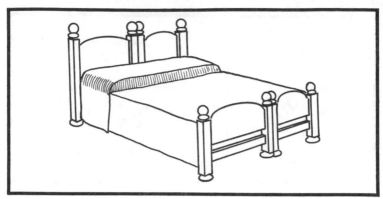

Fig. 4-3. Pivoting twins.

width of the leaves of these hinges will depend on the width of the head posts unless you bend the hinge leaves of longer hinges to an offset as shown in Fig. 4-5C or apply a filler block to the head rail as shown in Fig. 4-5D. If you do either of these, you can use 10 inch "barn door" hinges. Any of these methods will require reinforcement of the frames as shown in Fig. 4-5.

To reinforce the rails, run 2 inch thick reinforcements the full length inside the head and side and foot rails, fastening them to the existing rails with heavy woodscrews or bolts. The width of these 2-by reinforcements should, if possible, be 6 inches. At each corner, inside the reinforcement rails, install a reinforcing block (Fig. 4-5B). Bore two holes in each block at an angle so that large sized woodscrews will bite into the reinforcing rails and extend into the existing frame. Of course this short-cut method of pivoting existing beds is only a make-do conversion. There is nothing to anchor these beds in place and there is still another drawback.

Look at Fig. 4-6 and you will see this drawback for yourself. Even using one of the quick conversion methods, the heads of the beds are the standard 48 inches in width and their lengths will be 84 inches. In order for these beds to pivot so that the inner corners of the foot of one will swing approximately 5 feet away, the outer corner at the head must swing in an arc about 12 inches back toward the wall. If the beds are not set out that distance from the wall, especially if they are not anchored, the wall will get marred when they are pivoted.

Since this space must be left vacant in any case, why not utilize it for bed lights, blanket storage, a bedside library and knicknacks? At the same time a headboard unit will protect the wall and enhance the appearance of the "king-sized" bed.

Headboard Unit

In this discussion it will be presumed that the twin beds are 48 inches wide and have no head posts nor headboards of their own. From the dimensions given in Fig. 4-6, it is readily apparent that without requiring any more space you can build and set in a head-board unit that takes up 144 inches (12 feet) along the wall. This unit will occupy the 12 inches of space that the heads of the beds must be set out from the wall to allow for the pivoting. This will put this space to good use while it protects the wall from being marred. The lid of the middle section, appropriate for the storage of blankets, when closed, should be at an ideal height for separate reading lamps while the shelves on either side provide bookshelf space reachable from

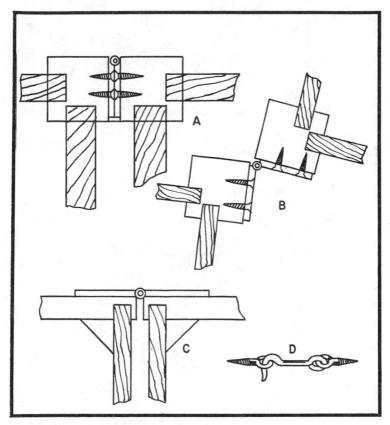

Fig. 4-4. Quick pivot conversions with sturdy frames.
    A. Hinged head posts, closed.
    B. Hinged head posts, open.
    C. Hinge linking head rails.
    D. Latch for foot of beds.

the beds. You can build the headboard unit whether you build the beds from scratch or use twin beds that you already have.

Note on Fig. 4-6 that at full pivot the arcs of the outer corners of the heads of the twin beds need almost 12 inches between their

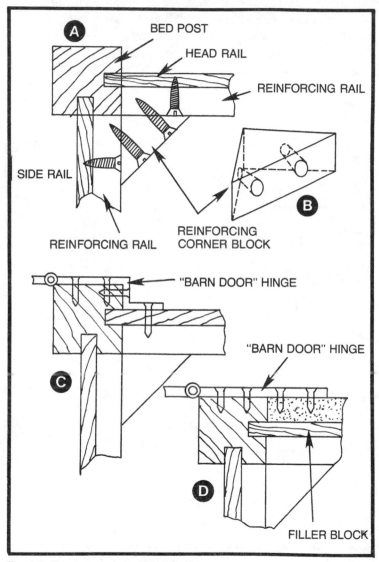

Fig. 4-5. Pivot conversion with reinforcing.
 A. Reinforcing the frames.
 B. Corner block.
 C. Contouring hinge.
 D. Filler block.

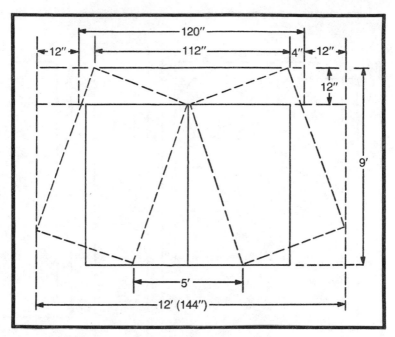

Fig. 4-6. Pivoting arcs space requirements.

unpivoted position and the wall. When fully pivoted, the outer corners of the heads will need a space nearly 124 inches wide while the outer corners at the foot will extend approximately 144 inches (12 feet) when the foot of the beds are about 5 feet apart. With these constraints in mind, it is evident that the headboard unit will require no additional space.

These dimensions presume that the beds being used are each 48 inches wide by 84 inches long. If the beds are of a different size, you will need only to adjust the dimensions given to accommodate the beds you are using. It is also presumed that the surface of both beds is no higher than 16 inches. If the beds are higher off the floor, you will need more escape room between the top surface of the beds and the bottom of the middle compartment of the headboard unit, also adjust the measurements of the pivot structure accordingly.

The fourteen components of the headboard unit should be cut from ¾-inch thick plywood to exact measurements. Six of these can be cut from plywood veneered on one side to match the other furniture in the bedroom, unless you prefer to paint all of the surfaces. Lightly sand any rough edges, insure that the edges are straight and the corners square, but take care that the veneer is not marred.

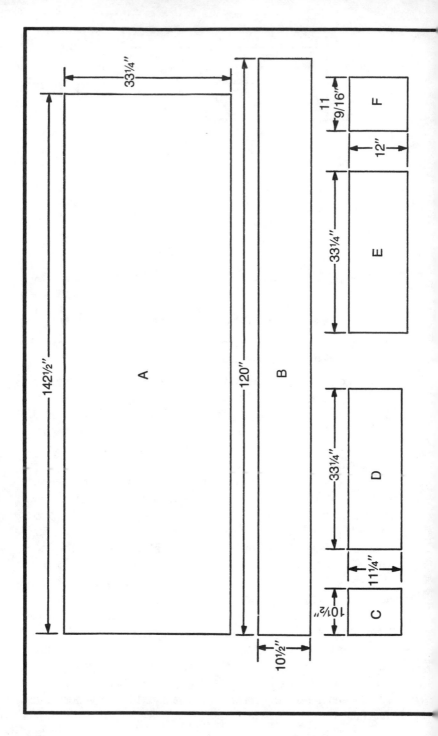

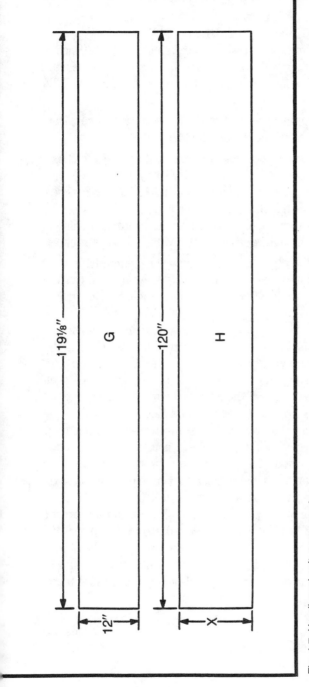

Fig. 4-7. Headboard unit components.
A. Back panel (1), plain.
B. Middle component shelf (1), plain.
C. End unit shelves (4), plain.
D. Inside side panels (2), plain.
E. Outside side panels (2), veneer one side.
F. End unit stops (2), veneer one side.
G. Hinged lid of middle compartment (1), veneer one side.
H. Facing (1), veneer one side.

Cut the components (Fig. 4-7) as follows:

From ¾-inch thick plywood, plain finish, cut:

(A)—One back panel 33¼ by 142½ inches

(B)—One middle compartment shelf 10½ by 120 inches

(C)—Four end unit side panels 11½ by 11¼ inches

(D)—Two inside end unit side panels 11½ by 33¼ inches

If you are using the veneered finish on the outside pieces, from ¾-inch thick plywood veneered on one side, cut:

(E)—Two outside end unit panels 12 by 34¼ inches

(F)—Two end unit tops 11 15/16 by 12 inches

(G)—One middle compartment lid 12 by 119⅞ inches

(H)—One middle compartment facing 120 inches long by a width to be determined after the headboard unit and both beds have been assembled with the pivot structure

In addition to the plywood pieces you will need four hinges (lid to back panel), about 30 feet of ¾-inch wide finishing tape (for the raw edges of the plywood), finishing materials, adhesive and finishing nails.

Assemble twelve of the fourteen plywood components shown in Fig. 4-7, laying aside the middle compartment shelf (B) and the facing (H) until the completion and assembly of the headboard unit, the beds and the pivot structure. Move them into place. The shelf (B) must be installed on top of the pivot structure and the facing (H) cannot be cut to size nor installed until the last thing.

In building the headboard unit use finish nails, setting their heads, and adhesive. Since many of the nails go into the edge thickness of the plywood, it is a good idea to first dip the nails into adhesive before pounding them in since they are apt to go between the plies. Be sure to wipe off any surplus glue before it can set.

To assist you in placing the pieces of plywood in their proper position, straight and true, it is a good idea to mark with a pencil and square the position of each component on the back panel. It will also help to draw in the center line down as far as the shelf. Be sure to note which pieces and on which side panels are veneered so that you will be sure to place the veneered side out.

Proceed to assemble the headboard unit as follows, referring to Fig. 4-8. Work on a clean, level place so that all bottom edges are even and the unit won't wobble.

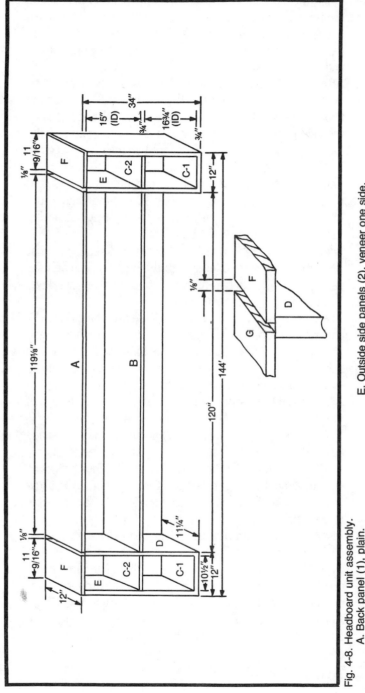

Fig. 4-8. Headboard unit assembly.
A. Back panel (1), plain.
B. Middle compartment shelf (1), plain.
C. End unit shelves (4), plain.
D. Inside side panels (2), plain.
E. Outside side panels (2), veneer one side.
F. Top of end units (2), veneer one side.
G. Hinged lid of middle compartment (1), veneer one side.
H. Facing (1), veneer one side.

249

1. Bring the two outside end section panels up and fasten them on the 24 inch edges of the back panel. The bottom edges of these panels should be even, the top of the end panels coming ¾-inch above the top edge of the back panel, and of course with the veneered sides out.

2. Attach the bottoms of the end sections inside the lower ends of the outside panels so that the unit will sit flat on the floor. The shelves (C-1) butt against the back panel (A) and the side panels (B). They need not be veneered and the three sides and back will be covered so that they need not be taped, only the front.

3. Insert the middle shelves of the end units (C-2) so that their bottom surfaces are exactly 16¾-inches above the top surface of the bottom shelves (C-1). Before attaching them check that they will be level.

4. Install the inner side panels (D) of the end section so that the bottom edges are level with the outer panels and the back panel. Check carefully that both shelves are level before attaching them.

5. The end section tops are next. These are designated (E) and are veneered on the top side. They go over the side panels and the back panel, however they should cover only half of the edge of the inside side panels, leaving a slight gap (about 1/16-inch) to allow the lid to close and rest on the other half of that edge. This is the reason why the tops of the shelf units are 1/16-inch short of the 12 inches.

6. The middle compartment lid (G) should fit into the space left between the two shelf tops if you have cut it exactly 119⅛-inches long. Center the lid and install four hinges as shown in Fig. 4-9, countersinking the hinges neatly to allow the lid to close down level when it rests on the facing that is to be installed later.

7. Install a lift knob on the center line of the lid an inch or so back from the front edge.

8. Using this knob, lift open and close the lid and make any needed alterations so that it will operate properly. Remember to be careful not to mar the veneer with sanding.

9. Apply the ¾-inch finishing tape to all exposed raw plywood edges. This tape should match the veneer. The following edges will need tape (Fig. 4-8):

   (1) Front of lid (G)

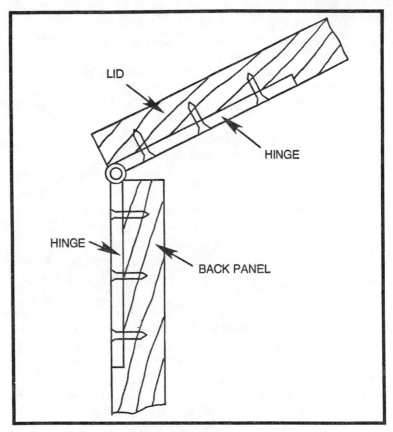

Fig. 4-9. Hinged lid installation.

     (2) Front and outer side of both end unit tops (F)
     (3) Front of the two outer side panels (E)
     (4) Front of the two inner side panels (D)
     (5) Front of the two bottom shelves (C-1)
     (6) Front of the two middle shelves (C-2)

10. Apply seal to all veneered surfaces and the tape.
11. Paint the other surfaces, preferably in a darker color for contrast.
12. Allow the seal and the paint to dry thoroughly and the adhesive to set while you build the pivot structure.

Pivoting Structure

The pivot structure for these twin beds requires the following materials:

One pivot post, 4-by-4, 18 inches high

Four angle braces, 2-by-4, 9½ inches long (plus allowance for angle cuts at both ends)

Two central braces, 2-by-4, 4½ inches long (plus allowance for angle cuts)

Two back spacers, 2-by-4, 14 inches long (plus allowance for angle cuts)

Four heavy hinges, preferably of the loose pin type

Screws, nails, glue and finishing materials

The heaviness of the pieces plus the weight of the headboard unit will help to stabilize the pivoting of the beds. This avoids the need of connecting any of the arrangements into the wall. However, if you do want to tie it into the wall, use butterfly bolts or others as appropriate. These can be placed anywhere along the two back stretchers (Fig. 4-10G) where they will hit suds or other structural members. These four small holes can be patched if the need arises later.

The height of the upright pivot (Fig. 4-10A) will depend somewhat on the height and structure of the beds. The taller this post is, the more shallow will be the middle storage compartment of the headboard until because the shelf of this compartment rests on top of the pivot post and the two topmost angle braces (Fig. 4-10B). The shelf is secured to these members by woodscrews and serves to anchor the headboard unit in place so that it will not require anchoring to the wall and thus entailing more holes.

Two heavy hinges attach each bed to the pivot post (Figs. 4-10 and 4-11). At the extreme of its arc the head of the pivoted bed will rest against the angle brace on that side. For this reason it must escape the middle compartment shelf that rests on top of the pivot post and the uppermost angle brace. This of course would be impossible if the beds have head posts or headboards. The length of the middle compartment of the headboard unit (Fig. 4-7) allows the outer top corner of the beds to swing to full pivot, leaving about 4 inches between the sides and the end units of shelves.

To assemble the pivot structure (Figs. 4-10 and 4-11) first find the center line of the beds, which will be along the meeting place of the two inner rails. Install the two back spacers, above and below against the wall, using the appropriate fasteners, so that they are securely fastened center line to center line. The ends of the two back spacers will have to be cut on the proper angle to take the angle braces (B) and allow their ends to also fit snugly against the wall. The angle of this cut will also be parallel with the back face of the pivot post.

Both ends of the angle braces (B) must also be cut to fit against the wall and the face of the pivot post (A). Connect the members of

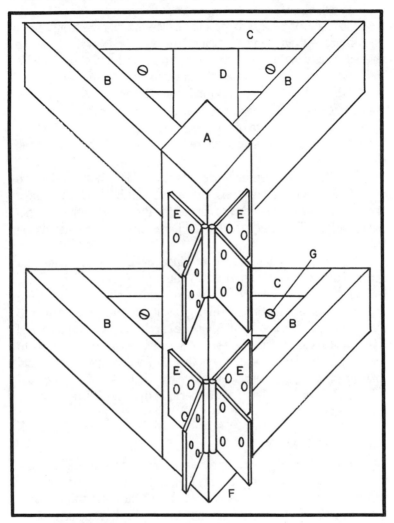

Fig. 4-10. Pivot structure.
    A. Pivot post (1).
    B. Angle braces (4).
    D. Back stretchers (2).
    D. Center braces (2).
    E. Hinges (4).
    F. Junction of wall and floor.
    G. Wall fasteners. (4).

the pivot structure using large common or box nails and sink their heads well into the wood. The pivot structure will not be visible from the room as it will be below the top surface of the beds and under the headboard unit, but at any rate, it should be painted a "shadow color" such as dull black.

Install the pivot post to the angle braces so that the front corner points directly out between where the two beds will sit and be aligned exactly to the center line out from the wall and at right angles to it. Now you can determine the angles at which the two central braces (D) must be cut to fit into and brace the pivot post (A) and the angle braces (B). To make these angles more accurately make a pattern by laying a piece of heavy manila paper on top of the back stretchers (C) and creasing it where it joins the angle braces (B) and the pivot post (A).

Install the two center braces (D) by nailing them to the two angle braces and the pivot post at the top and bottom of the pivot structure. Now you are ready to install the hinges. Heavy, loose pin door hinges will do very nicely, the loose pins making installation easier.

If you are using the type of hinge as has been suggested, remove the pins. It will be easier to get at the screws. Attach each leaf using long, heavy screws to the bed frame as shown in Figs. 4-10 and 4-11. Be sure that the screws go well into the reinforcing or 2 inch wood and get a good bite. Measure carefully, the way you would if you were hanging a door. After installing the leaves of the hinges to the beds and the pivot post, check that they will properly mesh and that the pins slip in easily. Now move the beds out of the way and bring in the headboard unit after checking that the finishes are dry and the glue set.

Putting It All Together

Position the headboard unit over the pivot structure against the wall so that the center lines are aligned. If the bedroom wall against which the pivoting twin beds with the headboard unit will sit has a baseboard that projects out from the wall, the back of the unit will sit out from the wall for that thickness above the baseboard. This space will give you the opportunity of further protecting the wall by gluing padding to the back of the back panel to fill this space. Felt or carpeting is a good filler and can be glued in spots to the back of the back panel to act as a cushion. This setout also enables the middle compartment lid to be raised without marring the wall.

254

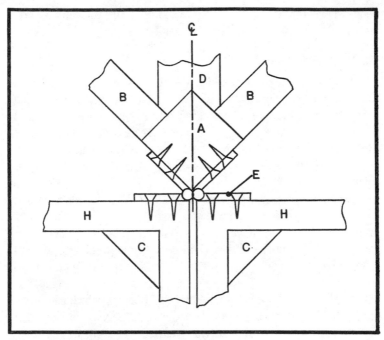

Fig. 4-11. Bed frame connection to pivot structure.
   A. Pivot post.
   B. Angle braces.
   C. Center braces.
   D. Pivot structure.
   E. Hinges.
   H. Bed frames.

When you have completed this precaution and located the headboard unit properly, install at least six heavy woodscrews through the middle compartment shelf down into the top of the pivot post structure, into the post and the top angle braces. When you have secured the pivot structure, complete installation of the shelf between the two inside side panels.

Some paint touchup may be needed, but do not place the beds yet. Paint the pivot structure, preferably a "shadow" color and the under side of the shelf that rests on it. The same "shadow" color can be used on the plywood surfaces that are not veneered.

When all finishes are dry, it is time to move up the beds into place and install the hinge pins. Check that the beds pivot properly and that all is in order. Now you have pivoting twin beds that close up to look like a king-sized bed with a handy shelf unit on each side for books and knicknacks and a bed reading light at the head of each bed. If you have done your carpentry elsewhere, like on a level garage floor, you've kept the sawdust out of the bedroom and can now flop on one of your pivoting beds for a well-earned rest.

GUEST CUBE SQUARED

In Chapter 3 we discussed how to build guest quarters, but in case you couldn't find such a place in your house that you could convert, here is another idea that will provide guest sleeping places with some measure of privacy. You need a large closet 8 feet wide by 6 feet six inches deep. Remove the door—you'll need the ventilation because few closets have windows. The door can be used as a partial partition (Fig. 4-12).

Stand the door up between the heads of the two beds and run a wire from the top of the door to the middle of the top of the door frame (Fig. 4-13), which we presume is located in the middle of the wall on that side of the closet. The doorway is probably about 78 inches high, which is high enough to provide privacy. On this wire hang a drape or a sheet, even a piece of muslin will do nicely. The entry doorway will not be blocked by this curtain, which can be as high as 18 inches from the floor. Although only 12 inches is allowed in Fig. 4-13 on either side of the dividing curtain, your guests can make their way to bed past this flexible barrier.

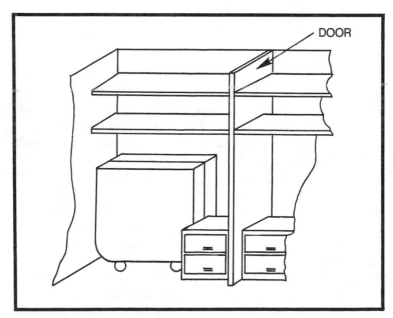

Fig. 4-12. Temporary guest cube.

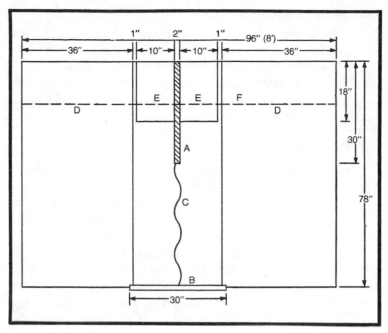

Fig. 4-13. Guest cube floor plan.
   A. Door partition.
   B. Removed from entry doorway.
   C. Curtain.
   D. Beds.
   E. Bedside built-ins.
   F. Existing shelves.

Presuming that the door that serves as a partial partition between the heads of the two beds is about an inch thick, a little over 10 inches will be left on either side between the door and the beds. In this space build a bedside table (Fig. 4-13E) extending outward 18 inches. Under the tabletop build two drawers. A bedside lamp can be attached to the wall or set on the tabletop by the head of each of the beds. Two hooks can be put up on either side of the door partition on which the guests may hang up clothing. This completes all of the necessities.

Should you want to use this area for storage again after your guests have departed, build everything the same only use fold-up beds as shown in Fig. 4-12. Fold-up beds can be pushed back by the built-in units, the wire and curtain taken down and the door rehung in its original place. In no time you have a storage closet again.

If you are building the two beds, keep them low and you won't need to remove any shelves (Fig. 4-13F) that the closet may have unless they are lower than 6 feet from the floor. If such a shelf exists across the back wall of the closet, saw out a slot for the door that you are using for a partial partition to slip into. This will secure it at the top. With two pieces of quarter round molding you can make a slot on the floor and just slide the door into these slots without the necessity of nailing it in place. When your guests depart, just slide the door out of the slot and return it to its original place as the door to the closet.

SLEEPING WEDGES

Using an even smaller area, sleeping wedges for three guests can be provided in a space as small as 6 feet wide by 6 feet, 6 inches long, providing there is an 8-foot high ceiling. Only one person will have to climb to his bed and then only 4 feet up (Fig. 4-14). This design is especially appropriate for studios and cabins.

Wedge four 2-by-4s between the floor and the ceiling so that they form a V. The poles from which sailcloth or canvas hang (Fig. 4-14C) are attached to the 2-by-4 V. These 2-by-4s separate the three foam mattresses, (Fig. 4-14A) on the floor and (Fig. 4-14B) set 4 feet up, and are secured on a ¾-inch thick plywood base in the crotch of the V. This bed is reached by a short ladder suspended from the outer end of the lower pole on the side.

The shelf above bed B is optional. It will be convenient for a bed light, a radio or a stereo. The area needed for these three beds will be determined by the width of the two floor level mattresses and the depth will be determined by the length of the mattresses or pads. These sleeping wedges are about as simple as possible to accommodate three individual sleepers in a small area.

ATTIC SLEEPER

Don't waste that space between the ceiling and a slanted roof. Many recreational cabins have such a space, and there never are enough beds to sleep all of the guests, to say nothing of the owners.

If the area is not floored, floor only where you need to step and where the bed will roll, the rest can be used for storage space and so it won't need flooring. Insulate the ceiling if temperatures get overly hot or cold. The heat will rise through the opening you need to make for access. Before flooring the area, check that the ceiling beams will take the weight, usually they will. If there is none, you will need an access ladder, permanently installed or removable.

Build a trundle bed (Fig. 4-15A) and mount it on easy rolling casters (not orbital because it should roll straight out and back).

Make the trundle bed sufficiently long so that when it is pushed back into its cubbyhole, it will protrude far enough to form a sofa. (Note the dotted lines.) In most cases the trundle bed can be a double to accommodate two people.

Into the angles formed by the slope of the roof, which is usually steep in cabins, you can build hang-up spaces for clothing, cabinets and shelves. Carpet the floor, install windows for ventilation, or portholes in the gables, and provide illumination (discussed in detail in the next chapter.) You will profit by this comfortable attic "found space."

FOLD-UP SLING PIPE BED

If you have the tools to work with pipe, including welding equipment, you can build a sling bed that will fold up and can be used indoors or out. When not in use, this sling can be folded flat (Fig. 4-16).

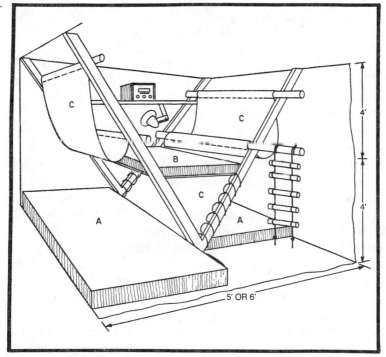

Fig. 4-14. Sleeping wedges.
    A. Floor level beds.
    B. Elevated bed.
    C. Sailcloth divider curtains.

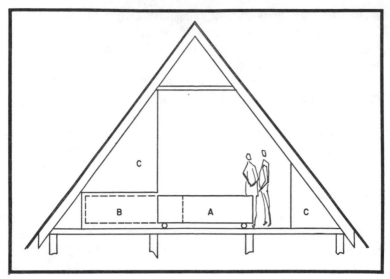

Fig. 4-15. Attic sleeper.
    A. Trundle bed.
    B. Bed push-back space.
    C. Shelf, cabinet and hang-up space.

A ¾-inch thick plywood base sits on the pipe frame (A) and on this base is placed a foam pad. The frame hinges on bolts through the standards (C) at the back side. The front corners of the frame rest on stops (B) that are welded to the front legs (C). Heavy chains (D) between both pairs of standards limit the spread of the legs and keep the frame resting on the stops.

Across the top between the two pairs of standards at E is either another heavy chain or a stretcher pipe. This should be welded to the inner of the two legs at each end. When the bed is used out-of-doors, a canvas can be thrown over this pipe or chain and hang down each side where it is laced. In this manner a poncho or other waterproof covering will protect the sleeper. Crutch tips (F), placed over the bottom ends of the pipe standards, will prevent them from marring the surface on which the sling sits as well as deter it from slipping.

The sling is made of ¾-inch common plumber's pipe or, if you prefer, heavy aluminum tubing. If iron or steel pipe is used, paint it with rust preventive paint. The bolts and chain used should match the material of the pipe. Never combine iron or steel with aluminum as it will set up an electrolytic action.

The sling pipe bed can be easily folded flat for storage in little space. The bed frame, after removing the plywood base to which the foam mattress should be attached, leaves only the bed frame and the collapsed two pairs of standards. Folded, the whole thing will only take up less space than the foam pad. Fold-up sling pipe beds are good to take along when you are camping.

SIESTA TREE HOUSE

For a quiet siesta or meditation there is nothing like a tree house. The design of this get-away spot must be adapted to the conformation of the particular tree you propose to use (Fig. 4-17). Holes and notches in the structure must be made for the protruding branches. You can protect the limbs with canvas sleeves and no nails need be driven into the tree since the platform is secured by lashing

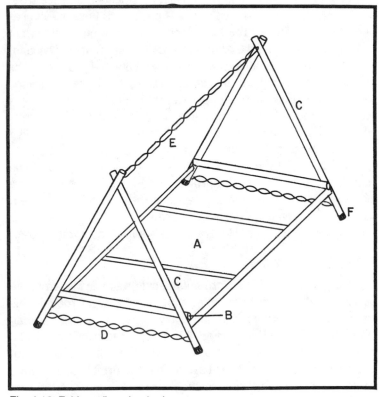

Fig. 4-16. Fold-up sling pipe bed.
    A. Frame for bed, plywood base (folds upward).
    B. Stop for frame to rest on.
    C. Standards hinged at top on bolt.
    D. Limiting chains, foot and head.
    E. Limiting chain or pipe top.
    F. Crutch tips.

with ¼-inch marine rope. This type of rope will not stretch. Before selecting these branches, be sure to test them for strength.

The dimensions of your siesta house will depend somewhat on the conformation of the tree, as will the size of the foam mattress and where it fits into the branches. The sleeping pad is shaded by a roll up bamboo blind from above. The blind rolls down the slatted framework from the peak, where it is secured. To keep the blind in place in spite of any wind, run a cord down each edge and tie it off. On the back of the framework, laths with spaces left in between will allow for ventilation.

Access to the siesta tree house is by ladder. The ladder should be built on a pole notched to take pole rungs secured by bolts. If you've ever tried to climb a rope ladder suspended under a tree, you'll understand why the pole type is preferred. For appearances only, tie raffia around the rungs and supporting pole but do not depend on this to hold the rungs in place, it just isn't strong enough.

It will be a good idea to arrange it so that once you are on the platform, you can pull up the ladder, locking the door so to speak. Most likely your siesta tree house can only support one person at a time safely. You should also be able to "lock the door" from below when leaving the sanctuary to prevent invasion by the curious. Just rig the ladder to pull up and tie off out of reach of youngsters.

You can paint the outside of the tree house a gay color if you want it to be seen from the ground. If you want it to truly be a hide-away, paint it a green that resembles the foliage of the tree. Since a soft green is condusive to meditation, the interior surfaces can be painted this tone. Decorate or leave it plain as you choose.

FOR FLOOR PEOPLE ONLY

If you and your friends are floor people, take an idea from the Japanese and furnish one room or a corner of a larger room in this serene Oriental manner. Around a low table supply large seating pillows that are called banjar (Fig. 4-18A), covered in muted Oriental prints. Line up several banjar pillows along the wall and back them with smaller cushions and you have built a comfortable sofa, that is, for people who enjoy sitting on the floor.

For guest sleeping, a Shiki can be spread on the floor. This is a thin sized, well-padded mat (Fig. 4-18B). Over the Shiki tuck a Futon. This is a soft but thick quilt (Fig. 4-18C). At the head place a Makura (Fig. 4-18D) for a head rest. While this three-piece set would cost you around $120 or more if it were store-bought, you can

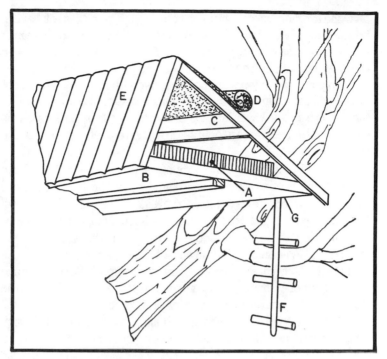

Fig. 4-17. Siesta Tree House.
   A. Foam pad attached to plywood base.
   B. Plywood bed base and floor.
   C. Frame of 2-by-4s tied to strong limbs.
   D. Roll up bamboo blind.
   E. Lattice.
   F. Ladder.
   G. Canvas sleeves.

make it yourself for much less if you can use a sewing machine, then you'll have just the spot for an overnight guest or for lounging, that is, if you're floor people.

To add to these, try to obtain a cable spool. These can be easily converted into a fine round, low table. Since these spools are made of fairly rough wood, I have learned the hard way, from experience, that it is just about as easy to cut it out of plywood and some 2-by-4s as to find and refine a genuine cable spool that will fit into your living room. I finally used mine on the patio where any roughness passes for rusticness. To find one you'll either have to be really lucky or haunt where they are building apartments, after the workmen have left. I did see one at a salvage yard once.

A cable spool table isn't all that difficult to build from scratch, providing that you can saw out the round top and bottom. Use ¾-inch plywood for these pieces, plain or veneered. The edges will have to be taped with ¾-inch, to match the veneer if you use that. No matter how well you can saw the plywood round, the edges will be too rough to leave unfinished. The tape should match the veneer.

To connect the top with the base, use either a 4-by-4 inch post or 2-by-4s placed in a circle. Build this structure about one-third of the way in from the lower, smaller circle that is the base. This leaves room for the knees when people sit up to the table. It should look like (E) in Fig. 4-18.

Another way to form the upright section of the table is to cut two circles about two-thirds the diameter of the base. Glue and secure with woodscrews to the bottom side of the top and the side of the base, exactly centered outside the supporting post, lattice or T&G flooring. If you use the flooring it can match the finish of the top and base. Use finishing nails and nailset them. If you use lattice, the vertical structure must be strong enough to support the table top and anything put on it; flooring is stronger. If you use lattice, it should be painted; stain generally looks spotty on this soft wood.

A square table will be easier to build. Cut the top from ¾-inch thick plywood and finish the edges with tape. Support this top by 2-by-6s on edge, crossed. Where they meet in the middle, you can cut them out to cross one over the other or merely cut off one and start it again on the other side, just be sure that it is level. The structures can be painted a dull black before applying the top. Leave the top surface unpainted if you are going to cover it. It is a good idea to install glider buttons near the end of each of these crossed legs and one in the center.

The top of the table can be covered with marble, which is striking but quite heavy. Plate glass is also heavy, but makes a good top. If you use clear glass, glue a sheet of gold paper under it. While glass won't scratch as easily as marble, it will break or chip, therefore the edges must be smooth. Look around the salvage yards for an interesting table top—you will be surprised at what will turn up.

The height of this table will depend on the height of the seats you will use with it. Even the pictures on the wall of that area should be lower in comparison to keep everything tied together.

ZOOM-ZOOM BED

Even the most recalcitrant child will zoom to bed in a zoom-zoom racing car bed at bedtime. Since children usually appreciate details, give the little fellow a bed that will capture his imagination

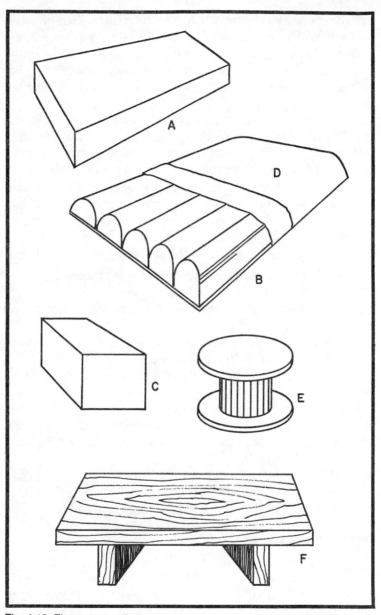

Fig. 4-18. Floor accessories.
    A. Banjar.
    B. Shiki.
    C. Futon.
    D. Makura.
    E. Cable spool table.
    F. Square low table.

and provide him with something to feast his mind on while he zooms off to sleep. This zoom-zoom racing car bed (Fig. 4-19) should go a long way in eliminating the complaint, "Do I have to go to bed?"

This design is presented in simple form. Elaborate on it as you will, just be sure to measure and cut accurately to make the bed practical.

As described here it will only require about 72 feet of 2-by-4 in usable lengths, less than two 4-by-8 panels of ¾-inch thick plywood, a 7-foot length of 6-foot wide ¼-inch thick vinyl floor covering that will accept paint, adhesive, box and finish nails, woodscrews, finishing materials, imitation leather (Nalgahyde) liner and a polyurethane foam pad. Plan your cutting to leave as little waste as possible. Make all of your measurements and cuts accurately, verifying each measurement several times before cutting.

Proceed a step at a time in the following order:

1. Build the 2-by-4 framing structure or chassis.
2. Cut out and install the base panel.
3. Make the pattern for the lining panels and the skin and transfer them to these surfaces.
4. Verify the fit of all components and make any needed adjustments before proceeding.
5. Cut out the lining panels for both sides and the back and install them.
6. Cut out the skin and glue it to the chassis, carrying it over the top and down inside on the lining panels.
7. Paint designs on the skin and all exposed wood, including the bumper.
8. Apply the inside skin and tail piece.
9. Install bumper and verify that all glued surfaces are secure.
10. Cut out and fit in the polyurethane foam pad.

Building the Chassis

First check the actual width of your 2-by-4s. If they do not measure exactly 1¾ by 3¾-inches, adjust the dimensions given to allow for the difference (Fig. 4-20). From two straight pieces cut two lengths exactly 80 inches long (A). Be sure that both ends are square. Rest them on the 1¾-inch edge and check that they do not wobble.

On the under surface starting at one end make cutouts to receive the uprights, 3¾-inches wide by ¾-inch deep (B–1). Do the same at the other end and the other 80 inch piece. Keep the cuts accurate and exactly at right angles. Do the same for upright B-2 at a distance 18 inches on center. Repeat on center at 21 inches for B-3 and B-4. Repeat on center 20 inches for B-5, which should take you to the end of the beam (A).

From 2-by-4 cut eleven uprights (B), being sure that the bottom is square and flat. These fit into the cutouts in A and will be the following heights:

Two B-1, 13 inches long with level top.

Two B-2, 16 inches at the front and slanted to 17 inches at the back on one end and flat on the bottom.

Two B-3, 21 inches at the front and slanted to 21½-inches at the back, flat on the bottom.

Two B-4, 24 inches, flat top and bottom.

Two B-5, 19 inches, with level top

One B-6, 19 inches with level top

Fit ten of these uprights into the slots along each side rail (A). The joints should be smooth. If there are any discrepancies, correct them before you continue. Nail each upright securely using box nails large enough to hold them firmly but short enough not to protrude beyond the outer surfaces.

Cut five 2-by-4s exactly 36 inches long with squared ends, one for each crossbeam. Check that all of these crossbeams are exactly the same length.

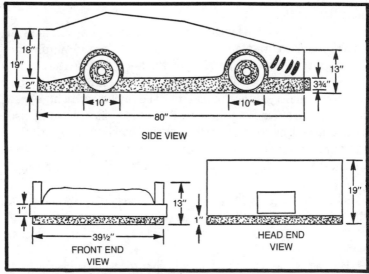

Fig. 4-19. Zoom-zoom racing car bed.

Cut out B-6 on the center line to receive the upright B-6 and install it. Install the assembled head crossbeam between the right and left longitudinal beams so that all surfaces are flush. Install the other four crossbeams between the upright center lines, with the 1⅜-inch edge uppermost. The crossbeam between the B-1 uprights should be even with the front end of the assembled longitudinal beams and their uprights.

From the 2-by-4 scrap, cut eight corner blocks (C), 6 inches down one side and the width of the board (3¾-inches) down the other. Drill two holes at angles for large woodscrews that will allow the threads of the screws to bite well into the framework. By using woodscrews you will avoid knocking any of the joints loose. While it is not necessary to reinforce all eight corners, it is a good idea.

The zoom-zoom chassis should now look like Fig. 4-21. Make any adjustments or corrections needed before proceeding. Lay aside a 42 inch long piece of 2-by-4 that is in good condition for the bumper.

From one of the plywood panels, ¾-inch thick, cut out the base panel 39½ by 80 inches. Notch to fit around the 2-by-4 uprights as shown in Fig. 4-22. Install using finish nails and nailsetting the heads neatly so that the base panel lays flat on the top edges of all lengthwise beams, the crossbeams and the corner blocks. The edges at what will be the head of the bed and the foot should also be even with the surrounding structural surfaces. Sand any rough surfaces.

Lining the Car

A pattern is needed for the inner lining panels as well as the skin to make them accurate and match at the top. It is easy to make mistakes that will spoil material if you trust only one measurement. The four silhouettes should match exactly for a neat looking job.

The two inner side liner panels must be cut left and right. These liner panels can be cut from one 4-by-8 sheet of ¾-inch plywood. Use the straight edges for the bottom of the panels and the cutouts toward the center as shown in Fig. 4-23. Cut it 14½ by 36 inches with square corners. Install against uprights (Figs. 4-20 B-5 and B-6).

The upper edge of the two side liner panels must be cut to the pattern as shown. Since these butt against the head lining panel, they will need to be shorter by its thickness of ¾-inch or 79¼-inches in length.

By placing the pattern or making your measurements for each of the side panels, the straight edge of one panel and the straight

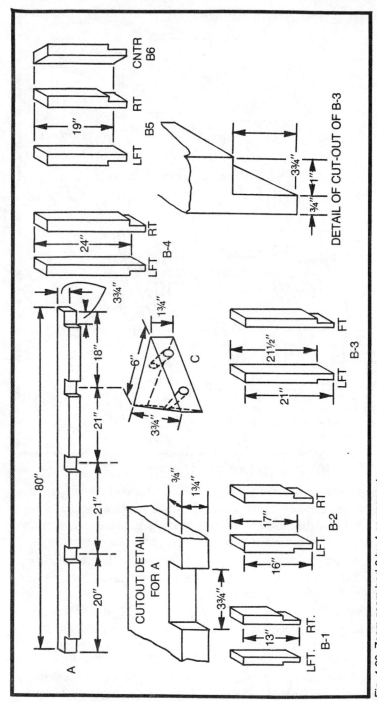

Fig. 4-20. Zoom-zoom bed 2-by-4 components.

269

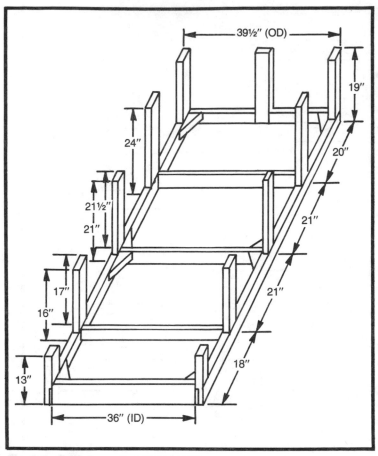

Fig. 4-21. Zoom-zoom chassis assembly.

edge of the other panel will be best if placed at opposite sides of the plywood panel for cutting so that all waste will come in the center, making it more usable. This is assuming that the edges of the plywood panel are square, in good condition and not splintery.

When you have carefully cut out the profile of both left and right side lining panels, and sanded the edges square, install them into the chassis using finishing nails and nailsetting the heads so that they are smooth with the surface. The 14½-inch straight edge butts against the head lining panel. The 8½-inch straight edge that installs against the uprights B-1 should come out even with the ends of the longitudinal beams on both sides.

When you have ascertained that everything so far fits snugly and is secure with no nails protruding, you are ready for the next

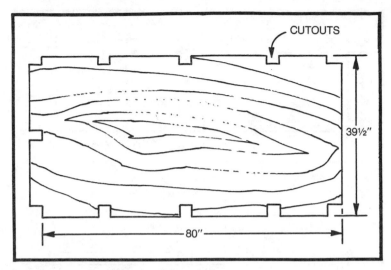

CUTOUTS

39½"

80"

Fig. 4-22. Zoom-zoom base panel.

step, applying the skin. You can use the same pattern for the top edge of the skin as you used for the plywood liner by adjusting its placement on the sheet.

Vinyl floor covering, ⅛ or ¼-inch thick, in a solid color is the best choice for the skin. It should be a metallic or bright color to carry out the racing car idea. The color of the skin should make a good contrast to the dull black painted along the bottom and the shadows around the bottom of the fenders and the tires, which can be white or with a white stripe. The hubcaps and the bumper should be painted some shiny color. Of course the vinyl must be able to take the paint, so get the advice of the clerk when you buy the material for the skin.

Vinyl flooring comes in 6-foot widths. If you plan your cutouts right, a piece of vinyl about 7 feet long should do the job, but check before you buy it.

The total length of the skin from head to foot is 80 inches plus 1¾-inch across (Fig. 4-23 B-1), plus ¾-inch, the thickness of the plywood lining panel, plus the turnback on the inside of about 1½-inches, for a total of 84 inches. The skin starts 1 inch up from the bottom edges of the longitudinal beams.

From there it covers the side of the uprights, which are at various heights, and bends over the top surfaces (1⅜ plus ¾ equals 2⅛-inches) and down on the plywood liner for 1½-inches. This means that, allowing for the ninety-degree bends, the width of the pattern must be increased a net of 2¾-inches over the total height

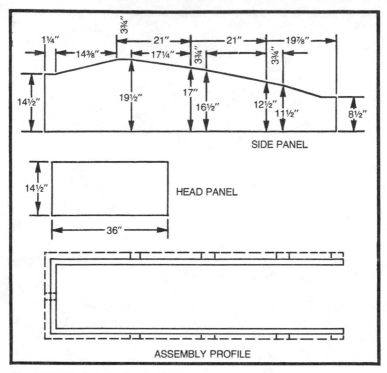

Fig. 4-23. Zoom-zoom plywood lining panels.

from the floor to the top edge. For example, the total height from the floor to the top of the upright is 13 inches; this will require a total (13 plus 2¾ equals 15¾-inches) of 15¾-inches of skin to cover at this point.

In case the structural members are a little off, it will be a good idea to measure the actual height and add 4 inches at the top to insure that the skin carries from 1 inch up from the floor, across the top of the uprights (of different heights) and down on the inside plywood lining to an even line below the top.

While the skin can be painted before or after having been glued to the chassis, if you paint it before installing it, you may have to do a bit of touching up afterwards. Do not use nails to apply the skin because they will be difficult to cover and will mar the skin. Anchoring wire brads may be used at the corners but they should be removed when the adhesive has set unless you are able to cover them so that they will not shine through the touch-up.

Since the skin at the head is square at the top, it is a good idea to start by applying this piece. You will find that due to the differences in

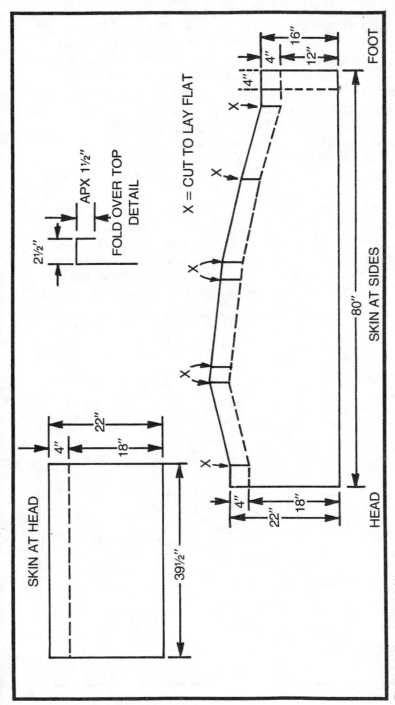

Fig. 4-24. Zoom-zoom skin patterns.

273

heights of the uprights on the sides it will help to cut down the 4 inch width of the turn down at the places marked X on Fig. 4-24. Rather than to allow one fold to lap over another, carefully cut away a portion. It will look neater if you cut away too little rather than too much, which will leave a gap in the covering skin. Just don't be in too big a hurry while you are cutting and applying the skin.

Allow the adhesive to thoroughly dry and set. Meanwhile you can be cutting out the fabric lining. Nalgahyde is the best material for this purpose because it can be wiped clean from time to time, but probably more important, it carries out the idea of automobile up-holstery.

The Nalgahyde lining should be glued to the inner plywood panel all the way around, starting at the base panel and extending up to cover it by at least 1½-inch. The outer skin that is turned down at the top should be covered by at least ½-inch. Since this is by way of a finish, it should be done very neatly. Verify the dimensions given in Fig. 4-25 before cutting the lining material. While the bottom edge

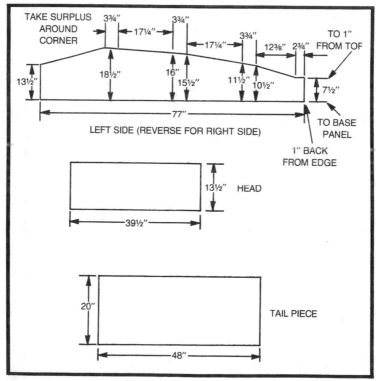

Fig. 4-25. Zoom-zoom finish lining.

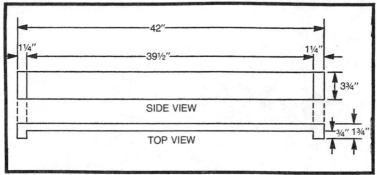

Fig. 4-26. Zoom-zoom bumper.

will be covered to the thickness of the polyurethane foam pad, it will show better workmanship if it meets the top surface of the base panel all the way around. Lay aside the tail piece for installation. Neatly glue in the liner to the head and both sides.

While this adhesive sets, cut out the bumper (Fig 4-26). Using the 2-by-4, 42 inches in length, that you laid aside, cut into its thickness the 1¾-inch way, 1¼-inch from each end, to a depth of ¾-inch. With a sharp wood chisel, remove the material until you have a smooth, straight, level cutout. Sand smooth and drill two holes for installation, centered about 3 inches in from each end. Finish the bumper in a bright color or a metallic with a shine. This should carry out the idea that it is metal. Allow the finish, which will be in several coats, to thoroughly dry.

A core type polyurethane pad at least 6 inches thick should be cut oversize so that it can just be crowded on the base panel into the width. Since you may want to remove this foam pad at some future time, do not glue it in. It should be held in place by being crammed between the side and head panels and at the foot by the bumper and the Nalgahyde foot piece.

Crowd in as large a mattress pad as possible yet keep the surface smooth. Do not take the pad up the sides beyond its thickness. If your little racer is a restless sleeper so that you fear he may scrape his elbows or knees against the sides, you can prevent this by gluing a thin sheet of foam onto the plywood panels at the sides under the Nalgahyde finish lining.

When the polyurethane mattress is in place, lay the finish tail piece of Nalgahyde (Fig. 4-27) well up onto the top of the pad, say about 12 inches, tuck it down on each side and bring it smoothly out of the opening at the foot down to about 3 inches from the floor

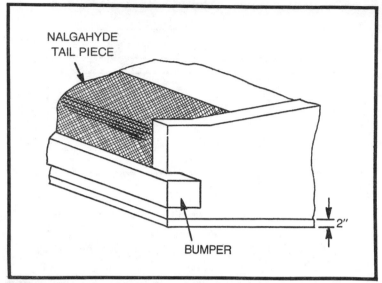

Fig. 4-27. Zoom-zoom bumper and tail piece installation.

where it will be covered by the bumper. Cross the brace and add several upholstery tacks and a few spots of adhesive. Should you ever want to remove the mattress pad, the Nalgahyde tail piece can be loosened at the sides, where it is not fastened, and folded out over the bumper. One end will be still held securely underneath the bumper.

With the Nalgahyde tail piece in place, install the bumper over it so that the lower edge of the bumper is 3 inches above the floor. In this position the bumper will cover, hold and protect the tail piece and the mattress pad. At the foot, sheets can be put on above or below the tail piece as you choose. Be certain that all adhesives and finishes are set and thoroughly dry before making up and using the zoom-zoom racing bed.

BOLTED ALL IN ONE SET-IN

The bolted set-in is for creating a cozy all in one living unit appropriate for a loft studio or an attic. This design can be bolted together so that it can be dismantled on moving day, presuming that the premises are rented. Other appropriate uses may occur to you.

The all in one frame includes a bed on the upper level, reached by climbing a self formed ladder, one on either side, a shelf on the lower level that can be used as a dressing table or a desk, and storage space that offers pull-out drawers, shelves and hanging space for clothing. Lighting, stereo and television can also be built-in or perhaps I should say built-on (Fig. 4-28).

If the occupant is heavy, the frame can still be made of 2-by-2s, providing at least two tension cables are installed. To prevent any tendency to sway under the stress of weight, these tension cables should be attached by turnbuckles to 2⅛-inch eyebolts, the kind that

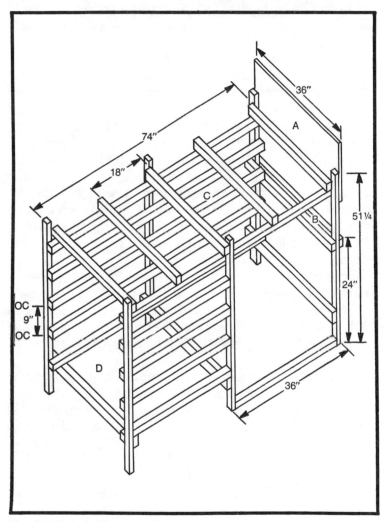

Fig. 4-28. Bolted all in one set-in.
    A. Headboard.
    B. Desk or vanity.
    C. Bed base.
    D. Space for drawers, roll-out bin and closet.

take a nut on the far side, not the screw-in kind. The use of 2-by-4s will take most of the tendency to sway out of the frame because more than a single bolt can be used at strategic joints to attach the members.

Since the dimensions given are suggested guides, vary them to fit the occupant and the space available. If the size is increased, however, 2-by-4s should be used to supply the needed strength for the longer span.

The headboard (Fig. 4-28A) should be of ¾-inch thick plywood and be the width of the unit. It will be stout enough to support a read-in-bed lamp and also a speaker, if one is desired.

The desk or vanity (Fig. 4-28B) is also the width of the unit and the headboard above it. This shelf should be of ¾-inch plywood and at least 18 inches wide. Place it at a convenient height although 24 inches is indicated on the drawing. If desired, this shelf can be at a slight angle. It is supported by arms or brackets.

The bed base (Fig. 4-28C) is ¾-inch thick plywood, on which is spot glued a thick polyurethane foam mattress. Safety rails are mounted on each side for half the length of the bed down from the head, leaving the half at the foot end open for the occupant to climb into the bed. This safety rail can be of rounded 2-by-2s, like the framing, or of aluminum tubing.

Into the space at the foot end and under the bed (Fig. 4-28D) you can build drawers, a roll-out bin and a hang-up clothes closet. The drawers and roll-out bin should face outward and the hang-up clothes closet face inward and have sliding doors. Not only will these come in very handy but they will assist in taking any sway out of the unit.

A shelf for a television, stereo or just an alarm clock can be extended out from the head of the bed or the foot of the bed, or both. A television or stereo will be heavy so the shelf must be well supported. Build it of ¾-inch thick plywood. To add a touch of the exotic, a blue glass mirror can be mounted on the headboard or above the bed itself on the ceiling.

Details for these accessories and their controls will be discussed later, also construction of the drawers and roll-out bin. Hang-up closets were covered in Chapter 3.

The all in one unit can be finished with stain or paint as desired. Privacy can be provided by pull curtains hung from the ceiling around the unit. This unit can solve the problem of creating a compact living area in a large open type space.

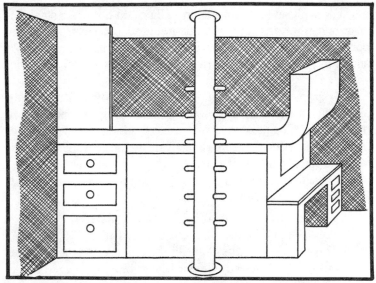
Fig. 4-29. Alternative set-in.

ALTERNATIVE SET-IN

For an alternative set-in that encompasses all of the needs of a bedroom in a compact space see Fig. 4-29. The bunk is reached by climbing up the pipe ladder. Below the bunk is a hang-up clothes closet, set off from the room by sliding doors. At one end of this enclosure are two drawers and a roll-out bin type drawer at the bottom. Under the other end of the bunk is a dressing table with drawers and a mirror or it may be used as a desk if you prefer.

Since the building of each of these items is discussed elsewhere, it will not be repeated here. The bunk can have springs, rope or leather lacing or just a thick polyurethane pad over a base board. If you prefer a hook-on ladder to the climbing pipe, build that.

A radio, stereo or television can find a resting place on the foot piece of the bunk, but be sure to ring it with sufficient molding deep enough to prevent it from falling off. The cabinet work should be of ¾-inch thick plywood, either with veneer on one side or plain and painted. The 2-by-4 structural frame is concealed by plywood.

ANOTHER FOLD-UP PIPE SLING BED

If you like to work with pipe and have the tools and welding equipment, here is a handy fold-up pipe sling bed (Fig. 4-30) that can be set up indoors or outdoors when you need an extra bed or just a place to relax. While common ¾-inch plumber's pipe is recommended, aluminum or steel pipe can be used.

If you chose to use aluminum tubing, do not use a steel limit chain or hardware as the combination will set up an electrolytic action between the two metals. In such a case you can use aluminum bolts and ¼-inch marine rope. Marine rope does not stretch like nylon will.

By capping the bottom of the legs with rubber crutch tips, the pipes will not mar the surface on which the sling sits and it will be more stable. For protection from above, when the sling is used out-of-doors, a canvas can be slung over the top pipe and tied on the inside to the legs below the bed frame.

To build this fold-up pipe sling bed to the dimensions given in Fig. 4-30, you will need:

> Common ¾-inch plumber's pipe as follows:
> Four pieces 36 inches long for the legs
> Three pieces 30 inches long for the top pole and the two sides of the bed, all exactly the same length
> Two pieces 30 inches long for the end rails
> One piece 27 inches long for the middle support of the bunk
> Two lengths of heavy chain, each about 32 inches long
> Six ¼-inch carriage bolts, washers and nuts
> Four rubber crutch tips
> Flat springs, lacing or a plywood base panel and thick polyurethane foam pad
> Finishing materials
> Canvas cover and lacing, if desired

Either weld or have welded the top pipe between the inner legs at both ends. The length must be exactly the same as that of the side poles of the bunk so that the bunk frame will swing upward between the two inner legs on ¼-inch bolts at either end.

The swing down bed rail should rest on bolts extended through the two outer legs. While the fit should be snug, it should not bind so as to constrict the folding upward of the bunk.

This extra bed will come in quite handy when you need another bed indoors or outdoors and can be easily set up almost anywhere. Meanwhile, the fold-up pipe sling bed can be stored in very little space alongside that set of golf clubs you've been too busy building beds to use.

BED OF ROSES

A bed of roses is certainly a conversation piece, even if it is only a bed covered with a rose print spread or cutouts from a seed

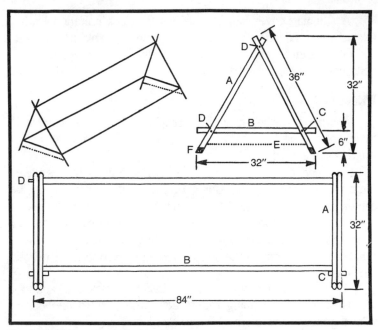

Fig. 4-30. Fold-up pipe sling bed.

catalogue applied to a plywood backing as head and foot boards. Roses can be appliqued to the coverlet or embroidered on it.

Apply appropriate floral designs in dressing the bed and its surrounds and give the bedroom the appearance of a garden bower. You can even enhance this by spraying the aroma of roses about the bedroom.

A BED OF NAILS

Here is another conversation piece, a bed of nails. When you mention your bed of nails, people will immediately wonder if you have gone in for East Indian mysticism, that is, until they see what you actually have. They will envision you lying on pointed spikes, but when you show it to them, they will see that instead you lie beneath a nail studded headboard or with your feet toward a nail studded footboard.

You can get plier-like punches that affix these studs into fabrics and shiny studs can be glued on or pounded into the head and foot boards. Apply them in designs to give the appearance of row upon row of nail points. You can tightly cover or merely spread the nail studded cover across the bed.

A stunning cover can be made from black imitation leather (Nalgahyde) studded with shiny chrome studs. The black "wet look" contrasts beautifully with the shiny studs. The surrounds in the bedroom that keep with the same idea will enhance the bed of nails.

WHEEL BED

A "when I take her out in the surrey" bed (Fig. 4-31) will also be a conversation piece. For that matter it can be done with any type of wagon or buggy wheels.

The width of wheels from old-time horse-drawn vehicles makes them more appropriate to single or twin beds, but they can be centered on double beds. Cut them into two pieces through the hub and use them as head and foot boards. The height of the head rail should lift the headboard wheel higher than that of the foot board. Build your bed by any of the designs already described and just add the wheels.

If you have difficulty in finding wheels to use as head and foot boards, a letter describing the wheels you want to one of the following may locate them.

Cumberland General Store, Rt. 3, Crossville, Tenn 38555

Glen-Bel's Country Store, Rt. 5, Crossville, Tenn 38555

Hoosier Buggy Shop, Rt. 2, Topeka, Ind 46571

Phillips and Son Buggy and Wagon Shop, 119 Cardinal Ave., Goleta, Calif 93017, telephone (805) 967-1966

Reinhardt's Harness Shop, Box 186, Hinsdale, Mont 59241

Southwest Wagon and Wheels Works, P.O. Box 738, Patagonia, Ariz. 85624, telephone (602) 394-2973 (Douglas A. Thaemert, carriage-smith proprietor, promises authentic, hand forged wagon and carriage parts and museum-quality restoration.)

Charles Van Valkenburgh, Castle Creek Road, Binghamton, N.Y. 13901 (He says he can furnish anything in wheels.)

IF YOU LIKE TO WHITTLE

An interesting bed can be made from fence posts, especially if you like to whittle. These posts will not all be the same diameter nor configuration, some will be slightly tapered. You can use these discrepancies to advantage by choosing the right post to fit the right part of the bed (Fig. 4-32).

The four bed posts can taper slightly toward the top. How small they can get is determined by how tall you want to make the posts.

However, there should be some uniformity in the shape and size of the posts for appearance sake. The taller you make them, the more they can taper toward the top.

Where the head, foot and side rails attach, the circumference of the head and foot posts should be sufficient to permit strong mortise and tenon joints. The top head rail and the blanket rail at the foot can be the smallest in diameter.

All that is actually needed are the fence posts and a sturdy, sharp hunting knife. Of course you will also need adhesive for the joints. If you want to make the springs of laced rope or leather thong, you will need a drill and a bit long enough to go all the way through the posts that serve as side, head and foot rails. This lacing will tend to keep the frame firmly together with its tension, but do not depend on this alone; glue the joints securely.

Make your fence post bed any size you want. It is only necessary that the head and foot rails are exactly the same length, also the two side rails; otherwise your bed will not be square. As with any carpentry, make all cuts square and your measurements accurate.

Select the four largest posts that pretty well match and saw their bottom ends square. These will be the two head and two foot

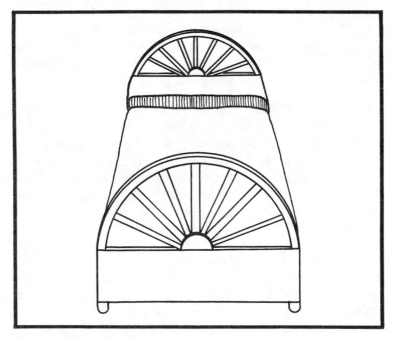

Fig. 4-31. Wagon wheel bed.

posts. Now select two matching posts for the side rails. These should be smaller than the four bed posts. The head and foot rails, while shorter, should be about the same diameter as the side rails. The top head rail and the blanket rail posts can be even smaller. That is all the fence post that you will need.

Cut the six rails so that the ends will dowel them into the posts. The dowels should be about half as long as the diameter of the post into which they fit. Whittle them so that they will curve up to the posts and the holes into which they fit after marking the limits carefully. The dowels themselves do not have to be exactly round, just make them to fit the holes reasonably snug. A little roughness on the side of the dowels is all right because it will allow the glue to distribute up and down the hole for a better hold. These dowels can otherwise fit so snugly that they have to be tapped into place.

If you plan to use lacings as springs, counterpunch and drill the holes in the rails before assembling them; it will be easier. Just be sure to make the holes exactly opposite each other. They should be from 6 to 8 inches apart.

A good way to insure this is to measure and centerpunch one rail, drill through it and then mark the opposite rail through these holes. Since lacing springs have already been discussed in this book, it will not be repeated here.

When the fence post bed has been assembled and the adhesive thoroughly set, apply wood seal. If you have left the bark on the poles, no further finish will be needed. The rustic furnishings of your cabin or summerhouse will benefit from this whittled fence post bed.

COAT HANGER TESTER

Bed draperies date back to the time courtiers were received in the royal bedroom with the royalty in a warm bed while the courtiers shivered in their boots, from cold and sometimes also from fear. If you fancy a bed with drapery at the head and don't want to go to all the trouble and expense of building a real tester bed, here is an easy way to do it.

Find a picture or sketch out how you want it to look. Figure 4-33 gives one suggestion as does Fig. 4-34.

Remember that lint will collect in the bedroom from the linens and the bedding as well as dust that comes in from the outside. For this reason the bed drapes should be made so that they can be taken down and laundered or cleaned once in a while.

Wire clothes hangers can be hung separately from screweyes embedded in structural members of the ceiling. The hangers can also

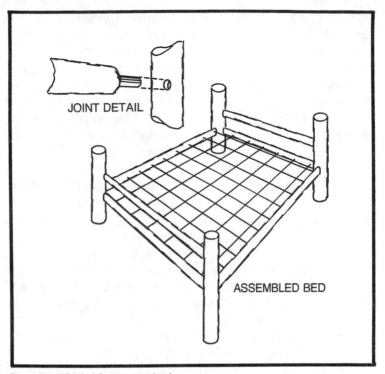

JOINT DETAIL

ASSEMBLED BED

Fig. 4-32. Whittled fence post bed.

be connected by cords that run through the heading of the draperies or on hangers connected in gangs.

Since you are using coat hangers, the drapery fabric should not be too heavy. The width of the tester will depend on the bed you propose to use. The height will, of necessity, be limited by the height of the ceiling of the bedroom. Since the tester hangs from the ceiling and the drapes fall to the floor, this must be the overall height. Such light-weight fabrics as chintz make excellent testers and they are also colorful.

One way of making the hanger for your tester is shown in Fig. 4-34, but experiment with the coat hangers. Perhaps you will only need two hangers; then you will only need to put two screweyes into the ceiling. Be sure to plan their placement so that they will bite into a structural member so that the whole thing won't come down on you some night. You will probably need screweyes with long threaded shanks(A).

Use hangers of uncovered wire (B). At the front they can be connected by cord (C) that is long enough to reach across the width of the bed and tie the ends of the hangers together. The valance across the front can be run onto this cord. Bend the hangers square around the front corners and their hooks closed on the screweyes.

Check the balance before bending the front corners square. Remember, the drapes at the back, being longer and therefore heavier will tend to keep the front from sagging and the drapes that fall to the floor at the back against the wall. Drapery hooks will make the hanging of the long draperies easier and the tops will be covered by the valance, which can be threaded on a cord. The heading of the valance should also conceal the screweyes in the ceiling.

Make the valance as well as the drapes with a lot of fullness. The drapes can hook onto the lower wire of the hanger where the drapery pins will be fully concealed. The lighter weight the fabric you use, the more fullness is needed. Chintz should have at least two and a half fullness and organdy at least three times the span.

The drapes that fall to the floor will need tie-backs. It will help to keep the tie-backs neat if you sew buckram into them. A small drapery ring at the back will hook the tie-backs to the wall by a small hook screwed into the wall.

You may be amazed at how well this coat hanger framed tester can be made to look at the head of the right bed.

Some of the suggested designs in Fig. 4-33 will require that more than two coat hangers be used in forming the tester frame. Remember that these hangers are made of not too heavy a wire and, if overloaded, will sag. A droopy tester will soon lose its style.

Wire coat hangers are easy to come by so use as many as is needed to strengthen the tester framework. Without doubt the French Dutchess tester will require a number of hangers and more than two screweyes in the ceiling because it extends further out than the single pair of hangers will reach.

These ideas should start you off on an interesting project if you fancy a tester bed. The only expense will be the draperies.

PERIOD BEDS

When we speak of period beds, we mean those that exhibit characteristics developed over a certain span of years. By style we mean the mood or influence of that period. There is one big drawback to the genuine antique articles, however, besides their age, cost and difficulty in finding. These old beds are seldom comfortable for twentieth century bodies. One way of satisfying a yen for an

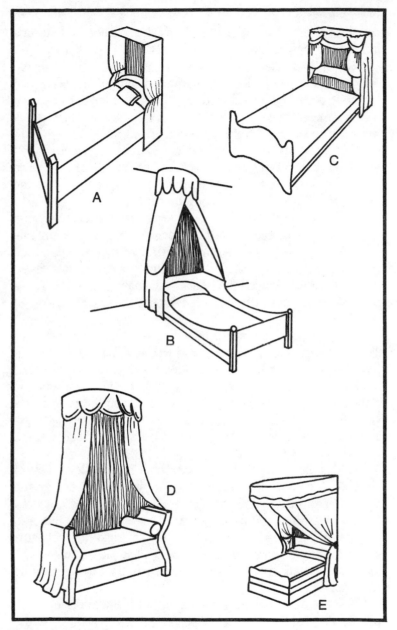

Fig. 4-33. Bed draperies for coat hanger testers.
    A. Plain
    B. Empire, German, 1810.
    C. 18th century French.
    D. French, influence of Napoleon's Egyptian Campaign.
    E. Dutchess, French.

antique style of bed yet be able to sleep in it in comfort, is to tailor a bed to your body's comfort but in the style that you want it.

Style in beds, like most other possessions of people, reflect the customs of the times, at least the customs of the various classes and economic strata of the society of the times. Primitive man sought only protection from the elements, from animals that might attack him while he slept and from his human enemies.

During the Middle Ages people moved around a lot and it wasn't safe to leave their furnishings at home while they were away. Too often when they returned home they would find that mauraders had made off with the furniture while they were absent.

Another influence, especially on beds, was the lack of central heating. Bedrooms might have had fireplaces, but as a general rule they were frigid, especially in Europe. In Poland some people solved this problem by putting their mattresses on stoves. In most cases, the wealthier surrounded their beds with heavy draperies. These also shut out the drafts that whistled through the stone corridors of the castles.

Unlike modern furniture, period styles each have their own distinctive curves, turns and decor as well as finishes. The decoration of beds by carvers of wood often documented the heraldric history of the family. An expert on such things can identify the period of the bed by its design, sometimes even the family for whom it was made. Sixteenth century beds, for example, had melon-shaped carving midway up square footed posts that quite often tapered at the top.

In England upon one notable occasion, Chippendale even went Oriental when he made a pagoda-topped, carved wood bed for the Duke of Beaufort at Badminton (Fig. 4-35A). Its deep red lacquered bedposts were touched off by gilt and pierced fretwork that also covered the high headboard. It had a green gilt and red roof and a small bedside stepstool. Some of these bedside pieces contained a convenient chamber pot. Those that survive today are often used as planters.

Beds of the Elizabethan period were usually massive, many with wooden testers supported by posts that were separate from the bed itself (Fig. 4-35B). In the Gothic era the bed posts supporting these massive testers were quite often entirely separate from the bed. Even the headboard was separate and a part of the wall paneling.

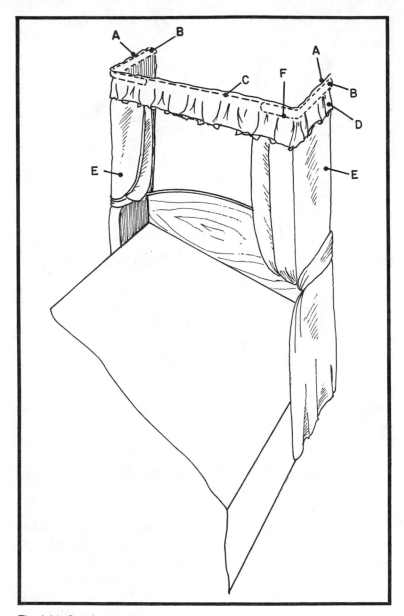

Fig. 4-34. Coat hanger tester.
A. Screw hook into ceiling.
B. Coat hanger, bent.
C. Cord.
D. Valance.
E. Drape.
F. Drapery hooks.

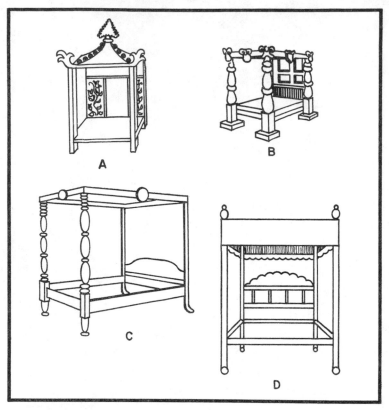

Fig. 4-35. Four early tester beds.
   A. Chinese Chippendale.
   B. Elizabethan Gothic with separate bed.
   C. Sheraton tester.
   D. Florentine 17th century forged iron four poster.

Early Bed Designers

Sheraton, among others, made tester beds (Fig. 4-35C). These had slightly tapered posts that were turned and carved with foliage, festoons, vases or rings. The roofs were carved and gilded. At the sides and the foot were plaques and often they had centered scrolls.

Duncan Phyfe (1768-1854) was not an innovator but specialized in stylistic details. It could be said that he was an interpreter of French and English styles, such as the Empire.

About 1855 cast iron moved indoors. These cast iron beds (Fig. 4-35D) featured delicate designs and were very costly even in those times. For a while there was a revival of Renaissance styles, especially Italian.

Into the eighteenth century the well-to-do French used their beds less for sleeping than for semi-reclining at social affairs such as small dinner parties. These beds were placed prominently and were richly draped to show off the wealth of the owner. The heraldry of the family was documented by hand wood carvings. Some of these beds were like outsized cupboards with spindled doors or shutters to provide privacy in the one room houses as well as protection from the cold of the rooms.

Beds have been built into alcoves for centuries. Such beds were found in Pompeiian ruins and were common in Northern Europe through the Middle Ages. Figure 4-36 shows an example of a heavily carved bed in a box-like enclosure. This one is of the late German Gothic Alpine period of about 1500.

Ancient drawings show stone, wood and bronze beds over which, no doubt, animal skins or textiles were thrown both to soften their hardness and for warmth. Some of these had hide or rope lacing and some were made to fold-up. It has been suggested that the head rests were carved so that they would not disturb the elaborate headdresses of the day.

Early Greek sculptures show beds with high frames and turned legs so this style was a long time in developing. Roman beds were even higher than those of the Greeks and had inlays.

Fig. 4-36. German Gothic Alpine.

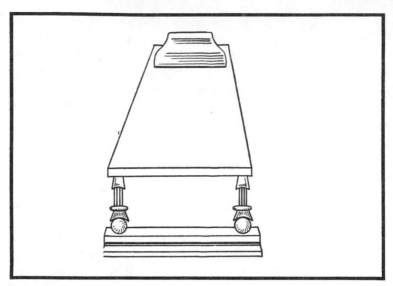

Fig. 4-37. Bronze Pompeiian bed.

A bronze bed was found in the ruins of Pompeii (Fig. 4-37), complete with a headrest. Perhaps there were softer coverings that were burned by the flaming lava that buried the town.

A box-like provencial Swedish bed (Fig. 4-38) has survived from the seventeenth century. This one was painted and was a refinement of a box filled with leaves or branches and covered with skins. By the early Middle Ages some bright soul tried stuffing

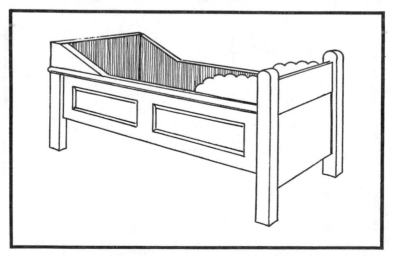

Fig. 4-38. Provencial Swedish 17th century bed.

mattresses with wool or hair and finally with feathers. Thus, the featherbed was born.

When people started traveling in the Middle Ages, some got the idea that if furniture was massive enough, it would not be stolen while they were away from home. This resulted in massive seventeenth century beds (Fig. 4-39). Today an antique reproduction of this bed sells for about $800, including the steps. Needless to say, bed steps today do not include the chamber pot (Fig. 4-39B).

Figure 4-40 shows a neoclassic sleigh bed for which Napoleon is credited; perhaps he got the idea during his Russian campaign. Katherine the Great had a sleigh bed. The ornamentation appliqued onto the darkwood of which the sleigh bed is made, were usually of brass or silver and in the form of stags, festoons, wreaths, laurel branches, torches or mythological figures.

Around 1840 papier mache came into popularity. Henry Clay, who was a japanner, patented this process in 1772. In 1825 Jenners and Bothridge patented a process for inlaying it with mother-of-pearl. This material was popular with those who liked the rococo until the 1860s. It was necessry to combine the papier mache with

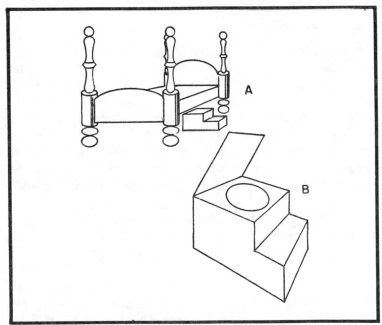

Fig. 4-39. Massive 17th century bed with steps.
    A. Bed with steps.
    B. Bed steps with chamber pot.

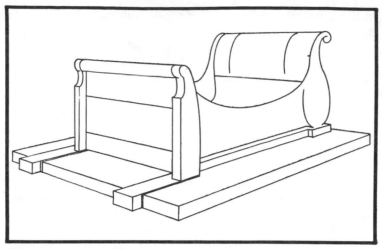

Fig. 4-40. Neoclassic sleigh bed.

wood or metal for reinforcement and strength because this soft material did not supply the strength needed for furniture. Figure 4-41 is a sketch of a papier mache foot board made in the 1850s that has survived and may be seen in the Victoria and Albert Museum.

American Colonial Beds

Beds of the American Colonial Puritan era mirrored what these people had left behind in their Elizabethan dwellings. The ships that carried the early American settlers across the Atlantic had little room for furniture, but these people carried in their heads the traditions and memories of what they had left behind. They had to build their furniture in the new land with what tools and abilities they could command and from the materials that they had at hand, so naturally the furnishings of their homes were simple. One wonders if the voluminous draperies didn't sometimes hide their lack of work-manship.

Many of the early American houses were of the one room variety, with perhaps a loft where the children slept. The typical early American under-the-eaves bed (Fig. 4-42) usually had rawhide springs.

Another bed that was popular was the slaw bed, slaw being a corruption of the word for curtains. The one shown in Fig. 4-43 can be folded up. It has 3 inch square, tapered bed posts at the head that are 6 feet, 2 inches to 7 feet tall. The tester frame, at the head only, is 24 to 30 inches from front to back and supports a pair of wide

Fig. 4-41. Papier mache footboard.

curtains that can be drawn to conceal the bed frame when it is folded up. These beds were popular mostly between 1775 and 1840 until other types of folding beds became available.

The tester frame, at the head only, consisted of strips of wood ¾ to 1 inch thick, braced by two short diagonals mortised to the head

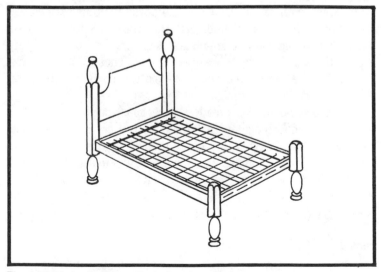

Fig. 4-42. Under-the-eaves Early American bed.

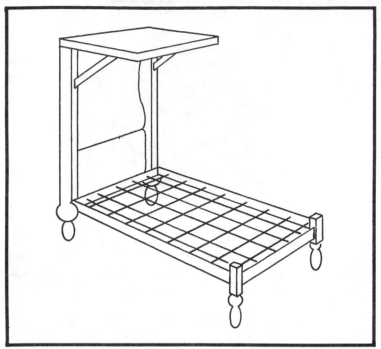

Fig. 4-43. Slaw folding bed.

posts. The low headboard has a straight top edge, 10 to 12 inches high. Sometimes the headboard has curved ends. The side rails are 16 to 20 inches from the floor and are bored for rope springs.

About 20 to 24 inches out from the head posts the side rails have knuckle joints that are wooden hinges, supported by turned, tapering legs that match the front posts at the foot. These foot posts only go 2 to 3 inches above the side rails and terminate in buttons or slightly rounded or flat knobs.

Particular housewives made the curtains that hung from the tester to the floor of linen that matched the coverlet and often embroidered the fabric with colored woolen yard in crewelwork. When the bed was not in use, the lower part was folded back behind the drawn curtains. These beds were from 6 feet to 6 feet, 6 inches long by 4 feet to 4 feet, 4 inches wide. They were usually made in New England from 1690 to 1760 of native hardwood, mostly maple.

Field or Tent Beds

The tent or field bed appeared in Philadelphia in 1780, spread throughout America and remained popular until 1830 (Fig. 4-44). It was invented by a New York cabinetmaker by the name of John Hewitt. The characteristic of these beds is the humped tester, sometimes called a serpentine canopy. It is thought that they derived their name from the tent beds used by the officers of Napoleon's army in the field.

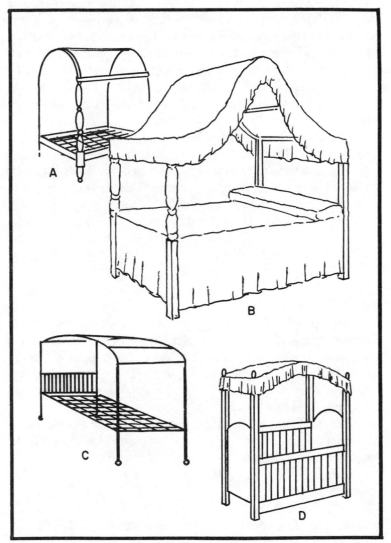

Fig. 4-44. Examples of tent or field beds.
    A. Typical field or tent bed.
    B. Hepplewhite Field Bed with spade foot and serpentine canopy.
    C. Iron tent bed.
    D. Tent crib.

These beds originally had posts 5 to 6 feet in height, surmounted by a humped tester frame with the side panels always in two parts, butt-hinged at the center. Replacement frames were generally less arched and in one piece. Perhaps as ceilings lowered there was less room for the high arches.

Some of these beds had four simple posts that were all alike or turned with a slightly vase-shaped taper. Some were more elaborate with the foot posts above the side rails urn-shaped and surmounted by vase-shaped elements that were reeded. Some had a spiral twist for the upper part. Below the rails the posts were sometimes square with bead-molded edges. On others the feet were box shaped or terminated in vase-and-ring turnings, while still others had turned peg feet.

The rails of the original tent beds were 24 to 28 inches from the floor and were either bored for rope lacing or had knobs to which the rope was attached. The headboards were 14 to 18 inches high with the upper edge either straight or slightly arched. Later tent beds sometimes had a matching foot board.

The tester arched 6 to 7 feet above the floor. These beds were 6 feet to 6 feet, 6 inches long by 4 feet to 4 feet, 4 inches wide. The favored woods were mahogany, plain or curly maple, cherry or birch.

Low Post Beds

The Belter bed of the middle 1800s named after a leading New York cabinetmaker of the time, John Henry Belter, introduced a headboard twice the height of the foot board. These beds (Fig. 4-45) were usually made from laminated rosewood. They resembled the sleigh bed (Fig. 4-45B) except that the sleigh bed had the same height head and foot boards.

A characteristic of the Belter bed was the bold quarter round corners and deep curve of the side rails that carried low to the floor at the lower edges. The feet were quarter round blocks, sometimes castered. Both head and foot boards were heavily ornate being carved in high relief.

Preceding the Belter bed by about twenty years, the sleigh beds were the American version of the European bed called French Napoleon. Both of these resembled a horse-drawn cutter or sleigh, hence the name. The head and foot boards were the same height and flared outward in cyma curves. Cyma curves are continuous, half concave, half convex. Both of these beds were low to the floor and

Fig. 4-45. Low post beds.
    A. Belter bed.
    B. Sleigh bed.
    C. Spool or Jennie Lind Bed
    D. Turned post bed.
    E. Three quarter high post bed.

set on block shaped feet, sometimes castered. The head and foot boards were from 44 to 55 inches in width. These beds were frequently made from crotch grain veneered mahogany.

Early Victorian spool beds are also known as knobby spool turnings and Jenny Lind beds (Fig. 4-45C). These beds come in two types: one had spool turned posts that terminated in urn-shaped or small ball-and-ring finials connected by two spool turned cross rails (Fig. 4-45D) or spool turned posts joined by spool turned top rails. Some have been found that have turned bottom rails featuring spool or spool-and-vase turned spindles. The top of the headboard may be spool turned or in one piece 18 to 20 inches high, although some have been found with the headboards 4 to 6 inches higher than the foot boards. The side rails are 6 to 8 inches in width and made fast by countersunk bed screws or concealed iron catches. The slats for the bed springs fit into strips on the lower edge of the side rails. These beds usually are made of maple, birch or a native hardwood with a pine headboard. They are frequently painted or stained to simulate black walnut or rosewood.

Tester Beds

Then the heights of beds started climbing again with such beds as the three-quarter high posts (Fig. 4-46D). Godey's Lady Book did much to spread the popularity of tester beds. Many of these were elaborately carved although some were simple, except for the draperies, which were elaborately contrived.

The rich carving ran from foliage, such as ocanthus leaves (Fig. 4-46A) that often decorated the feet. The tapered or turned posts were often reeded or fluted. Reeding is a series of vertical, rounded, closely set parallel lines—the opposite of fluting.

Chippendale made some of his beds with heavily carved knees that could be removed (Fig. 4-46B). Some testers were wooden canopies and required no draperies (Fig. 4-46C). On some high-post beds the tester frame could be lifted off and the bed used with or without draperies (Fig. 4-46D).

Furniture designers of the day combined all sorts of moldings, turnings and carvings in decorating their beds and making them attractive to buyers (Fig. 4-47).

The moldings shown in Fig. 4-47 are:

A. Ovolo
B. Cavetto
C. Torus
D. Roll
E. Scotia
F. Cyma recta
G. Cyma reversa

The posts of the beds of this era were seldom without ornamentation. Those that didn't have reeding usually had fluting. Both of these striations run up and down the post, the reeding forming parallel humps and the fluting being concave ruts alternating with outward flat areas.

Turnings were just as varied and ornate. Those turnings shown in Fig. 4-47 are called:

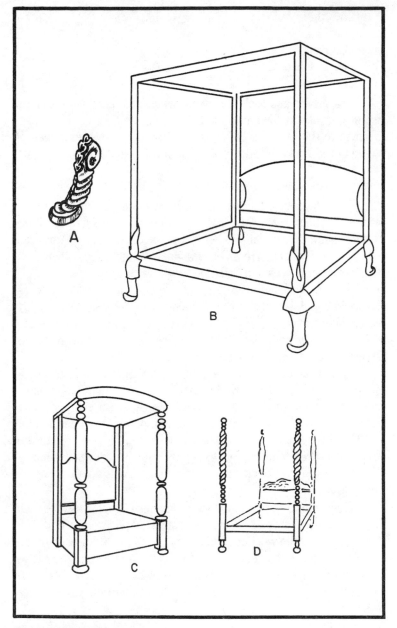

Fig. 4-46. American tester beds.
A. Conventional carved leaf foot.
B. Chippendale Queen Anne tester with Dutch feet and detachable carvings.
C. Hepplewhite with wooden tester.
D. American Empire with tester removed.

A. Melon bulb
B. Vase
C. Knob
D. Bell-and-reel
E. Spool

Imagination and tools that were available were the only limits when it came to hand-carved finials. These designs were also adapted to the feet. Those shown in Fig. 4-47 were examples of some of the Early American hand carved finials.

When Tastes Change

Following the American Revolutionary War public taste turned against anything that was English. Since many English furniture makers were heavily influenced from France and Italy, American furniture designs began to favor straight and simple lines rather than the European curves and furbeloes.

George Washington might well have slept in such a bed as shown in Fig. 4-48, except that this one is a 1978 bed. This canopy bed is built of hardy pine and today sells for around one thousand dollars. It can be truly said that this bed represents "a melting pot of styles" that is truly American.

By the end of the 17th century, caster making had become a distinct trade in England. Early casters were made of wood; later they made them of leather or brass. By the 18th century some furniture makers utilized the casters as a part of the design (Fig. 4-49) as they had distinctive feet. It was not, however, until the invention of the orbital caster that beds could be easily pulled in any direction, even over thick carpeting, without the danger of marring the flooring.

The Shakers had an influence on modern furniture styles with their simple designs and the use of casters. They are credited with the invention of the wooden clothespin as well. The simplicity of the Shaker designs with even more naturalism than those of the Victorian period, have been called "religion in wood." Figure 4-50 contrasts the extreme styles in bed posts. All of them, however, were hand carved.

Partly due to the changing status of furniture in households, as well as the changing popularity of styles, more ornate furniture was usually discarded and replaced. That was before the antique craze. When these items came into demand again and were found to be scarce, up went their prices. It is said that the price asked by a

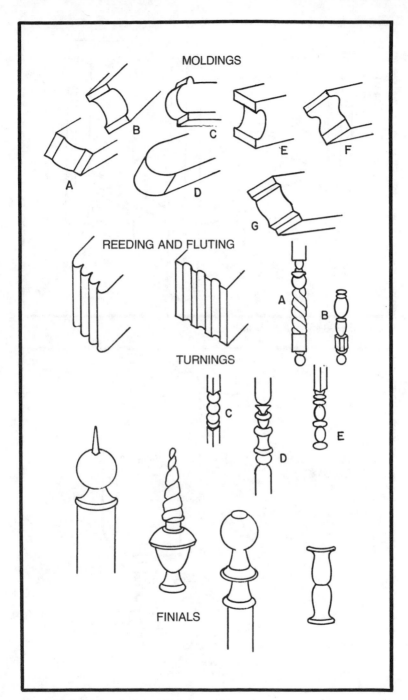

MOLDINGS

REEDING AND FLUTING

TURNINGS

FINIALS

Fig. 4-47. Typical period wood turnings and carvings.

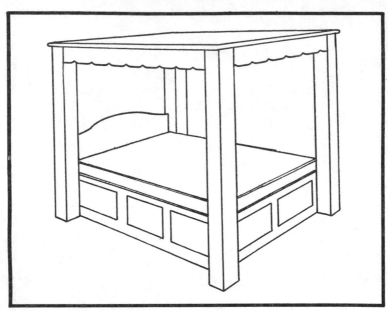

Fig. 4-48. 1798 style canopy bed.

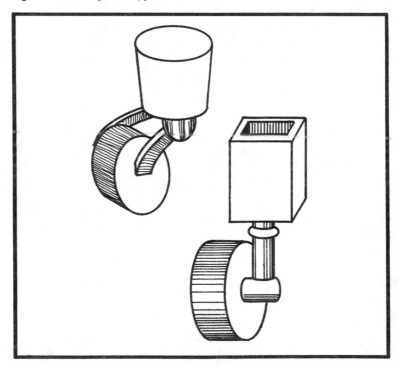

Fig. 4-49. Early casters.

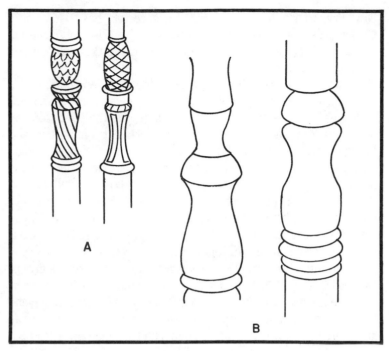

Fig. 4-50. Contrasting bed post styles.
    A. Hepplewhite (1794).
    B. Early American turned.

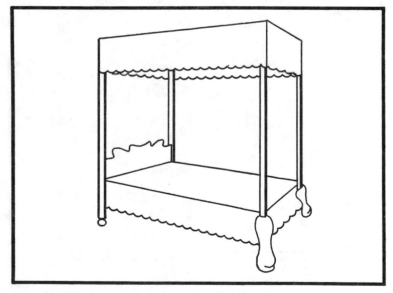

Fig. 4-51. Chippendale tester with removable carved kneecaps.

Newburyport family was $50,000 for a certain bed. This was a Chippendale mohogany four poster made in the 1750 to 1780 period in Philadelphia (Fig. 4-51). It had removable carved kneecaps, which made it a rare specimen.

The most commonly used hardwoods for these period beds came from large leafed trees or, if soft wood was used, from trees with small leaves or needle-type foliage. In the 18th century mahogany pretty much supplanted walnut. Do not confuse this with Philippine mahogany, which is not of the same species. Philippine mahogany can be quarter-sawn for striped or ribbon effects in the wood. Other hardwoods used were oak, maple, birch and gum.

When these hardwoods grew scarce, the furniture makers sometimes couldn't get a full piece from one piece of wood. These resourceful artisans solved this shortage by cutting parts out piecemeal and gluing them together (Fig. 4-52).

Furniture artisans have always been a resourceful group. Dovetailing (Fig. 4-53A) was not developed until around 1680 however. Veneering, so common a practice today, did not reach England from the Continent until after 1660. There seems to be no record as to the origin of doweling, but specimens of double doweling (Fig.

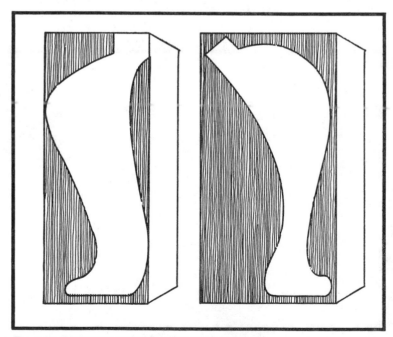

Fig. 4-52. Piecemeal cutting for gluing pieces together.

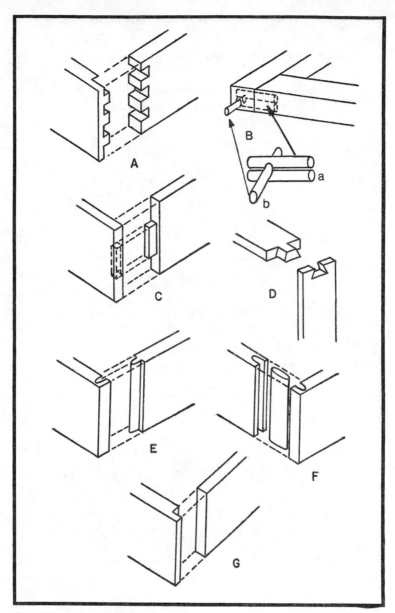

Fig. 4-53. Joining techniques.
    A. Dovetail.
    B. Double dowel with locking dowel.
    C. Mortise and tenon.
    D. Dovetailed mortise tenon.
    E. Tongue and groove.
    F. Splined.
    G. Rabeted.

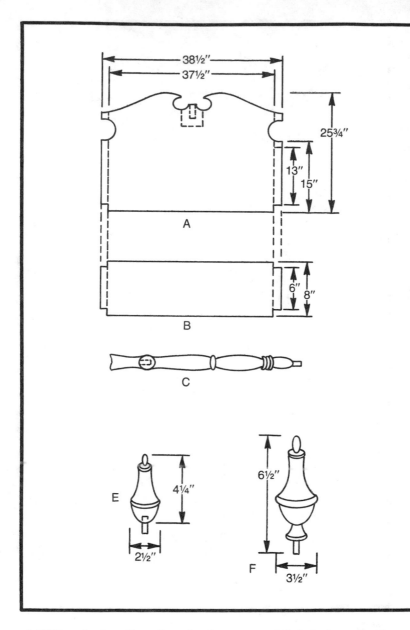

4-53B) can be found in antique furniture, especially in beds, probably to offset the gyrations of our overweight ancestors who used them. They even inserted a locking dowel to prevent the joint from failing and letting down the occupants of the bed with a disagreeable jolt. They also invented ingenious attaching hardware and used many of

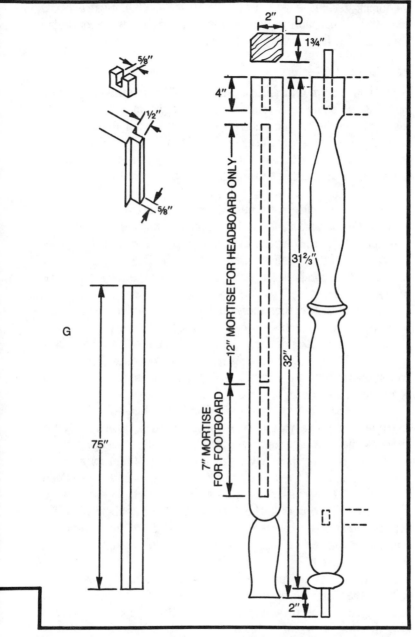

2"

D

1¾"

5/8"

1/2"

5/8"

4"

12" MORTISE FOR HEADBOARD ONLY

7" MORTISE FOR FOOTBOARD

31⅔"

32"

2"

75"

G

Fig. 4-54. Tester bed components.
    A. Headboard.
    B. Footboard.
    C. Half of turned blanket rail.

D. Posts, each in two parts (4).
E. Post finial (4).
F. Headboard finial (optional).
G. Side rail (2).

the joining techniques still used today (Fig. 4-53C). Figure 4-53D shows a modern improvement that strengthens joints by combining dovetailing with a mortise and tenon.

How To Build A Tester

If you want to reproduce a period bed that is authentic in style, you must do some research. Seriously study that period in books that you can find at the public library. Then visit museums and antique stores and study the examples of that period in detail. All of this is presupposing that you have the tools and the ability to use them, and of course that you are able to find a source for the proper wood.

Unless you will be satisfied with a reasonable likeness, or to end up with one you have frankly designed out of your own head, you will really have to study the period you have selected and all of the beds you can find of that particular period in depth. The information you will accure from this will really be of value, especially if you are interested in antiques.

The bed posts of these period beds need to be turned or carved from suitable wood; lumber 3 to 4 inches square is needed. The rails should match the bed posts in width and thickness so that they will fit up neatly when the tenons are inserted in the mortises. The tenons are on the ends of the side rails and the mortises cut into the bed posts, head and foot.

The original rails of these period beds also had holes for lacing the rope springs every 6 to 8 inches apart or small, turned knobs for attaching the rope. The rope was stretched tightly on these knobs by means of a rope wrench or wooden level about 2 feet long.

The canopy of these tester beds usually consisted of wooden strips about 1½-inches wide by ¾-inch thick. These strips were lap-joined at the corners and held in place by iron pins about ¼-inch in diameter that were inserted into the top ends of the bed posts. Sometimes the holes bored in the finials took iron pins over which the tester slipped.

Since rooms appropriate to canopied beds usually have high ceilings, the tester can be around 6 feet high. At this height the depth of the tester can be anywhere from 18 to 36 inches. If the ceiling is low, the draperies can be hung from a 1-by-2 inch frame that is fastened to the ceiling.

The base, springs and mattress will be covered by the bedclothes, so think of your comfort or reproduce the antique bed

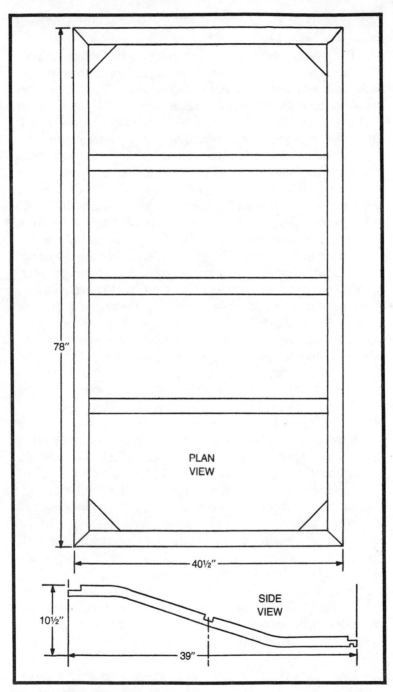

Fig. 4-55. Canopy for tester bed.

entirely as they built them in the olden days. Laced springs have been discussed at length already so we won't repeat it here.

The posts for your tester (Fig. 4-54D) should be turned. Start with four square stocks, 1¾ by 2 inches, and make your posts in sections. Dowel these sections together securely. If you make them in two sections, the bottom one should finish to 32 inches long and the top section to 31 2/3-inches. Use ⅞ by 2½-inch dowels to join the top and bottom sections, embedding the dowels 1 inch into the top section and 1½-inch into the bottom section of the bed post.

Remember that all four of the posts should match, but if you can't manage to do that, at least the two head posts and the two foot posts must match. This is often the most difficult part of the job for the amateur woodworker. It may be that you will be able to find posts already turned. If so and you want to forego this part of the job, match them up to the specifications. By doweling and the use of today's superior adhesives, you can often piece together ready-made turned parts and come out with a good set of bed posts.

Rip the head and foot rails from 1¾-inch stock. Cut 1⅛-inch tenons at each end to fit into matching holes in the posts. Be sure to design the posts so that they are wide enough where the rails join to take these tenons. For single occupancy the bed needs only be 37½-inches wide, 40½-inches overall. If you are making a double bed, you must adjust the width dimensions given in Fig. 4-54. The same thing goes for the length, which is given as 78 inches overall, like the original beds that you are copying.

Foot and head rails can also be in two sections, joined by 4 inch long dowels because they must be strong. Glue all dowels and mortise them securely using a good adhesive.

If you cannot find a large enough piece for the headboard, 25¾-inches in height by 37½-inches in width, you can join two pieces together. It does not have to be the same wood as the posts, but the joints must be strong and smooth enough not to show when finished. For precision you should use a table saw to cut tenons on each side ⅝-inch deep, ½-inch wide and 12 inches long, starting 1 inch up from the bottom edge and again at the top flange of that edge.

Cut the footboard exactly the same width and with tenons on each side exactly the same depth. If these dimensions are off in the least, the bed will not be straight and square. Measure at least twice every time before you cut anything.

Attach the bed rail supports with carriage bolts, reinforced by metal brackets. It only takes a very little spread at the rails to allow the slats to drop out. Anchor the bed rails into each post with steel pins.

If you want a solid wooden roof canopy, make it of ½-inch thick plywood in sections glue dowelled or splined together to form the hump characteristic of these beds. The canopy must be supported by a frame (Fig. 4-55). The two endcross pieces of the frame and the two side pieces should be no smaller than 1¼ by 1¼ for strength. The three middle cross pieces can be as small as 7/16 by 1¼. Mortise the four corners and strengthen them with corner blocks. The dowel at the top of each bed post fits into a hole in the corner of the frame of the canopy.

If you prefer to cover the canopy with fabric instead of plywood, the weight would be considerably lightened. The fabric, however, will need laundering from time to time so it must be removable.

The last step in building the tester bed is to make the finials (Fig. 4-54E). The four finials that top the bed posts should be exactly alike. The headboard finial (Fig. 4-54F) is optional and should be larger than those at the top of the bed posts. All of the finials should be glued in place. In the olden days, however, the holes for their dowels were deepened so that they could be used as a hide-away for valuables. It wasn't long before burglars got wise to this practice.

The tester bed should be finished so that it has an Early American appearance. Spray the wood with an orange colored stain. When this is dry, apply a semigloss lacquer. Steel wool this when it has thoroughly dried and apply a final coat of clear lacquer.

Now all that remains is to tailor the fabric canopy. It should cover the entire bed or consist only of ruffled valances on all four sides. If you choose to use the latter type of fabric canopy, anchor the draperies to the posts by ties.

The style of bedspread should match that of the canopy. The spread should cover the bolstered pillows and fall in full ruffles to the floor.

Complete the Early American picture with a colorful afghan or a crazy quilt folded over the blanket rail at the foot of the bed.

Chapter 5
Custom Beds and Surroundings

There is no law that a bed must have a headboard, or for that matter, a footboard either. If the bed is to have a headboard, it need not be attached to the frame. Headboards can be attached to the wall or merely stand alone between the wall and the bed frame. However, since the foot of the bed is customarily out in the middle of the room, footboards need to be attached to the frame.

HEADBOARDS

A freestanding headboard, as distinguished from the cabinet or shelf type, can be built in several ways. The simplest of these is a panel of plywood, hardboard or any type of sheet for that matter that can stand upright on an edge. It can be painted, stained, veneered, decorated or covered with fabric. It should extend at least 36 inches above the surface of the bed when it is made up, and at least 8 inches beyond the sides.

This requirement means that you can't just slide a 4-foot panel in against the head of the bed because most of these panels come in 4-foot widths. The standard 8-foot length is sufficient for beds up to 80 inches in width. To make such a headboard look right it must be elevated on legs.

Since these legs will be hidden behind the head of the bed, they do not have to be anything fancy (Fig. 5-1). Four 1-by-3s with the top portions extended up behind the panel to or near to the top edge will raise the panel to the needed height. These legs can be screwed to the back of the panel, providing the screws do not penetrate to the front surface. If Masonite or paperboard is used, the legs must be held to the headboard panel by adhesive alone. If it becomes necessary to nail or screw from the front side of the panel, the heads of these fasteners can be covered by molding.

Even when ¾-inch thick plywood is used for the panel, it is a good idea to dip the woodscrews into adhesive just before you install them to insure that they hold to the plies. If you prefer to bolt on the legs, countersink for both head and nut and then cover them. You

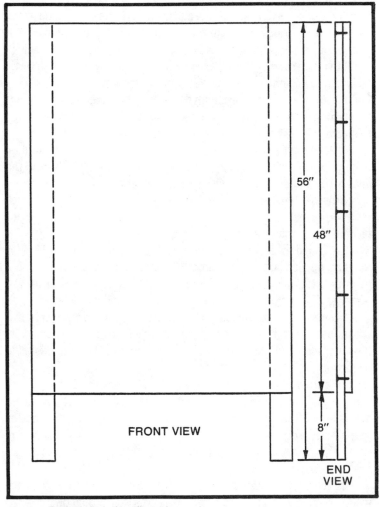

Fig. 5-1. Typical set-in headboard.

can do this with molding glued on in a design or cover the entire panel. If plywood is used for the panel and the panel is to be left uncovered or decorated with molding, you have a choice of painting or staining it, but the raw plywood edges must be finished with tape or narrow molding.

I made one stunning set-in headboard for a pair of twin beds using ¼-inch thick plywood. I set it on 1-by-3 legs and then covered it with a bedspread that matched those used on the beds, only larger so that it covered around the edges of the panel. Flat on the plywood it lacked something so I stapled on a pad 1½-inches thick. At evenly spaced intervals I inserted upholstery tacks with decorative heads in a pattern. Where I carried the spread around to the back of the panel, I just stapled it, being careful not to stretch it too tightly but let it billow out between the tacks in little tufts. The effect was stunning.

If you are one of those people who like the "wet look," and it is fashionable in some circles, cover the headboard with a shiny black imitation leather, such as Nalgahyde. Apply this in the same manner. If you choose to do this, the "wet look" should be carried over for the bed covering as well. It can be quite effective.

If for some reason you do not want to put your headboard on legs, it can be hung on the wall at the right height. In this case the lighter the weight of the panel, the better, except that it should not be easily dented. For this reason the lighter weight ⅛-inch thick plywood or hardboard will do nicely, but don't plan on covering or piecing these materials.

A ¾-inch thick plywood headboard can serve as the backing for mirrors, applied squares or framed sheets. Mount and framed sheet mirrors with appropriate molding, remembering that mirrors are heavy and you won't want to run the risk of having it fall out.

Some people prefer mirrors that have a blue tint, others like those that are shot with gold. If you incorporate any sort of mirror, do not place a light so that it shines on it and casts an undesirable reflection of the beam.

In framing a mirror with molding the corners should be mitered (Fig. 5-2). The convolutions of some moldings are tricky to miter neatly so get the advice of the saw man where you buy it or better yet, have him do your mitering for you. You can often save money by doing this because you don't pay for molding if it is wasted by miscutting.

In building a traditional style headboard you should use a hard wood or at least a veneered plywood. The sides should be morticed into the head posts at each side or at least dowelled into them.

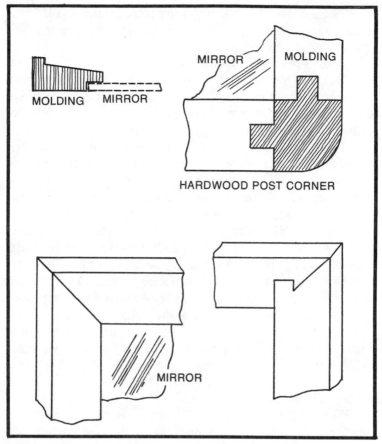

Fig. 5-2. Mitering mirror frames.

Unless you use plywood and the headboard is not over 48 inches in height you will have to piece the boards together. When you do this back up the resulting panel with 1-by-3 battens or cut them out of plywood at least ½-inch in thickness. This will prevent the pieced boards from separating. Be sure the boards are perfectly straight on the edges so no gap will be left between them where they join (Fig. 5-3).

The highest point of the headboard is usually at the middle and can be 44 inches above the top surface of the made bed. This leaves only 4 inches below if the panel is 48 inches wide. If the headboard is attached to the head rail of the bed frame or hung on the wall, the length of the 8-foot panel can be used for the width of the headboard. Allowing 8 inches beyond the bed means the bed area can be as much as 80 inches in width without having to piece the panel. If the headboard is attached to the bed frame, the panel should be mortised or dowelled into the head posts.

Headboards can be of various designs and freestanding, attached or hung from the wall. Those suggested in Figs. 5-4 and 5-5 are shown with dowels. Figure 5-4 suggests more unconventional headboards. These appear to be incorporated into the frame because the doweling does not show.

The designs shown in Fig. 5-4 can be built into freestanding headboards, or hung from the wall. They can be duplicated by applying half round moldings and cutouts to a base panel or the profiles accented by painting them in contrasting colors. In the case of the Colonial style headboard with twin mirrors (Fig. 5-5), the headboard should be incorporated with the bed frame. The mirrors will be heavy and so need the substantial support of a ¾-inch thick plywood backing. With the mirrors applied to the front, the headboard will tend to tilt forward. This headboard should be firmly kept in place by a large tongue of a tenon inserted into the head posts.

Free form headboards (Fig. 5-6A) should have profile (thickness) to set them off. This profile should be at least 3 inches deep. Such a headboard will be enhanced if it is upholstered and will adapt nicely to tufting (Fig. 5-6B). Since we have already discussed tufting of walls and the same procedure applies to any flat surface, we will not repeat it here.

When you build a headboard, it will probably occur to you to question: does the bed or do the beds need a footboard? Some styles of beds do, especially replicas of old-fashioned ones; but, if you choose to go modern, the footboard is entirely optional.

Usually the footboard is lower than the headboard (Fig. 5-7). If there is a footboard, however, it should somewhat repeat the design of the headboard.

The design of the headboard is influenced more by decorative considerations than by convenience or necessity. For this reason, when having a headboard at all you must take into consideration the other furnishings and the decor of the bedroom, just as you do when choosing a bedspread.

I heard of one man who got a big kick out of usng his bed as a conversation piece. He called it "Japanese Colonial," and that was as good a description for it as any. The frame was of a pink plastic material imitating bamboo. The bed sagged in the middle into a deep curve, somewhat like a hammock, except that the occupant could

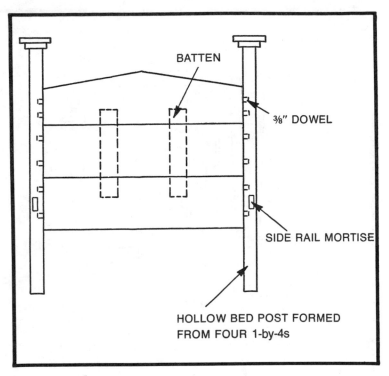

BATTEN

⅜" DOWEL

SIDE RAIL MORTISE

HOLLOW BED POST FORMED
FROM FOUR 1-by-4s

Fig. 5-3. Traditional headboard.

hardly fall out of it. To gild the lilly, it was covered by a white bear skin that had been dyed pink to match the plastic. He claimed that it worked better than etchings because everyone wanted to go up and see that bed.

Another headboard design features a cane inset. You will need a sheet of cane from the supplier of upholstery materials.

Build a sturdy frame with mitered corners held by glued-in dowels, strong enough to take the strain when the cane shrinks as it dries. Cut a groove ¼-inch wide and ⅜-inch deep about ⅝-inch in from the inside edges of the frame. This groove is for driving in the cane webbing and the wedge strip.

You will need a sharp knife to trim the sheet of cane, a good grade of adhesive that will not show when it has dried and a hammer or, better still, a wooden mallet. If you use a hammer, place a scrap of soft wood between the hammer and the spline wedge to act as a protective buffer.

Install the sheet of cane as follows:

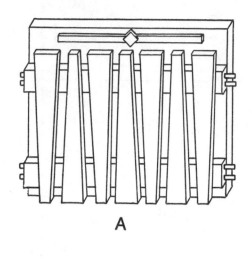

A

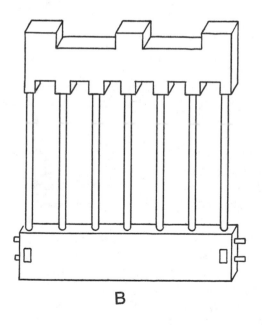

B

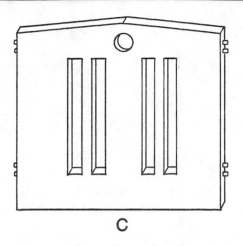

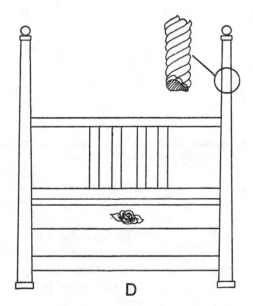

Fig. 5-4. Various designs for conventional headboards.
   A. Ripped 1-by-6s applied to panel.
   B. Greek key and post.
   C. Varied verticals.
   D. High post headboard.

Fig. 5-5. Colonial style headboard with mirrors.

1. Put the spline in cold water to soak at least an hour before installing. The cane webbing should soak for ten to 15 minutes.
2. While these are soaking, cut a wedge spline from scrap hardwood with one edge tapered from ¼ to a little under ⅛-inch. Then cut a groove in the frame completely around the opening. This groove should be barely large enough to take the tapered spline when it wedges in the cane webbing. These splines will not go around corners satisfactorily so it must be neatly mitered. It can usually be coaxed around a wide, flat curve.
3. When the cane has soaked sufficiently, lay it over the opening and cut it 1½-inches larger.
4. Brush the adhesive generously into the groove.

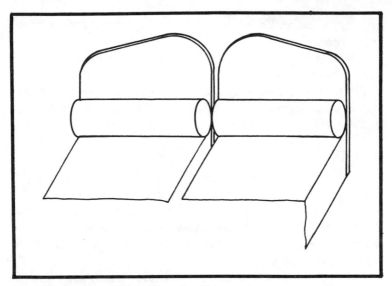

Fig. 5-6A. Free form twin bed headboards.

5. Lay the cane webbing squarely over the opening and pound it into the groove with the wedging spline without stretching either one. Both should still be wet or they may break. As the cane dries, it will tighten. As you drive in the wedging spline, add more glue as needed.

6. While both the cane and the spline are still damp and pliable, fold back the excess cane and cut it off neatly next to the spline.

If this whole process is done from the back side, there will be less danger of tiny spikes of cane sticking out beyond the spline; these can be sharp and prickly. Unless you intend to stain both the frame and the cane inset, finish the frame before installing the inset. Allow the finish to thoroughly dry before proceeding. Customarily the frame is stained a darker color than the cane inset, which may or may not be left natural.

ROOM DIVIDERS

A headboard that is at the same time a room divider that does not obstruct the free flow of air can be fashioned from bamboo poles. Larger poles are wedged between the floor and the ceiling and smaller poles are criss-crossed between them and secured by raffia windings. While this headboard will not withstand too much pressure against it, it does make an attractive room divider that fits in with an oriental decor.

Another headboard and room divider can be made by mounting shutter doors, permanently or on hinges, between upright 2-by-2s. Wedge the uprights between the floor and the ceiling if you do not want to install them permanently in a frame for more stability. The shutter doors do not have to extend all the way up to the ceiling.

LET THERE BE LIGHT!

Nearly everyone likes to read in bed, or at least everyone needs a light that he or she can turn on before getting in and out of bed to see sufficiently not to bark shins or fall over things in the dark. Headboards should provide an electrical outlet unless one is available nearby. This is in addition to the general room illumination controlled right at the entrance door.

While lighting fixtures can be modified to alter their intended purpose, it is better to select and use the right sort of fixture to fulfill the specific purpose. There are four types of household illumination in general. They are:

1. Direct lighting: a beam of white light that is centered on the work area or the page you are reading. usually supplied by incandescent light from a bulb.
2. Indirect lighting: a concealed light source from which a beam or multiple beams are directed at a reflective surface, such as a wall or the ceiling, and is reflected back into the room. Incandescent bulbs or fluorescent tubes can supply this type of lighting.
3. Diffused lighting: the source is concealed behind a semi-transparent or translucent material, such as milk glass, parchment, a thin, cloudy plastic, paper or a thin fabric.
4. Mood lighting: produced by a dimmed source, colored light bulbs or fluorescent tubes. Ideally, mood lighting resembles candlelight.

Domestic lighting frequently combines all of these. Quite often lamps are used only for decorative purposes. Incidentally, if you feel that a room is short on lamps, place one in front of a mirror and it will give the appearance of two lamps because of the reflection. To prevent unwanted spots of reflected light, move up a plant and let the foliage run interference. That will also result in interesting moving shadows. By directing a too bright light from a fixture or a lamp so that the light bounces off the wall or the ceiling, it will become

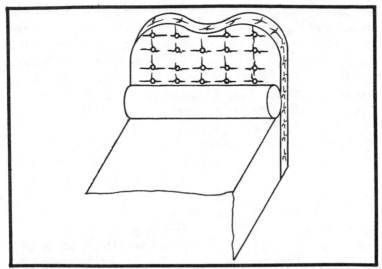

Fig. 5-6B. Tufted free form headboard.

somewhat diffused. The darker and duller the surface from which you bounce the light beam, the more it will be diffused.

There are electric fixtures appropriate to all of these needs, as well as other purposes. There are also different types of switches, including wall switches that not only turn the light off and on but dim it. There are also noiseless switches and delayed action switches that allow you to get out of the room before it turns out the light. There are time switches that can be set to turn a light off or on at given times. These are most convenient if you are going to be away from home and don't want the house to be in total darkness. Lights going off and on in a house will discourage burglars, according to police.

There are a number of choices as to the location of switches. Sockets may have push switches on the side. The key-type that you used to have to turn seems to have gone out of style. Then there are the switches that mount on the extension cord and those that are installed on the lamp base. Choose the switch that will be most convenient for your purpose.

If you light the whole bedroom by one or more lamps, to avoid a trip across the room in the dark and fumbling under the lamp shade to find the switch, by all means plug at least one lamp into an outlet that is controlled by a wall switch right by the entry door. This general illumination lamp should not be the same one that you want controlled by your bed. You will need direct lighting for reading in bed.

Take full advantage of the great variety of lighting facilities that are available. You do not have to put out money for storebought lamps when you can build them for yourself to serve your special purpose. Build a direct light for reading in bed, either a pole lamp or one that sits on or attaches to the headboard. For general lighting you can use indirect or mood illumination. A combination of these types of lights will help you enjoy the room a lot more, so don't rob yourself by skimping on the lighting.

People who have allowed their eyes to become lazy usually demand more intense lighting so they can see. It is amazing how many people who are otherwise exercise fanatics fail to excercise their eyes, which have muscles too.

This discussion involving electricity applies to 110 to 120-volt household current customarily supplied in the United States. The precautions, however, apply to any electricity. One of the precautions is that *electricity can bite*, and that bite can be fatal, especially if you are standing in water or on a conductor. Always be suspicious of any electrical wiring until you have ascertained that the main switch has been pulled, not just the fuses removed. Don't take someone else's word for it.

The main switch is emphasized because a number of circuits run out of a main fuse box. All of them are supposed to be fused, but you never can tell which of the circuits is "hot" or on which circuit the outlet you are working on is on. The only safe way to protect yourself is to throw the main swtich to *off*.

The main fuse box will have several circuits running out from it with each circuit protected by a screw-in fuse or a circuit breaker. House wiring circuits carrying 110-volts are each fused separately. A 220-volt circuit for an air conditioner or any other motor is separate and should be dealt with only by a licensed electrician. The fuses are rated for the maximum current that should be drawn on the line. The fuse and wires that they protect should never be asked to carry more than their labeled amperage. In adding outlets, never overload a circuit.

To figure the safe electric load, add up the wattage of all lights and appliances that will be drawing current on a particular circuit. This will determine the load that the wiring can safely carry. Use this formula:

$$W = VA$$

when W is watts (appliances and light bulbs are marked)
   V is volts (house current is 110-120-volts)

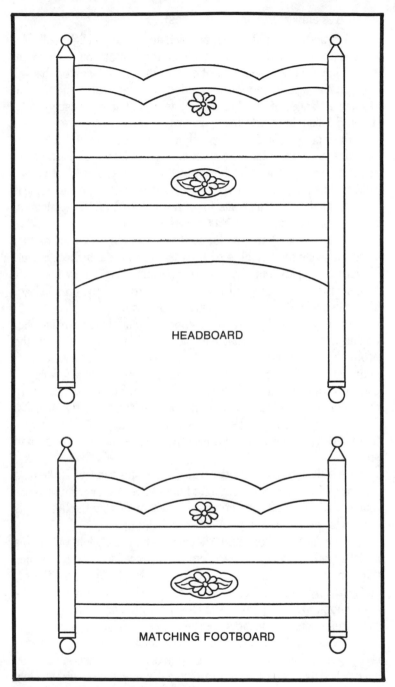

HEADBOARD

MATCHING FOOTBOARD

Fig. 5-7. Matching head and foot boards.

A is amperes (marked on fuses)

Add up the wattage given on each appliance and light bulb on a circuit. Don't forget to include all of the outlets on a circuit to determine if there is a chance of overloading it. In addition this will tell you the size of the wires needed to safely carry the current without a danger of overheating, blowing a fuse or causing a fire. Table 5-1 lists both safe loads and wire sizes.

Fuse capacity and wire size should be coordinated. The larger the wire the smaller the size number and the less the resistance to current flowing through it, therefore the less heating. Most household circuits are protected by 15-AMP fuses and the house wiring is No. 14 solid wire. This calls for a normal load of 1500 amperes, absolute safe maximum of 1800 watts on a circuit.

When a fuse blows you know that something is wrong on that circuit; usually the circuit is overloaded or there is a short circuit. Never attempt to remedy it by merely installing a new fuse of a higher rating; the wiring will only be asked to take too great a load. This can cause a fire in the ceiling or the wall.

Whatever you do never put a copper penny (if you can find one) behind a screw-in fuse that has blown. That will take away the protection that a fuse should supply and will be asking for trouble. If your fuse box uses screw-in fuses, keep a supply on hand where you can put your hands on them in the dark. Be sure that these fuses are of the correct amperage. If your fuse box, instead of screw-in fuses, has rows of toggle switches, the same thing applies. Do not turn them back to until you have located the trouble that caused them to snap off.

Less dangerous than overloading or a short circuit is the heat generated by an incandescent light bulb. Never spray paint on more than half of a light bulb or the filament will melt from the heat. This heat must be allowed to pass off by radiation.

Never screw a heat bulb, thermal bulb or spot-light bulb into a metal sheathed socket. These demand a porcelain socket. Another thing, never let a heavy lamp or fixture dangle by its light cord; support it by a chain. Never make electrical connections behind a ceiling nor a wall except inside an UL-approved connection box, with the wires connected using solderless connectors.

Obviously, the electrical connection should be done when there is daylight so that you can see what you are doing. Remember, you have pulled the main switch so no artificial light will be available. Only in an emergency should you try to make a hook-up by flashlight.

Table 5-1. Safe Loads and Wire Sizes.

FUSE CAPACITY		NORMAL LOAD		CORRECT WIRE SIZE
AMPERES	WATTS	AMPERES	WATTS	
7	840	5	600	No. 18
10	1200	8.3	1000	No. 16
15	1800	12.5	1500	No. 14
20	2400	16.6	1900	No. 12

Then there is the problem of how to heat the electric soldering iron with the current turned off.

Solderless Connectors

Soldering wire connections is no longer necessary in ordinary household wiring. UL-approved wire connectors that require no solder are available at electric supply stores. These connectors are little porcelain cones with a metal lined hole down the center into which the twisted wires are pushed. The house wiring, which uses solid wires, and the fixture or extension wiring, which should use a strand wire, are cleaned of insulation just back to the inside of the insertion hole, no farther. If any of the bare wires or even a strand extends beyond the porcelain connector, a short circuit can result. To prevent this it must be wrapped with approved insulation, but if you did the job right, this is not necessary.

Color Coding and Troubleshooting

Customarily, three wires come into the main switch box for 110, 120-volt service. These wires are supposed to be color coded. The third wire is the ground wire and the insulation is white. The other two wires carry the current, but you can get a shock by touching any of these wires.

The household 110-volt current is obtained by using one of the wires with dark insulation and the white-insulation ground wire.

While there should be a schematic diagram on the inside of the main fuse box showing which circuits serve which outlets, this may have been torn off or the circuits changed without noting the change on the diagram. This is one reason why you should pull the main switch before working on any wiring.

A good weekend project and one that will pay off some time in the future is to supply or update the schematic so you will be certain in the future which outlets are protected by which fuses. This is not a difficult job, however it is time consuming, because you must locate every outlet in the house.

Deactivate all but one of the circuits by pulling the fuses by throwing the toggle switches to *OFF*. Make an outline drawing of the whole house and mark each outlet. This requires a thorough search. It is a good idea to label the circuits by number; this will help you to check that you have covered every one of them.

Now you are ready to check which outlets are on the circuit that you have left "live." Test each outlet, and if it lights, mark that it is "hot" on that circuit. Repeat the process with each circuit until you have covered all of them. Now when a fuse blows, you will immediately know which outlets are on that circuit and to look for the trouble at one of them. I like to use a different colored pen or pencil for each circuit; it makes it easier to trace.

Sometime when you are trying to trace a short circuit this schematic will come in handy. When a fuse blows, you know the trouble will be on that circuit. Inspect all the outlets on that circuit and you should be able to locate the trouble, at least you can pull all the plugs on that circuit until the trouble that caused the fuse to blow has been corrected.

If you cannot find the trouble by sight inspection, there is a way to locate it, although it will probably cost you a fuse. Turn off all of the switches on the circuit and pull all of the plugs. Put in a new fuse and then reconnect the plugs, one by one, and turn on the switches. When the fuse blows again, you will have found the trouble, which may be an overload at some outlet and not a short circuit at all.

Ceiling Connections

One of the most difficult electrical connection jobs is the ceiling connection because all of the work must be done from a ladder and in a cramped space. Ceiling connections really call for the services of a licensed electrician because the ceiling connection box is usually stuffed with wires, in addition to several other problems.

Insurance companies and building inspectors will frown on the householder doing this wiring because it is not plugged in. Should they have occasion to inspect the house wiring and find that it is not done in the approved manner, they can make you tear it out.

The anatomy of the standard ceiling connection is shown in Fig. 5-8. All house wiring connections made in a ceiling or a wall must be within a connecting box. The conduit encasing the solid house wires

(Fig. 5-8A) enters the box where it is secured by a collar. Since the house service is carried by heavily insulated solid wires, it must be connected to the strand wires of the extension that leads to a fixture. The connection box (Fig. 5-8B) is secured to a structural member by screws. These boxes may be square, oblong or hexagonal in shape.

Formerly the solid house wires were connected to the strand wires (Fig. 5-8D) by soldering, but today solderless connectors (Fig. 5-8C) are UL-approved. The box is closed by a lid and in turn concealed behind a ceiling plate (Fig. 5-8E). At the center of this decorative plate is a ring fixture (Fig. 5-8F) that screws into the plate. The top link of the chain (Fig. 5-8G) that supports the fixture hooks into the ring. At the center the wires pass through a hole and are woven in and out of the links of the supporting chain to the fixture's socket.

All hanging lights need to be supported by a chain and not hang only on the wire. This puts too much stress on the wire, even more if the socket has a pull-type switch. The strand wire is not intended to be that strong. It is soft copper that carries electricity because that

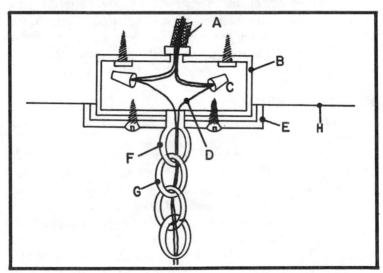

Fig. 5-8. Typical ceiling connection box.
    A. Conduit encases solid house wires.
    B. Connection box installed to a structural member.
    C. Solderless connector.
    D. Strand wire carrying current to fixture.
    E. Ceiling plate.
    F. Screw-in ring.
    G. Wires intertwined through links of fixture supporting chains.
    H. Ceiling line.

offers a low resistance and heats up slowly. If the soft strand wire is jerked loose, it will come out from under the terminal screws in the socket and is almost sure to cause a short cirucit. To further protect the extension wires, tie an UL-approved knot in it just after the wires have entered the collar in the cap of the socket.

Figure 5-9 shows how a UL-approved knot is tied, in this case in a plug, but it is the same for a socket. When the knot is drawn down it will take up very little space if properly tied. Such a knot is especially needed in the plugs of extension cords. While no informed person will pull out a plug by jerking on the cord, some people do not know any better or are careless. To pull a plug from an outlet, always grasp the plug itself the same as you would in putting it into the outlet.

In installing a hanging light, first determine the height that you need the light bulb in order to produce the desired illumination before you cut the wire. If a fixture is involved that has more than one bulb, it may help to hold it up to decide just how high it should hang.

When it comes to installing a connection box where the house wiring does not already exist, call in a licensed electrician to at least put the house wiring in the ceiling or wall. The swag lamp is popular because it hangs from a hook with the suspension chain festooning to the wall, yet carries the extension wires to a wall socket that is already installed. By hooking the links of the chain onto the hook, you can adjust the height of the hanging lamp fixture easily.

Hooking Up an Outlet

Hooking up an electrical outlet may appear to be a simple matter for anyone who has a screwdriver, but there is a right way and a wrong way to do it. Always use UL-approved parts. It is especially important that all the wiring around your bed is done in a correct manner; that is the last place that you want to have a fire start.

One of the most important and least observed procedures involves what would appear to be the simple way of connecting a wire to a screw terminal. This is required in hooking up sockets, switches, plugs and outlets, yet few amateurs know how to do it correctly. It consists of three easy steps plus a final inspection and can prevent a lot of trouble in the future.

Always follow this procedure in hooking up wires to screw terminals (Fig. 5-10):

1. Strip the insulation from the wire back just far enough to form a hook in the wire that will go around the shank of the screw terminal under the head of the screw. This should

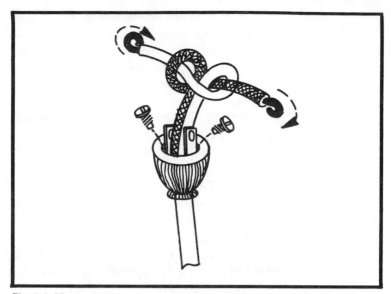

Fig. 5-9. UL-approved knot.

leave about ½-inch of bare wire beyond a clean cut of insulation.

2. Bend the wire into a hook, put it around the shank of the screw and close up the hook. The wire should not overlap but stop as it meets itself around the screw. If the wire is the strand type, be sure that none of the individual strands of the wire stick out beyond the others or from under the head of the screw.

3. Put this hook around the shank of the screw *clockwise*. This is very important because that is the way that the screw

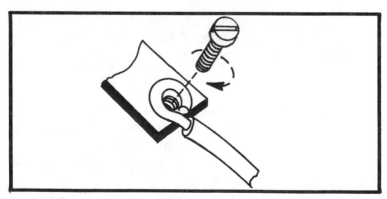

Fig. 5-10. Forming wire into a clockwise hook.

tightens down. If you put the wire around the screw counterclockwise, when you tighten the screw, it will be forced out from under the head or be doubled back on itself. Either of these can result in the wire touching either the other wire or a part of the conductor and a short circuit can result.

4. Be sure to tighten the terminal screws down snugly. A loose connection can heat up and damage the fixture.

5. Always inspect the connection thoroughly after you have made it and before you reassemble the fixture. Finally, plug it in and test it out.

Never use solid wire for an extension or a hanging fixture. Since switches and wall outlets are heavily insulated within the house structure, solid wire running through conduit is properly used. The strand wire is flexible and less apt to break while the solid wire is usually strung in a straight line so it does not need to be flexible. The solid wire is less likely to heat, however.

In running solid wire within ceiling or wall spaces do not permit it to kink or touch structural wood or plaster. Use porcelain insulators to hold it firmly away from structural parts. Should the wires heat, the danger of charring flammable material will be minimized. Be sure that the insulation is intact. All such wiring should be run through conduit.

Connecting Sockets

The standard metal clad electric socket will consist of four basic parts (Fig. 5-11):

(A) Metal sheath
(B) Insulating liner
(C) Screw socket for bulb
(D) Wire terminal screws
(E) Cap with threaded collar
(F) Set screw
(G) Extension cord

The correct way to hook up a socket is as follows:

1. Remove the cap (E) from the sheath (A). Do not remove or damage the insulting liner (B) that is inside the sheath.

2. Slide out the porcelain or plastic part to which the screw socket (C) for the bulb is attached.

3. If the socket is to be mounted or attached to a threaded tube or fixture, screw the cap onto it and tighten the set

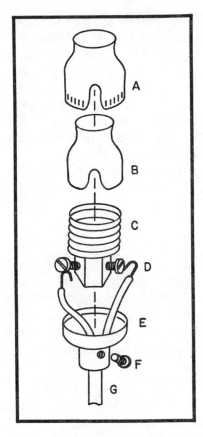

Fig. 5-11. Electric socket assembly.

screw (F) so that the socket will not turn when you screw in the bulb.

4. Using a screwdriver that is square on the end, turn the terminal screws counterclockwise to loosen them. These screws don't usually have a stop to prevent them from coming out and getting lost when unscrewed, so turn them only enough to get the wire under the head.

5. Free the ends of the extension wires from their outer sheath so you can separate them and tie them into the UL-approved knot (Fig. 5-9) that should fit under the cap.

6. Strip each wire of its insulation back about ½-inch using a sharp knife. Press the blade against the insulation while rotating the wire with the other hand, holding the knife blade perpendicular. If the blade is sharp enough, the insulation will be cut through cleanly and you can coax it off the wire in one piece. If you whittle off the insulation, a

ragged edge will result that can allow contact with the other wire, resulting in a short circuit, the bane of the householder because it not only blows fuses at the most inconvenient times, it also damages sockets and sometimes even causes fires.

7. Bend the ½-inch of wire into a hook that will fit snugly around the shank of the screw terminal (Fig. 5-10). Position this hook clockwise around the screw and under the head. The tip of the hook should curve to the right, the same way as the screw turns to tighten it down.

8. Inspect the connections before reassembling the socket and putting it into use.

Hooking Up a Wall Outlet

If the wires to be hooked up to a wall outlet have come down or are up inside of the wall, they should be the solid kind encased in conduit. Remove the insulation back ½-inch and form the bared wire into a hook that will fit around the terminal screw shank under the head (Fig. 5-12). Place it around the shank of the screw clockwise and close up the hook so that the top meets the incoming wire where the insulation was cut. None of the bare wire should be visible if you have done this properly. Screw down the terminal screw tightly; remember, a loose connection will heat up or flicker.

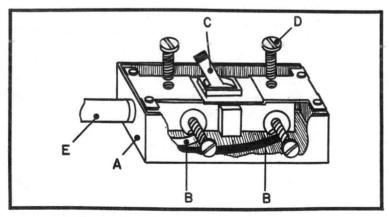

Fig. 5-12. Wall outlet.
    A. Connection box.
    B. Duplex plug-in outlet.
    C. "Hot" wires formed into hook for connection to screw terminals.
    D. Cover plate screw.
    E. Conduit carrying service into box.

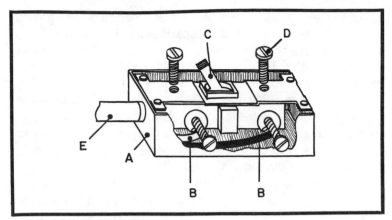

Fig. 5-13. Wall toggle switch.
    A. Connection box.
    B. Service wires formed into hooks for connection to screw terminals.
    C. Toggle of switch.
    D. Cover screws.
    E. Conduit bringing "hot" service wires.

In the case of the wall outlet no UL-approved knot is needed as the incoming wires come through the wall. Anyway, you don't tie solid wire in such a knot. Wall outlets should be encased in a UL-approved connection box, protected by a lid. Usually these are rectangular to fit the switch unit and a decorative plate is screwed on that fits against the surrounding wall. Be sure to check all connections over before putting on the lid and the plate.

Hooking Up a Wall Switch

There are several types of wall switches: toggle switches that click (Fig. 5-13) and those that are operated silently. There are also wall dimmer switches controlled by a knob that you push and then turn to control the dimness or brightness desired. All of these wall switches are hooked up similarly, much like the wall outlet.

While the same precautions should be taken as with any other wall hook up, usually only one "hot" wire enters the switch box. This means that if the two wires to be attached to the screw terminals were to touch it would be the same thing as turning on the switch.

Installing a Plug

Although Fig. 5-14 shows a round plug, they are sometimes rectangular in shape. Plugs are made of rubber or plastic, but their innards are much the same: two prongs with screw terminals attached to them, unless a third prong is provided to make a ground contact. This type is usually only used on extensions to which tools are attached. The rectangle casings are designed so that more plugs can be crowded into the outlet, but that only encourages overloading and is not a wise practice.

In hooking up a plug remove the outer sheath of the extension wire so that the two wires can be separated and tied into an UL-approved knot. Strip the wire insulation back neatly ½-inch as described for a socket. The insulation should protect the wire right up to the head of the terminal screw (D).

Bring the insulated wire out of the UL-approved knot and around the prong (B) to which it is to be connected (D). Form the bare tip of the wire into a hook that will just circle the shaft of the terminal screw and place it around the screw clockwise under the head. Tuck in any loose strands of the wire so that nothing sticks out from under the screw head when you tighten it down. All of this should be done precisely in the small space in which you have to work so do not rush the job.

Pull the extension cord outward from the plug so that the tightened knot rests snugly into the hole in the plug. Check the connections you have made and then replace the thin insulation piece (A) that fits over the prongs. This piece is for the purpose of protecting the face plate of the outlet in the event of a short ciruuit.

Other Electrical Connections

Make all electrical connections in a like manner, observing all of the precautions against short circuits. Leave no chance for bare wires to contact each other or a common conductor. Make certain that you have tightened all connecting and terminal screws and that they are firmly seated. Loose connections can cause sparks and heating.

Never undertake an electrical connection job when you are in a hurry. These jobs should be done carefully and with care and you will be rewarded by years of trouble-free service. Keep in mind that crossed wires cause fires and as I said, if there is any place that you don't want a fire, it is around the bed. If you meticulously follow directions and use only UL-approved parts, there will be less reason for you to hire a licensed electrician unless the job involves installed house wiring.

Just remember that if you monkey with the house wiring in back of the plug-in outlet and the insurance company finds out because of a

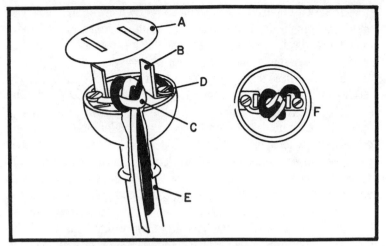

Fig. 5-14. Plug connection in process with insulative cover.
 A. Cover.
 B. Prong.
 C. UL-approved knot.
 D. Screw terminal.
 E. Outer two wires sheathed.
 F. Completed connections.

fire, they can cancel your insurance and the inspector can make you tear out the wiring, costing you plenty for the services of a licensed electrician to put it all back in service.

The householder can legally do his own electrical work to his heart's content providing it is outside a plug-in. One time I installed the complete stage lighting for a little theater, including a switch board with several banks of dimmers that was fully approved by both the insurance company representative and the building inspector because I had a licensed electrician install plug-in outlets at three fuse boxes to which I plugged in cables, like extension cords. Two of these cables were even dropped down an unused elevator shaft from the floor above where additional circuits were available. The stage lighting required the combined amperage furnished by all three of these lines. Before I did this the little theatre had been plagued constantly by blackouts from blown fuses as the result of overloads.

It took an unrelated fire on the floor below that was occupied by a printing plant to bring about an inspection of the entire building. This revealed the little theater's electrical troubles. When their stage was left in darkness by the removal of their illegal connections, they asked me for help. At the time I was lighting and effects director for the community theater and I came to their rescue.

Electricity operates according to its own laws, and alibis just aren't acceptable. Even household 110-volt current has no respect of people and will bite anyone who handles it carelessly. It will even start a fire when precautions are not observed.

Electrical fires seem to so often start when no one is around to quickly pull the plug or to throw the main switch to *OFF* until the source of the trouble has been remedied. Some acquaintances of mine who had a miniature Pomeranian dog had left it at home alone one evening when a wall outlet developed a short circuit and started to throw off sparks. The tiny dog rushed into action, probably attracted by the sparks and the noise they made. He took the cord attached to the sparking plug in his teeth and pulled it out of the outlet. When my friends returned home and found the room in darkness, they investigated. The little dog proudly displayed the offending plug that he had pulled. However, few of us have such intelligent dogs so we must take our own precautions.

BUILDING LAMPS

A table lamp is not too difficult to build. You can make such a lamp out of practically anything. It is a good way to use your favorite vase or a wine bottle, even a statue to advantage. The shade will be the most expensive component but, even with the fittings added to this cost, the whole thing will only amount to a fraction of the price of a store-bought lamp. Figure 5-15 shows the components of a typical table lamp.

If you are using a vase, for example, and you do not want to risk breaking it by putting a hole in the bottom, you can use the type of socket that lets the wire out of its sheath at the side. It still will have to have a collar that threads onto the cap so that it can be mounted on the fitting. Otherwise the wires would run down to the base through a threaded brass tube.

If you will want to use a three way bulb in the lamp, get a three way socket. This socket looks like the one way socket but the switch turns in three positions so that the bulb burns in three intensities of wattage and off. This type of socket is preferred to using three sockets in your lamp. Any time you want to use a single intensity bulb with one of these three way sockets you can, but it will only light the bulb when the switch is turned to one position.

The components of the lamp as shown in Fig. 5-15 can be found at almost any electrical fitting counter. The shade is held secure by the brass screw-on finial that comes in several sizes and designs.

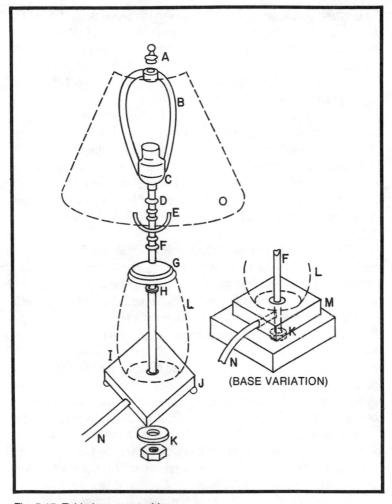

Fig. 5-15. Table lamp assembly.
 A. Screw-in finial to hold shade.
 B. A harp goes around bulb to support shade.
 C. Socket.
 D. Nut.
 E. Harp holder.
 F. Threaded brass tube.
 G. Cap to fit mouth of vase.
 H. Nut.
 I. Base.
 J. Feet.
 K. Nut and washer.
 L. Vase, bottle or jar.
 M. Wooden superimposed base.
 N. Extension cord.
 O. Shade.

This fitting should screw on tightly to the threaded projection at the top of the harp that goes around the bulb and fits into a holder assembled on the brass tube core of the lamp. Customarily harps will take up to 100-watt bulbs and leave nearly an inch of space between the glass of the bulb and the metal shade supports. Do not use a bulb so large that it touches the harp.

Unless you are not making a hole in the bottom of the vase or bottle that you are using, you will need to determine how long a brass threaded tube will need to be for the core to carry the wires down to the base and to act as the spinal column for the lamp. The components screw onto this brass tube. While the vase or bottle helps to keep the tube perpendicular, each screw-on fitting needs to be tight to prevent the weight of the shade at the top from throwing it out of balance.

The weight and mass of the vase or bottle aids in keeping the tube upright, but the base plays an important part by providing stability. This generally requires the base to be of several tiers.

A piece of marble will supply the weight needed if it is sufficiently large, but that presents another problem. It is no simple matter to put a hole neatly into marble, let alone a transverse hole in which to run the extension cord out to the side. A base with two or more tiers of a hard wood can be drilled not only perpendicularly but horizontally so that the brass tube can be inserted through the middle and the extension wires carried out to the side. Since the bottom must be flat, the washer and nut on the bottom of the tube must be countersunk. Rather than drill a horizontal hole for the wire, a groove can be routed from the countersink well to the edge for the extension cord that runs down the brass tube. This tier is glued onto the marble lower tier of the base.

Regardless of how you make the base, the brass rod must be secured to it if it runs through the vase or bottle. To help prevent the tube from wobbling, tighten the washer and nut at the bottom and the top of the vase or bottle. The nut at the top that impinges on the stopper for the mouth of the vase need not be countersunk but the one at the bottom must be so that the base will sit flat. The threaded brass tube has been concealed above the harp attachment, below that it may need a decorative sleeve.

It may be that to place the bulb at the right height, the threaded brass tube must be extended between the screw-on pieces. If so, install decorative screw-on pieces or a decorative sheath. You will find quite an assortment of these fittings at the electrical department counter. The threaded collar on the socket cap has a set screw; tighten it to prevent the socket from turning when you screw the bulb in or out.

Your decision on the length of the threaded tube will depend on the height of the vase used and the height you want for your lamp. This threaded tube should run the full height of the lamp. In deciding how tall the lamp should be, keep proportions in mind. The larger the vase used, the larger the shade should be.

It may be a good idea to take the vase you are going to use along with you, or at least the dimensions. You need to have the size of the opening at the top of the vase when you buy the cap. This cap must

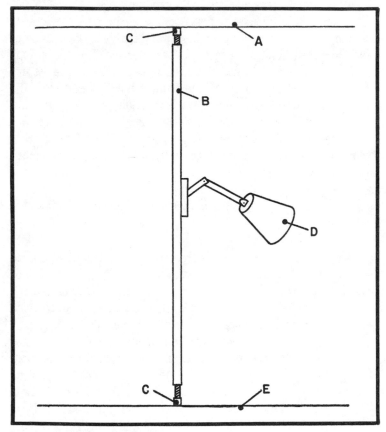

Fig. 5-16. Bedside pole lamp.
    A. Ceiling.
    B. Tube or pole.
    C. Adjustable wedge.
    D. Reading lamp.
    E. Floor.

343

stabilize the tube at this point and unless it fits snugly inside or outside of the opening, you will have to shim it. If you are making a ceramic bowl or wide mouthed gardineer into a lamp, you probably won't be able to find a cap large enough and will have to make one to fit. The best way to do this is to cut a pattern and saw out a piece of ¾-inch thick plywood. Make it just a wee bit larger and gradually sand it down to a close fit. Paint or stain the plywood.

I was making such a lamp using a large wine bottle and couldn't find a cap small enough to fit so I tried to whittle a cork down to size but it broke when I was putting the hole down the center. Then I tried wrapping the brass tube in foil to shim it out to a tight fit; this lasted only until I was able to find a cap that fit.

I have learned from experience to take all the measurements of the lamp, especially the overall height and the girth of the vase or bottle with me when I go shopping for a lamp shade. The salesperson in the lamp shade department should be able to advise you on the size of shade that will best show off the lamp. After all, the shade is the most visible portion unless you use an outstanding vase for the body.

The material of a lamp shade is flammable and must be kept at a very minimum of 6 to 8 inches away from the bulb. An incandescent bulb gets very hot and throws off a lot of heat. A flow of air is needed around the bulb to carry off this heat, otherwise the heat will discolor the shade and deteriorate it quickly.

Proceed to assemble the lamp components (Fig. 5-15) as follows:

1. Insert the extension cord through the base and up the threaded brass tube, leaving enough slack at the top to form the UL-approved knot. All fittings will have to be threaded onto the rod, so lay them out in the order in which they go to be sure you don't omit one.
2. Screw on the washers and nuts above and below the base and tighten them up, keeping the threaded tube perpendicular. If this tube leans to one side, the whole lamp will be crooked. If the vase you are using for the body of the lamp has a large enough mouth for you to get your hand into it, so much the better as it will make tightening up the nut against the bottom easier. The washer and nut on the bottom side of the vase needs to be countersunk into the base. That is why the top tier of the base should be of wood even if the lower tier is of marble.

3. Set the vase or bottle in place. Adhesive can be used on the bottom to assist in holding it steady.

4. A nut can be threaded on the tube below the cap to steady it in place and another nut tightened above it so that the tube is held firmly between the two nuts. The mouth of the vase is not closed either by the cap or the wooden plug you have made.

5. Slip the harp on over the tube and secure it firmly in place with a nut. The harp should be totally concealed by the shade.

6. If any portions of the threaded tube will be left uncovered, slip a piece of decorative sheath tubing over it so that it is anchored by screw-ons.

7. Thread the wires up through the collar of the socket cap, tie the UL-approved knot in it and connect them to the terminal screws as previously described. Draw the surplus extension wire down through the threaded tube and out of the base and assemble the socket.

8. Inspect your wiring job and test it out after having hooked up the plug as already described.

9. When you are assured that all is correct so far, mount the harp on the holding arms, the shade on the threaded finial screw atop the harp and screw on the finial.

10. If it turns out that you have slipped up somewhere and the lamp is too low, do not despair. It can be raised by adding a layer or two at the bottom of the base, even at this late date.

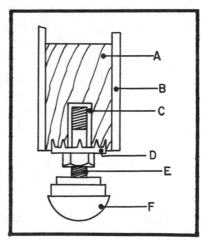

Fig. 5-17. Adjustable T-nut wedge.
A. Wooden plug.
B. Aluminum tube.
C. ⅜-inch diameter hole.
D. T-nut.
E. ¼-inch bolt.
F. Rubber tip.

If the shade is a deep one so that it is difficult to reach up inside of it to turn or push the switch on the socket, you can remedy this in two ways. One good way is to leave the socket switch on and plug the extension cord into an outlet that is controlled by a wall switch. Another way is to install a line toggle switch just beyond the lamp base so that it can be reached easily. You now have built yourself a lamp that would have cost you plenty had you bought it.

Building a Pole Lamp

Where beds have no headboards on which to set a reading lamp, a floor-to-ceiling pole lamp (Fig. 5-16) can be located just about anywhere you want it. While these lamps can be bought, you can build your own for a lot less. This will require only the purchase of the materials and the lamp to be attached or at least the shade or reflector.

The pole can be wooden or aluminum and wedged between ceiling and floor by an adjustable unit in the bottom and the top. The poles are available in 6 and 8-foot lengths that will reach most ceiling heights.

The pole can be wedged between the ceiling and the floor by insertion of either of two adjustable wedging devices (Fig. 5-16). While there are devices that depend on a spring for the wedging action, I have found two to be more reliable and, incidentally, less expensive.

The T-nut device (Fig. 5-17) can be installed on either a wooden pole or into an aluminum pole. Because an aluminum pole is hollow, it must have a wooden plug driven into the ends. The tite-joint device requires a sufficient wood thickness on the receiving side to insert the hex nut that locks the carriage bolt at the desired height (Fig. 5-18).

The pole can be round or square, even rectangular if you use a 2-by-4 for the pole. If you use a round pole, it should be at least 1½-inches in diameter. Two inches is even better. It must be straight to begin with and should be sealed so that any dampness will not tend to cause it to warp. When I lived by the ocean, I used a 2-by-4.

Install the T-nut device as follows:

1. At the exact center of the pole, drill a ⅜-inch hole about 1 inch in depth.
2. Exactly over this hole tap in the T-nut (D) so that the holes correspond.

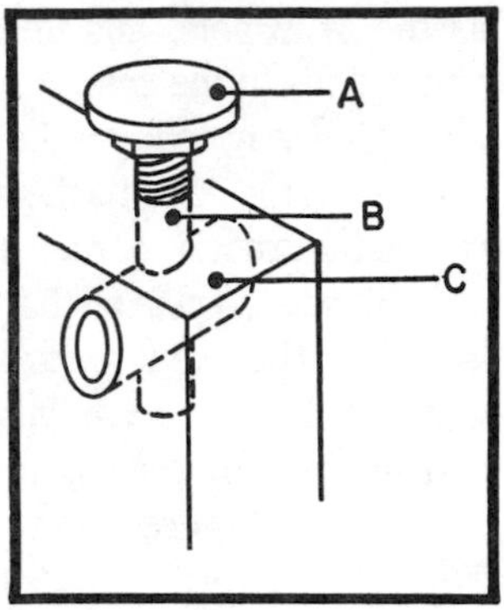

Fig. 5-18. Adjustable tite-joint wedge.
    A. Hard rubber washer is glued on.
    B. 12 inch long carriage bolt.
    C. Hex nut tite-joint fastener.

3. Screw the rubber-headed ¼-inch bolt (F) into the nut, through the T-nut (D) and up into the ⅜-inch hole.
4. When you have done this at both ends of the pole, fit the pole between the floor and the ceiling, being sure that it is exactly perpendicular. To insure this use a bubble level.
5. Adjust the bolts at bottom and top until the lamp pole is tightly wedged in place.

It is presumed that before putting up the lamp pole you have attached the light fixture you are going to use. This means that the extension cord has been run into a hole, if a hollow tube is being used

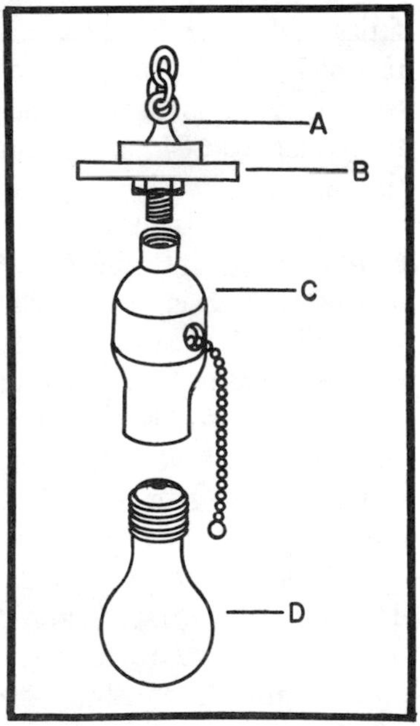

Fig. 5-19. Drop light.
    A. Hanger ring fixture.
    B. Top of lantern.
    C. Socket.
    D. Light bulb.

347

as the lamp pole, and up or down according to where it is to be plugged in. In the case of a wooden pole, the wire is stapled to the pole. One way to keep the wire from being too noticeable is to use wire the same color as the pole or weave it in and out of the links of a chain and drape it across to the wall and the outlet.

Be sure to plan so that the switch that controls the bedside pole lamp is within easy reach of a person in the bed. The light fixture itself can be of several types, but the beam should be confined to a narrow area for reading in bed.

There is no reason why the pole should not support a second lamp for general illumination of the room. This one can be trained on the ceiling for reflection. If you use a 2-by-4 lamp pole, you can install a small fluorescent fixture up and down for general lighting.

Building Slatted Lanterns

A slatted hanging lantern is easily built and will cast interesting shadows about a room.

Cut the base and top from ¾-inch thick plywood. The base should be 6 to 8 inches square. The top can be the same or a little smaller. Either one can have more than one tier, especially the top from which hangs the socket and light bulb.

In the exact center of the top bore a hole for a ⅜-inch hanger fitting. If the top is too thick, such as having used two thicknesses of plywood, the fitting may have to be extended by screwing on another threaded piece so that it extends far enough to screw into the cap of the socket. These fittings must have a hole down the center to carry the wire to the socket.

In making a lantern the socket and bulb hang downward and the wire comes out at the top (Fig. 5-22). The top fitting has a ring that attached to a chain from which the lantern is suspended. The wire weaves in and out of the links of the chain, which is attached either at a ceiling plate or hook. The wire is hooked up in this case at the ceiling connection box. If the wire is to go to a wall outlet, it continues to weave in and out of the links of the chain, which is festooned across to the wall, and from there it goes to the wall outlet.

If you want to be able to turn the light off or on at the lantern, use a socket with a pull chain switch and bore a hole in the bottom for the pull chain or cord to hang down through. In either case the socket switch can be left turned on and the light controlled by the switch that controls the outlet to which it is attached. Do not plan to use the socket switch if it is the type that you push at the socket because it will be difficult for you to get your hand through the slats of the lantern.

The lantern should be somewhere from 12 to 18 inches tall, depending on its width. Cut the slats from smooth lattice and tack them between the top and the base with wire brads.

The lantern can be square (Fig. 5-20), triangular (Fig. 5-21), round (Fig. 5-22) or hexagonal. The square lantern can have either 12 or 9 slats; the round one 4 to 6 slats. Use more slats if you do not

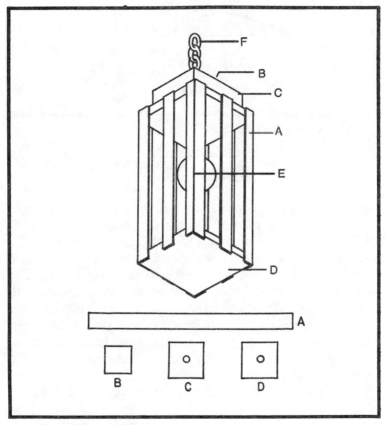

Fig. 5-20. A square slatted hanging lantern.
    A. Lath.
    B. Top, upper tier.
    C. Top, lower tier.
    D. Bottom.
    E. Light bulb.
    F. Hanger ring fixture.

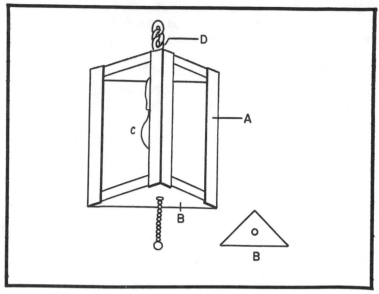

Fig. 5-21. A triangular slatted hanging lantern.
  A. Lath.
  B. Bottom.
  C. Light bulb.
  D. Hanger ring fixture.

plan to line the lantern. Such a lantern can be lined with any transparent or translucent material or left open with a decorative light bulb.

The base can be slightly smaller than the top and the lattice slightly angled, but do not allow this difference to be more than ½-inch or the lattice is liable to pull away from its fastening. The plywood edges must be finished with tape to make them look smooth across the plys. When completed, the lantern should be painted.

A standing lamp can be built on the same idea as the slatted lantern. It too can be square, triangular or round, but the socket and bulb must come up from the base (Fig. 5-23) and the switch should be on the extension cord, just beyond the base.

The lattice lamp can also be left open or enclosed by transparent or translucent material the same as the lantern. Since most of the heat from the light bulb will be flowing upward, if you plan to enclose the sides, put two or three vent holes in the top for the heat to escape. Heat tends to rise and will be mostly radiated upward from the rounded end of the light bulb.

Note in Fig. 5-20 how the extension cord may be taken out through the base from where it comes down the center from the

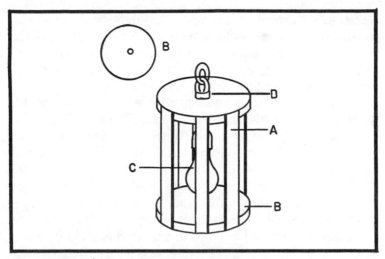

Fig. 5-22. A round slatted hanging lantern.
    A. Lath.
    B. Bottom.
    C. Light bulb.
    D. Hanger ring fixture.

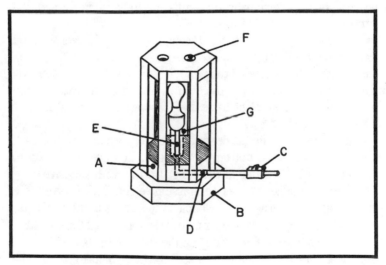

Fig. 5-23. Standing slatted lantern.
    A. Top and top tier of base.
    B. Bottom tier of base.
    C. Line toggle switch.
    D. Extension cord exit.
    E. Threaded tube and fittings.
    F. Air vent holes.
    G. Brass sleeve.

socket. As with any lamp, the base needs to be heavy enough to prevent the lamp from toppling over easily. If the base has at least two tiers, the extension wire can be brought out between them in a routed-out groove, otherwise the base must be thick enough to permit having a hole drilled horizontally for the wire.

Figure 5-23 shows such a lamp with a hexagonal base, but just as with the lanterns, the base may be square, round, triangular or even free form. Make as many latice upright pieces as you want. The more of these, the closer together and therefore the less light, but the shadows are interesting.

The supporting threaded tube goes into the hole in the center of the top base and is secured in the countersink on the bottom side by a nut. This countersink should be deep enough so that there is room for the extension cord to turn into the horizontally routed groove and out at the side of the top tier of the base, yet set flat on the bottom or at least next lower tier of the base. This method is much simpler than to make the extension wire turn a right angle inside of a horizontal hole, which requires a much thicker upper base.

A toggle line switch should be installed just beyond the base. It will be more convenient here than having to reach in through the lattice pieces.

Secure the threaded tube to the upper base. Slip over the tube the decorative sheath that is to extend up to the socket. Screw the socket cap on the threaded tube and tighten the set screw so it will not turn when you screw in the bulb. Now thread the wires up the tube, allowing enough slack to tie the UL-approved knot and connect it to the terminal screws.

Hook up the socket as described previously and draw the slack of the wire out at the bottom of the base. You are now ready to assemble the bottom tier of the base. Do this with adhesive.

After the adhesive has set, assemble the lattice using wire brads dipped in glue so they will hold in the edges of the plywood.

Note that holes have been made in the top so that the heat from the bulb can escape. If you close up the sides of the lantern so that you cannot get your hand in to install the bulb, install the top with wood screws so that you can remove it when it becomes necessary to change the bulb.

If you want, you can install legs beneath the base. This will lift the height of the lamp, make sure that elevating it on legs does not give it the tendency to top. If the lower tier of the base is marble, it will help the lamp to keep its balance.

Plastic Bottle Lamp

Clever lighting fixtures can be fashioned from large polyethylene bottles, but never use larger than a 60-watt bulb in them or they may melt. Usually these containers will have removable labels, at worst the printing will be only on one side. You can cut out that portion and use the remainder as a reflective shell when

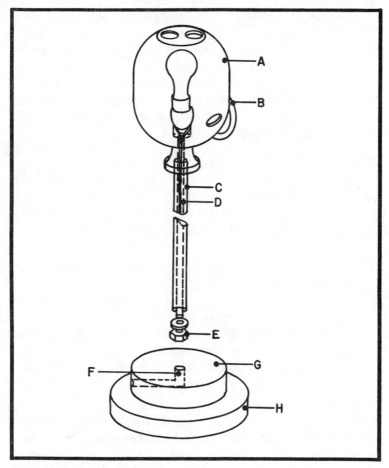

Fig. 5-24. Plastic bottle floor lamp.
    A. Polyethylene bottle.
    B. Socket, threaded brass tube to carry wires and fittings.
    C. Aluminum tube.
    D. Threaded tube carrying wire.
    E. Fittings to secure tubes.
    F. Routing for wire.
    G. Top tier of wire.
    H. Heavy lower base.

mounted upside down (Fig. 5-24). Turn the cut-out side toward the wall and you will have a soft, diffused illumination.

At the electrical fitting counter of your supplier you can find candle-like sheaths that are fine for concealing the threaded tube that carries the wire from the socket. These are nonmetallic and so do not carry the heat to the plastic, but you can use a brass sheath if you prefer.

Cut the base, round, square, triangular or hexagon in shape. Figure 5-24 shows a round two tiered base, the lower one preferably of a heavy material such as marble or metal. You will not need to make any holes in it as it can be glued to the upper tier or tiers.

The extension wire should be brought out at the upper tier of the base as discussed for the slat lamps. Plastic bottles make good floor based lamps, and the same idea can be used for a hanging light used for general illumination.

Hi-Lo Intensity Lamp

Some people who like to read under an intense light, will probably enjoy this high intensity lamp that operates on 6 or 12-volts. It can be fashioned from a small, preferably aluminum frying pan. Some people prefer this type of lamp for in-bed reading.

To build this type of lamp you will need:

One inexpensive or recycled metal frying pan, preferably a 6 inch aluminum one

One transformer, 6 or 12-volts, with a secondary coil of the same rating as the size of the bulb you plan to use

One three way toggle switch with positions marked for HI, LO, OFF (or you can mark these)

One socket and matching bulb (these can be the automotive type)

A rectangular sheet of Lucite that will fit into the pan. If the frying pan you are using is aluminum, shine up the interior surface. The back can be painted with heat-resistant enamel. If the pan is of another metal, spray the inner surface smoothly with aluminum to obtain the shiniest surface possible. If this surface is not smooth so that it will reflect the light well, line the inside of the pan with smooth aluminum foil. Aluminum is the most efficient reflecting surface and for a high intensity lamp you want all the light reflected.

Bend the handle of the frying pan as shown in Fig. 5-25A to form a stand for the back. Using heat resistant adhesive, install the transformer near the lower end of the handle, but do not block the

354

hole at the end of the handle intended for hanging the pan up. Use this hole to carry away the extension cord.

Check that the Lucite face plate will fit snugly into the pan; if it does not, trim it as necessary so that all of its edges that contact the inside of the pan touch. Do not glue the Lucite in yet.

To mount the socket for the bulb and the toggle switch, holes must be bored in the Lucite (Fig. 5-25B). Mark switch positions for HI, LO and OFF.

It may be that the top edges of the Lucite may need to be contoured to fit against the pan so that the glue will hold it firmly. The intense light will heat the pan metal making it necessary to use an adhesive that will not be affected by heat and will hold the Lucite firmly to the aluminum. Make the wiring hook up. The lamp will now look like Fig. 5-25C with the bent handle and the Lucite balancing it in an upright position.

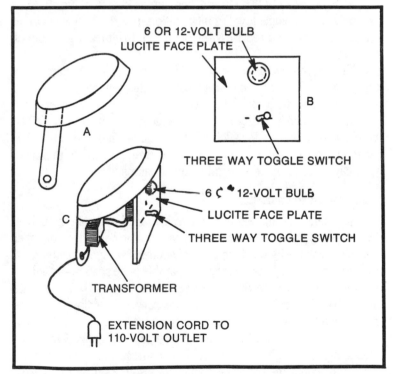

Fig. 5-25. High intensity bed lamp.
    A. Bend the handle.
    B. Mount the socket and toggle switch.
    C. Completed lamp.

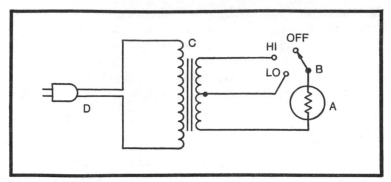

Fig. 5-26. High intensity lamp three way circuit.
    A. Hi-lo 6 or 12-volt bulb.
    B. Three way toggle switch.
    C. Transformer.
    D. 110-volt extension cord.

For the HI-LO-OFF circuit, hook up as shown in Fig. 5-26. If you only want a single level of illumination, use the two way circuit and components that go with this (Fig. 5-27). In either case solder all connections.

Should you use a larger than 6 inch frying pan, the lamp may tend to pitch forward. To counterbalance this tendency to tip, add some weight to the back of the bent handle, toward the lower end.

Using a high intensity beam for reading is habit forming. When you habitually read under such a light, you may find that you will be wanting to do other close work under the intense beam. In this case, you may want to make several of these lamps.

Using Japanese Lanterns

Most interesting and decorative illumination can be contrived by the use of Japanese lanterns for shades. They are made of paper and held in shape by toothpick-sized wooden "wiring." Incidentally, they are more inexpensive than comparable lamp shades and light in weight. They do have one disadvantage however, they are quite flammable. For this reason it is necessary that a flow of air be maintained between the lantern and the light bulb, especially when the bulb is over 40 watts. Even small wattage bulbs like Christmas tree lights, although they are of small wattage, can heat up sufficiently to scorch the paper lanterns and possibly set them on fire.

Speaking of Christmas tree lights, even though these strings divide the line wattage by the number of bulbs, they can give a striking effect in white or colors. Since the bulbs are connected in

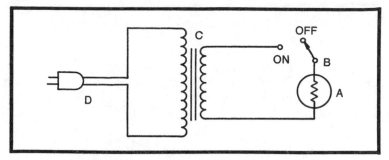

Fig. 5-27. High intensity lamp two way circuit.
　　A. Off-on 6 or 12-volt bulb.
　　B. Two way toggle switch.
　　C. Transformer.
　　D. 110-volt extension cord.

series, however, when one burns out all go out. Outdoor strings sometimes are connected in parallel, each bulb using the full 110 volts. In this case one bulb can burn out and not affect the others on the string. Not only do these lights use more current but they heat up more. This increased heating requires more air flow space to not endanger the paper lantern.

Figure 5-28A suggests a string of eight lanterns of graduated sizes with one of the tiny bulbs in each. In Fig. 5-28B larger lanterns are used and each contains two bulbs. Both styles of strings can be suspended from the ceiling with the extension cord festooned entwined in a chain to the wall outlet. Since these strings are light in weight, a heavy chain is not necessary.

The Japanese lanterns can be all white, figured or in various colors. The tiny bulbs can also be all white, of one color or a variety of colors that will show off the lantern that encloses it. Make certain that no bulb touches the enclosing lantern and hang the string so that it can be retracted if one of the bulbs must be replaced. One way to do both of these is to attach the string to an ordinary wash line cord so that you can pull it out at the top. The lanterns can be glued together by their thin wooden collars with the solid base removed. This accelerates the flow of air between them.

Japanese Pole Lamp

Getting to the effective use of Japanese lanterns, I once used such a lantern that was just over 18 inches in diameter, suspended from a decorative bracket attached to a pole, a little over halfway up. The pole was wedged between the ceiling and the floor (Fig. 5-29).

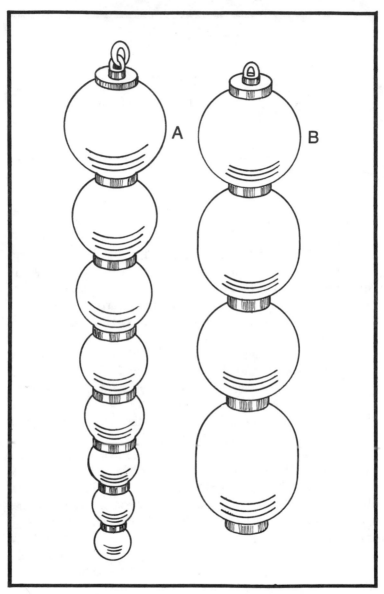

Fig. 5-28. Christmas tree lights in Japanese lanterns.
    A. One bulb per lantern.
    B. Two bulbs per lantern.

The lantern used in this manner should be at least 12 inches in diameter or it will look dinky. The larger the diameter the smarter it will look. To find a large Japanese lantern you will probably have to do a lot of shopping; I know I had to. I finally found one nearly 19 inches in diameter; it was pure white.

This large a lantern required a bracket about 24 inches long to set it out from the pole several inches. Due to the size of this paper lantern, it only needed several links of chain to suspend it from the bracket. Each link was about an inch long.

I found 21 inch brackets although I had searched several places for a 24 inch one that was decorative looking. For the pole I chose to use a 2-by-2 that was perfectly straight and well seasoned. It was hard wood.

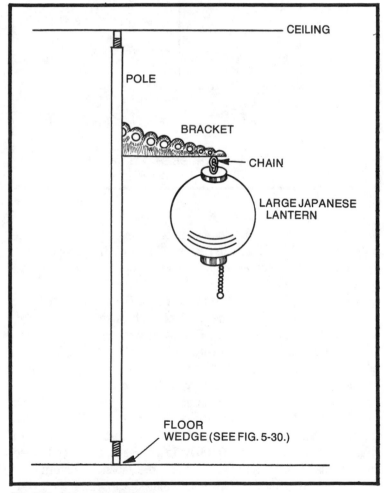

Fig. 5-29. Japanese pole lamp.

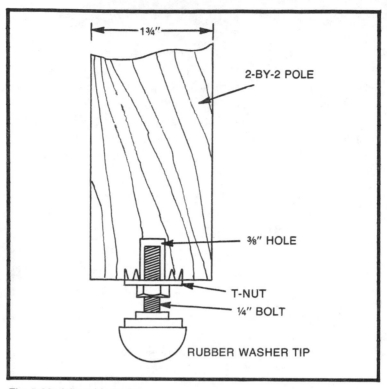

Fig. 5-30. Adjustable wedge.

I carefully measured from floor to ceiling and sawed off the 2-by-2 an inch short of that. In each end I bored a hole about an inch deep exactly in the center (Fig. 5-30) and tapped a T-nut in so that the holes coincided.

To prevent the wedges from marring the floor or the ceiling, I glued a rubber washer on the head of each of two ¼-inch bolts. These were just plumber's washers that had no hole through them. When the adhesive had set, I screwed the bolts into the T-nuts on either end of the pole far enough to raise the pole exactly perpendicular between the floor and the ceiling. I checked this with a carpenter's level so that the pole was parallel with the nearest wall. I had already installed the bracket on the pole a little over halfway up from the floor. About an inch back from the tip of the bracket, I inserted a link of a brass chain, the bracket having a brass finish. Then I added another link of chain from which I hung the Japanese lantern.

Before installing the pole, I had painted it to match the woodwork. Measuring the needed length of an extension cord, which matched the color of the pole, I wound the wire in and out of the links of the chain that held the lantern to the bracket. To do this I found that I had to remove the plug at the other end of the extension cord since I had not thought that far ahead.

Stapling the cord up the pole on the back side, I only had take it over to the wall outlet. Luckily I had bought a length of chain long enough to reach so I twined the wire in and out of it.

Since it was a rented apartment with a fussy landlady, I took the precaution against leaving a spot on the ceiling from the rubber tip of the wedge by inserting a small piece of white blotting paper between the rubber and the ceiling. As it turned out, however, the landlady was so taken with the lamp that she paid me for it so I would leave it when I moved.

If you want to use an aluminum pole, there is the problem of attaching the bracket and of finding a bracket of aluminum. In this case I would recommend that you use a wooden pole, but the whole effect will be spoiled if the pole is not perfectly straight.

Glow Worm

While not using Japanese lanterns, an interesting and novel light can be made that will supply general mood illumination. It is made from a plastic drayer hose and a string of Christmas tree lights. The plastic dryer hose can be found in at appliance departments or hardware stores. It usually comes in 6-foot lengths and is 4 inches in diameter (Fig. 5-29).

For the best effect insert a string of frosted white Christmas tree lights, wound about a piece of cotton cord to keep the bulbs from touching the sides of the tube. The low wattage bulbs cast an interesting mood glow and a flock of glow worms make novel party lighting.

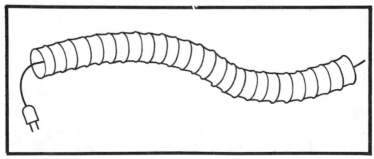

Fig. 5-31. Glow worms via Christmas tree lights.

Styrofoam Ball Fixture

Styrofoam does not come in large enough balls to make this fixture. Since styrofoam tends to melt with heat, no larger than a 60-watt light bulb should be used when it is within 40 inches of the material.

You can build a ball of any size you wish by attaching styrofoam cups together. The wastebasket by any office coffee machine will yield enough of these cups to make a good sized ball. The size of the cups you use will determine the size of the ball to some extent, or you can use more of the smaller sized cups.

The smallest size of these cups is similar to a shot glass. These can be made into a ball about 26 inches in diameter. The largest size, like those in which they serve milk shakes, can be formed into a ball as large as 6 feet across. This size ball requires some 250 of the large cups.

Use a white adhesive, such as Elmer's Glue, because the styrofoam is sparkly white. This glue sets fast but to avoid having to wait for the glue to set, hold the cups together with clothespins until you are sure that the glue is dry enough so that they won't slip. Any glue that adds even a tinge of color will spoil the sparkly white appearance of the styrofoam and some adhesives even tends to melt the foam.

Start making the ball by gluing two cups together, side by side and keep adding. The spherical shape is attained by gluing the sides of the cups together with the solid bottoms turned outward. Leave a hole at the top and circle it with a hoop formed out of heavy enough wire to support the ball, socket and light bulb.

Suspend the bulb so that you can pull out the socket should you need to replace the bulb if it burns out. This is a novel fun light fixture that will become a conversation piece, especially if it is hung in a large area. Use your imagination and you will be able to contrive other types of mobiles for lighting fixtures using wire and many types of materials.

Large Wattage Bulbs

When you use bulbs of large wattage they must be held at a safe distance from surrounding surfaces. Look over the assortment of clips and holders that you will find at an electrical fixture store. Some of these clamp onto shelves, some attach to poles. Then there are the photo-flood reflectors with clamps that you can find at the photographic supply store. It is designed for a large light bulb, has a reflector that is usually aluminum and a heavy clamp that will slip over a thick shelf.

All sorts of clamps and holders can be used to safely hold the larger bulbs, even spotlight bulbs. Shop around and you will be amazed at what you can come up with. Some of these holders are shown in Fig. 5-32. These are designed to hold a socket, bulb and the shade, mounted on a rod that can be slipped into the holes.

In the case of A, B or C, any crooking of the light must be provided by the holding device on which the socket is mounted.

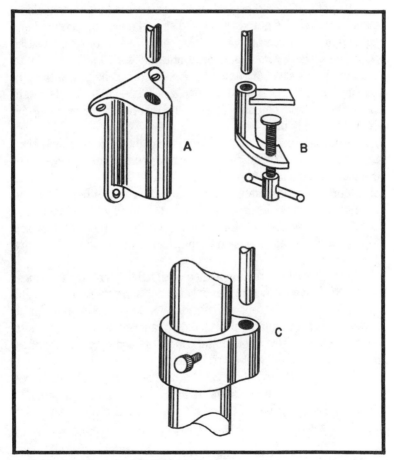

Fig. 5-32. Clamp and holders for direct lighting.
    A. Screw-on mount.
    B. Clamp-on mount.
    C. Pole mount.

Clamp B can also be had with a thumb screw that controls the tilting arrangement. Should you want to use the light in several places, a bracket can be mounted at each place and the lamp moved to each place and plugged into a nearby outlet.

Recessed Lights

When a light is recessed so that there is little air flow, do not use larger than a 60-watt bulb. Fluorescent tubes are much better for this purpose and consume less electricity. Neon tubes do not heat up like incandescent bulbs; this makes them safer.

If spotlights are recessed, ventilating arrangements should be made. These bulbs get very hot and should never be screwed into metal sockets, especially when they are 100-watts or over. Use porcelain sockets with spot lights and therapeutic bulbs. The latter are not always red but they are labeled on the bulb. Speaking of labeling, once in a while you will find a bulb label that directs you to install it up or maybe down. If you do not heed this instruction, the bulb will quickly burn out.

When an electric light flickers, suspect a loose connection. Check immediately, first see if the bulb is completely screwed into the socket. If the flickering is caused because the filament is about to burn out, a gentle thump of your fingernail will either cause the filament to reweld itself or the bulb will burn out immediately. Troubleshooting beyond this should never be without first pulling the plug if it is on an extension, or pulling the main switch if it is on a direct line.

The intensity, direction and color of lighting creates an atmosphere. Soft warm lighting lends enchantment while harsh, cold lighting or glare destroys all romantic mood. Harsh lights can be softened by reflecting the illuminating beam off of walls, mirrors or ceiling surfaces. The whole effect can be enhanced or destroyed by the illumination used and its placement.

Not only mirrors but reflections on shiny surfaces will produce glare unless mitigated in some manner. Only when you want to provide for reading, writing or doing close work do you want to use a direct lighting source. That is why blue tinted mirrors are used in the bordellos of Europe.

Mirrors can add depth. They can be large, square, rectangular, framed or unframed, or small 6 or 12 inch squares that are installed with tape or adhesive. Some are shot with gold or tinted. Using this technique, mirrors can be installed on top of built-ins, with a reflective acoustical panel suspended above them if the ceiling is not the right height.

Small pools of light create interest and a feeling of isolation. Glaring light creates an uncomfortable feeling. White or ivory surfaces will reflect the most light after aluminum. These are just a few useful hints in the use of light; use them in planning your bedroom.

Fluorescent Bed Light

One of the most pleasant lights by which to read in bed is a pinkish fluorescent lamp. You can install such a light under the shelf at the head of your bed (Fig. 5-33). Fluorescent tubes come in various lengths and with fixtures to fit them. A 14-watt, 14 inch, warm white tube will give you plenty of light and no added heat. It will also save you a lot on your electric bill if you read in bed often. The fixtures usually have a switch installed right on them. If it is a double bed and your bed partner also likes to read in bed, install one at the head of each of you. The soft light from one of these is not as disturbing as an incandescent lamp if your partner wants to go to sleep.

FOR THE EARS

Many people enjoy listening to stereo or the radio or watching television while they relax in bed. To do this you need to plan so that the listening and seeing is satisfactory and you are comfortable.

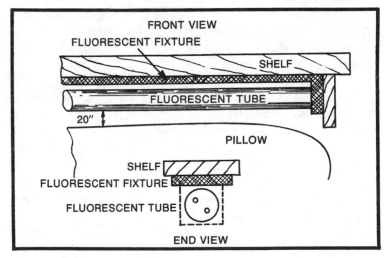

Fig. 5-33. Fluorescent bed light.

Audio engineers are quite fussy about the setup of a stereo system, especially the location of the speakers. Not only do they want good speakers, correctly adjusted, but they want them up off of the floor and facing the longest axis of the room and at the correct angle and distance.

Placement of Stereo Speakers

Since this discussion is principally concerned with beds, we will presume that the listener's ears that are to receive the sounds from the stereo speakers will belong to the occupant of the bed. After all, the listener's ears must be considered as a part of any stereo system.

At least in this discussion the bed is the center of the listening environment. This complicates matters, especially if the bed has a tester, whether it is drapery or wood. To test an area for its acoustics, place yourself in the center and clap your hands sharply. If you can hear an echo, you can be assured that the room is too "live" acoustically for slow or heavy music, for concert or orchestral music, for light and lively tunes or vocal and instrumental music. If you will be listening exclusively to beat and rock, the room will be all right acoustically. If when you clap your hands sharply, the clap ends with a dull thud, the room is acoustically "dead" for any kind of stereo sound. Try this test from the middle of the bed where you will be listening.

Bouncing of sound or resonance can be alleviated by changing or modifying the arrangement of furniture, moving the bed or the location of the speakers. If the music from the speakers sounds like you are in a hole when you are in the middle of the bed, probably the speakers are too far apart.

If you hear odd noises at times, do not be too quick to blame the speakers; investigate first. The source of these sounds may be sympathetic vibrations originating from a piece of bric-a-brac, a loose fixture or some such item. Try moving likely items slightly and tighten up anything that may be slightly loose. If the sound disappears, you have found its source. Likewise, a hum may be caused by an incomplete housewiring ground or interference from some appliance. Do not be quick to blame the speakers or the adjustment of their controls in this case either.

Acoustical problems will enter the picture whenever you plan to incorporate a stereo system, even radio or television, in a bed area. Let the instruction manual guide you in your installation and operation of the controls. Here are a few bits of advice that may be of assistance:

"Dead" surfaces will rob sounds of their brilliance.

Hard surfaces not only bounce sound back but will tend toward strident amplification.

Since there are almost bound to be some "dead" surfaces around a bed area, position "live" surfaces opposite them to balance and temper the sound. Square or rectangular corners can also set up acoustical resonances and cause sounds to bounce back and forth so that one sound wave steps on the one ahead of it and bumps into others that are returning on their bounce.

This is a glimpse of some of the problems involving the placement of two stereo speakers; consider how a four speaker stereo system will multiply these problems. While far be it for me to tell you where to place the speakers, Fig. 5-34 may be of some help.

Other Installations

Not only do engineers have ideas about stereo systems and the proper way to install them, but so does every "stereophyle," if you can so classify those who make it a hobby. These notions multiply

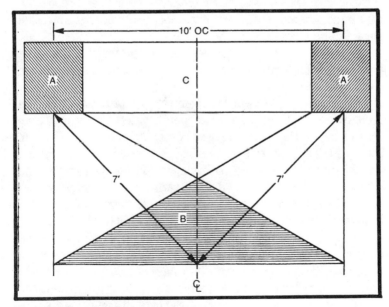

Fig. 5-34. Area of best stereo sound balance.
     B. Best sound reception area.
     C. Other units.

when it comes to quadraphonic systems, but the principles of acoustics remain the same and a balance of sound is what they all are striving for.

When a sound system is incorporated into the bed area where the space is confined, the controls should be placed conveniently so that they can be reached without the necessity of the occupant of the bed having to get up. This can be done by incorporating the controls in the headboard as in Fig. 5-35.

This arrangement may not place the speakers in an advantageous position. Some manufacturers offer combinations, such as Panasonic (Fig. 5-36), that put the turn table on the top shelf where it is insulated from the AM/FM radio and the player controls to prevent pickup of any hum. They think that this arrangement has an advantage over others that may be chosen by the installer. Then they put the stereo speakers so that they are likewise insulated from both the controls and the record player, at either end to complete the compact unit. The records and tapes are stored on the shelf between the speakers and below the shelf on which rests the controls.

There are certain restrictions in the installation of a stereo system. These restrictions mainly have to do with acoustics in a confined area such as a bed. However, vibrations and resonance must be considered. The safety of the electrical work that is involved must also be considered.

To combat heating, ventilation must be provided. This can be done by allowing air to circulate freely and avoiding crowding of the components.

Acoustically, the ideal arrangement will place the speakers about 10 feet apart with the listener approximately 10 feet away from each of them. This, I am assured, produces the best balance of sound. As was shown in Fig. 5-34, this requires an equilateral triangle with all three sides 10 feet apart. These distances can be varied as much as 3 feet by a slight variation in the angle of both speakers toward each other. Sometimes this variation may even improve the sound depending on the other acoustical influences.

While the instructions furnished by the manufacturer of the equipment should guide you in installation of the stereo system, a certain amount of trial and error will be necessary since the manufacturer cannot be aware of the constructions in your particular case.

Resonance must be avoided at all costs. It can be partly prevented by the use of glue and proper nailing in building the shelf for the equipment. The arrangement of the equipment is important in

Fig. 5-35. Integral sound system in the headboard.

addition to partitions between the amplifier and the turn table to prevent the photograph cartridge from picking up the hum of the amplifier transformer.

Further precautions will reduce the chances of acoustical feedback and hum. These include isolation of the low level leads between the components of the system. These leads can be identified by their woven metallic shielding, which should be grounded at the ends.

When lining up the stereo components on a shelf, probably about 10 feet in length, the equipment will weigh quite a lot so the shelf will have to be well supported. For sufficient support, ¾-inch thick plywood will work for the shelf. The raw front edge of the plywood will have to be finished with tape of course, or molding. To further guard against resonance glue a sheet of 1/16-inch thick cork on the top of the wooden surface.

Before you decide on how long and how wide the shelf should be, measure the equipment, allowing for the divisions that we have advised. Hi-fi and stereo equipment keep getting more and more compact so it may be possible that by the time you build your shelf, a shorter shelf may be sufficient.

In lining up the components, for example, place the speakers with their woofers and tweeters at each end. Between them set the

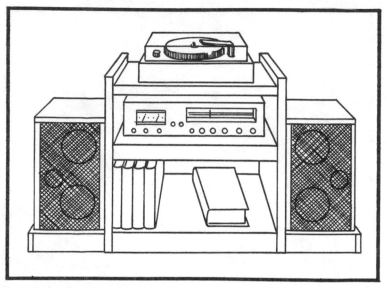

Fig. 5-36. Stereo combination.

record changer and tape recorder, the AM/FM broadcast tuner, the combination preamplifier and controls.

You may want to add a tape recorder and a phantom third channel, possibly with separate speakers. If so, place them in the middle or build a second shelf for them. The second shelf can be an additional help in solving the problem of dissipating the heat generated by the extra equipment.

The chances of a hum or acoustical feedback can be further reduced by running the low level leads between the units along the bottom of the shelf on which the components rest. By routing out grooves along the bottom of the board or plywood shelf and running these wires in them, they will be hidden from view. This means that the shelf must be of a material that is thick enough not to be weakened by the routing.

You have the option of leaving the equipment exposed to view or of hiding it in cabinets. If you put it in cabinets it is necessary that you provide for adequate ventilation so that the heat will be able to pass off. These cabinets should be closed by sliding doors. The doors can be best made of hardboard (Masonite) ⅛-inch thick. The controls, however, should be located so that they can be easily reached without getting out of bed.

The turn table and tape recorder will mean that record and tape storage is needed. This can be supplied integrally or as a separate unit. You can easily build the record storage rack shown in Fig. 5-37, which has the additional advantage of being portable. While not shown, a tape storage shelf can be run between the legs on one side of the rack.

The length of this rack will depend on the number of records you want to have by your bedside. The width of the V-shaped sides should be about the diameter of the largest record. Lace leather thongs of ⅛-inch cord from side to side just far enough apart to take record. Records should always be stored on edge; storing them in stacks will cause them to warp. A warped record will produce distorted sounds.

The legs and crossbars can be made from 1-by-2s. Spread the V so that the largest record will fit in comfortably and you will have sufficient space in front for a shelf on which to store tapes. If you also have smaller records, add lacings deeper down the V to hold them.

Some people believe that you can best hear and appreciate stereo or quadraphonic music in the dark. Where else can one find a darkened environment more comfortable than in bed?

TOTAL INVOLVEMENT

In the days before central heating, bed chambers were seldom heated, and when they were, it was only by a fireplace that was drafty. This luxury was at best only provided in some castles.

The idea of beds that provided total involvement provided the master of the castle with some measure of comfort while his courtiers shivered as they stood about in the chilly room. With this in view, beds were built into alcoves and protected by heavy draperies.

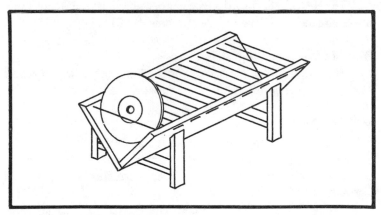

Fig. 5-37. Record storage rack.

However with all of these measures the sleeper was more apt to spend the night in a "pleasant state of semi-asphyxiation."

In those bygone days there was no central heating or air conditioning, but today total involvement means the addition of many conveniences to the bedside scene. Here are suggestions that will make for more luxury within arm's reach of the bed.

The old objection to "crackers in bed" can be avoided by building in shelves within reach. There are a number of types of shelves for different purposes so select the ones that best suit your in-bed habits.

Headboard Hook-Over

You can make a handy shelf that hooks over the headboard of the bed from ¾-inch plywood. The dimensions shown in Fig. 5-38 can be varied to suit your use, such as for books, alarm clock, a glass of water, or whatever that you want within reach when you are in bed.

The width of slot (A) should be so that it will slip snugly over the top of the headboard. If you like it can be padded with flannel. The depth of the slot will depend on the height of the headboard and how far down you want the shelf to hang. While this should be within reach, it should not be so low that you will bump your head on it.

If you plan to load the shelf with books, build it heavy enough to take the load by reinforcing the hook. This can be done by inserting a good sized woodscrew (B) above the slot. To further prevent marring the headboard you can glue the felt all the way down the back side as well as in the slot.

The shelf (D) needs to be 8 inches in width to hold the books and at least 12 inches in length. Use two dowels (C) in gluing it into the uprights at both ends. Finish to match the headboard. Tape the front edge of the plywood to match.

The advantage of this hook-over shelf is that you can move it, remove it or carry it into the other room when you want.

Bedside Hook-On

This shelf will enable you to remove edibles and drinkables from the sleeping surface, yet have them within arm's reach. It hooks over the bed rail and is balanced to remain there steadily (Fig. 5-39). The side rail of the bed must be the type that comes up level, or nearly so, with the surface of the bed. The shelf will be steadiest on a thick bed side rail.

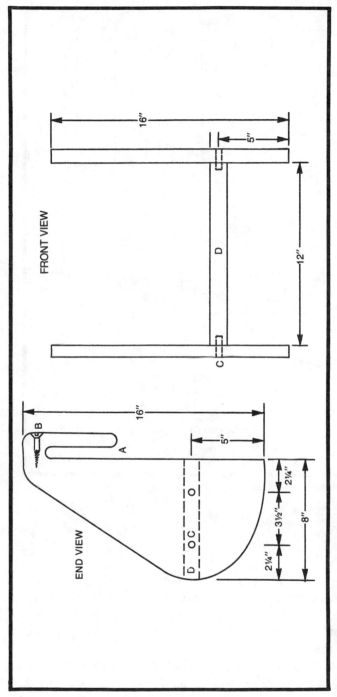

Fig. 5-38. Headboard hook-over shelf.
A. Slot that slips over headboard.
B. Reinforcing screw.
C. Dowels.
D. Shelf.

373

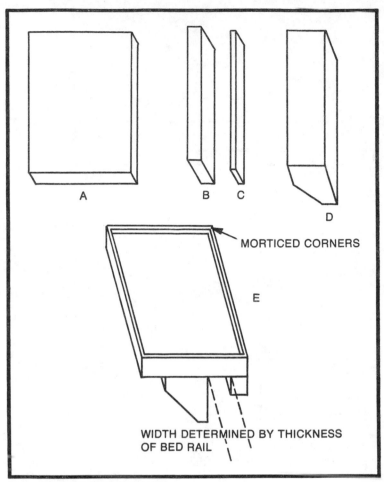

Fig. 5-39. Bedside hook-on shelf.
- A. Tray.
- B. Hook-on.
- C. Flat edge molding.
- D. Hook-on.
- E. Assembled shelf.

A thin, flat molding can be used to finish the edges of the tray so that it discourages things from slipping off of it. The hook-on arrangement should be placed to help balance the tray. The space should allow the hook-on to slip snugly over the bed rail so that the bottom of the tray rests on it.

No dimensions are shown so make them to fit your needs and your bed rail. The shelf, however, should not be so wide that it counterbalances and pulls out the piece that fits down between the side rail and the mattress.

Reading-Eating Bed Rack

People who read magazines or large books in bed will appreciate this rack. If you write or work crossword puzzles in bed or eat from dishes in bed, this rack can be folded flat (Fig. 5-40).

This rack can be made from ½-inch thick plywood or even hardboard. Alter the dimensions as you wish.

The width of the V-shaped leaves should be the same. They can be hinged at the top so that they will lie flat when folded, using 3 inch binding tape, tiny butt hinges or glue on a piano hinge. The ½-inch plywood or hardboard is too thin for nails so assemble the rack with adhesive. A limiting cord or light· chain is needed to prevent it from collapsing under the weight of a heavy book or the pressure of your hand.

All edges should be taped or at least sanded smooth. The mouse trap springs attached to the outer edge of the lip hold the book or magazine steadily upright. When folded flat for writing, the mouse trap spring side can be placed uppermost to hold the paper or crossword puzzle on which you are working.

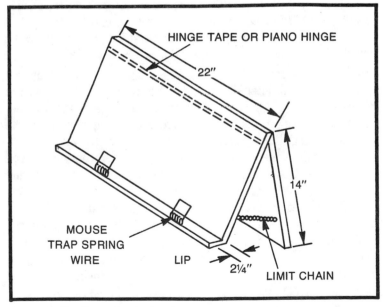

Fig. 5-40. Reading-eating bed rack.

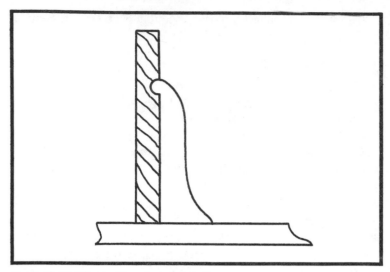

Fig. 5-41. Stabilized wider slip-proof shelf.

Shelves

Bedside shelves are generally built for books. Occasionally they will also hold lamps or bric-a-brac. While the average book will only require that the shelf be 6 inches deep and 8 inches high (paperbacks even less), book shelves in the bed area should be 8 to 10 inches in depth and 12 inches high to accommodate the exceptions.

Adjustable shelf hardware is available at hardware and building supply stores. These consist of metal U-strips that are affixed to the wall, using the proper fasteners. These strips have slots up and down for hooking in shelf brackets to allow for the height of the shelves. These ready-made shelf components come with instructions for installation. Just make sure to put them up straight on the wall and so that the brackets will hold the shelves level.

The shelves themselves are available in several finishes, or you can buy boards and finish them to your liking. Both brackets and shelving come in a variety of widths.

If you already have one of these shelf assemblies but find you need wider shelves than will fit on the brackets you have, you can make the shelves slip proof (Fig. 5-41), although they extend over the hump at the end of the bracket. Of course the metal strip to which the bracket is attached must be properly attached to the wall using the correct fastener and the fastening, if possible, should be into a structural member.

Get a board the width you need for the shelf and have a groove routed along its length or a hollow made where the brackets come. The dimple will do just as well if you can manage to get it where the bulging end of the bracket comes. This knob will prevent the shelf from slipping just the same as it holds the intended width shelf.

There is one objection to this method of supporting the shelf: only the wieght of the shelf and whatever is on it, plus gravity, holds down the shelf. In most cases this is sufficient, unless a shelf is accidentally bumped upward. Such accidents usually occur when someone hastily and carelessly removes a big book from the shelf below and gives the shelf above a healthy swipe.

Drawers

Drawers are merely enclosed boxes, but building them takes a lot of precision know-how. Few things are as annoying as a sticking drawer. No matter how smoothly it pulls out, however, everything in a drawer seems to roll or slide to the back. You get it all straightened up and push it back in and everything slides to the front. There is only one way to overcome this and that is with partitions crosswise.

Because of the stress to which drawers are subjected as they are pushed and pulled, they must be built so that they are strong. They must be truly squared at the corners and be reinforced with corner blocks to maintain their squareness.

The best type of corner reinforcing block is made by cutting a 2-by-2 lengthwise. This makes two triangular sections the height of

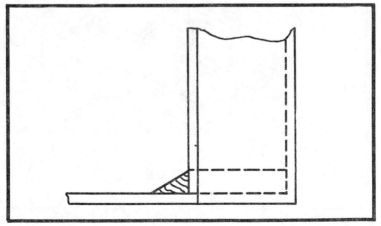

Fig. 5-42. Drawer corner post.

the drawer (Fig. 5-42). When the drawer is completed, glue these corner posts in each corner and allow the adhesive to thoroughly set before subjecting it to any stress.

Another feature that applies to all drawers and roll-in bins is a stop that prevents it from pushing in too far. The simplest way to provide this and also a neat closure is to make the front face of the drawer wider than the opening into which it slides. How far the front face should impinge beyond the opening will depend on the design. Often the face extends below, above and at both sides.

Be sure to use well seasoned wood so that it will not swell and spoil all of the pains you have taken to insure a good fit. If you use soft wood, it is a good idea to coat it with a seal first because soft wood is more subject to ills caused by dampness.

If the sides, ends and surrounds are built from ¾-inch thick plywood, there is less chance of warping. Store-bought drawers usually have a thinner bottom. The sides of the drawers are then usually routed to take the entire length of the bottom as a tenon. This, however, will not prevent the thin bottom from sagging down in the middle, even from pulling out of the routing, especially if the drawer is heavily loaded. To prevent this from happening, reinforce the bottom with a piece underneath down the middle. This measure will also help to correct a sag. Too deep a sag can catch on the surrounds and prevent the drawer from operating properly.

Drawers must be supported in some manner and this can be done in several ways. A drawer can have slats on the bottom that

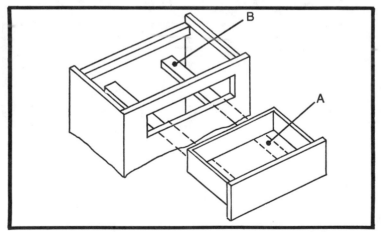

Fig. 5-43. Sliding drawer.
   A. Slats.
   B. Cleats.

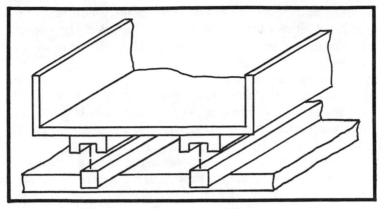

Fig. 5-44. Glide tracks.

ride on cleats that are anchored to the surrounds at the back and the front (Fig. 5-43). These drawers should not be too heavily laden and the sliding contacts need to be soaped.

If the drawer glides are built with tracks as shown in Fig. 5-44, there will be less chance of it wedging due to sidewise slippage. This method should have a solid base below the drawer or heavier tracks.

Still another method (Fig. 5-45) is to rabbet the sides of the drawer (B) with the drawer bottom (D) as the tenon. The drawer is supported on glide cleats (C) and guided from above by another set of cleats (A). The drawer slides between the upper and lower cleats.

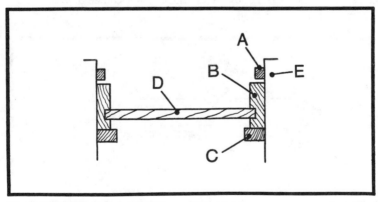

Fig. 5-45. Drawer on upper and lower glide cleats.
   A. Stability cleat.
   B. Side of drawer.
   C. Support of cleat.
   D. Bottom of drawer.
   E. Surrounds.

If the drawers are not too heavy (Fig. 5-46), glide bars (C) can be rabbeted between the surrounds (A) and the sides of the drawer to provide a track. In this case the bottom of the drawer should be rabbeted between the two sides.

If drawers are to be heavily laden, they will need the assistance of rollers. Figure 5-47 shows two types of drawer rollers.

The simple single roller type (A) is installed on the bottom of the drawer near the front and the back. To obtain a balance, four should be used.

These single type rollers do not prevent sidewise movement of the drawer, they merely help to support it, but the drawer can still wedge sidewise. The triple roller type (B) not only rolls on the top of the stabilizing strip but along each side. This prevents the sidewise movement that allows the drawer to wedge in the surrounds.

Many of the better steel letter file drawers use an expensive glide suspension system. One of these (Fig. 5-48) consists of a set of metal gliders with ballbearings (sometimes they are nylon), on each side of the drawer. The gliders roll on double tracks (B). Due to the cost of this system, *it* is seldom used on wooden drawers.

Occasionally when more drawer space is needed, you can fit another one into a corner or around an obstruction. Figure 5-49 offers two suggestions. There is no law that says that all drawers must have square corners. When you need to avoid pipes, for example, see (A). This will also work for other obstructions. If only a corner is available, (B) shows how the drawer can be built in there. No space need be wasted.

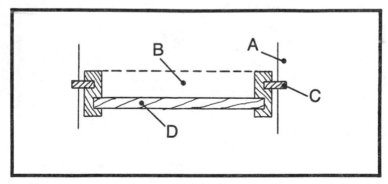

Fig. 5-46. Rabbeted drawer glide bars.
    A. Surrounds.
    B. Drawer.
    C. Glide bar.
    D. Bottom of drawer.

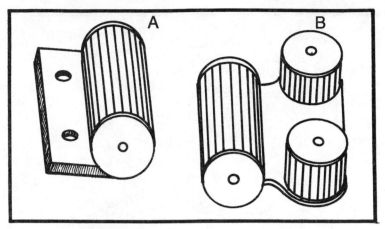

Fig. 5-47. Two types of drawer rollers.
    A. Rolls on top of stabilizer strip.
    B. Rolls on top and on each side of lower stabilizer strip.

Rolling Bins

    To store toys, bedding or other larger or heavier items, there is nothing like a roll-out bin (Fig. 5-50). The bin is built similar to a drawer except that it does not have to be supported. Put four casters under a bin and it rolls out on the floor. No track is needed if you use casters that do not turn.

    Bins can be built as the lowest tier in a cabinet or under a bed. In the latter case, either the bin most be low enough to fit under the bed or the bed raised to make room for it.

    As in building drawers, the measurements must be accurate to the ¼-inch or the bin will stick or wedge sidewise. If the bins are

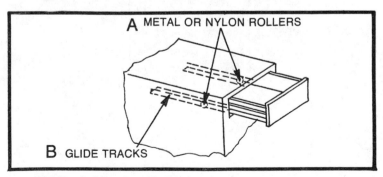

Fig. 5-48. Metal glide suspension system.
    A. Metal gliders.
    B. Tracks.

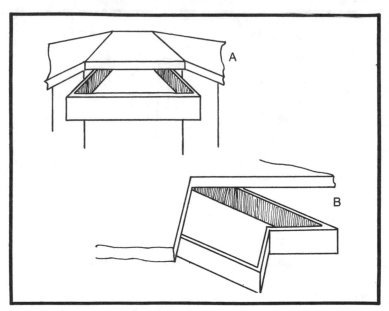

Fig. 5-49. Drawers to fit corners or obstructions.
   A. Drawer angled to clear a pipe.
   B. W-shaped drawer utilizes inside corner.

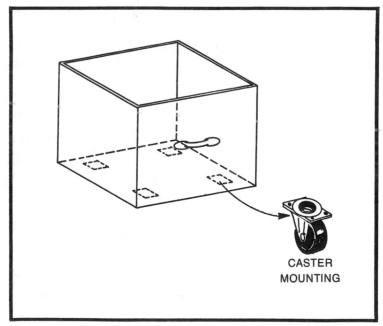

CASTER
MOUNTING

Fig. 5-50. Roll-out bin.

under a bed, they must be recessed to lessen the likelihood of the front being scratched, barking your toes or heels against it or catching on the pull.

Like drawers, bins should be built from well seasoned wood to avoid shrinking, warping or swelling that will change the fit. The corners of bins must be well reinforced as discussed with drawers. Since the bin is usually deeper than a drawer, the corner reinforcement should run all the way up and down each corner. Don't forget to seal each component before assembling it.

Anything that is pushed into surrounds needs stops to prevent it from going in too far. To prevent this the front face of the bin, like the drawer, should be larger than the opening in the surrounds. In making this decision, consider how it will look when closed. A front face of greater area, even if you have to add on an extra facing (Fig. 5-51), is the best stop. It certainly is a lot easier than trying to install stops inside the surrounds at the back.

Bins should be built of at least ¾-inch thick plywood and well reinforced. When building any drawer or bin, plan it all out on paper with accurate measurements, close to the ⅛-inch. After you have rechecked the measurements, it is time to go out and buy materials.

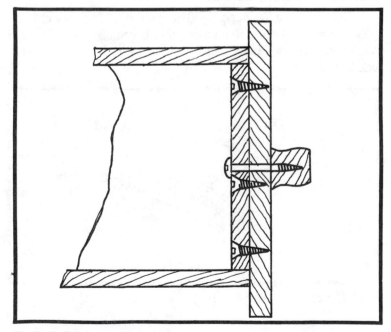

Fig. 5-51. Reinforced drawer facing.

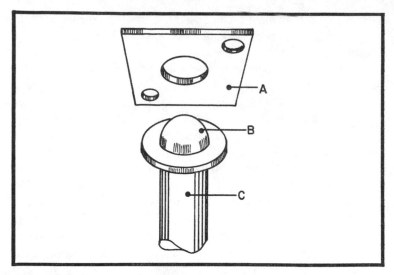

Fig. 5-52. Cabinet door bullet latch.
    A. Indentation.
    B. Catch.
    C. Dowels into door.

Hardware for Drawers and Bins

Bins will need heavier pulls than most drawers; they are not only larger but heavier. Remember that if you use two pulls, one hand won't pull it out; it will take two and that can be inconvenient if one hand is full.

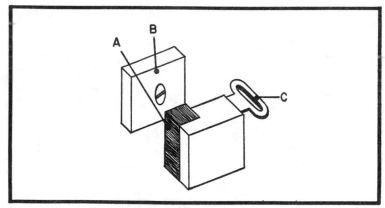

Fig. 5-53. Cabinet door magnetic catch.
    A. Magnet.
    B. Steel plate.
    C. Adjustable screw slot.

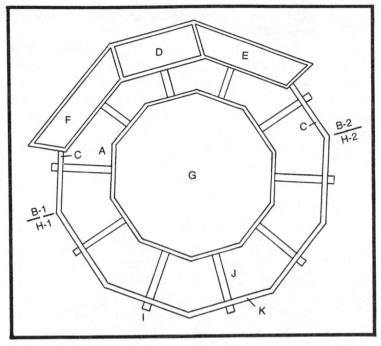

Fig. 5-54. Plan view of the BioAquatic Bed.
    A. Waterbed area.
    B. 1 to B-2. Five sided headboard.
    C. Mirrored panel.
    D. Cabinets.
    E. Stereo unit and controls.
    F. TV and controls for vibrator and waterbed heater.
    G. Overhead mirror.
    H. H-1 to H-2. Open sided.
    I. Bed posts.
    J. Rafters.
    K. Stereo speakers in pedestal.

Never select hardware with sharp corners or edges. Because pulls are classfied as hardware does not mean that they cannot be wood or plastic. They should be mounted by a bolt that goes through the face and fastens securely on the inside. Pulls can be fashioned from sewing thread spools, but heavy drawers and bins should have handled pulls that you can get a good grip on. The larger the drawer, the larger should be the pull. Attaching bolts should be countersunk on both outer and inner side.

When it comes to catches, seldom will drawers or bins need them; cabinet doors, however, do need them. Easier to install and certainly much easier to use are the bullet and the magnetic catches (Figs. 5-52 and 5-53).

Here is another tip so you won't be rudely awakened by an avalanche of books toppling out on you some night. String a couple of thongs or small cord across the face just far enough apart to be able to extract one volume at a time but so that it will not fall out by itself. It is sometimes surprising how inanimate objects can move themselves around.

Now that we've discussed the surroundings, let's get back to beds.

BIOAQUATIC BED

Bio- means total living; -aquatic is water, so now we have a waterbed for total living, created by Robert Martens. You could call it a Honeymoon Bed because that is what he is building it for, but it will serve him and his bride long after the honeymoon with all the comforts and luxuries that they could want.

Martens' BioAquatic bed is dexagon-shaped, 9 feet across and topped by a tester lined with clear mirrors. You just have to see it to believe it.

The BioAquatic bed has ten sides, 9 feet across (Fig. 5-54). It will look much like the sketch in Fig. 5-55 when it is finished.

The creator and builder, Robert L. Martens, like the postman who goes walking as a hobby, is the owner of Universal Waterbeds, with factory and show room at 13057 Garvy, Baldwin Park, CA 91706. He also has a retail show room in West Covina, CA 91791.' His business includes custom designing waterbeds and surrounds, making components and selling the leading brands. He ships these nationally.

If the section in this book on waterbeds inspires you to build one for yourself and you want to buy parts, you can get them from Bob. Should you find yourself in too deep water and need help, he can supply information or components. You'll find him at the other end of the telephone when you dial (213)337-2188.

Bob's BioAquatic bed, like many of the ones he and his men in the shop make for sale, is of Ponderosa pine, stained walnut and finished in hard gloss urethane. He is having a special "Captain's" waterbed mattress and liner made up by the Marina Marine people who specialize in these items. When completed, he estimates that his BioAquatic bed will be worth in the neighborhood of $3000.

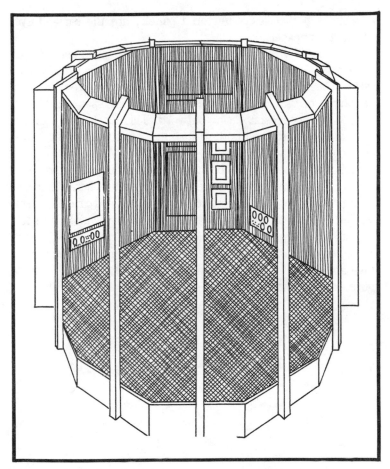

Fig. 5-55. The BioAquatic bed.

Five sides of the bed comprise the headboard (Fig. 5-54 B-1 to B-2) and five sides are left open (H-1 to H-2). The bed is 9 feet across from one flat side to the opposite one. In the middle of each of these flat sides a 2-by-4 post runs from the floor to support the canopy, which is the same sized dexagon as the base.

From the top of each of these posts ten beams (J) run like the spokes of a wheel to support a large dexagon clear mirror that forms the center of the canopy. Overall the bed is 7 feet in height.

The headboard has a panel with a large mirror on either end (C). The middle panel of the five (A) contains a cabinet divided into sections for a wine rack, wine and water glass cabinets, a bottled cold water dispenser and book shelves. On either side of this panel, next to the perpendicular mirrored panels, are the ear and eye entertainment panels.

Into one of these panels (F) is set a television screen and the controls for it, also the controls for the vibrator and the water-mattress heater. Behind the other panel (E) is the stereo unit with the controls on the face of the panel. Quadraphonic speakers (K) are installed in the pedestal, facing outward. This location is with the intent of flooding the bedroom with sound, or as Bob puts it, "surrounding the bed with music."

Since elsewhere in this book waterbed construction has been discussed at length, we will not repeat these details here. Illumination is provided for the BioAquatic bed by lamps and candle holders installed on the bed posts. These will be alternated with holders for the pots of small plants.

When I remarked that his bed had everything but the kitchen stove and sink, Bob agreed, adding, "I'd include those if I could figure out where to put them."

Glossary of Terms

Air-dried lumber. Lumber that has been piled in yards or sheds for any length of time. For the United States as a whole, the minimum moisture content of thoroughly air-dried lumber is 12 to 15 percent and the average is somewhat higher. In the South, air-dried lumber may be no lower than 19 percent.

Backband. A simple molding sometimes used around the outer edge of plain rectangular casing as a decorative feature.

Batten. Narrow strips of wood used to cover joints or as decorative vertical members over plywood or wide boards.

Beam. A structural member transversely supporting a load.

Bearing partition. A partition that supports any vertical load in addition to its own weight.

Bearing wall. A wall that supports any vertical load in addition to its own weight.

Blind-nailing. Nailing in such a way that the nailheads are not visible on the face of the work—usually at the tongue of matched boards.

Blue stain. A bluish or grayish discoloration of the sapwood caused by the growth of certain moldlike fungi on the surface and in the interior of a piece, made possible by the same conditions that favor the growth of other fungi.

Bodied linseed oil. Linseed oil that has been thickened in viscosity by suitable processing with heat or chemicals. Bodied oils are obtainable in a great range in viscosity from a little greater than that of raw oil to just short of a jellied condition.

Boiled linseed oil. Linseed oil in which enough lead, manganese, or cobalt salts have been incorporated to make the oil harden more rapidly when spread in thin coatings.

Bolster. A short horizontal timber or steel beam on top of a column to support and decrease the span of beams or girders.

Brace. An inclined piece of framing lumber applied to wall or floor to stiffen the structure.

Butt joint. The junction where the ends of two timbers or other members meet in a square-cut joint.

Casing. Molding of various widths and thicknesses used to trim.

Conduit, electrical. A pipe, usually metal, in which wire is installed.

Construction, frame. A type of construction in which the structural parts are wood or depend upon a wood frame for support.

Coped joint. See **Scribing.**

Corner boards. Diagonal braces at the corners of frame structure to stiffen and strengthen.

Dado. A rectangular groove across the width of a board or plank. In interior decoration, a special type of wall treatment.

Decay. Disintegration of wood or other substance through the action of fungi.

Density. The mass of substance in a unit volume. When expressed in the metric system, it is numerically equal to the specific gravity of the same substance.

Dimension. See **Lumber dimension.**

Direct nailing. To nail perpendicular to the initial surface or to the junction of the pieces joined. Also termed **face nailing.**

Dressed and matched (tongued and grooved). Boards or planks machined in such a manner that there is a groove on one edge and a corresponding tongue on the other.

Facia or fascia. A flat board, band, or face, used sometimes by itself but usually in combination with moldings.

Filler (wood). A heavily pigmented preparation used for filling and leveling off the pores in open-pored woods.

Fire-resistive. In the absence of a specific ruling by the authority having jurisdiction, applies to materials for construction not combustible in the temperatures of ordinary fires and that will withstand such fires without serious impairment of their usefulness for at least 1 hour.

Fire-retardant chemical. A chemical or preparation of chemicals used to reduce flammability or to retard spread of flame.

Flat paint. An interior paint that contains a high proportion of pigment and dries to a flat or lusterless finish.

Fungi, wood. Microscopic plants that live in damp wood and cause mold, stain, and decay.

Fungicide. A chemical that is poisonous to fungi.

Furring. Strips of wood or metal applied to a wall or other surface to even it and normally to serve as a fastening base for finish material.

Gloss enamel. A finishing material made of varnish and sufficient pigments to provide opacity and color, but little or no pigment of low opacity. Such an enamel forms a hard coating with maximum smoothness of surface and a high degree of gloss.

Gloss (paint or enamel). A paint or enamel that contains a relatively low proportion of pigment and dries to a sheen or luster.

Grain. The direction, size, arrangement, appearance, or quality of the fibers in wood.

Grain, edge (vertical). Edge-grain lumber has been sawed parallel to the pith of the log and approximately at right angles to the growth rings; i.e., the rings form an angle of 45° or more with the surface of the piece.

Grain, flat. Flat-grain lumber has been sawed parallel to the pith of the log and approximately tangent to the growth rings, i.e., the rings form an angle of less than 45° with the surface of the piece.

Grain, quartersawn. Another term for edge grain.

Gusset. A flat wood, plywood, or similar type member used to provide a connection at intersection of wood members. Most commonly used at joints of wood trusses. They are fastened by nails, screws, bolts, or adhesives.

Joint. The space between the adjacent surfaces of two members or components joined and held together by nails, glue, cement, mortar, or other means.

Joint cement. A powder that is usually mixed with water and used for joint treatment in gypsum-wallboard finish. Often called "spackle."

Kiln dried lumber. Lumber that has been kiln dried often to a moisture content of 6 to 12 percent. Common varieties of softwood lumber, such as framing lumber are dried to a somewhat higher moisture content.

Knot. In lumber, the portion of a branch or limb of a tree that appears on the edge or face of the piece.

Lattice. A framework of crossed wood or metal strips.

Lumber. Lumber is the product of the sawmill and planing mill not further manufactured other than by sawing, resawing, and passing lengthwise through a standard planing machine, crosscutting to length, and matching.

Lumber, boards. Yard lumber less than 2 inches thick and 2 or more inches wide.

Lumber, dimension. Yard lumber from 2 inches to, but not including, 5 inches thick and 2 or more inches wide. Includes joists, rafters, studs, plank, and small timbers.

Lumber, dressed size. The dimension of lumber after shrinking from green dimension and after machining to size or pattern.

Lumber, matched. Lumber that is dressed and shaped on one edge in a grooved pattern and on the other in a tongued pattern.

Lumber, shiplap. Lumber that is edge-dressed to make a close rabbeted or lapped joint.

Lumber, timbers. Yard lumber 5 or more inches in least dimension. Includes beams, stringers, posts, caps, sills, girders, and purlins.

Lumber, yard. Lumber of those grades, sizes, and patterns which are generally intended for ordinary construction, such as framework.

Miter joint. The joint of two pieces at an angle that bisects the joining angle. For example, the miter joint at the side and head casing at a door opening is made at a 45° angle.

Moisture content of wood. Weight of the water contained in the wood, usually expressed as a percentage of the weight of the ovendry wood.

Molding. A wood strip having a curved or projecting surface used for decorative purposes.

Mortise. A slot cut into a board, plank, or timber, usually edgewise, to receive tenon of another board, plank, or timber to form a joint.

Natural finish. A transparent finish which does not seriously alter the original color or grain of the natural wood. Natural finishes arae usually provided by sealers, oils, varnishes, water-repellent preseratives, and other similar materials.

Notch. A crosswise rabbet at the end of a board.

O.C., on center. The measurement of spacing for studs, rafters, joists, and the like from the center of one member to the center of the next.

Paint. A combination of pigments with suitable thinners or oils to provide decorative and protective coatings.

Partition. A wall that subdivides spaces within any story of a building.

Penny. As applied to nails, it originally indicated the price per hundred. The term now serves as a measure of nail length and is abbreviated by the letter d.

Pigment. A powdered solid in suitable degree of subdivision for use in paint or enamel.

Pith. The small, soft core at the original center of a tree around which wood formation takes place.

Plough. To cut a lengthwise groove in a board or plank.

Plumb. Exactly perpendicular; vertical.

Ply. A term to denote the number of thicknesses or layers of veneer in plywood, or layers in built-up materials, in any finished piece of such material.

Plywood. A piece of wood made of three or more layers of veneer joined with glue, and usually laid with the grain of adjoining plies at right angles.

Pores. Wood cells of comparatively large diameter that have open ends and are set one above the other to form continuous tubes. The openings of the vessels on the surface of a piece of wood are referred to as pores.

Preservative. Any substance that, for a reasonable length of time, will prevent the action of wood-destroying fungi, borers of various kinds, and similar destructive agents when the wood has been properly coated or impregnated with it.

Primer. The first coat of paint in a paint job that consists of two or more coats; also the paint used for such a first coat.

Putty. A type of cement usually made of whiting and boiled linseed oil, beaten or kneaded to the consistency of dough, and used in sealing glass in sash, filling small holes and crevices in wood, and for similar purposes.

Quarter round. A small molding that has the cross section of a quarter circle.

Rabbet. A rectangular longitudinal groove cut in the corner edge of a board or plank.

Raw linessed oil. The crude product processed from flaxseed and usually without much subsequent treatment.

Resorcinol glue. A glue that is high in both wet and dry strength and resistant to high temperatures. It is used for gluing lumber or assembly joints that must withstand severe service conditions.

Sand float finish. Lime mixed with sand, resulting in a textured finish.

Sapwood. The outer zone of wood, next to the bark. In the living tree it contains some living cells (the heartwood contains none), as well as dead and dying cells. In most species, it is lighter colored than the heartwood. In all species, it is lacking in decay resistance.

Scribing. Fitting woodwork to an irregular surface. In moldings, cutting the end of one piece to fit the molded face of the other at an interior angle to replace a miter joint.

Sealer. A finishing material, either clear or pigmented, that is usually applied directly over uncoated wood for the purpose of sealing the surface.

Seasoning. Removing moisture from green wood in order to improve its serviceability.

Semigloss paint or enamel. A paint or enamel made with a slight insufficiency of nonvolatile vehicle so that its coating, when dry, has some luster but is not very glossy.

Shellac. A transparent coating made by dissolving lac, a resinous secretion of the lac bug (a scale insect that thrives in tropical countries, especially India), in alcohol.

Stud. One of a series of slender wood or metal vertical structural members placed as supporting elements in walls and partitions. (Plural: studs or studding.)

Toenailing. To drive a nail at a slant with the initial surface in order to permit it to penetrate into a second member.

Tongued and grooved. See **Dressed and matched.**

Trim. The finish materials, such as moldings.

Turpentine. A volatile oil used as a thinner in paints and as a solvent in varnishes. Chemically, it is a mixture of terpenes.

Undercoat. A coating applied prior to the finishing or top coats of a paint job. It may be the first of two or the second of three coats. In some usage of the word it may become synonymous with priming coat.

Under layment. A material placed under finish coverings to provide a smooth, even surface for applying the finish.

Varnish. A thickened preparation of drying oil or drying oil and resin suitable for spreading on surfaces to form continuous, transparent coatings, or for mixing with pigments to make enamels.

Vehicle. The liquid portion of a finishing material; it consists of the binder (nonvolatile) and volatile thinners.

Veneer. Thin sheets of wood made by rotary cutting or slicing of log.

Wane. Bark, or lack of wood from any cause, on edge or corner of a piece of wood.

Water-repellent preservative. A liquid designed to penetrate into wood and impart water repellency and a moderate preservative protection.

Wood rays. Strips of cells extending radially within a tree and varying in height from a few cells in some species to 4 inches or more in oak. The rays serve primarily to store food and to transport it horizontally in the tree.

Appendix A
Details of Common Nails

PENNY SIZE	LENGTH (INCHES)	GAGE	NUMBER PER POUND
2	1	15	840
3	1¼	14	540
4	1½	12½	300
6	2	11½	160
8	2½	10¼	100
10	3	9	65
12	3¼	9	65
16	3½	8	45
20	4	6	30
30	4½	5	20
40	5	4	17
50	5¼	3	14
60	6	2	11

Appendix B

Wood Screw Holes

GAGE	SHANK DIAMETER (INCHES)	PILOT HOLE DIAMETER HARDWOODS	(INCHES) SOFTWOODS
2	0.086	3/64	–
3	0.099	1/16	–
4	0.112	1/16	–
5	0.125 (1/8)	5/64	1/16
6	0.138	5/64	1/16
7	0.151	3/32	1/16
8	0.164	3/32	5/64
10	0.177	7/64	3/32
12	0.216	1/8	7/64
14	0.242	9/64	7/64
16	0.268	5/32	9/64
18	0.294	3/16	9/64
20	0.320	13/64	11/64
24	0.372	7/32	3/16

Appendix C

Fastenings

In the best furniture construction most joints are fitted and glued and have no metal fastenings. Where metal fastenings are needed, these are screws rather than nails, except in places that will not be seen. In less important furniture there may be more use of screws, nails, and other metal fastenings.

Many modern glues have such strong adhesion that they can be relied on even in places where they do not have the benefit of cut joints to relieve the glue of some of the direct load. With some glues the joint may be stronger than the wood, so wood fibers give way before the glue line in a test to destruction.

GLUES

Until World War II the common woodworking glue was made from bones, hooves, and other animal products. There were liquid glues in cans and tubes, but most glue was heated for use. It had adequate strength, as shown by the many old pieces of furniture still in sound condition; but this type of glue weakened to the point of becoming useless in damp conditions and would also soften if it became hot. Animal glue is obsolescent, but it might be needed to match existing glue in restoration work. It is not compatible with modern glues, so any remaining in a failed joint should be scraped away before using another glue.

Another glue that dates from before World War II and is still in use is casein (*Casco* is one trade name). This is derived from milk. It is usually supplied as a white powder to mix with water into a paste. It has reasonable strength and some resistance to dampness, but immersion will soften it (although strength might return when it dries out). Casein still has uses for large laminations and other constructional woodwork inside buildings, but for furniture construction the craftsman in the home shop will find other glues more useful.

Synthetic Resins

Most woodworking glues are synthetic resins. As they are often known only by trade names, it is not always easy to identify them. Careful reading of the description or instructions will give a clue to the type. If an adhesive is described as being suitable for fabric, paper, and other things besides wood, it is unlikely to have the maximum strength needed for joints in furniture construction, although it may be quite satisfactory for light decorative work or toys. If the glue is in two parts, that is a sign that it is a strong, waterproof one. If it is a one-part glue and the information on the container only mentions wood, it is also likely to be a good glue for furniture joints, although it might not be a good choice for anything that will be exposed to rain.

One of the powerful synthetic resin glues is resorcinol. Its glue line is a reddish-brown color, which makes it undesirable on some woods. It is used in plywood and some commercial production, but it needs a close-fitting joint and must be clamped tightly. It does not bond to the resins used with fiberglass, so it may be unsuitable for furniture that combines wood and fiberglass. Although it may have some uses in the home shop, there are other glues more generally useful.

A good, general-purpose two-part synthetic resin is based on urea. It is not so fully waterproof that it will withstand very prolonged immersion, but otherwise, once it has set it will retain a strength at least as great as the wood in any conditions furniture is likely to meet. In one form the glue is a syrup with a shelf life of a few months. Alternatively is may be a long-life powder to mix with water to make the syrup. With this there is a catalyst (hardener), which is a mild acid. When catalyst and syrup are brought together, a chemical reaction drives out the water and the glue sets permanently. The process cannot be reversed. The catalyst may be mixed with the syrup before use; then the mixture must be used in the time specified by the marker (20 minutes is typical). Alternatively the syrup may go on one surface and the catalyst on the other so that reaction does not start until they are brought together. In another form both catalyst and glue are in powder form and may be together in one container. So long as the powder mixture is dry, the glue has a long storage life; but when water is added, reaction commences and the glue has to be used in the time indicated on the container.

Urea glue is best used with a reasonably close joint, but this is not as critical as with resorcinol. Great pressure is not needed—clamping need only be enough to maintain a close contact. Setting time varies according to the catalyst and temperature. In most cases the joint may be handled and worked within a few hours, but strength continues to build up, probably over several days or weeks. Urea glue may be used with wood and fiberglass.

There are glues with bases other than urea. If in two parts, they may be assumed to be at least as strong as urea. The glue with the greatest strength and versatility is based on epoxy, but it is expensive and so is not usually chosen when another glue will do. It is a two-part glue that not only joins wood to wood but will join almost any material, including metal, to the same or some other material. Most synthetic glues have to be used above certain minimum temperatures (normal room or shop temperature is satisfactory), but epoxy can be used close to freezing.

Using Glue

Some woods will discolor if the glue parts are mixed in a metal container or applied with a metal-bound brush. Mixing in a throw away plastic container and applying with a piece of wood is better. Mix glue and catalyst by hand. A power mixer may introduce too many air bubbles. If any joint is too open or there is a part to be built up, sawdust can be mixed with the glue until it has the consistency of putty. This can be pressed or molded to shape and will have a strength comparable to the plain glue. If plain glue is used in bulk, it will craze as it sets and will have no strength. With sawdust the glue is employed bonding the tiny particles of wood, and it does not craze. Using this mixture instead of plastic wood or other filler provides strength, but a filler would only provide shape.

SCREWS

Wood screws are described by their length from the surface of the wood, their thickness by gauge number, the type of head, and the material. There is no easier way of familiarizing oneself with screw sizes than by examining a selection, since the gauge numbers do not represent sizes easily visualized. Except in the smaller sizes, the even-number gauges are more easily obtained than the odd-number ones. Some generally useful sizes are ½ in. by 4, ¾ in. by 6, 1 in. by 8, and 1½ in. by 10; but all lengths may be had thicker or thinner.

Unless there is a need for something else, flat-head screws are commonly used (Fig. C-1A). Round-head screws (Fig. C-1B) are not often used directly with wood, but they are suitable for some metal fittings. The oval head (Fig. C-1C) also looks well where the screw head is visible on a fitting. If a panel has to be removed occasionally, oval-head screws through cup washers (Fig. C-1D) make a good choice.

General-purpose screws have straight slots, but Phillips and other comparable screws have star-shaped recesses (Fig. C-1E). These are intended to prevent slippage with power screwdrivers in production work, but there are hand screwdrivers to fit.

Most screws are bright steel. There is a risk of rusting, not only from dampness in the air but from chemicals in some wood; so in the best cabinetwork it is usual to have brass screws, which are less likely to corrode. A rusted steel screw in some oak may seize so it cannot be withdrawn, and it will eventually corrode to the breaking point. Stainless steel, bronze, and other metals, and some plastics, are used for screws for special purposes, and most metal screws

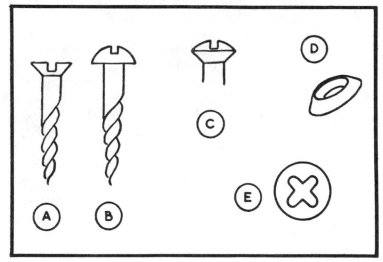

Fig. C-1. The variety of heads screws can have.

may be obtained plated to match the finish of the fittings they pass through.

Except for the smallest screws in softer woods, it is important to drill first. A screw usually has to pull two pieces together by squeezing the upper part between the screw head and the lower part gripped by the thread. Consequently there should be a clearance hole through the top piece (Fig. C-2A). If the plain shank of the screw will continue into the lower piece, the clearance hole should go that far as well. There is no fixed size of lower hole for each screw, as the type of wood affects it. A small screw that does not have to go far in a softwood may cut its own way in, or a bradawl hole may be sufficient.

In harder woods the hole should be made about the same as the core diameter of the thread. The screw can be left to cut its own way for perhaps two threads (Fig. C-2B) in many woods, or the hole may have to go the full depth in really hard woods.

A flat head will pull in flush in softwoods and some plywood. Hardwoods will require use of a countersink bit, but even then there will be slight pull-in, so be careful not to countersink too much.

Screwdrivers should have ends which make a reasonably close fit in the screw head. This means having several screwdrivers. A long screwdriver is easier to use than a short one, but in furniture construction there are often places where a long screwdriver will not go. A collection of plain screwdrivers is worth having. Additionally there may be ratchet and pump-action (Yankee) types with various points. A pump-action screwdriver may also take small bits for making the screw holes.

Sometimes the screw heads must be hidden. In this case the screws can be counterbored to put the heads below the surface. A hole is drilled larger than the screw head, and this is plugged after the screw has been tightened (Fig. C-4). For the best effect the plug is cut cross-grained from a piece of wood that matches that being screwed. This can be made with a plug cutter, which is like a hollow bit used in an electric drill stand.

Keep the ends of screwdrivers filed or ground so they do not have rounded corners or edges. A worn screwdriver or one of the wrong size may jump off the screw and mar the adjoining wood.

NAILS AND TOOLS FOR NAILING

Nails are described by their length. Although they are made to gauge thicknesses, there is usually little choice, and the thickness

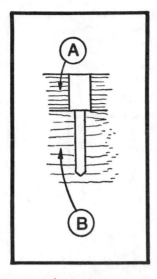

Fig. C-2. Holes should be drilled to clear the screw shank (A) and be the tapping size for the threaded part (B).

usual for a particular length will have to be accepted. There is a system of *penny* sizes for nails—2d. is 1 in. long, 60d. is 6 in. long. It is probably better to avoid this system and order nails by length.

There is a very large range of nails available, mostly for purposes other than furniture making. Common box nails have flat heads (Fig. C-5A). These are usually bright steel. The head gives a safe grip, particularly for a piece of thin plywood at the back of a cabinet or similar construction. There are different sizes of heads, but none is likely to be acceptable on a finished exposed surface.

Nails may be bronzed or otherwise treated to improve their appearance. There are brass, copper, aluminum, and other metal

Fig. C-4. A screw head can be sunk below the surface of a piece of furniture and concealed with a plug.

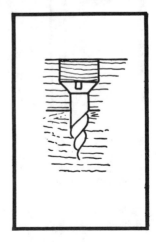

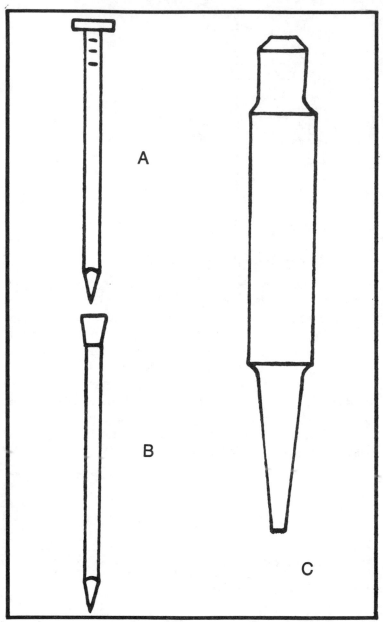

Fig. C-5. Box nails (A) can't be easily concealed, but a casing nail (B) can be driven below the surface with a punch (C) and covered with stopping.

nails, but some of them are inclined to bend or buckle if holes are not drilled.

Some nails are obtainable with ringed shanks. The rings give the nail something of the grip of a screw, but if it has to be withdrawn, it will tear up the surrounding surface.

If nails are to be used in a place where the surface is visible, there are nails with only slight heads. Larger ones are *casing* nails (Fig. C-5B) and finer ones are *finishing* nails. These can be driven below the surface with a nail punch (Fig. C-5C) then the head can be covered with stopping. In good furniture, nailing is to be kept to a minimum, but sometimes molding or a decorative piece has to be fixed in this way. The strips holding glass in a cabinet door may also be nailed. If furniture is to be fixed to a masonry wall and nails are used instead of screws in plugs, there are hardened-steel masonry nails which can be used. Screws are preferable to nails for most furniture construction.

Nails in general carpentry are usually driven without any pre-drilling, but in the hardwoods and sometimes in narrow sections used for furniture, it is often advisable to drill for nails, particularly if the nail is to come near an edge. The hole in the upper piece may be

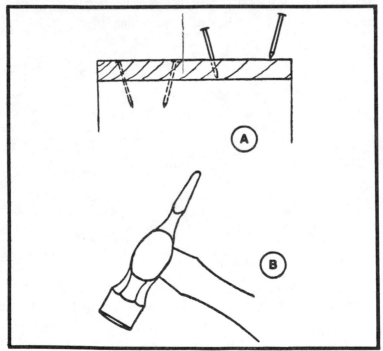

Fig. C-6. Driving nails at opposing angles makes strong joints (A). A hammer with a narrow cross peen (B) is useful for fine nails.

just slightly undersize, while the one in the lower part may be about half the nail diameter and not taken the full depth. Much depends on the wood.

If a nail bends when being driven, it is usually wiser to withdraw it and use another than to straighten it and continue. Pincers or a claw hammer will remove the nail, but be careful that surrounding wood is not damaged in the process. Put a piece of thin wood where the pincers will be levering.

The spacing of nails or screws is a matter of experience. When covering a framework with plywood, spacing around the edges should be closer than fastenings driven into intermediate frames, and at the edges it may be advisable to have a few closer fastenings near the corners. Nails driven alternately at opposite angles (Fig. C-6A) in dovetail fashion will have an increased grip.

Almost any hammer will drive nails, but if one is bought for furniture work, it is useful to have a cross peen (Fig. C-6B), which will go between finger and thumb when holding a small nail or hit in a recess that will not admit the flat peen. Nails in awkward places are best driven with the aid of a punch. For the pinlike nails often used in cabinetwork, a very light hammer (about 4 oz) is best.

Appendix D
Finishing

Items of the types described in this book will have to be finished in ways that are the same as, or compatible with, existing finishes of the room itself and things in it. It will not always be easy to identify existing finishes. Where investigation does not conclusively identify what has been used or even what the base wood is, it may be better to use a finish on the new work that is compatible the old than to try to get an exact match. A finish that does not quite achieve the match attempted is often less acceptable than one which is different than, but complementary to, the existing colors.

In general, it is usually unwise to mix more than two colors, except for white and black, which may be used sparingly in addition to other colors. A natural wood look, either genuine or simulated in plastic, may come alongside painted work, either directly or with a narrow line of black between. A bold color may be associated with a neutral or pastel shade of another color. People's tastes differ, and what may be too violent a contrast in the eyes of one viewer may be very attractive to another. Almost all combinations of color have been used by someone who regards the result as satisfactory, despite breaking all usual rules. If possible, try panels of the intended finishes in position and judge the effect before actually treating a piece of furniture.

For most furniture the beauty of the wood grain is the best decoration. It may be strained or given a clear finish. There are places where a painted finish is preferable, and then the basic material can be a cheaper and less attractive wood or a plain manufactured board.

There are not many items that can be left untreated. Because it is porous, wood absorbs dirt and becomes unattractive. There are just a few woods that contain natural oils and resins that give them a resistance to this. Teak for example, has an oil, and furniture made from it may be left untreated at first; but, later, treatment with special oil or polish will be needed. Some cedars contain a resin that makes them durable without treatment, but the appearance is not good enough for indoor furniture, and this wood is better used outdoors or in a shop.

WHY FINISH?

There are several reasons for applying a finish. The first is appearance. Attractive wood becomes more attractive under a clear glaze. It may look even better if a stain is used to bring out the beauty of the grain or emphasize the color.

Another reason for finishing is to give a surface that will facilitate cleaning. Without the protective finish, the wood might be marked by liquids and dirt. Bare wood is almost impossible to keep clean, even with frequent scrubbing—and that would not be appropriate for most furniture.

The finish may also be applied to prevent moisture absorption. This may not always be important especially if the furniture is always in an environment of equable temperature and humidity. Elsewhere, moisture absorption can cause expansion and contraction and warping. Most finishes seal the pores of the wood and reduce the absorption of moisture to a negligible amount.

Finishing may be done to give a uniform appearance. Even when a piece of furniture is made completely from the same wood, there can be variations in appearance. If different woods have to be used, something has to be done to give them a matching appearance, unless different colors are desired. There are stains and other treatments that make almost any final shade possible. A cheap wood can be made the same color as a more expensive wood, although its grain may show the expert that it is not genuine. Most staining is done to emphasize the existing color. For instance, the natural redness of some mahoganies can be deepened. It is unusual to use a color that is foreign to the wood. It is advisable to use stains normally associated with a wood unless special effects are required.

Painted finishes completely obscure the appearance of the wood or other material underneath. Their purpose is otherwise the same as for clear finishes: protection, waterproofing, and easy cleaning.

SURFACE PREPARATION

Whatever the finish, its final effect is largely dependent on the quality of the surface underneath. The actual application of the finish may be of much less importance. Although paint covers differences in color and shade, flaws left in the surface may become very apparent, particularly with a high-gloss paint.

Planing followed by thorough sanding is the usual way of preparing a surface. If the grain is the type that tears up no matter how it is planed, scraping should follow planing. If torn grain is dealt with by sanding only, not only is the process tedious, but the surface may be hollowed and the fibers bent instead of cut as they would be with a scraper. The eventual finish should be kept in mind during construction. Many parts are easily sanded before assembly, yet adequate sanding might be difficult later. Final sanding of exposed surfaces is best left until after assembly, when any risk of marking from construction work will have passed.

Although power sanding has its uses, final sanding is best done by hand, using abrasive paper wrapped around a block of wood or cork. The grade of abrasive should suit the wood and have sufficient cut to do what is intended. This means a coarse grade on softwoods, most of which soon clog fine papers. Sanding with the paper loose in the hand should only be done on curves. Final sanding of any surface should be in the direction of the grain. Looking across the wood toward a light will show any crosswise scratches that might show through a finish.

It may be necessary to use stoppings and fillers to get the wood to a satisfactory state. Although there are ways of making your own, it is probably wiser to buy them already prepared. Making your own really only pays when a large amount of furniture is being handled or there is no prepared material available.

Hollows where nails have been punched and similar small holes are best dealt with by a stopping, which is squeezed or pressed in the left to harden. Usually the top should stand very slightly above the surface so it can be leveled after it hardens. For larger cracks and places where joints may not fit as closely as you wish, there is plastic wood which is used similarly.

With some open-grained wood it is advisable to use a filler, otherwise the open grain and pores may show as minute holes and hollows in the finished surface. Most fillers are pastes. They are rubbed over the wood with a cloth and allowed to dry, then the surplus is sanded off.

Stoppings and fillers may take stain, or they may be obtained in colors to match the wood. For a painted finish there are stoppings which the makers advise using after the first coat of paint, not on bare wood. There are fillers for painted finishes which are used on very coarse-grained wood to hide the markings, but such woods are more likely to be used for exterior work than in built-in furniture.

STAINS

If the wood is to be stained, it is usual to use separate stains on the wood before applying the finish. There are colored varnishes and other finishes that might be considered to combine the processes, but the effect is not as good. A stain applied separately enhances the appearance of the wood as it penetrates the surface. With a colored varnish, the stain is in the finish and not the wood, so the grain is less enhanced. Also, as the varnish loses color with wear the appearance will be affected.

Stains may have water, spirits, or oil as solvents. A stain with an oil solvent is convenient. It soaks in to a good depth, and the color is even. It does not raise the grain. There is a slight risk of it seeping through some finishes.

Water stain comes as a powder to mix with water. Almost any shade or color is possible. As the water tends to raise the grain, it is advisable to dampen the surface with water as a preliminary treatment to get the grain raised in advance, then sand this after it has dried and before staining.

A spirit stain uses alcohol as the solvent, which makes it quick drying. This may be an advantage in some circumstances, but it makes staining a large area difficult, as parts will dry and causes streaks when new stain is brought alongside. A spirit stain is convenient for touching up and for treating carvings and moldings, but it is not a good choice for the overall staining of a large piece of furniture.

Prepared stains are usually provided with instructions, which should be followed, but it is always advisable to experiment on an inconspicuous part of the furniture or a scrap piece of the same wood. The color is affected by the original color of the wood and sometimes by chemicals in the wood. When a clear finish is applied, this may also alter the color slightly.

CLEAR FINISHES

Traditionally furniture was finished by waxes, oils, and resins. The beauty and patina of much old furniture is due more to use and polishing over the years than to the original surface treatment. There was time when most furniture was French-polished. In more recent years there have been brushed and sprayed finishes.

Waxing was once done with beeswax, and oiling was done with linseed oil. To get a satisfactory finish with these involves hard rubbing, then a pause of maybe a week and a repeat of the process, and so on for a long time. Neither process has much place in modern finishing of new work.

Shellac may be bought as flakes to dissolve in alcohol, or it can be bought already in solution. The natural color is orange-brown, but there is a bleached shellac more suitable for very light woods.

Shellac may be brushed on as a varnish. It will also act as a sealer under other finishes, closing the grain so the other solution does not soak in. It can also be used on resinous wood to prevent resin seeping through paint or some other finish. Even if shellac is not used all over a surface, brushing over knots is advisable before painting.

Shellac dries quickly. Quite a good brush finish can be obtained by applying up to six coats at about 2-hour intervals. The shellacked area can be rubbed with steel wool (or pumice stone) and oil to give an attractive, durable finish. Shellac applied by brush should be worked thinly and quickly to avoid problems of one part drying before an adjoining part is covered.

Shellac is also the material for *French polishing*. The polish (thinned shellac in alcohol) is put on a pad of batting (cotton or wool wadding), which is enclosed in a lint-free cloth. This is rubbed over the wood with a steady motion. At first the aim is to build up layers of polish. The rubbing motion causes the alcohol to evaporate quickly so the surface soon dries ready for another coat. When a sufficient surface has been built up, further steps are done with less polish and more friction to build up a sheen on the surface. A spot of mineral oil may be added to the pad occasionally to prevent sticking. Later stages are done with the polish thinned still more.

VARNISH

In recent years there have been considerable changes in the makeup of varnishes and similar finishes. Some of the older varnishes, dependent on natural resins, would not dry properly, or their surface was affected if working conditions were not right. Modern synthetic varnishes are much less troublesome, but it is still advisable to work in a fairly warm, dry place and to avoid dust for at least a few hours. Some of these synthetic finishes may be described as furniture sealers as well as varnishes, but the results are similar.

Use a clean brush that has never been used for paint or other finishes. The slightest contamination with another finish may affect the appearance of varnish. It is usually helpful to warm the varnish before use, preferably by standing the can in hot water. Runs down the outside of the can can be avoided if a piece of wire is put across the can to wipe the brush against (Fig. D-1A). Between coats, it is best to keep the brush suspended in varnish or thinners (Fig. D-1B).

Read the directions on the can. Extensive brushing is inadvisable for synthetic varnishes, since it may cause air bubbles, which dry as little pinpoints in the surface. Some makers advise "flowing on" the varnish. This may be ideal from their point of view, but on anything except a horizontal surface, this will result in runs or curtains.

A first varnish coat may be thinned slightly to aid penetration of the wood. Thin sparingly—a very small amount of thinner has a surprising effect. The first coat may be brushed in several directions before finishing along the grain (Fig. D-1C). Further coats should be brushed with just enough strokes to spread the varnish, almost entirely in the direction of the grain. In all cases, make a final brush stroke back towards the previously wetted area and lift the brush in one sweep as it passes over the area (Fig. D-1D). This minimizes the risk of brush marks in the dried surface. On vertical or sloping surfaces, work from the top, but let final brush strokes each time be upwards over the previously covered part.

Coats of varnish should be allowed to dry completely before applying more coats. In many cases, the surface may have to be left overnight before the next coat is applied. However, follow the maker's instructions. Formulas change, and there are some varnishes with which a following coat may come before complete hardening. Normally, when a coat has hardened, it should be rubbed down with steel wool or pumice. This removes any flaws and removes some of the gloss to give the next coat a better grip with less risk of runs. Any particles of abrasive or the dust they cause should be removed with a tack rag or a cloth moistened with thinner.

The number of coats needed will depend on the varnish and the desired finish. Usually the first coat soaks in, the next coat builds up somethings of a body, and the third coat shows what the finish is capable of. For some purposes, three coats may be enough, but the quality improves with a few further coats, providing rubbing down between coats is adequate.

Fig. D-1. Preservation of brushes and the proper method of brushing are important in achieving the best paint or varnish finish.

LACQUER

Much commerically produced furniture has a sprayed-lacquer finish. Lacquer gives a hard, clear gloss that resists most of the usual conditions in the home. Lacquer is formulated with various ingredients, all of which dry quickly. There are brushing lacquers, but lacquers are most satisfactory when sprayed on.

Several coats can be sprayed on in a matter of hours. Lacquer should not be used with other finishes, since lacquer over most other finishes acts as a solvent and will soften or dissolve them to give an unsatisfactory result. Of course, skill is needed to get a satisfactory sprayed finish. Ripples on the surface may give an orange peel effect due to the spray not atomizing properly. Sags and runs are caused by an excess of lacquer. Blushing is caused by moisture in the lacquer.

PAINT

Like varnish, paint has undergone many changes in recent years. Of course, paint is basically varnish with colored pigment and a few other changes to suit the opaque finish, so changes brought by the introduction of synthetics affect paint as well as varnish. Use a complete paint system from one manufacturer so the different coats are compatible, and follow the directions of your chosen make.

The first coat of paint does little except to form a seal and to bond to the wood surface. Some hardboard and plywood makers recommend a sealer to use before the first coat of paint. This prevents excessive paint absorption. When nothing else is advised, the first coat should be a *primer* paint, much of which will soak in. This gives a good bond to the wood and reduces the risk of paint peeling at a future date.

There may have to be two priming coats on some very absorbent woods. The next coat is the *undercoat*. This has more body than the primer, and it dries with a matte surface ready for the *topcoat*. Many makers supply an undercoat paint of a color that matches the topcoat, but is not quite the same color. Thus there is little risk of missing a part, as there might be if both coats were exactly the same color.

Some surfaces may need two undercoats, rubbed down between coats. This is better than applying two topcoats. The topcoat, particularly if you use a gloss paint of the modern synthetic type, needs all the precautions mentioned for varnish. Spread enough to avoid runs and sags; finish strokes over previously wetted parts (going in the direction of the grain is not always essential). Usually it is better to make final strokes lengthwise on a panel. On a vertical or sloping surface, even when the length of a panel is the other way, it may be better to work from the top down and make final strokes upward, to reduce the risk of sags or runs.

Where there are molded edges, inset panels, carvings, or other shaped parts that adjoin flat panels, it is usually best to brush surplus paint or varnish onto the flat parts so as to remove paint away from the intricacies, which might trap excesses. If panels are painted first, there is nowhere for any excesses on the shaped parts to be spread.

If more than one color is to be used, the lighter one should be applied first. If it spreads to the area that is to be painted darker, it is more easily covered than a dark color under a light color. The best way to get neat joins between adjoining colors is to use masking tape, but make sure the paint the tape is stuck to is absolutely dry, or the tape may mar the surface.

If parts are to be given a clear finish, do this before painting nearby parts. Paint accidentally applied to bare wood will almost certainly leave a mark that will show through a clear finish, but if it splashed onto a clear-finished surface, it will wipe off without leaving a mark (providing it is not allowed to dry).

OTHER FINISHES

Veneer panels may be obtained to be ironed on or otherwise fixed to a surface. Formica and similar materials make good working surfaces, and these may be used directly on bare wood or used to supplement similar surfaces already on manufactured board.

There are decals that simulate inlays or other wood patterns. These are not popular with craftsmen any more than any imitation. However, nursery tale or other suitable decals may be used in a child's room. Usually it is advisable to apply all but the last coat of varnish and then fix the decal and give it time to dry before the final varnishing.

Self-adhesive flexible plastics useful as shelf or interior linings and in places where stripping and replacing at some later date may be done, possible for hygienic reasons. A suitably patterned piece may form a door panel, as could wall covering that matches that on the walls of the room.

There are plastic and cloth panels that could be used on furniture around a headboard or bar. Decorative plywood panels intended for walls may be included in furniture.

There are ways to make variations on the commoner finishes. Flock can be sprayed to give a clothlike finish. Lacquer can be treated to give crackle or wrinkle surfaces. Some of these treatments may harbor dirt and resist cleaning, so this should be considered before finishing wood in an unusual way.

Appendix E
Wood For Your Bedroom Furniture

Although many man-made and other materials are now used in furniture, wood is still the first choice, particularly for structural parts. There is an attractiveness about wood that is lacking in most other materials. Apart from its appearance, it can be worked without great skill and without the need for elaborate equipment. Manufactured and natural forms of wood make up the bulk of materials used in making bedroom furniture.

CHARACTERISTICS OF LUMBER

Wood varies in appearance, quality, characteristics, and flaws. These variations provide much of its attraction. They can be made use of to provide interest and beauty.

As wood comes from trees, possible sizes depend on the original tree. Some trees grow tall and slender and so produce long, narrow boards. Others tend to have thick trunks of no great height, so that boards may be of considerable widths but no great length. Most furniture-making woods are available in all sizes likely to be needed, but it sometimes happens that a particular choice of wood may result in suitable sizes being unavailable.

In any tree a part of the wood is *heartwood*, and around it there is *sapwood* (Fig. E-1A). As the tree grows, more layers are formed on the outside, and some of the inner sapwood changes into heartwood. The annual rings form the grain marking. In some woods there is a pronounced difference in appearance between sapwood

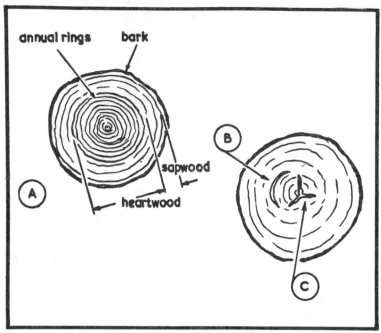

Fig. E-1. The middle of a tree produces heartwood (A) the most durable wood, but there may be flaws: cup or ring shakes (B) and heart or star shakes (C).

and heartwood. In other woods it is difficult to distinguish them. In general, heartwood is much more durable than sapwood, but there are some woods in which there is little difference durability. Where possible, all wood used for furniture should be heartwood.

As a tree grows, *shakes* may develop. These are cracks that may go around the grain as cup or ring shakes (Fig. E-1B) or across the grain as heart or star shakes (Fig. E-1C). These do not affect the quality of the wood, but furniture wood has to be cut around them. When a tree has been felled, it has to be seasoned to dry out the sap to a controlled small amount. Cracks may develop during drying, particularly at the ends. These do not affect quality or other characteristics, but they will have to be allowed for and cut around when preparing furniture parts.

Wood will always absorb and give up moisture with changes in humidity. This affects the stability of the wood. There is little effect along the grain, but a board may expand in its width as it takes up moisture and shrink as it loses moisture. It will also warp, and the risk of warping and its probable direction is related to the way the board is cut from the tree.

CONVERSION OF LOGS TO LUMBER

If boards are cut straight across the log, a board with the grain marks across the thickness is unlikely to warp at all (Fig. E-2A); but boards nearer the circumference will tend to become hollow (Fig. E-2B). If the end of a board is examined, the board's relation to the whole section of tree can be visualized and the risk of warping estimated. A convenient way to remember what may happen is to consider the curved grain rings as trying to straighten out (Fig. E-2C). If the wood is in a round or square section, distortion is likely to be a shrinking in the direction of the grain (Fig. E-2D) as the wood dries.

Sometimes wood is cut to give the best grain appearance. To get the maximum number of boards with attractive markings, they

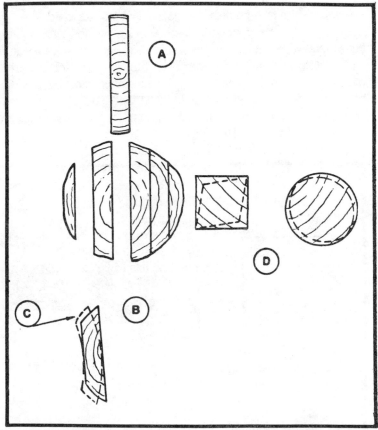

Fig. E-2. Freshly cut boards warp and shrink as they dry, but this is less obvious if the grain lines are across the thickness.

are cut from the outside inwards (Fig. E-3A). Besides grain there are *medullary rays*, which radiate from the center outwards. In many woods they are invisible, but in some woods they are sufficiently prominent to provide a decorative effect if the wood is cut along their lines. This is particularly so in some types of oak. A radially cut board is then described as *quarter sawn, figured oak, wainscot oak,* or *silver grain* (Fig. E-3B). Cutting many boards exactly radially results in much waste so it is more usual to make the cuts in layers (Fig. E-3C) so that all but the outermost boards may be expected to show markings from the medullary rays. Wood cut this way will be more expensive, but in suitable types the effect is very attractive.

LUMBER SIZES AND GRADES

Much furniture-grade wood is sold in nonstandard sizes or prepared to suit the customer. The owner of a shop with suitable equipment will find it most economical to buy wood in stock sections and cut it down to suit his needs. Even then, if stock sections from the local yard can be used, there will be a saving in cost and effort. Standard sizes are most applicable to lumber used for house construction and similar work, but may be found with the higher quality woods needed for furniture.

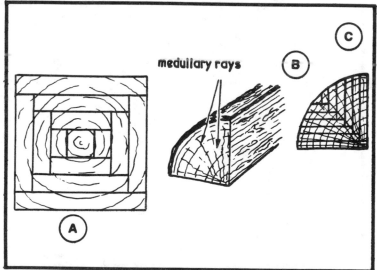

Fig. E-3. Wood may be cut to get the best appearance of grain (A), or to use the figuring of rays of oak and some other woods (B and C).

Grades

Lumber may be offered in two grades: *select* and *common*. Select may be subdivided into A, B, C, and D in decreasing quality. Common lumber starts where select leaves off and is graded into 1, 2, 3, and 4 in descending quality. The main difference between select and common lumber is in the ability to take a finish where the grain shows through. Grades A and B obviously are just about free of blemishes or defects in the grain, but these may be more obvious in grades C and D. Common grades are suitable for use where they do not have to take a finish or where appearance is unimportant. Grades 1 and 2 have uses in internal work in furniture, but grades 3 and 4 may have too many defects—such as large knots, knotholes, or confused, rough grain—to be used in furniture.

It is possible that a board with a low grade because of a defect in one place may yield wood of adequate quality in another part. For economy the buyer may not want to buy wood of a higher grade than necessary. If you have an opportunity to look over the stock in a lumberyard, it is often possible to find economical pieces you can use by cutting around defects yourself.

Sizes

Lumber is sized as it is sawn. Machine planing takes off at least ⅛ in. This means that a piece of lumber described as 2 by 4 in. which has been machine planed all round will actually be about 1¾ by 3¾ in. The term *board* is applied to wood for sale that is over 8 in. wide and less than 2 in. thick. Smaller pieces may be called *strips*. Larger sections may be called *timbers* although in some places *timber* is a word used as an alternative to *lumber*.

Lumberyards that may not cut the wood to size on the premises may keep stock lengths in multiples of 2 ft, from 6 ft upward. Purchases should be arranged to allow for this. Charges may be according to length and section, but it is advisable to know what is meant by *board foot* in case that is the method of quoting prices. This reduces the size to the equivalent of a square foot 1 in. thick. Hence a piece of wood 1 ft square and 1 in thick is one board foot. So is a piece 2 in. wide and 6 ft long by 1 in. thick. A thicker piece has to be reduced to 1 in. by increasing the surface area, so a piece of wood 2 in. thick need only be half a square foot on the surface to represent one board foot.

There is an advantage in buying in quantity rather than just getting wood for the project at hand. There are certain stock sections that find a use in many pieces of bedroom furniture, and it is economical to build up a store so you can take wood from the shelf or rack as needed. It would be false economy to buy unusual material that might never be needed again, but even then, much of the joy of amateur craftsmanship is in designing furniture around available material.

Because of difficulty in obtaining long or wide pieces in some woods (caused by the sizes of trees), extra wide or long pieces may cost proportionately more than smaller pieces. It is always advisable to visit a lumberyard armed with your detailed cutting list, then wood from stock may be found to suit items economically. This is much better than totaling all the pieces of a certain section and asking for one long piece, which may carry a premium because of its length.

Similar arguments apply to widths. It is usually most economical to accept the narrowest pieces that will suit your purpose rather than to ask for wider boards to cut down. However, there are exceptions. Very narrow pieces may be cut from the waste from cutting large boards and may be sapwood. Narrow strips may be cut from branches. A wide board has to be cut from the trunk of the tree and should be all heartwood. The best wood is more likely to be in the wide piece, and if this is particularly wanted, it may be advisable to buy a wide board and cut it down, even if it costs more than the equivalent narrow pieces.

WOOD TYPES

Wood is very broadly divided into hardwoods and softwoods. Although most hardwoods are harder than most softwoods, the names are not really very apt. Hardwoods are those trees that have broad leaves, nearly all of which are lost during the winter. Softwoods are trees with needle leaves, which are mostly retained during the winter. It is the pines, firs, spruces, and similar trees that make up the softwoods that the average woodworker will handle. All the better woods that are used for furniture, particularly where a polished finish is used, are hardwoods.

It is difficult to keep track of all the kinds of wood. Although certain woods are accepted for particular purposes and are in fairly regular supply, there are many others that are equally suitable for the same purposes. There are supposed to be upwards of 3000 separate species of trees with commercial value, so any advice on woods can only be regarded as a guide.

Quite often a piece of bedroom furniture will have to match some existing furniture, and that will settle what wood is to be used, at least for the visible parts. Sometimes, however, contrasting wood can be quite effective. A room with dark furniture may benefit from building in something with light facing, or vice versa.

The use of the furniture should be considered. Something in a child's room may get rougher treatment than a similar thing elsewhere, so the wood should be one that will take knocks without showing them much and should certainly not be likely to splinter. A corner cupboard may not be at much risk from knocks because of its position, so a softer wood could be sufficiently durable.

Some of the more choice woods are very expensive. They may still be worth having, but it is sometimes possible to use a cheaper wood with a sufficiently similar grain marking, then finish it with stain and polish to produce an effective piece of furniture at a much lower price. Of course, if the final finish is to be paint, it is more important to have wood that will finish smoothly, with no pronounced grain.

Softwoods

Although softwoods grow in many parts of the world, those used by woodworkers are mostly from the northern temperate zones of America, Europe, and Asia. Unfortunately, common names are not always the same, and the same wood may have a different name if it comes from a different place. Some are listed below with their alternate names.

Cedar, Western Red. Soft, reddish-brown, straight grained, and available in long lengths.

Cypress. Grows in swamps. Has a greasy feel and a sour smell. Straight-grained, light brown. Will withstand heat and moisture. Does not take glue very well.

Columbian Pine, Douglas Pine, Oregon Pine, Douglas Fir. One of the harder softwoods, straight-grained, reddish-brown. Raised grain and resin make the wood unsuitable for face work, but it may be used structurally in furniture.

Hemlock. Does not take a fine finish and is more of an external wood than one for furniture.

Larch. Medium texture, easily worked, light orange-brown color.

Pine, Parana. Brazilian wood, pale straw color, and available in wide boards.

Pine, Pitch. Heavy because of considerable resin. Has pronounced grain. Difficult to bring to a good finish.

Other Pines. Eastern white pine and ponderosa pine are light, with little strength. Sugar pine grows into large trees; it will finish smoothly despite large knots, which may be used as a decorative feature. Western white pine is similar. None of these is very durable if exposed.

Redwood, Yellow Deal, Red Deal, Red Pine, Scots Pine, Northern Pine. Reddish-brown, straight-grained, some resin. Suitable for internal construction.

Sequoia, California Redwood. Very large trees, so great lengths and widths obtainable. Rather open and porous, reddish-brown, and straight grained. Not very strong.

Spruce, Sitka, Silver Spruce. A combination of lightness with a strong, straight grain makes this a choice for aircraft construction and yacht spars. Not a furniture choice unless easily obtained.

Spruce, Whitewood, White Deal. Sometimes considered a poorer quality redwood. Near white, with some knots and resin pockets.

Hardwoods

Although a great variety of hardwoods are native to North America, many others are imported because of their special qualities. Distribution varies according to geography and climate. When making traditional furniture, the indigenous wood of the region is often chosen. Some of the woods indigenous to various regions are listed below, but these lists are not exhaustive, and some trees spread over into other regions.

Northern Region. Ash, aspen, basswood, yellow birch, butternut, cherry, elm, hickory, locust, hard maple, oak, walnut.

Central Region. White ash, basswood, beech, buckeye, chestnut, cottonwood, American elm, hackberry, shagbark hickory, locust, hard maple, white oak, sycamore, yellow poplar, walnut.

Appalachian Region. Ash, beech, red oak, white oak, hard maple.

Southern Region. Ash, basswood, beech, birch, cottonwood, elm, hackberry, hickory, locust, maple, red and cherry-bark oak, pecan, sweet and red gum, sycamore, black willow.

There are some very hard woods, such as greenheart, which will sink in water; but these do not have furniture uses. The softest and lightest of what are technically hardwoods is balsa—which is softer and lighter than most softwoods. It has no normal furniture application.

The woods listed below are hardwood examples, which may provide comparisons when other woods are being considered.

Ash. Straight, rather coarse grain. Valued for its springiness and bending qualities.

Basswood, Lime. Light, close-grained; easy to work and suitable for carving.

Beech, Red or White. Tough, close grain. Used for tools. Very good for turning on lathe.

Chestnut. Looks and works like oak, but has no figuring when quarter-sawn.

Elm. Durable, with confused grain that resists splitting. Not of much use in furniture except trasitional designs.

Gaboon. Nondurable African wood that looks like mahogany. Used for lightweight plywood.

Red Gum, Sweet Gum, Satin Walnut. Soft, even brown color with little sign of grain. Stains well. Twists and warps if not built into other parts.

Maple. Varies from light yellow to brown.

Mahogany, Spanish and Cuban. Rich brown with close grain. Original furniture mahogany, but there are many more.

Mahogany, Honduras; Baywoods. Lightweight with light brown color. A furniture wood.

Mahogany, African. There are several of these, and not all true mahoganies; but some are suitable for furniture.

Red Oak. The usual open-grained brown oak, with a pink shade present. Has figuring in quarter-sawn boards. Large boards obtainable.

Oak, English. The oak used for medieval ships and furniture. Brown, open-grained, with prominent figuring when quarter-sawn. Very strong and durable.

Oak, Japanese and Austrian. More mellow and easier to work than English oak. Good furniture woods.

Popular, yellow; Canary Wood; American Whitewood. Even, close-grained, yellow wood. Varying quality, but usually easy to work. Similar to basswood and sometimes confused with it.

Sapele. Looks like mahogany. Its attractive grain may be difficult to work. Used for making plywood.

Sycamore. Whitish-yellow, close-grained wood with sometimes a figure or ripple marking visible in the grain. Good for turning on lathe. Its near white color makes it suitable for use with food.

Teak. This is a dark brown wood that bleaches to near white in the sun. It may be difficult to work because of its resin. It is very durable even when not treated in any way. Not usual for furniture.

Walnut, American Black Walnut. A shade of purple mixed with dark brown. Takes a good finish.

Index

Index

A

All in one set in, bolted	276
American colonial beds	294
Attic sleeper	259

B

Baby box cradle	94
Bassinet, folding	105
knockdown	114
Beanbag bed	234
Beds, American colonial	294
beanbag	234
bioaquatic	386
children's no frill	56
converting existing twin	241
field or tent	296
low post	298
period	286
pivoting twins	238
quickie lounge	59
rocking chair	16
roll up bolster	53
scooter	131
Siamese twin guest	156
sling	22
stacked	144
taste in change	302
tester	300
wheel	282
zoom zoom	264
Bed couch, bundle board	62
Bed couch, convertible	64
Bed designers, early	290

Bed light, fluorescent	365
Bed projects, no frills	11
Bed rack, reading-eating	375
Bedroll, converted	14
Bed dimensions	70
Bed in a box	150
Bed of nails	281
Bed of roses	281
Bedside cradle	119
Bedside hook on	372
Bins, rolling	381
Bioaquatic bed	386
Bolted all in one set in	276
Box, bed in	150
Broomstick roll up cradle	112
Buck saw cot	55
Building a pole lamp	345
Building slatted lanterns	347
Building lamps	340
Built ins	186
Bulbs, large wattage	362
Bundle board bed couch	62
Bunks, yoke	137

C

Car, lining	269
Casters, orbital	239
Ceiling connections	330
Chair, waterbed pillow	234
Chair bed, foldup	14
lean to	19
Characteristics, lumber	417
Chassis, building	268

Children's no frill beds 56
Clear finishes 411
Closet, hang up clothes 185
Coat hanger tester 285
Coil springs, tying 44
Color coding & troubleshooting 329
Connecting sockets 334
Connections, ceiling 330
Connectors, solderless 329
Conversion of logs to lumber 419
Converted bedroll 14
Convertible bed couch 64
Converting existing twin beds 241
Cots 51
Cot, buck saw 55
    peg block 53
    rustic 54
Covering for head foot slings 26
Covering the flat base sling beds 36
Cradle, baby box 94
    bedside 119
    broomstick roll up 112
    flat base sling 42
    rock-a-bye 117
    swinging 100
Crib, egg cup reversible 58
    fiber drum 57
    gated 126
    half gated hinged 129
    side hinged 129
    sliding side 130
    spool 131

D

Dimensions, bed 70
Dividers, room 324
Doll cradle, shaker style 89
Doors, shutter 184
Dowels 80
Drawers 377

E

Early bed designers 290
Egg cup reversible crib 58
Electrical connections 339

F

Family fun project 81
Fiber drum crib 57
Field or tent beds 296
Finishes, clear 411
Finishing 407
Finishing nails 96
Finishing reasons 408
Fixture, styrofoam ball 362
Flat base sling beds 30
Flat base sling beds, covering 36

suspension methods 33
Flat base sling cradle 42
Flat springs, tying 46
Floor people 263
Fluorescent bed light 365
Foam padding 49
Folding bassinet 105
Folding luggage rack 192
Fold up chair bed 14
Fold up pipe sling bed 279
Fold up sling pipe bed 259
Framed slings, head foot 23
Futon 13

G

Gated cribs 126
Glow worm 361
Glues 398, 400
Grades of lumber 421
Guest cube squared 256

H

Half gated hinged crib 129
Hammocks 20
Hang up clothes closet 185
Hardware for drawers & bins 384
Hardwoods 425
Headboards 314
Headboard hook over 372
Headboard unit 244
Head foot framed slings 23
Head foot framed sling cradle 29
Head foot slings, coverings 26
Head foot slings, sus-
    pension methods 28
Hi-lo intensity lamp 354
Hooking up an outlet 332
Hooking up a wall outlet 336
Hooking up a wall switch 337
Hook on, bedside 372
Hook over, headboard 372
How to build a tester 310

I

Installing a plug 337

J

Japanese lanterns 357
Japanese pole lamp 357

K

Knockdown bassinet 114

L

Lacquer 414
Lamps, building 340

430

building a pole	345
hi-lo intensity	354
Japanese pole	357
plastic bottle	353
Lanterns, building slatted	347
Japanese	357
Large wattage bulbs	362
Lean to chair bed	19
Library, portable	191
Light	324
Lights, recessed	364
Lighting the Siamese twin guest	
quarters	197
Lining the car	269
Logs, to lumber, conversion	419
Low post beds	298
Luggage rack, folding	192
Lumber, characteristics	417
grade	421
sizes	421
Lumber sizes & grades	420

M

Metal springs	42

N

Nailing, tools & nails for	404
Nails	79
Nails & tools for nailing	404
Nails, bed	281
finishing	96
No frills bed projects	11

O

Orbital casters	239
Outlet, hooking up	332
hooking up a wall	336
Out sized bed platforms, simple	66

P

Padding, foam	49
Paint	414
Panels, veneer	416
Partitions, shoji	177
Peg block cot	53
Period beds	286
Pivoting structure	251
Pivoting twin beds	238
Plastic bottle lamp	353
Play pen	123
Play pen, multilevel	124
Plug, installing	337
Portable library	191
Preparation, surface	409

Q

Quickie lounge bed	59

R

Reading-eating bed rack	375
Reasons for finishing	408
Recessed lights	364
Resiliency	72
Resins, synthetic	399
Rock-a-bye cradle	117
Rocking chair bed	16
Rollon bins	381
Roll up bolster bed	53
Room dividers	324
Rose, bed	281
Rustic cot	54

S

Scooter bed	131
Screws	401
Screws, wood	77
Set in, alternative	279
Shaker style doll cradle	89
Shelves	376
Shoji partitions	177
Shutter doors	184
Siamese twin guest beds	156
Siamese twin guest quarters,	
lighting	197
Side hinged crib	129
Siesta tree house	261
Sizes, lumber	421
Sleeper, attic	259
Sleeping tubes	56
Sleeping wedges	258
Sliding side crib	130
Sling beds	22
Sling beds, flat base	30
fold up pipe	279
Sling cradle, head foot framed	29
Sling pipe bed, fold up	259
Sockets, connecting	334
Softwoods	423
Solderless connectors	329
Spool crib	131
Springs, metal	42
Stacked beds	144
Stains	409
Stereo speaker placement	366
Stretcher, webbing	48
Style influences	288
Styrofoam ball fixture	362
Surface preparation	409
Suspension methods for head	
foot slings	28
Swinging cradle	100
Switch, hooking up a wall	337
Synthetic resins	399

T

Taste in beds change   302
Tatame   12
Tester beds   300
Tester, coat hanger   285
　　how to build   310
Tree house, siesta   261
Tubes, sleeping   56
Tying coil springs   44
Tying flat springs   46

V

Varnish   412
Veneer panels   416

W

Waterbeds   199
Waterbed pillow chair   234
Webbing stretcher   48
Wedges, sleeping   258
Wheel bed   282
Whittle   283
Wood screws   77
Woodtypes   422

Y

Yoke bunks   137

Z

Zoom zoom bed   264

Vegetation

The jacaranda raised its froth
of transmarine splendor,
the araucaria, bristling with spears,
was magnitude against the snow,
the primordial mahogany tree
distilled blood from its crown,
and to the South of the cypress,
the thunder tree, the red tree,
the thorn tree, the mother tree,
the scarlet ceibo, the rubber tree
were earthly volume, sound,
territorial existence.

A newly propagated aroma
suffused, through the interstices
of the earth, the breaths
transformed into mist and fragrance:
wild tobacco raised
its rosebush of imaginary air.
Like a fire-tipped spear
corn emerged, its stature
was stripped and it gave forth again,
disseminated its flour, had
corpses beneath its roots,
and then, in its cradle, it watched
the vegetable gods grow.
Wrinkle and extension, sown
by the seed of the wind
over the plumes of the cordillera,
dense light of germ and nipples,
blind dawn nursed
by the earthly ointments
of the implacable rainy latitude,
of the enshrouded torrential nights,
of the matinal cisterns.
And still on the prairies,
like laminas of the planet,
beneath a fresh republic of stars,
the ombú, king of the grass, stopped
the free air, the whispering flight,
and mounted the pampa, holding it in
with a bridle of reins and roots.

Arboreal America,
wild bramble between the seas,

from pole to pole you balanced,
green treasure, your dense growth.

The night germinated
in cities of sacred pods,
in sonorous woods,
outstretched leaves covering
the germinal stone, the births.
Green uterus, seminal
American savanna, dense storehouse,
a branch was born like an island,
a leaf was shaped like a sword,
a flower was lightning and medusa,
a cluster rounded off its résumé,
a root descended into the darkness.

II

Some Beasts

It was the twilight of the iguana.

From its glistening battlement
a tongue
darted into the verdure,
the monastic anteater trod
the jungle with melodious feet,
the guanaco fine as oxygen
in the wide brown heights
was wearing boots of gold,
while the llama opened candid
eyes in the delicacy
of the world covered with dew.
The monkeys wove
an interminably erotic thread
on the shores of dawn,
leveling walls of pollen
and startling the violet flight
of the butterflies from Muzo.
It was the night of the cayman,
the night pure and pullulating
with snouts emerging from the ooze,
and from the somnolent swamps
an opaque thud of armor
returned to the earthy origin.

The jaguar touches the leaves
with its phosphorescent absence,
the puma bolts through the foliage
like a raging fire,
while in him burn
the jungle's alcoholic eyes.
Badgers scratch the river's feet,
sniff out the nest
whose throbbing delight
they'll attack with red teeth.

And in the depths of the almighty water
lies the giant anaconda
like the circle of the earth,
covered with ritual clays,
devouring and religious.

III

**The Birds
Arrive**

All was flight in our land.
The cardinal, like drops
of blood and feathers,
bled the dawn of Anáhuac.
The toucan was a lovely
box of shining fruit,
the hummingbird preserved
the original sparks of dawn,
and its minuscule bonfires
burned in the still air.

Illustrious parrots filled
the depths of the foliage,
like ingots of green gold
newly minted from the paste
of sunken swamps,
and from their circular eyes
yellow hoops looked out,
old as minerals.

All the eagles of the sky
nourished their bloody kin
in the uninhabited blue,
and flying over the world

on carnivorous feathers,
the condor, murderous king,
solitary monk of the sky,
black talisman of the snow,
hurricane of falconry.

The ovenbird's engineering
made of the fragrant clay
sonorous little theaters
where it burst forth singing.

The nightjar kept
whistling its wet cry
on the banks of the cenotes.
The Chilean pigeon made
scrubby woodland nests
where it left its regal gift
of dashing eggs.

The southern lark, fragrant,
sweet autumn carpenter,
displayed its breast spangled
with a scarlet constellation,
and the austral sparrow raised
its flute recently fetched
from the eternity of water.

Wet as a water lily,
the flamingo opened the doors
of its rosy cathedral,
and flew like the dawn,
far from the sultry forest
where the jewels dangle
from the quetzal, which suddenly
awakens, stirs, slips off, glows,
and makes its virgin embers fly.

A marine mountain flies
toward the islands, a moon
of birds winging South,
over the fermented islands
of Peru.
It's a living river of shade,
a comet of countless
tiny hearts
that eclipse the world's sun